Outstanding praise

for Charles Casillo and *Elizabeth and* ...

"Elizabeth Taylor and Montgomery Clift are hardly unknown quantities and still they benefit from a fresh re-examination in Charles Casillo's tandem biography. Casillo doesn't treat Clift and Taylor as pristine people and he can be quite dishy at times . . . The author approaches them both with sympathy and comes away with a melodrama as good as any that they ever starred in. I mean it as the highest possible compliment when I say that it would all make excellent source material for a future Ryan Murphy TV series." —*The New York Times Book Review*

"As Charles Casillo's touching *Elizabeth and Monty* underscores, theirs was a relationship of equals. Not a screen romance, exactly, but the longing was mutual, and that truth still shines out from those long-ago close-ups." —*The Washington Post*

"This dual biography is so jammed packed with sex, pill popping, alcoholism, affairs, breakdowns, suicide attempts and multiple brushes with death that most readers will want to read it in one greedy, high-caloric gulp. Readers may come for the nonstop scandals but what will keep them reading is Casillo's deeply empathetic and nuanced portrait of two Hollywood stars who forged a loving and loyal friendship." —*Shelf Awareness*

"Loved *Elizabeth and Monty* by Charles Casillo. Insightful, surprising, a great read." —Andrew McCarthy, author of *Brat: An '80s Story*

Please turn the page for more outstanding praise for *Elizabeth and Monty*!

The praise for *Elizabeth and Monty* continues!

"Well chronicled and abounds with details never before brought to light. For those who are enamored by the lives of movie stars—this is a great read of the behind-the-scenes antics." —*Sun News Austin*

"A well-researched work that will appeal to readers who like their celebrity biographies juicy." —*Library Journal*

"Traces the professional and personal triumphs and tragedies of two Hollywood icons, focusing as much on their private peccadilloes as on their career-defining, and in Clift's case, career destroying roles." —*Booklist*

"There is a tremendous amount of love, friendship, life, tragedy and triumph in Charles Casillo's biography, *Elizabeth and Monty*. Casillo has done a magnificent job." —*Rage Reviews*

"We're looking forward to diving into the worlds of these stars' lives in Casillo's new tome. If it's even half as dramatic and moving as the films they dazzled us in together, we have a feeling we're in for quite the read." —*Southern Living*

ELIZABETH AND MONTY

The Untold Story of Their Intimate Friendship

CHARLES CASILLO

KENSINGTON PUBLISHING CORP.

www.kensingtonbooks.com

KENSINGTON BOOKS are published by

Kensington Publishing Corp.
119 West 40th Street
New York, NY 10018

All Kensington titles, imprints, and distributed lines are available at special quantity discounts for bulk purchases for sales promotion, premiums, fund-raising, educational, or institutional use.

Special book excerpts or customized printings can also be created to fit specific needs. For details, write or phone the office of the Kensington Special Sales Manager: Attn. Special Sales Department. Kensington Publishing Corp., 119 West 40th Street, New York, NY 10018. Phone: 1-800-221-2647.

The K logo is a trademark of Kensington Publishing Corp.

ISBN: 978-1-4967-2481-6 (ebook)

ISBN: 978-1-4967-2480-9

First Kensington Hardcover Printing: June 2021

First Kensington Trade Paperback Printing: June 2023

10 9 8 7 6 5 4 3 2 1

Printed in the United States of America

For Anthony

CONTENTS

PROLOGUE

WHEN ELIZABETH THOUGHT OF THAT NIGHT, SHE REMEMBERED the blood and how it must have felt as he lay trembling in her arms—broken and ruined—on a lonely, dusty road.

It was Montgomery Clift in her arms, one of the most handsome and celebrated movie stars of the day. He had been driving home from a small dinner party at the home of his best friend, Elizabeth Taylor, when he crashed his car into a telephone pole, smashing his finely chiseled face into the dashboard.

Elizabeth had rushed down the road with some other guests to the place of the accident. She climbed into the wreck and cradled Monty's head. "He was bleeding so much that it looked like his face had been halved," Elizabeth recalled many years later. "I probably shouldn't have touched him. His head was getting bigger and bigger . . . and he opened his eyes and [the whites] were bright red—so that the blue of them looked even bluer. He looked like an alien."

Monty's suffering was conveyed by low, steady moaning. He tried to mumble something, but he immediately started gagging. "What is it, my love?" Elizabeth whispered. "What is it, baby?"

At first, Elizabeth thought he was choking on blood—it was gushing out of his mouth. Then Monty uttered something about teeth. Realizing he was choking on his teeth, she instinctively stuck her fingers down his throat and pulled out two broken teeth, clearing the passageway. The others watching, Rock Hudson, Michael Wilding, and Kevin McCarthy, said she saved his life.

There was still one tooth hanging from some skin on his gums. He asked Elizabeth to remove it. Fighting off revulsion, she did that, too. "Save it," Monty muttered. "I might need it." Later he would give the tooth to Elizabeth as a souvenir.

She could smell the blood and feel the warmth of it as it flowed from his wounds and pooled in her dress—she was momentarily able to push her revulsion about blood aside, although she would remember it for the rest of her life. The quickly flowing blood of her friend, the smell of it, and the feel of it drying on her horrified her—from now on she would be haunted by nightmares.

But it was nothing compared to what lay in store for Monty.

"That," a friend stated later, "was the beginning of the end."

1

DEVELOPING MONTY

He didn't talk about his childhood a lot. He found it unpleasant to talk about. He said he must have been a very depressing child.
—**Jack Larson**

*R*ESEARCHERS ARE ALWAYS COMBING THROUGH MONTGOMERY Clift's childhood history, searching for the cause of his later unhappiness—as if there had to be one particular incident or reason for such a gifted person to become so self-destructive and unhappy.

It often comes down to his mother, Sunny, who separated him from what was considered a normal childhood and put too much emphasis on what he should be, rather than what and who he was. The damage she did was insidious, if not overt. That's not to say she didn't love him. She loved him terribly. Simply not in the way he needed to be loved.

Many people go through an unhappy childhood and in adulthood are able to leave it behind. But some unusually sensitive people cannot overcome it. It's something they have to live with, something that spills into their lives, staining everything. That's how it was for Monty.

Montgomery Clift's mother, Ethel "Sunny" Fogg, was born in 1888 in Philadelphia, Pennsylvania. Sunny grew up believing she was an orphan. She was raised by a couple who had adopted her at the age of one, a Mr. and Mrs. Charles and Mary Fogg. The Foggs led her to believe she had been born illegitimately and abandoned and frequently told her she had been an unwanted child. It wounded her, though something deep inside her told her they were wrong. She was a somebody.

When she was eighteen, however, the doctor who had delivered her, Dr. Edward Montgomery, told her the true story. Her biological parents were Maria Latham Anderson and Woodbury Blair, both wealthy, both from socially prominent families who were against the couple marrying. In the days of extreme class distinctions, these families' names were a very big deal.

Maria's father, Robert Anderson, had been a Union colonel in the Civil War. Woodbury's father had been a postmaster general for Abraham Lincoln. Maria's mother was particularly opposed to the marriage, mostly because she was a lonely widow and she wanted her daughter to stay with her. The couple eloped, but even after Maria became pregnant, the powerful families had the marriage annulled and put the newborn up for adoption. For her first year, the child lived with Dr. Montgomery as he searched for a couple suitable to raise her. He became extremely fond of the girl and nicknamed her "Sunny" because of her lovely lilting laugh.

When Sunny became of age, Dr. Montgomery informed her of her true lineage. The news stunned her. Her instincts had been right—there was something special about her. She had not come from nothing—she was descended from a noble lineage of aristocrats. At once she tried to contact her biological family, but they refused to see her. She was completely shut out. She wrote letter after letter, trying to reveal herself, attempting to get her real family to like her and then, maybe, accept her. But they refused even to acknowledge her.

It devastated Sunny to know that a whole part of her true identity—and her claim to her aristocratic origin—was being kept from her. She would spend the rest of her life attempting to prove her value—eventually attempting to transform her children into the living embodiment of her lost aristocratic heritage.

Despite her frustration, she was bright and ambitious and won a scholarship to Cornell University. In school Sunny was lovely and popular: men seemed to be caught in her spell, transfixed by her luminous eyes, lush dark hair, and intoxicating laugh. Sunny was a Quaker, so her clothes were tasteful but not provocative, and she wore only the tiniest bit of makeup. She had a way of coming across as charming and proper, but she made you feel as if—although she was worlds above you—she was willing to meet you on your level and like you, anyway.

One of her admirers was fellow student William "Bill" Clift, who was studying mining engineering but planned eventually to get involved in investment banking and trust companies. Born in 1886 in Chattanooga, Tennessee, Bill was the son of a judge. Of Irish/English descent, he was a slight man with soft features. He wasn't the most dashing of Sunny's admirers, but he was the most ardent, driven, and practical, and he had a calming effect on her. She was filled with compelling contrasts—at once insecure and imperious—which he noticed she covered up with a grand air of unapproachable manners and breeding—showing vulnerability was out of the question. Bill longed to take care of Sunny—and to be taken care of by her. They became engaged after she graduated.

After they married, the couple settled in Omaha. In 1919 their first son, Brooks Clift, was born. The following year Sunny was pregnant again. Montgomery Clift, however, was unexpected. This time it was a tough pregnancy, and after Sunny gave birth to a daughter, Roberta, she leaned back into the pillows, exhausted and satisfied. She now had a boy and a girl.

"Wait a minute," the doctor exclaimed suddenly. "There's another one in there!"

Sunny had been given no indication she was carrying twins. "Oh no, no," she sighed. "I don't want another one." But a short while later her second son was born.

"I was always the gentleman," the adult Monty Clift would always say. "I let my sister see the moon before I did."

Edward Montgomery Clift was born on October 17, 1920.

Sunny perhaps named him after her biological grandfather, who still had not accepted her into the family.* He would never be called "Edward." Everyone knew him as Monty.

Despite her annoyance at the surprise appearance of Monty as a twin, he soon became Sunny's favorite. She realized there was something exceptional about him. Even as a baby, he possessed a preternatural beauty and a way of observing people with his blue-green eyes that seemed the embodiment of her aristocrat ancestry. Because of this, she doted on the boy—to the point of suffocating him.

Social standing was paramount in her view of success, and Sunny wanted her children to view themselves as aristocrats. She considered her children "thoroughbreds," and she became obsessed with raising them in a way she saw fit. Omaha, Nebraska, was not the social milieu in which they could cultivate the kind of worldliness Sunny wanted for them. Therefore, she took to traveling so that her children could attain a worldly air and a top-notch education.

Instead of having them befriend neighborhood children, allowing them to play with toys and games, and enrolling them in school, she traveled with them to Bermuda and then to Europe. They always had private tutors, who taught them to speak French and German and instructed them in classic literature, art, and music. Manners and politeness came foremost. As for their athletic training, they were taught to skate and swim and even fence. While Sunny traveled with the three children extensively, Bill stayed home in Omaha, working as an investment banker to pay for his family's extravagant lifestyle.

The children's playmates and competitors were each other,

---

*It cannot be known if Sunny named her second son Montgomery after her real paternal grandfather, Montgomery Blair, or after Dr. Edward Montgomery, the family doctor who had been kind to her. Perhaps it was a stroke of fate that allowed him to be named after both. In an interview, Brooks Clift stated emphatically that Monty was named after Dr. Montgomery.

their tutors were their outside socializing, and their mother had the final word on everything. This way of life became smothering. "We were forced to swallow our opinions in front of Ma and agreed to her demands," Monty said. "We were never allowed to trust our own judgment or experience."

There is no reason to believe that Sunny wasn't raising her children with the best of intentions—giving them the things of which she had been deprived. But at the same time, she had something to prove—that she was indeed an aristocrat. The way of life she forced on her children did not make them feel privileged in adulthood. They felt unusual, isolated and, in their later years, traumatized.

The way the three grown Clifts responded to their childhood suggests that something more terrible than just the isolation and aloneness of it scarred them. When Monty's movie career was just starting, gossip columnist Hedda Hopper, trying to shed light on his enigmatic personality, asked him to describe his life so far in one sentence. "I've been knifed," he responded bluntly. But what it was that made his life so torturous remained a secret. To state exactly what did happen to Monty, to all of them, would be speculation, since there is nothing on record that pinpoints the reason for such unhappiness.

All three of the Clift children, Brooks, Roberta, and Monty, would state in adulthood that they simply couldn't remember much about their childhoods—big chunks of time were completely blocked out. "Psychologically, we couldn't seem to take the memories, so we forgot," Brooks stated. All they remembered was the lingering unpleasantness, and although they were obsessed with their childhoods, they would talk about it only to each other, desperately trying to remember. "It caused us to weep, when we were drunk enough, when some minor detail from our past was released." Brooks recalled.

In the stock market crash of 1929, Bill Clift lost most of his money, and Sunny and the children were forced to return home. Their life, for a while at least, would have to be lived as a typical middle-class family in Highland Park, Illinois. Unfortunately, nothing in the children's upbringing so far had prepared them to intermingle in an average middle-class residential neighborhood in America.

Everything about them reflected their cultured European up-bringing: they had stiff, formal manners, which made them seem remote, and they rarely spoke in English, which made them appear to be out-of-place misfits. In addition, they were completely at odds with the American way of life.

After a while, Bill stabilized the family income and was once again financially secure, the Clifts moved to Florida and then to New York. Brooks assimilated himself into life in the United States enough to go off to Harvard. Roberta, too, felt secure enough to attend Bryn Mawr College.

On the other hand, Monty felt like too much of an outsider to face an academic environment. He loved to learn, but he preferred to choose his subjects on his own terms. He hated to be force-fed what other people thought he should be educated in. He decided not to pursue any sort of higher education—life, he thought, would be his teacher. This allowed Sunny to focus totally on him. She had always felt that there was something special about Monty—something mysterious and appealing that set him apart—and now she considered him a prince. He was a strikingly beautiful boy. His looks mixed with his brooding nature and cultured manners gave him an intriguing aura, a charm that aroused people's curiosity and admiration.

Sunny thought that modeling would be a successful way for him to market these qualities, but Monty hated it—he found standing around, striking poses, boring and vacuous. The only thing that really seemed to interest him was photography. He loved taking pictures and would remain a consummate photographer for the rest of his life, documenting moments in the lives of strangers, friends, and colleagues.

Once the Clift family was settled in New York, Monty was introduced to the theater, and he thought he might like to be an actor. When he was thirteen, he joined a local theater group and appeared in an amateur production called *As Husbands Go*. Monty found he felt an ease on the stage. He stated, "The theater is my calling." Sunny recognized his aplomb on the stage and started to think that there was a career in this for Monty. Bill was not so sure that acting was a good profession for his son. He knew it was an unpredictable way to make a living. But because he always wanted to please his wife, he encouraged his son to explore the possibilities.

In 1934 Bill heard of a summer-stock play that was auditioning teenage boys, and he suggested to the producer that his fourteen-year-old son might be right for the role. The comedy *Fly Away Home* revolved around three mischievous children who plan to get their divorced parents back together. Monty auditioned and got the part. The play was a success, and when it moved to Broadway, fourteen-year-old Monty found himself a part of the legitimate New York theater scene. Coming from a life where he had never felt as if he fit in, he found a comfortable refuge on The Great White Way.

Monty was living up to Sunny's image of him as a prince. His regal bearing, his intoxicating good looks and his seemingly calm demeanor collectively suggested royalty. With Monty becoming a stage success, Sunny found a place to direct her longing for respect and recognition. Because she had no sense of self, Sunny attached herself to Monty. Her identity became exclusively that of Montgomery Clift's mother. She accompanied him everywhere, choosing who was suitable and who was not suitable to be friends with her son. Monty was too young to know there was something seriously wrong with this, that his own self-identity was being sacrificed to his mother's distorted ambitions.

Sunny became the quintessential stage mother—tagging along with Monty to meetings with agents and managers and coaching him into becoming elegant in the ways she was elegant.

She formed a protective bubble around Monty, attempting to keep him from getting too close to anyone else. Sunny wanted to be his mother, friend, confidante, and advisor. As far as she was concerned, no one lived up to her standards for Monty, no one, really, except herself.

Perhaps part of Sunny's protectiveness derived from her belief that he needed protecting. Many years later, she confided to her firstborn son, Brooks, that despite Monty feeling at home in the theater, she had been warned against allowing him to pursue acting. Apparently, she had talked to a medical professional regarding a career on the stage for her sensitive son. The doctor had said, "Mrs. Clift, I want to advise you to take him right out of the theater. It is no place for him. He doesn't have the nerve, constitution, to stand it, and he will break down. I should say about forty."

Bill Clift also had reservations, concerned that his sensitive son might be susceptible to homosexuals, who were known to be a big part of the theater community. There is some evidence that Monty had already experienced some homosexual activity by that time. "You see, Monty was a homosexual very early," Sunny confided to her son Brooks years later. "Oh, I would think he was about twelve or thirteen." Whether she was aware of homosexual encounters he had at that age or had just perceived some gay traits in Monty, she didn't say. Despite their concerns, Sunny and Bill allowed Monty to continue with his stage career and even seemed to turn a blind eye to the possibility of any sexual activity with men.

During the run of *Fly Away Home*, two English actors in their early thirties did take a troubling interest in Monty. Considering that Sunny had her hand in all aspects of Monty's life, it is curious that she did not interfere in the relationship of her fifteen-year-old son and these older actors, who were not in the play. A family friend, Phyllis Bamberger, saw dark forces at work. Recalling her concern for Monty at the time, she later said, "They would wait for Monty at the theater a lot. I told Bill Clift about the two men. I told him he ought to be worried about these two actors' relationship to Monty because they were old enough to be his parents and were obvious."

Fly Away Home ran for seven months—a healthy run for the times—and made Monty a known young personality in the theater. Soon after the run, he was cast as a prince in *Jubilee*, a Cole

Porter musical. With his looks and talent and that little extra dash of specialness, Monty was noticed.

Monty realized for sure by now that he preferred life on the stage to real life. If he was an actor, he would be able to reinvent himself again and again. All Monty wanted to do was perfect the pretend life that occurred within the pages of a script. And he became very good at it.

What mattered most to Monty was the work he was doing. In order to turn himself into fictional characters, he became a keen observer of life on the streets. For instance, while sitting in a diner, he would people watch for hours, as various New York City denizens came and went. When someone caught his attention—man or woman—he would focus in on them, observing the way they moved, spoke, ate. If when walking down the street, he found someone particularly interesting, he might follow them for blocks, imitating the way they walked but also observing where they stopped, where they might be going, until he felt he became that person and, for a while, inhabited their life.

2

FORMING ELIZABETH

Had I been raised in England, my life would have been completely different. Because my family settled in Los Angeles, I became a movie star. It wasn't a normal life, of course. The demands, particularly on an emotional level, were killing.
—**Elizabeth Taylor**

*T*HE CONNECTION BETWEEN ELIZABETH TAYLOR AND MONTGOMERY Clift was forming years before they met—with the parallel experience of a controlling mother living a large part of her life through an extraordinary child.

Elizabeth's mother, née Sara Viola Warmbrodt, was born in 1895 in Arkansas City, Kansas. Sara was a bubbly, attractive girl with bobbed hair and large dark eyes that dominated her pretty oval face. Sara's dream was to be an actress, and she dropped out of high school to pursue a career on the stage. She changed her name to Sara Sothern, and over the next decade, she appeared in several plays across the country, which led to her Broadway debut at the age of twenty-seven in the religious play *The Fool*. She made a strong impression in that role, and she toured with the production across the country and even played an engagement in London's West End. Stardom felt very close.

But after this success, "her long runs in 'the Fool' were not duplicated on her return to America," the *New York Times* noted in 1926. "A jinx . . . seemed to hang over her," and the next few plays she appeared in were flops. Show business can be cruel—stardom comes to only a few. In 1926, after one unsuccessful audition too many, Sara began to look for an alternative to her acting career, thinking, maybe, that the safest thing to do was to make a traditional life for herself—perhaps settle down and get married, if the right opportunity came along.

Enter a young man, Francis Taylor, whom she had known slightly back in Arkansas City. Sara was still unemployed and looking for her next role when she ran into Francis at the El Morocco club in New York City. Francis was stylishly dressed, handsome, and respectable—and from a good family.

He was born in 1897 in Springfield, Illinois, and a short time later his family moved to Arkansas City, where Sara originally met him. Although she was two years older, Sara couldn't help noticing Francis in their hometown. Everyone was taken by his striking good looks, particularly his sparkling blue eyes and thick, dark lashes. "All the young girls thought he was marvelous," one friend recalled, "but he didn't seem to notice."

When Sara met up with him again, Francis was working as an art dealer in Manhattan. His wealthy uncle, Howard Young, had got him started in the business and had brought him to New York, where the two men ran Howard's successful gallery. (Francis and Sara would later name their son after this uncle.)

At twenty-nine, Francis was already stepping into an age when people questioned why he wasn't married. If there are many threads that lead to Elizabeth's great love with Montgomery Clift, perhaps the first one started with her father. His romantic dalliances with men weren't well known—and even in the sophisticated art world, homosexuality was denounced in the 1920s and 1930s. Francis and Sara were married in 1926. For the first three years, they traveled extensively for Uncle Howard Young's business, buying European paintings for the American market.

If the relationship wasn't passionate, it was at least comfortable. Each personality contributed and enriched the whole entity they became as a couple. He was passive but suave and successful, and his career put them in the center of an artistic, affluent circle. She was outgoing, strong willed, and attractive, and it made a better impression for Francis to be married to such a woman. They made a pleasant public impression and stayed out of each other's way.

By 1929 Sara was ready to start a family, and the Taylors settled down in the UK, where Francis managed an art gallery in Mayfair, London. Even before the London art gallery was established, the Taylors were afforded a very comfortable lifestyle. Luxury was guaranteed to them because of their friendship with Victor Cazalet, a millionaire Conservative Party member of Parliament who had a passion for fine art and for Francis Taylor. It has been said that he became Francis's benefactor and lover. Apparently, Sara didn't mind. Sara, writes biographer William J. Mann, liked gay men. A quality Elizabeth would inherit.

Their son, Howard, was born in 1929. If Francis was a somewhat aloof father, Sara compensated by being a devoted mother. However, she longed for a daughter she could coddle and shape into a great lady with a thrilling life. So, in 1931 she was thrilled to discover she was pregnant again. Her son, Howard, had been born with the big eyes and finely sculpted features of a Botticelli angel—Sara imagined a girl would be even more gorgeous.

Elizabeth Rosemond Taylor, destined to become one of the most dazzling stars in Hollywood history, was born in London, England, on February 27, 1932. However, Elizabeth Taylor was not born beautiful. The great screen goddess was, at first, a most unusual-looking infant. Upon hearing that the newborn was a girl, Sara was over the moon. But with Elizabeth, at first, something seemed to have gone wrong. "As the precious bundle was placed in my arms, my heart stood still," Sara later remembered. "There inside the cashmere shawl was the funniest-looking baby I had ever seen. Her hair was long and black. Her ears were covered with thick black fuzz and inlaid into the sides of her head."

The newborn's head and body were covered with black hair, like a soft coat of fur. The excessive hair on newborn Elizabeth was diagnosed as a rare condition called hypertrichosis, most probably lanugo, because this type of body hair in infants falls out after a week or two, and this is precisely what occurred with Elizabeth. On top of that, her eyelids were tightly shut, as if glued together. The doctor tried everything to open the infant's eyes, but it seemed Elizabeth wasn't ready to look at the world yet. A visiting family friend, art dealer Ernest Lowy, commented bluntly, "The infant looked like a little monkey."

To Sara's great relief, after ten days the dark body hair Elizabeth was born with had fallen out. That was one concern out of the way. Then, when the baby's eyelids snapped open at last, they revealed the violet-blue eyes that she would become famous for. It was almost as if by sheer will, Sara made her daughter beautiful—transforming the ugly duckling into a baby swan—and at last she had the lovely baby girl she had envisioned for herself.

The baby's bright eyes seemed even more astonishing because they were framed by black fringes of long lashes. In her first few weeks, it was also discovered that the infant was born with another unusual trait: a genetic mutation called distichiasis, which causes the person to grow a double set of eyelashes. When told of this, Sara looked into her daughter's eyes and remarked, "Well, now, that doesn't sound so terrible at all." In Elizabeth's case, it wasn't. The double set of thick black lashes that framed her crystal-blue eyes would become a trademark of her beauty and would greatly enhance her exquisite features.

By the time she was a toddler, Elizabeth was startlingly beautiful. When Sara was strolling with Elizabeth on the streets or browsing with her in shops, strangers would stop to marvel at what a gorgeous child she was, admiring especially her flashing, violet-blue eyes. It all just bolstered Sara's intuition that this child was special, destined for great things, and that with the proper grooming, Elizabeth may one day grow up to make a mark on the world.

Elizabeth would always remember her early years in London as a happy time, calling it "idyllic." The Taylors were still living in the cottage on Victor Cazalet's estate in Kent, and they also had a house in Hampstead Garden Suburb, London. This house was 5,082 square feet and included six bedrooms and servants' quarters, and the property featured a tennis court. It was here young Elizabeth developed a love for animals, as her two residences allowed her to keep a variety of pets. "I had chickens, and I had my pony," she recalled. "I loved anything that walked or crawled."

She and her brother, Howard, kept rabbits, turtles, lambs, and goats—and a golden retriever she gave the foreshadowing name Monty. The pony she learned to ride on, Betty, was a gift from Victor Cazalet, who remained a patron to Francis and would be named Elizabeth's godfather.

Sara adored both her children, but she paid particular attention to Elizabeth. One reason Sara doted on Elizabeth was that from the very beginning, she had planned great things for her. Things she herself had never achieved. Sara, like Monty's mother, Sunny, had a nagging feeling that her life was only half lived, that she had not been given the opportunity to reach her full potential. She intuitively looked to Elizabeth to be the vessel by which she could fulfill her own destiny.

In England of the 1930s, real celebrity came from social status rather than show business, and Sara's ambition for Elizabeth was to have her grow up to be a cultured lady and eventually marry a titled gentleman. By most, Sara was considered a charming lady, but some saw her as too class conscious, as a social climber who was always exaggerating her status. She didn't do this for herself: she wanted to secure a grand and privileged future for Elizabeth.

Although never shy around animals, Elizabeth could be bashful around people. To help her develop social graces, Sara enrolled her in deportment classes and dance lessons. (Sara also tried to get Howard interested in dance, but when he rebelled, Sara allowed him to drop out. This enabled her to devote more attention to four-year-old Elizabeth.)

When the time came for the dance recital, Elizabeth was included. Wearing a butterfly costume, she joined the other little girls backstage, who were all dressed as tiny butterflies, as well. Sara worried that Elizabeth might be too intimidated by an audience to perform, but she made it through the entire dance routine, doing the basic, perfunctory dance steps taught to young children.

It was after the dance recital was over that Sara discovered her daughter had inherited her ability to captivate an audience. After the other children departed the stage, the tiny butterfly named Elizabeth stayed front and center, bowing and blowing kisses, as the enchanted audience clapped and cheered, "Bravo!"

This was most likely a turning point in her young life, though Elizabeth was too young to realize it at the time. As a star looking back on the event, she would recall the mixed bag of exhilaration: "the isolation, the hugeness, the feeling of space and no end to space—and the applause bringing you back into focus, and noise rattling against your face."

In 1939, shortly before the outbreak of World War II, the Taylor family thought it best to leave their beloved England and return to the United States. Sara and the children set sail first, and Francis would follow soon after.

On the ship sailing to America, mother and daughter saw a movie with the foreshadowing title *The Little Princess*, starring eleven-year-old Shirley Temple. Elizabeth was mesmerized by the all-dancing, all-singing moppet, who got to be a princess to boot. From then on, she was a fan of movies and movie stars and saw a movie whenever possible. Sara's wheels started turning right there on the ship. Shirley Temple was a lovely little girl, a child star beloved by millions, and Sara had a lovely little girl of her own, and at that very moment the two of them were on their way to Los Angeles.

The Taylor family first settled in Pacific Palisades, in a house very near the beach. Elizabeth and Howard were enrolled in a school that was attended by the elite children of Hollywood bigwigs. "I went to a school where every kid's father was a producer, director, or an actor," Elizabeth would recall.

Sara figured that her children's real development would come not from the kind of education they were getting, but from her hobnobbing with show-business royalty. She devoted her time to networking—on the Hollywood landscape that was essential to getting anywhere, and networking was Sara's strong point.

In a town that valued beauty above all else, young Elizabeth garnered attention immediately. As they did in London, people would stop mother and daughter on the street to marvel at Elizabeth's ethereal loveliness, adding that "she should be in movies," as if the thought had never crossed Sara's mind. *Gone with the Wind* had just started production in early 1939, and it was the talk of the town. After a massive search, Vivien Leigh was chosen to play Scarlett O'Hara, and photographs of her were constantly appearing in newspapers and magazines. Sara was quick to ask anyone who stopped to admire Elizabeth, "Doesn't she look just like Vivien Leigh?"

She devised a plan to get Elizabeth cast as Scarlett and Rhett's daughter, Bonnie Blue, in the epic film. She pressed on, full steam ahead, making friends with casting directors and lunching with the wives of directors. Always, Sara's daughter, Elizabeth, would come up in conversation, and the inevitable photo would come out of the purse. When it came to getting Elizabeth into the movie industry, Sara seemed to have a one-track mind.

She was well off, had a handsome husband and two healthy, beautiful children. But she never forgot that glorious moment in time when she was singled out on Broadway. For her, that was a beginning, and she had never achieved the ending. A feeling of unfulfillment festered. "I gave up my career when I was married," she liked to say, giving the impression she had retired as a success.

Meanwhile, Francis Taylor opened a new art gallery in the Beverly Hills Hotel, and his earliest clients were some of the biggest stars in Hollywood. Among those who would stop in to browse and buy were Alan Ladd, Vincent Price, James Mason, and Greta Garbo.

But the customer who caught Sara's attention most, and whom she made a point to befriend, was gossip queen Hedda Hopper, who, along with Louella Parsons, reigned over celebrity gossip. It was to the gossip columns and movie magazines that the public went for information on their favorite stars. Through their columns Hedda Hopper and Louella Parsons reached millions of people, telling them which stars were hot, which movie they should see, and uncovering the scandal of the day. It was not lost on Sara that Hopper was one of the most powerful names in the movie industry.

Hopper had been a minor actress in the movies, one who never quite made a big name for herself. But once she started reporting about the business she herself had floundered in, she really found her calling (first, on the radio, then as a syndicated columnist for the *Los Angeles Times*, with thirty-five million readers around the world). When she really gained notoriety as a columnist, she was past forty and not particularly alluring, but she compensated by calling attention to herself with outrageous, extravagant large hats. Hats became her trademark. She was going to get heads to turn for her one way or another.

Sara sucked up to Hopper, and as a result, little Elizabeth got into her good graces. In her column she plugged the art gallery, but more importantly to Sara, Hopper also mentioned Sara Taylor's glory on the stage and her "beautiful eight-year-old daughter, Elizabeth." At one point the columnist noted that producer David O. Selznick had not yet cast all the smaller roles in *Gone with the Wind*. Hopper told her readers (including Selznick) that Elizabeth seemed an excellent choice to play Bonnie Blue, the daughter of Scarlett O'Hara and Rhett Butler.

Unfortunately, Selznick didn't bite, but Sara had made an important connection for her young daughter. Hopper would have a love/hate relationship with Elizabeth Taylor for the next fifteen years. In her last years, she did everything in her dwindling power to destroy Elizabeth's career.

In all of this jockeying for position in Hollywood, Francis Taylor became somewhat lost inside the family unit. Sara's focus was completely on Elizabeth. Francis very much wanted to be close with his daughter, but Sara kept a tight fence around her, isolating her even from her father. The days that he did have Elizabeth to himself became very special to him. They would go on excursions: he would spoil her, treating her like his own little princess by taking her shopping and buying her anything she wanted, and then they would end the day at the ice-cream parlor. Elizabeth came to love these father-daughter days, too—it was one of the few times she got to be a carefree kid.

Some saw Sara as too pushy and aggressive, because that's the way she represented herself. But her immediate family realized that she was just unfulfilled and wanted her daughter to have the things she had never had—and that she wanted a piece for herself, too.

3

SURROGATES

He had every gift that God could give a human being.
—Billy LeMassena

*M*ONTY'S STRIKING LOOKS AND EASE ON THE STAGE GARNERED him the attention of theater directors, and his Broadway career continued to blossom. It was his charm and naturalness that made the far-fetched 1938 Broadway play *Dame Nature* work. The play is about a fifteen-year-old boy who discovers he's going to be a father but doesn't know how it happened. When exploring a character, he already had developed a way of bringing in pieces of his own character traits to add detailed touches of realism.

Through his teen years, Monty had acquaintances in the theater, but no one he was close with. His sensitivity and his loner status made him seem somewhat weird, but the kind of exquisite beauty he possessed made even this weirdness very attractive. But he was still uncomfortable with people, and he had never really had an opportunity to learn how to ease into a friendship. His isolation made him come across as haughty. Between his own uneasiness with most people and Sunny keeping him from becoming close with those she felt were unsuitable, Monty became more closed off.

It was lonely in the cocoon Sunny kept him in. And in that

loneliness, he held on tighter to his relationship with his mother. He was dependent on her, but he resented it and always would. In later years he made no secret of his disdain for his mother. There was a lot of speculation about Sunny and the seventeen-year-old Monty; it was hard to understand that a young man as talented and promising as Monty would allow himself to be so domineered by his mother.

When the first biography of Monty, by Robert LaGuardia, came out, Sunny was upset and angry. She called Brooks and implored him to write a book himself, one contradicting LaGuardia's. "If I hadn't gone to the extremes in doing things for Monty, I probably wouldn't feel it quite so hard," she said, her voice shaking. "It's tough. I gave everything I had." Brooks taped the conversation, as was his habit, and listening to it, you can't help but feel for her. Here was a woman who did the best she could, who wanted what was good for her children, and was well meaning.

More acclaim came to Monty in 1938, when he took the role of the returning son in the Broadway play *There Shall Be No Night*, performing opposite the highly esteemed husband and wife acting team of Alfred Lunt and Lynn Fontanne. The couple spotted his specialness the moment Monty walked into the audition. "I guess that's the boy," Lunt said upon spotting him. Lynn Fontanne readily agreed. They grew to love Monty, even signing a photo to him with the inscription "From your *real* parents."

Meanwhile, with regard to his other "real parents," Monty started taking stabs at independence, dabbling in self-exploration, trying especially to free himself from the stranglehold Sunny had him in. Longing for male companionship, he started a sexual relationship with another actor in the play, William (Billy) LeMassena, who would remain a close friend for life. Shocked at Monty's indiscretion, and speaking as a father figure, Alfred Lunt warned Monty that, for his career's sake, he should find a nice girl and settle down—that is, hide his sexuality behind the respectability of matrimony, just as he himself had done. "You can't ordinarily be a pansy in the theater and survive," he warned. Insiders assumed that Lunt was gay and the older Lynn Fontanne was bisexual, and that the union was a lavender marriage, or a white marriage, to shield them from gossip.

It would have been easy for Monty to go along with this ruse. With his blue-green eyes (Monty called them "cat eyes"), dark, sculpted brows, and delicate, handsome features, more and more women were drawn to Monty, and he genuinely loved the company of women. One female friend claimed Monty was so easy to talk to, it was almost like talking to "another girl." Female audience members started waiting for him at the backstage door after shows. Monty would always stop and take the time to chat politely with them. Sometimes he would make dates to meet one of them and then not show up.

Monty welcomed friendships with women, and he was very affectionate with them. As a result, whenever he spent a lot of time with a woman, onlookers would say he was having an affair. Sometimes even the woman he was seeing wondered if they were having a romance and if it would soon involve sex. It wouldn't.

It should be noted that Monty, particularly earlier in his career, liked to give the impression that he was heterosexual or bisexual. Many of the women he was close with and appeared to be dating would later state that the relationship had been completely without sex. Those closest to him suspected he was primarily gay. The concrete evidence that he was bisexual isn't concrete at all: Certainly, he had close emotional attachments with female friends and a fascination with strong older women, he enjoyed going to burlesque houses to watch strip shows, and he was very fond of kissing and kissed lovers, friends, men, women, sexually, nonsexually. But early in life he tried his hand with women but discovered he liked men better—at least in bed. (That doesn't mean that he never slept with a woman.) Thus, the safest thing to conclude is that Monty was gay.

In 1938 Monty did spend a great deal of time with a young, dark-haired, fresh-faced actress who seemed to be more serious than the rest. Phyllis Thaxter was an understudy in *There Shall Be No Night*, and friends viewed her and Monty as a couple. And he even brought her home to meet his mother. For once, Sunny approved. From all outside appearances, this was a hot and heavy romance. The two became so close that they sometimes slept in the same bed together. Sunny would serve them breakfast in bed when Phyllis spent the night.

But after some time of her "relationship" with Monty leading nowhere, Phyllis confided to a girlfriend that although she loved Monty, she had to settle on being friends with him. "It was a romantic kind of love," she said, "but we never went to bed together." Even without any sexual relationship whatsoever, the two talked about marriage and becoming a great acting team. Then Monty did a complete about-face and declared he could never marry her.

Phyllis would later reflect that being young and naïve, she had thought Monty "liked both men and women." She said, "He was wonderful to women. He felt tremendous empathy. But I also sensed he lived a very separate life when I didn't see him—a life I had no part of and didn't ask about."

Part of that separate life had to do with Broadway conductor Lehman Engel. Monty met Lehman casually through a mutual friend, and there was an obvious powerful attraction between the two of them. Monty became assertive in pursuit of a relationship. Discovering that Lehman would be giving a lecture in Connecticut, Monty surprised him by showing up and sitting in a front seat. Afterward, Monty asked if Lehman would mind if he accompanied him on the two-hour train ride back to Manhattan, and the relationship started from there. Unlike Monty's relationship with Phyllis Thaxter, this one was sexual.

Thirty-year-old Lehman was madly flattered to be pursued by the handsome Broadway prince, who was ten years younger than him. Interestingly, even Sunny approved of the relationship. It was as if she was terrified of losing Monty to a female fling that might inevitably lead to marriage, but a relationship with another man—particularly one who was a cultured individual and a rising conductor—was fine with her. In fact, when Lehman was leaving for a vacation in Mexico, it was Sunny who called him and ask if

Monty might join him (or perhaps Monty asked Sunny to call him). She even went so far as to book a suite for them on the boat over.

It was during that trip that Monty came down with an intestinal condition called amoebic dysentery. They had to cut the trip short and head back to New York. Monty's condition turned into chronic colitis, which would ravage his insides and come back to haunt him for the rest of his life. He had to go on a diet of almost-raw steak and milk—it was the only food that didn't give him stomach cramps. From this point on, he had terrible trouble with his stomach, which often tormented him, and he began taking a great many pills, trying anything to get some relief. "He would double up in pain, in agony," his friend Jean Green would later recall. This was an important, busy time in his life. He couldn't allow his illness to hold him back. It was because of this condition that Monty was exempted from military service during World War II.

To combat his illness, he did his best to keep his body strong; even when feeling weak, he worked out at Stillman's gym. But Monty also started taking painkillers. Because of the variety of medications he began taking, this period marks the beginning of his addiction to pills. His friend Kevin McCarthy stated, "Because he was in pain very frequently, Monty would go in the drugstore, go behind the counter where the pills were, and he would charm his way with the clerks, so he'd get his pills to kill the pain. All his life, it was misery."

More than anything, his relationship with Lehman made Monty realize the need to sever ties with his parents, particularly Sunny. Now he didn't feel the need to bring every new person in his life to meet his mother, and he became secretive about who was in his life. He found a small apartment above a Laundromat on East Fifty-fifth Street. It was only a few steps away from his parents' place, but it was a start, as it was his own. Although he continuously tried to separate himself from his mother, there was a deep current of unexpressed emotions that kept them connected.

Sunny never felt that she was in the dark about what was going on in Monty's life. "I knew right away that he was addicted to little boys," she said. "It shocked me, and I told him so, and I said it would weaken him artistically. His father was furious. 'How could a son of mine stoop to this?' he asked. He said I was entirely too gentle about the matter." On the other hand, Sunny didn't mind the fact that Monty was gay. She felt it would keep him closer to her.

After his relationship with Leman, Monty started a relationship with a young actor, one about his own age, who was known as Josh. "When we were alone, it was like Monty and I were shut away from reality for a couple of hours," Josh recalled. "It was a disorientating experience. Alone, we would be emotional and passionate, but outside we had to hide our feelings. Naturally, we felt guilty about what we were doing, but we couldn't help ourselves. We were violently attracted to each other and knew we had fallen in love." According to Josh, Monty exhibited agitation about having to keep this relationship secret. Josh would recall, "One of the things that was starting to torture Monty back in 1940 was the fact that he had to hide his sexual feelings. He despised deception, pretense, and he felt the intolerable strain of living a lie."

In April 1942 Monty was cast in *Mexican Mural*, a play penned by Ramon Naya. The play is a series of sketches focusing on various characters in Vera Cruz during the Shrove Tuesday carnival. It would be one of the most remarkable projects of Monty's life. A noncommercial, experimental piece, it was not remarkable for the quality of the script or even Monty's performance. What made it such a milestone in Monty's life was the four people he met during the short run of the play, fellow performers who would be carefully woven into the fabric of his life.

As Monty was breaking away from his mother, these four friends became surrogate family members, each taking a role in his life that fulfilled something he needed. One of the actor's in the play, Kevin McCarthy, would become one of Monty's closest friends and would remain so for more than a decade. "We got to be friends almost instantly," McCarthy recalled. Monty bonded with him over a sort of theatrical elitism. They believed that the theater was producing too much mediocrity. They had little respect for most of the acting and the theatrical productions of that time period. They felt that they, of course, could do much better. "We must have assumed that we were more intelligent or something," McCarthy said. Not surprisingly, they developed an affinity for a new style of acting and writing that soon emerged, and Monty was the natural leader of this new wave.

Monty also befriended a young actress in the cast of *Mexican Mural*, Augusta Dabney, who was dating Kevin at the time. (They would soon marry.) The couple's lives would remain entangled with Monty's for more than ten years. "He was a remarkable person," Kevin stated, "and the fact that he was interested in us and liked us so much was flattering to us." Reflecting upon the phenomenon that was Monty, Kevin said, "He seemed the personification of the young prince. He had all the best qualities."

Also in the cast of *Mexican Mural* was a thirty-three-year-old Russian actress, Mira Rostova, whom director Robert Lewis cast as a fake witch doctor. Birdlike, delicately pretty, her voice heavily accented, Mira always maintained throughout the years that a sexual relationship or a romance of any kind was never a part of her and Monty's friendship, but Monty never denied or confirmed that. He seemed to enjoy having people guess about his love life.

One way to interpret this is that Monty no longer got along with his mother, but he needed a mother figure, so he always seemed to try to re-create one. He and Mira Rostova shared a love of the same books and music and plays—and they were both powerfully dedicated to the craft of acting. Mira would go on to coach Monty. More than just an acting coach, she became a sort of life coach. What was probably most important in Monty's life is that Mira was devoted to him. For years to come, her career was to devote herself to him, to fine-tune his brilliance, to make him look good. Monty came to monopolize a large portion of her life, as she took on a bigger and bigger role in his career, not just coaching him line by line, scene by scene, but also discussing the scripts he should accept and in which direction he should steer his career.

Professionally, he became completely dependent on Mira. When he started making movies, he would bring her onto the set, and as it turned out, she was on the set for most of his films. His movie directors would come to loathe her, because Monty would look to her after each take, seeking her approval over that of his directors.

Also colliding with Monty during the production of *Mexican Mural* was the notorious Libby Holman, one of the most interesting and controversial players in Monty's life. She became a major influence on him. Born Elizabeth Lloyd Holzman in Cincinnati, Ohio, in 1904, hard-drinking, chain-smoking, husky-voiced Libby was one of the more suggestive torch singers of the era.

Her sexuality was predominantly lesbian—her lovers are said to have included Tallulah Bankhead, Billie Holiday, and DuPont heiress Louisa d'Andelot Carpenter, with whom she had a long-lasting relationship—although she did have a weakness for extremely handsome younger homosexual (or sexually confused) men with a desire to be dominated.

Libby's first taste of fame came as a torch singer, owing in part to her throaty renditions of blues songs like "Moanin' Low." She wasn't beautiful, but she was a striking woman and seductively flashy, with kohl-lined eyes, penciled arched eyebrows, and bright red lipstick above and beyond the natural contours of her stern mouth. Her olive skin and long dark hair added to her exotic appearance.

With her smoky voice, raunchy humor, and uninhibited sexuality, Libby was able to ensnare men and women in an erotic spell—particularly when she was onstage. But years of smoking, alcohol abuse, and hard living eventually coarsened her sultry looks, leaving her rough and hard looking. Her once smooth complexion became ruddy and deeply lined.

Although her sexual appetite was mostly for women, Libby had a particularly strong fetish for sensitive younger homosexual men with a self-destructive bent. With Monty, she hit the erotic jackpot. The mere sight of Monty hit her like a gut punch. "I was burning up," she later told a friend. "Just looking at him made me feel like I would catch an incurable fever." Libby's biographer,

Jon Bradshaw, suggested that with these boys, "the sexual act itself was not what captivated Libby. She sought instead its ensuing intimacy, its friendship, and camaraderie."

Libby's true notoriety came from her marriage to twenty-year-old Zachary Smith Reynolds, an heir to the R. J. Reynolds Tobacco Company empire and seven years her junior. In 1930, six months after their wedding, Reynolds was found with a bullet hole in his head in an upstairs bedroom of the family estate. According to some stories, the couple had argued when Libby revealed that she was pregnant (Libby had been promiscuous throughout their marriage, while Reynolds had impotence problems). Was his death a suicide or murder? That was the question that dominated headlines. It was brought out that Reynolds had suffered from wild mood swings and depression and that his homosexual impulses (he was having an ongoing affair with a mechanic) had stymied any normal sexual relations with Libby.

The medical examiner at first declared Reynolds's death a suicide, but Libby was later indicted for murder. The Reynolds family, however, wanted the scandal off the front pages and used their considerable wealth to get the charges dropped. The case never went to trial, and the death was ultimately ruled a suicide. Libby later gave birth to Christopher "Topper" Reynolds, who became an heir to the Reynolds fortune. The marriage left her rich, but her husband's mysterious death became her defining characteristic.

Tragedy seemed to follow her closely. In 1945, at the age of twenty-nine, her second husband, Ralph Holmes—also suspected of being gay—was found dead from a barbiturate overdose. So by the time Monty met Libby, she already had two younger gay husbands who died by suicide.

With his beauty, youth, sexual ambivalence, and openness to manipulation, Monty couldn't have been more Libby's type if he had been computer generated. During rehearsals for *Mexican Mural*, other cast members looked on, fascinated, as they grew increasingly close. Unlike his chemistry with Mira, which came across as an intense friendship, Libby and Monty gave off an erotic charge. She understood his type. And Monty was corruptible.

What kind of sex life Monty had with Libby would be speculated about for years to come. Monty's friend William LeMassena observed, "The idea of the handsome young idol of Broadway going to bed with an unattractive older woman was repulsive."

Libby and Monty spent a great deal of time together in New York City and at her Connecticut estate, and in the coming years their relationship became fueled by alcohol and pills. All the while, Monty was involved with a number of men and cruised the streets and bars.

While the play *Mexican Mural* ran for only a few selected performances, the impact it had on Monty's life was enormous. These costars would help shape his future.

4

THE MOST ASTONISHING-LOOKING CHILD

My life was overscheduled and overdisciplined. When I was shooting a picture, I had to be on the set, ready to go. And when I wasn't before the camera, I had to go to school on the [movie] lot. It was an impossible way to grow up. But it did make me tough.
—Elizabeth Taylor

*T*HROUGHOUT 1940 AND 1941, SARA KEPT MAKING THE ROUNDS with Elizabeth and urging Francis that when a studio executive came into the art gallery, to be sure to mention his beautiful, talented daughter. Later in the year, a chairman at Universal Studios saw promise in Elizabeth's unusual beauty and signed the nine-year-old to a six-month contract at one hundred dollars a week, with an option to renew.

Hedda Hopper carried an item about Elizabeth's first contract in her column, at the same time plugging Sara's brief career: "If there is anything in heredity, Elizabeth should be a hit." But it was months before she landed her first small role in the low-budget comedy *There's One Born Every Minute*.

The hook for the movie at the time was that it had in the cast

Carl "Alfalfa" Switzer, of the popular *The Little Rascals* movie serial. The hook for history is that the film gave the world its first glimpse of Elizabeth Taylor on-screen. Nine years old at the time, Elizabeth did fine in her few scenes in the tedious picture, but she was ignored in the reviews, and the movie sank without a ripple just when she was up for review with her six-month option.

The studio casting director, Dan Kelley, saw no future for Elizabeth as a child star. He thought her specialness wasn't marketable. Elizabeth's half-child, half-woman face confused him. In a memo he wrote, "This kid has nothing. Her eyes are too old. She doesn't look like a kid." Universal promptly dropped her, which turned out to be a blessing in disguise. It is true that you could already see the face of the gorgeous woman she would become in the face of the child she was, which made her beauty unusual and arresting but difficult to categorize.

Sara, the quintessential stage mother, wasn't deterred by her daughter's first rejection. She pushed forward for a movie career for Elizabeth, but she didn't have to push very hard. Elizabeth was recognized as special almost from the start. Through producer Sam Marx, Francis heard that MGM was looking for a young girl to play opposite teen actor Roddy McDowall. Sara wasted no time in researching the role and what the studio was looking for.

She discovered that the young actress who had been cast opposite Roddy McDowall in *Lassie Come Home* had turned out to be too tall for the part. The producers were looking for a replacement. The two specific attributes they were looking for were that the young girl should speak with a British accent and she could not be taller than Roddy. Elizabeth was certainly petite, and her early years in England made her qualify on both counts. She was brought in for a screen test.

Elizabeth did her first screen test opposite a mop. She had studied the script carefully, and in the scene her character was supposed to be talking to Lassie, the world-renowned collie. When she arrived on the set in costume and makeup, they told her to say her lines to the mop, a stand-in for the dog. "The mop was supposed to be Lassie," Elizabeth laughed.

Apparently, both Elizabeth and the mop were convincing. In only her second film, she got her first real starring role in what would become a classic, *Lassie Come Home*. The movie was based on the popular children's novel, and MGM shot it with a big budget and in color, which was relatively rare for films in the 1940s.

Roddy McDowall would never forget his first encounter with Elizabeth. "They brought this little girl on the set," he recalled. "I began laughing, because she was so extraordinarily beautiful. Very mature face for a child. The most astonishing-looking child I had ever seen." Roddy was four years older than Elizabeth, and the two formed a strong bond on the film set, a bond that would last the rest of their lives. Elizabeth came to see him as another older brother—someone to confide in and share her dreams with.

At the same time, her mother was always on the set. She stood on the sidelines, giving Elizabeth secret hand signals throughout a scene and attempting to coach her between takes.

Lassie Come Home was a big hit. It was in color, and it gave Elizabeth a chance to show some acting chops. Her mother's coaching aside, Elizabeth's acting seemed instinctual. She was a born actress. Most importantly, Elizabeth's performance caught the eye of MGM head, Louis B. Mayer. Respected, feared, and powerful, Mayer could recognize talent, and he understood how to develop it. "More stars than there are in heaven," his studio boasted.

He signed Elizabeth to a seven-year contract, starting at one hundred dollars a week. Elizabeth was now primely positioned for the training and grooming necessary for stardom. MGM was renowned for its glamorous stars—the most talented and charismatic actors in Hollywood and some of the most beloved personalities to come out of the studio system.

Almost overnight, Elizabeth's life changed completely—MGM was now her school, her workplace, and her one source of contact with children her own age. Elizabeth would no longer attend traditional classes. She would now be educated at the famous Little Red Schoolhouse on the MGM lot.

Elizabeth would usually arrive at the classroom in the morning, already in makeup and costume for the movie she was working on. She'd be schooled for two or three hours; then a tutor would accompany her on the set and teach her in between takes. In an attempt to hold on to a small part of her childhood, Elizabeth would bring one of her beloved pets to work. Often there would be a cage housing a chipmunk or a hamster in a corner of the soundstage. "She would always come on the set with two or three dogs or a squirrel in a cage, which they'd have to put off the set because it was always making noise all the time," an MGM friend remembered.

When in a more bitter mood, Elizabeth would look back at that time and say, "Constantly faced with adult situations and denied the companionship of my peers, I stopped being a child the minute I began working in pictures." Although still a little girl, she was already having big demands put on her. A third of her salary went to her parents. Sara also got her own salary as Elizabeth's chaperone, but she took the role a few steps further, also acting as her daughter's unofficial publicity agent, acting coach, and manager.

MGM kept capitalizing on their investment. Not having any immediate roles that she was suited for, the studio loaned Elizabeth to Fox for another important movie, the screen adaption of *Jane Eyre*, starring Orson Welles and Joan Fontaine. In her role in *Jane Eyre*, all the qualities that made her a child star are evident. Fox didn't name Elizabeth in the credits, but she was given a memorable entrance.

In the film she plays Helen, a friend of young Jane in the orphanage. Jane Eyre is set up to be viewed as a bad child and to be isolated and hated by the cruel headmaster. She is left standing on a stool in the courtyard. Hours later, while she still stands there, Elizabeth comes down a staircase toward Jane. She casts a large shadow over the scene before we see her. Then there is a close-up. What a close-up! Her angelic face is instantly recognizable. Although she was only eleven at the time of filming, the close-up has the impact of the adult Elizabeth Taylor. "I brought you this from supper," she says, handing Jane a crust of bread.

The students had been warned to avoid Jane, and so Elizabeth's character represents kindness in a cold and indifferent world.

Back at MGM she was reteamed with Roddy McDowall in *The White Cliffs of Dover* (1944), but the talk of the MGM lot was their upcoming production, *National Velvet*, the story of a teenage girl, Velvet Brown, who wins a horse in the lottery and disguises herself as a boy to ride it in England's Grand National Steeplechase. Elizabeth decided she had to have the role of Velvet Brown. It was not only a star-making role, but she also felt that she deserved the part. With her affinity to animals, her strong love of horses, she literally was Velvet Brown.

But when she approached producer Pandro Berman about playing the character, he told her that at eleven she was too young to be cast as the teenage Velvet. Studio executives agreed, citing that, although she was highly promising, she wouldn't be believable as an adolescent. They even pointed out that the petite Elizabeth was still flat chested. Elizabeth was undeterred. "Don't worry. You'll have your breasts," she declared defiantly and stormed out of the office.

She wouldn't allow the top brass to forget her, reminding them almost daily that she wanted the part and she was on a vigorous campaign to "grow up fast." It was more likely a stroke of good timing—or the effect of a very strong will—rather than the workouts and the high-fat diet she put herself on, but in three months she had several growth spurts. In just twelve weeks, she grew three inches and developed into a B cup. Elizabeth got the part, and she was determined to do it justice. This was a career-making movie, and she knew it. So did Sara, and she was just as anxious for Elizabeth to shine. On the set Sara would stand behind the camera and coach her daughter with hand signals and gestures, most likely imagining herself doing the role.

During the shooting of *National Velvet*, Elizabeth fell off the horse and suffered a serious spinal injury. Terrified she would be replaced, she never let on that she was in a great deal of pain and soldiered on through the rest of the filming. But the injury would give her painful problems for the rest of her life. In the long run, all the hard work, pain, and anxiety were worth it. When *National Velvet* was released in 1944, it was a huge success, and audiences were captivated by its striking star.

Louie B. Mayer realized he had a major goddess in the making on his hands, but Elizabeth was at an awkward age—too young to play a leading lady and too adult looking to be the typical child star. The studio kept her off the screen completely in 1945 but kept up a steady stream of publicity about her, and she contributed to it by writing a book, called *Nibbles and Me*, about her pet chipmunk. In 1946 she was back on the screen with a canine for a costar in *Courage of Lassie*.

It was at this time that Elizabeth began to feel a wedge driven between herself and her father. If it is true that a girl's first love is often her father, that was certainly the case with Elizabeth. Yet Francis became more distant from her, and he began to drink and stay away from home more often. Elizabeth was too young to understand the myriad of reasons behind his change, one of them being that he suddenly felt belittled by her success. His young daughter was making more money than he did—and she was shooting to fame and fortune. Now he barely paid any attention to her, and when he did, he was drunk and would become abusive and "bat [her] around a little."

At the time, little Elizabeth wondered what had caused this change in a man she had always considered "proud, beautiful, and dignified." Now he was solitary, inscrutable. But she loved her father dearly and longed to connect with him again.

Some in his circle thought Francis seemed more comfortable with his male friends. He was at times uncomfortable in the family, as his marriage covered up a secret homosexual life. There would soon be a new man in his life, costume designer Adrian, who was involved in a lavender marriage with film star Janet Gaynor. "Of course, Taylor is a gay icon known for her close friendships with gay, bisexual actors, like Monty Clift, Rock Hudson, James Dean, Roddy McDowall, Laurence Harvey, etc.," showbusiness columnist Lee Graham observed. "But it goes further back than that, since her father was gay."

Years later, when she was twenty-one, Elizabeth was still hoping to forge a close relationship with her father. She called Francis one day and asked him to come over to the house she had just bought. "We went into the kitchen and I sat on his lap and I put my arms around him and buried my head in his neck and we both sobbed," she said wistfully. "And we bonded for the first time since I was nine." She went on to say that from that day up until the day he died, they were extraordinarily close.

5

A TROUBLED, COMPLEX GUY

He had a kind of mad, wild, crazy way about him. And witty. Very witty. The combination of the two was just . . . sheer wonder. Sheer delight . . . You became alive. He made everything alive.
—Jean Green

*O*VER THE NEXT SEVERAL YEARS, MONTY TOOK THE LEAD IN A NUMber of Broadway plays, including *The Searching Wind, The Skin of Our Teeth, Our Town,* and *Foxhole in the Parlor.* During this time, members of the film industry continually tried to coax Monty to Hollywood. He rejected every offer. He loved to act, but he preferred the stage. His passion was for Broadway. As with any growing young star, new horizons, were inviting, but he instinctively felt that the timing wasn't quite right to venture into movies.

In New York, Monty's professional life was soaring, and in his personal life, he was venturing out—deepening his friendships and exploring his sexuality. Like many magnetic people who become more in demand, Monty began instinctively to box away different areas of his life. Often his friends from one part of his life didn't meet or overlap with people in another.

In one boxed-off area, Kevin McCarthy and his wife, Augusta

Dabney, were particularly close to him, and Monty became a part of their family, having meals with them, staying overnight, traveling together, eventually playing with their children like an uncle. "Monty was always there," Kevin recalled. "Very often he wanted to be like part of our family. We welcomed him into it, and he would often invite us to come along when he was traveling."

Most people could find little negative to say about Monty during this period of his life and career. He had the magic, the elusive magic that true stars are made of, even though he wasn't a movie star yet. He had a distinctive gift for charming those around him. "I never had that experience since in my life," Augusta observed. "There was something very special about Monty. He really treated everyone, I mean individually, not in a group, as though one was of great value to him."

In spite of their relationship being void of a sexual component, many people in the theater felt that Monty had actually fallen in love with the chisel-jawed, hazel-eyed Kevin McCarthy. Many people, including Tennessee Williams and Truman Capote, would assert that Kevin was "the true love of Monty's life." Through the years Kevin stated many times that there was never anything sexual between them, yet befriending the couple and ingratiating himself into their household would certainly be a way for Monty to be near Kevin continuously. And they certainly developed what would be called in today's vernacular a bromance.

Looking back on his unusual place in their marriage, Augusta came to a realization regarding Monty's closeness with her and the wives of his other friends. "Every woman was crazy about Monty, and he seemed to be in love with all of us, individually," Augusta recalled. "But I don't think it was a coincidence that each one of us was married, so that the relationship was protected."

It wasn't until years later that these women realized that their marriages had formed a wall of protection for Monty. He could get as close to them as he liked and have them fall for him, but the relationship would not be brought into the romantic realm. Monty was also close friends with their husbands, and he would never cross the line with a pal's wife, and they knew that. This allowed for these relationships to run very deep without ever becoming sexual or confining. It also removed a lot of the complications that develop between lovers. "The odd thing about him is, both men and women, both sexes, loved him," Augusta observed.

Another couple, Fred and Jean Green, had a similar relationship with Monty. Years later, Jean tried to explain the dynamics of the couple's relationship with him, remembering what it was like when Monty would stay at their house. The minute Monty arrived, "this magic would start," she remembered. "Just his being there . . . It all became fun. We had one bedroom in that house, with twin beds. We were living in it and fixing it up. And [we had] an old terrible couch in the living room, which Monty was assigned to. We'd be exhausted at night, and we'd fall into bed. Monty would appear in the doorway like a child and say, 'I'm lonely out there. It's lonesome out there. It's dark.' He'd either get into bed with Fred or he'd get into bed with me. Or we'd push the beds together, and we'd all get in the same bed. In the strictest sense, it certainly wasn't sexual. There were no sex acts involved . . . We were like children."

Energy, charisma, optimism, and a sense of adventure poured from Monty like sunshine. Broadway was very excited about his future, and major playwrights, like Thornton Wilder, were inspired. When in charming mode, Monty was full of amusing expressions and had a unique way of describing things. Once, when he was going to the dentist, he explained, "He's just filling in the decay in my soul, that's all." Later, he quipped that his long telephone conversations with Elizabeth Taylor were "Elizabethan discussions." All the things he truly disliked were "vomitable." When depressed, he would describe himself as being "none too gorgeous."

Even though he remained on Hollywood's radar, the theater remained the most important thing for him, and over the next few years, he appeared in some very prestigious productions. He was directed by Elia Kazan in the original production of *The Skin of Our Teeth*, a play by Thornton Wilder, and performed opposite Tallulah Bankhead. He appeared as the poetic Canadian flyer in *You Touched Me!*, a collaboration between Tennessee Williams and Donald Windham, both of whom would become friends. He was also memorable in Lillian Hellman's play *The Searching Wind*. (By now his friend and coach Mira Rostova was ensconced in his dressing room during performances.)

Monty began to develop a mysterious and complicated sexuality, which many around him speculated about. But Monty was learning to make the moral constrictions of the time work for him in a private way. As frustrating as having a secret life could be at times, it also gave him the opportunity to inhabit different worlds and covertly slide in and out of each depending on his moods and his cravings.

He began to embrace his double life. Cruising for men in Times Square, in restrooms, bars, gyms, and diners was considered the dark side in the 1940s, and Monty found exploring it fascinating and exhilarating. "I'd really like to go down to the dregs of life in some way, Dostoevsky in *Notes from the Underground*, and see what that's like—and then get back," he told Kevin McCarthy.

However, as Monty became more sexual, an embarrassing, inescapable reality tormented him. He—who was so desirable in every other facet of his life—had a small penis, and he was "extremely embarrassed" about it. "He talked about it all the time to me," said Ben Bagley, a music-producer friend. "I think it was the secret tragedy of his life. A lot of homosexuals gossiped about Monty's problem, because gays put great importance on the size of their cocks." Some of Monty's partners agreed with the actor's assessment. "He had the ugliest cock I'd ever seen," recalled the producer Frank Taylor, who had sex with Monty later in his life. "This beautiful face, you know, but there was no cock really. It was all foreskin."

In the final years of Monty's life, the book *Hollywood Babylon*, by Kenneth Anger, came out, and it described Monty as "Princess

Tiny Meat." Monty saw the publication and is said to have cried out, "Jesus H. Christ! Is nothing sacred!" His lawyers had the reference cut out of future editions of the book.*

To attract men, Monty relied on his beautiful face and slight but defined, muscular body. In the evenings he would wander around Times Square, courting a sexual encounter. He'd wear an old tweed jacket, the pockets filled with pills and capsules of all kinds, in a variety of colors. The pills were just loose in the pockets. He was still frequently in pain because of amoebic dysentery, but he also used the pills, which he was easily able to get his hands on, recreationally—to wall off hang-ups, insecurities, and inhibitions. He also started drinking—a lot.

Sometimes in the late-night and early-morning hours, Monty would go to a twenty-four-hour greasy spoon on Fifty-first Street and Lexington, where he could pick up guys. He'd sit at a table and gaze at himself in a hand mirror—that was a signal that he was sexually available. Eventually, a hookup would be made. Anonymous sex made him an adventurer, a hunter in a secret world, and his friends from that scene were sure he did a lot of cruising.

After a night of anonymous sex, he might visit with Kevin and Augusta and talk about his hopes of playing Romeo and Hamlet on the stage and discuss whether or not he should go to Hollywood. But it was imperative that his worlds never collided. When he stayed with his "couple" friends, they'd hear Monty sneak out of his room after everyone had gone to bed, and then they would hear the front door open and close.

As an actor, he liked having different worlds he could exist in; he was a different person in all of them. In another corner of his life, Monty started a very well camouflaged affair with dancer-choreographer Jerome Robbins. Robbins was conflicted about his homosexuality, and Monty was discreet about his. Many of

---

*Years after Monty's death, forensic pathologist Michael Baden allegedly entertained dinner guests by describing Monty's less-than-generous endowment.

Monty's friends from the straight world didn't know anything about the relationship, although Robbins' notebook for 1946 shows that the two were seeing a great deal of each other. The twenty-eight-year-old choreographer fell deeply in love with Monty, and something legendary was born of that romance.

Robbins told composer Leonard Bernstein that the idea for *West Side Story* came to him when a friend told him he was considering an offer to play Shakespeare's Romeo. Robbins's "friend" was Montgomery Clift—his current lover. The couple was on Fire Island when Monty complained that the character of Romeo seemed too passive. He was wondering how he could bring him to life. They started talking about what a great musical a modern-day *Romeo and Juliet* would make—which planted the seeds for *West Side Story*. Robbins brought the idea to Leonard Bernstein and playwright Arthur Laurents.

By 1946, Monty's Broadway reputation had grown to the point that Hollywood was breathless in anticipation to have him—and was willing to take him on his own terms. In spite of his protestations, Monty really did want to be a movie star. Monty's agent, Leland Hayward, convinced him to fly out to Hollywood to at least check out what the studios were offering.

Monty met with Louis B. Mayer, Harry Cohn, and Darryl Zanuck. Each studio head was eager to get him under contract, but Monty hesitated. It wasn't that he was afraid of failure. In fact, in his mind Monty was certain he could be a movie star if he chose to be. What turned him off was the notion of being trapped in a long-term contract, with the studio calling all the shots in his career and life. He dreaded the fan magazines, the autograph hounds, and the loss of his privacy. In New York he could be a star in the theater and slip off the stage and into a private night.

As curious as he was about venturing into films, Monty loathed Hollywood. In letters to friends back home, he referred to it as "Vomit: California." In one letter he wrote, "Hollywood is a terrible place, and I shall want an explanation when I get back as to why the hell I am here."

A Hollywood offer that seemed ideally suited for him came when producer Howard Hawks offered him sixty thousand dollars to play John Wayne's adopted son in the 1948 Western *Red River*. It tells the story of the first cattle drive down the Chisholm Trail, with Wayne as a tyrannical cattle rancher and Monty as his sensitive, rebellious son. The contract committed Monty only to the one movie, so if he found the movie business intolerable, he would be free to return to Broadway.

Monty accepted the offer. The fact that he chose a Western for his very first movie was unexpected, and his part would be particularly challenging. Since the characters are at odds for much of the film, Howard Hawks thought the hulking, macho John Wayne and the slender, sensitive Monty would make an interesting father-son dynamic. As it turned out, Monty couldn't find much in common with Wayne or the rest of the *Red River* cast and crew. He would say, "They laughed and drank and told dirty jokes and slapped each other on the back . . . The machismo thing repelled me because it seemed so forced and unnecessary."

The sensitivity and vulnerability that Monty displayed in his leading-man role was something new to audiences. Janet Maslin later noted, "In his very first scenes in the film, as he languidly rolls a cigarette while eyeing John Wayne, Clift establishes himself as an altogether subversive element in the film's very masculine scheme."

Red River wouldn't be released for over a year. In the meantime, Monty agreed to play a young soldier in Fred Zinnemann's 1948 motion picture *The Search*, under the condition that he could rewrite his dialogue. The screenplay tells the plight of European orphans after World War II. Monty plays an American soldier who comes into contact with a nine-year-old Czech boy who has been in a concentration camp and has been separated from his mother. Assuming the mother is dead, Monty takes the boy under his wing and plans to take him back to America.

Zinnemann shot the film in a semidocumentary style, and Monty's natural performance would garner him his first Academy Award nomination. *Red River* was released several months after *The Search*, and Monty's acting in both films caused tremors throughout the entertainment industry. Suddenly, Monty was the most enigmatic and sought-after male star of 1948.

Variety observed that Monty was "one of the most unusual rises to stardom in all of Hollywood history . . . [W]ith only two films released, *Red River* and *The Search*, and with no studio backing, he has already become one of the two or three most in demand male players in Hollywood, and can pretty much have his choice of parts at any studio." Stacks of fan mail from teenyboppers started arriving regularly. Montgomery Clift fan clubs sprung up across America. Girls would swoon over this handsome, sensitive man with the mysterious sexuality.

With Monty's handsomeness and naturalistic acting style, in the coming months, both his visibility and value rose. Determined not to repeat the kind of roles he had played thus far, for his third film Monty chose to play a sinister yet sexy fortune hunter in nineteenth-century New York in *The Heiress*, directed by William Wyler. The part put him opposite Olivia de Havilland. Monty rarely liked his performances, but he felt particularly uncomfortable in this role, and some critics thought it showed. As one critic noted, "He seems wholly unaware of the *mores* of the play's period." Nonetheless, his dashing appearance in the film's period costumes was more than enough for his new fans.

Next, he costarred with Paul Douglas in *The Big Lift*, directed by George Seaton. Filmed on location in Berlin, Germany, it tells the story of two American air force sergeants who are sent to Germany during the 1948 Berlin airlift.

From Hollywood's beginning, actors were supposed to look a certain way, act a certain way, fit into specific categories. If you were attractive and charismatic enough, you would play the leading man or the leading woman. If you were unattractive (by popular standards) or offbeat looking, you became a "character actor." Offbeat actor types might play comic supporting roles, the plain sister, the dotty uncle, the wisecracking roommate. Few actors asked if it was right or wrong. Instead, they tried to find their "role" and fit into it.

In Monty's era, the typical leading man was tough and hypermasculine—actors like Clark Gable, John Wayne, Gary Cooper, and Humphrey Bogart were the top-billed male stars. The thing was, Monty didn't fit into the role of a leading man. He wasn't particularly virile looking or macho. He didn't come across as heroic in the traditional sense. On the screen Monty seemed alienated, vulnerable, and beautiful. Women wanted to love him, mother him, protect him. Monty was a different kind of leading man. He inspired very different feelings in audiences than the traditional leading man. "No one had ever seen an attractive man who was so vulnerable," Jane Fonda noted. "The cultural importance of Clift was that you could be a man and you could still cry and you could still be sweet and vulnerable and like a wound. And it was very, very appealing."

After he had spent a year making films and reluctantly giving interviews, Monty's public image emerged. Talented and great looking, but aloof, casual, and strange. The industry started labeling him a young rebel. Monty protested, "I am neither a young rebel nor an old rebel nor a tired rebel, but quite simply an actor who tries to do his job with the maximum of conviction and sincerity." He found that with his public image cemented, he had to field many questions. "I'm asked all sorts of personal questions now," he said. "I don't mind answering them, but it embarrasses me to talk about myself. I'd much rather talk about my work. I'm really quite dull."

In truth, he did mind answering them, and his reluctance made journalists view him as cagey. Monty took his privacy to a new extreme for a celebrity, and it only made the media speculate more about him, looking for a scoop. "He is friendly, agreeable, and smiles easily, but he lets you know that he has a mind of his own," a reporter declared. "He gives straightforward but sometimes sketchy answers to personal questions."

Monty made it clear that he wasn't interested in the trappings of Hollywood success, and publicists sold it as a charming quirk. One publicist noted, "Leather jacket a favorite. A bachelor, he lives in a one-room apartment with a pull-down bed which squeaks. He drives a fender-dented, paint-scarred 1940 convertible." Part of Monty's schtick—which was real—was that he hated the trappings of celebrity. He liked to convey that he was just a normal guy who happened to act. His melancholy and need for privacy were incorporated into that image, as was his disinterest in clothes, cars, and houses.

Because he didn't court publicity or bow down to it, he became a curious figure. Hollywood staples, like Hedda Hopper, resented Monty for not giving Hollywood politics the respect she felt it deserved. He drove a used car. He didn't attend parties. "Look," Monty would protest, "I'm not odd. I'm just trying to be an actor, not a movie star, an actor."

He would show up for interviews unkempt. It irked the media that he refused to talk about his dating life. Naturally, his publicity people tried to put a positive and quirky spin on it. "He is not engaged to be married but does not consider himself a 'confirmed' bachelor," one publicity man noted. "He feels that marriage is a very serious proposition and not to be entered [into] lightly. He doesn't believe in parading his personal life in nightclubs or other public places, is upset when his name is linked romantically in the gossip columns with some friend merely because he took her to lunch."

More sophisticated journalists deduced that he was gay, but in accordance with the times, they wrote about it in a roundabout way, one that hinted and accused rather than revealed. WHO'S A FREAK? asked one magazine headline accompanying a profile about Monty. Another stated simply, HE WANTS TO BE ALONE. Eventually, reporters became more explicit. WOMAN HATER OR FREE SOUL? asked a headline with the subheading "Monty's reluctance to wed is one of the most intriguing mysteries of our time."

For years, when others described Monty's feelings about his homosexuality, the word *guilt* would invariably come up. "I think he was struggling with his homosexuality," playwright Arthur Miller observed. "He lived in a period, unfortunately, when these things were unacceptable in any disguise . . . [T]his struggle that he secretly fought caused him great guilt." That was a misreading or simplification of Monty. He didn't feel personal guilt. He didn't see anything to feel guilty about. If anyone was guilty, it was society, for having such narrow-minded views.

What bothered Monty was having to hide part of his nature—that's where guilt came into play. It exasperated him that he had to pretend in order to be accepted. It particularly tormented someone like Monty, who was committed to honesty. In the coming years, he certainly became self-destructive. How much of his eventual decline was a result of being gay in that era can never be known, since Monty told different things to different people and was someone different with everyone in his life.

More recent generations sometimes don't grasp how dangerous it was to be a homosexual in earlier eras. It wasn't a matter of pride. It was a matter of survival. A gay person in the mid-twentieth century was considered mentally ill or dangerously perverted. Living life in the shadows was necessary to function in society. To be a known homosexual, for the most part, was to be a reviled outcast. It was one of the worst insults you could hurl at someone.

You could be beaten up in the streets for being gay, and you could be arrested—and the vast majority of citizens would think it was your just deserts. A suspicion of homosexuality stymied careers and open lifestyles. Even the most comfortable of gay people knew that they were marginalized. "At the time it was a criminal offense, and you could be sent to prison," Monty's friend Jack Larson observed. "A lot of people's lives were ruined." In America in those days it was impossible to be an openly gay public figure. If Monty had been "out" to the public, there wouldn't have been a Montgomery Clift.

In the movies, homosexuality was merely hinted at, presented in vague, veiled ways. Alfred Hitchcock wanted to cast Monty and Cary Grant in the 1948 psychological thriller *Rope*, about a homosexual couple who commit a murder simply for the thrill of it (based on the infamous Leopold and Loeb gay murder case), but, as Patrick McGilligan explains in his Hitchcock biography, "since Grant was at least bisexual and Monty was gay, they were scared to death, and they wouldn't do it. It hit too close to home.

Monty confessed to Hitchcock he would never do a role that 'raised eyebrows.' At least when it came to questioning his sexuality in a public forum."

At this time, Monty was very concerned about choosing roles that might be a key for the public to gain entry into his private life. Because of this fear, he made perhaps one of the biggest mistakes of his career by pulling out of his commitment to star in Billy Wilder's upcoming film *Sunset Boulevard,* for Paramount. It tells the story of an aging actress who falls in love with a much younger writer, whom she finances. The brilliant Wilder had written the script with Monty in mind.

Two weeks before shooting was to start, Monty dropped out. He explained that he didn't think he would be convincing when making love to a woman twice his age. But it was apparent to many that the script simply hit too close to home. Everyone knew of his romantic obsession with Libby Holman, who was sixteen years older. Monty didn't want to destroy his romantic image with his fans by portraying a young man dominated by an older woman. Comparisons to his real life inevitably would be made.

Libby also had some say in the matter. She threatened to kill herself if Monty played the role. For her, Monty gave up what he knew was an extraordinary role. But he was being offered every good role available, and at that moment he turned his attention to being cast in George Stevens's screen adaptation of *An American Tragedy.*

6

CHEMISTRY

He was vulnerable, introverted, hysterically funny. Monty was also intelligent beyond words. In his acting, nothing happened by accident. He always knew exactly what he was doing.
—**Elizabeth Taylor**

Liz is the only woman I have ever met who turns me on. She feels like the other half of me.
—**Montgomery Clift**

*I*T IS SAID THAT WHEN MONTGOMERY CLIFT DISCOVERED WHO HIS love interest in *A Place in the Sun* would be, he exclaimed, "Who the hell is Elizabeth Taylor?" The comment was more likely a put-down of the notion of a "Hollywood star" than a real question. It is unlikely he didn't know who the lovely seventeen-year-old actress was. Everybody in the country, if not the world, did. Still, in spite of her glamour and fame, a personality like Elizabeth represented everything that he despised about Hollywood. In Monty's view, she was a commodity rather than a serious actress.

The director George Stevens knew what she represented. Her image was the reason he chose her for the role. Elizabeth Taylor was "the girl on a candy box cover"—that's how the director envisioned the character Angela Vickers. Tempting. Sweet. But with an allure that was capable of corrupting. The kind of woman men dream about but who always seems to remain slightly out of reach. The director even briefly considered naming the movie *The Prize*, because a girl like Elizabeth, in a young man's mind, would be just that, the grandest reward of all. He felt that if Elizabeth played Angela opposite Monty's character, George Eastman, it would make sense that the thought of winning such a girl would be "staggering as far as his equilibrium is concerned."

Elizabeth was more visible than the publicity-shy Monty. You couldn't help but come across her photo in any magazine or newspaper. Always, she came across as being poised, beautiful, and somewhat vacuous. She was perfectly posed and perfectly guarded and, it seemed, always camera ready. Monty was the enigmatic one. He equaled Elizabeth in terms of beauty, but he also had mystery. Monty would get star billing.

On hearing that she would be starring opposite Montgomery Clift in a George Stevens movie, Elizabeth felt somewhat intimidated. There were a lot of stories about Monty going around show-business circles. The articles she had read about him in movie magazines stated that he was a "misfit," even a freak. Mixed in with his good looks, this made him seem exotic. But more than anything, he was considered a serious actor from the New York stage. Suddenly being a Hollywood film star seemed small in comparison.

After she was cast in the film, Stevens invited Elizabeth to his office to meet Monty for the first time. Elizabeth had been terrified to meet Stevens—she was in awe of the intellectual director. And she was just as intimidated about meeting Monty. "I was so scared," she said. "I thought, *Oh God, here's this accomplished New York stage actor, and I'm just a Hollywood nothing.*" She had already heard that Monty intended to spend the night in an actual state prison to see what it felt like to be on death row. Elizabeth had never considered the importance of researching a character. She acted on a completely instinctive level.

In Stevens's office, when Elizabeth first saw Monty, she was dumbstruck. "He was the most gorgeous thing I'd ever seen," she said. "I remember my heart stopped when I looked into those

green eyes, and that smile, that smile, that roguish, boyish smile."
The director slyly remained silent after the initial introduction,
letting an uncomfortable moment pass when no one said a word.
Elizabeth would recall Stevens acting like a "puppeteer," playing
one off the other and see how they reacted to each other. He observed Monty and Elizabeth check each other out.

Monty was also impressed with Elizabeth, at least physically. He
could see the value of such a woman in the role of Angela. She
gave his character, George, something to obsess over. He would
tell Mira that he had never before seen anyone who was so petite,
so delicate. Her skin was like porcelain, and she had big blue eyes
framed by pronounced, perfectly shaped eyebrows. She stood
only five feet two, but her posture was at once regal and sensual.

"How did you ever get into movies with a face like *that*?" Monty
finally joked.

Later, Elizabeth would say, "Monty was so funny, and he just put
me at ease. That's when I discovered we had a similar sense of
humor, which was also slightly perverse. We liked each other!"

A Place in the Sun was adapted from Theodore Dreiser's 1925
novel *An American Tragedy*. During the meeting, Monty mentioned that he had wanted to play the part of George Eastman
ever since he first read *An American Tragedy* five years before.
Stevens replied that Shelley Winters—who had been cast as the
third lead—had told him the same thing. Elizabeth didn't respond. She came to the part because it was assigned to her by
MGM. She hadn't yet read the book.

In *An American Tragedy*, Dreiser's underlying theme is the false-
ness of the American dream, and the novel is a denouncement of
materialism and the corrupting influence of power and money.
Stripped to its essence—without the social commentary—*A Place
in the Sun* is not a complicated story. It's a romantic triangle. The
plot places Monty as the man in the center—bewitched by Elizabeth and pursued by Shelley.

A poor boy, George Eastman (Monty), moves to Chicago to
work in his rich uncle's factory. There he meets a plain, poor girl
named Alice Tripp (Shelley Winters). Both are lonely and they

begin to date and she becomes pregnant. When he meets the very rich and very beautiful Angela Vickers (Elizabeth), there is an instant attraction between the two. Overcome with passion for Angela, he starts to think about killing Alice to get her out of the way. During an outing at a lake, George gets Alice into a boat, with the intention of drowning her, but at the last moment he changes his mind. Ironically, at that moment, she stands up in the boat, it turns over, and she falls into the water and drowns anyway. After her body is discovered, George goes to trial and is sentenced to the electric chair for the "murder."

In its adaptation for the screen, *An American Tragedy* became a story of alienation, ambition, and love. The human desire for more. The longing for a chance at success and love and happiness. The action pivots on a man who is willing to murder, to destroy whatever gets in his way, in order to attain what he desires. In the script, the feelings and relationships between the three lead characters develop very fast, over a short period of time, so it was of utmost importance that the actors be authentic in their emotional connections. The film had to be perfectly cast in order for audiences to believe in and care for the characters.

Shelley Winters—who had arrived in Hollywood by way of Brooklyn in the early 1940s—desperately wanted to play the role of Alice Tripp, the doomed factory worker who becomes pregnant. But her brassy image worked against her. After many pleas from her agents to test her for the part, Stevens finally agreed to meet with her, mostly to get her off his back. He set up an appointment to meet her in the lobby of the Hollywood Athletic Club. To prepare, she dyed her blond hair brown, put on a drab dress and sensible shoes, and went to the meeting, clutching a brown paper bag containing a sandwich. She sat in the corner and waited for Stevens to arrive.

When Stevens appeared in the doorway, he looked around but didn't see Shelley Winters. He sat in a chair, opened a newspaper, and waited. Shelley sat there, nervously fidgeting with her lunch bag. Every once in a while, she observed Stevens look at his watch and scan the room. After some time had passed, Stevens folded

up his newspaper and got up to leave. It was only then that he noticed that the mousy brunette sitting by herself in the corner was
Shelley Winters. Stevens was impressed. Shelley wasn't playing the
character Alice Tripp—she had *become* the character for him to
observe. He arranged for a screen test for Shelley, with Monty,
and eventually he gave her the role of Alice Tripp.

The first scenes for the movie were shot at Lake Tahoe in late
October of 1949. As usual, Monty had Mira Rostova in tow. Of
course, Sara was there with Elizabeth, to keep watch on her during the location filming. When they arrived at the location, there
was snow on the ground. This caused a problem for the outdoor
shooting, since the film's lake scenes take place during the summer. The crew's first job was to knock the snow off tree branches
and hose down the patches of snow in the grass until there wasn't
a visible sign of white. The very first scene filmed was between
Monty and Shelley. It was the important scene in which George
rents the boat, with the intent of killing Alice.

Elizabeth wasn't on call that day, but she was curious about the
filming. She showed up to the location, wearing no makeup and
with her hair tied back in a scarf, and positioned herself on the
sidelines to watch. The first thing she noticed was the concentration between the two actors and the casual, natural way they responded to each other. It wasn't just waiting for your cue and
then saying a line; it was listening and responding—a completely
different way of working than she was used to. The reactions, she
noticed, were just as important as the way a line was read. She
hurried back to her room to go over her lines again.

The following day she nervously reported for work. In Elizabeth and Monty's first scene together at the lake, their characters
were already deeply in love. As written, the couple was to strip
down to their bathing suits and jump into the water. Right off the
bat, Monty refused to bare his torso. He wasn't about to offer up
his body on the screen for appraisal.

He was self-conscious about what he considered his skinny legs
and "virtually nonexistent butt," which he often padded. Monty
also had a hair problem—his entire body was covered with a long,

thick carpet of it. He would go to electrolysis to have it removed throughout the 1940s, but a session never rid him of the body hair for very long. The hair always grew back very quickly. He and Elizabeth bonded when she confessed that she, too, was hairy and went to electrolysis.

Stevens rewrote the scene on the spot. Now Elizabeth would strip down to her bathing suit, run into the water alone, swim, splash around, squeal with delight, and run back to Monty, who would be waiting for her with a towel to dry her off. Although the scene takes place on a hot day in August, it was October, and the lake really was freezing. Just before the filming of the scene began, Sara took Stevens aside and asked the director to please go easy on her daughter.

"She's in grave danger," she whispered.

"Danger?" Stevens said in a surprised tone. "What's the matter? Can't she swim?"

"Of course she can swim," Sara replied huffily. Then her voice took on a confidential tone and she informed Stevens that in addition to enduring the uncomfortably chilly weather, Elizabeth was menstruating that day. Too much physical activity would make her cramps worse, her mother explained. In addition, Sara had come to believe that a menstruating woman's future fertility would be potentially compromised if she submerged herself in cold water.

Stevens ignored her and instructed Elizabeth to jump in and swim and splash around joyously in the water. Elizabeth complied, but after several takes, the director was dissatisfied with the way the scene was going. He was shooting in close-up and wanted her to convey spontaneous joy, and to him, it looked like she was merely following the instructions to act joyful. He had Elizabeth do take after take, while a stone-faced Sara watched from the sidelines.

"Cut! Do it again, Elizabeth," he instructed.

Freezing and humiliated, Elizabeth was also baffled. She was doing what she had always done, following direction and doing what was asked of her. Normally, for such a simple scene, the director might ask for two or three takes and then would move on to something else. Stevens spent the whole morning on the scene, and when he was finally satisfied with Elizabeth's performance, she felt strangely pleased. As if she had passed some kind of a test.

In between takes, Elizabeth and Monty sat close together under a blanket near a smudge pot, whispering and laughing. When she finished the day's work, Elizabeth left feeling exhausted but exhilarated by the challenging day. Her mother was furious. Shelley Winters would remember Sara going around for days to come, complaining that Elizabeth may be unable to have children because of Stevens's treatment of her.

Elizabeth was eager to go back to work the next day to continue with the scene at the lake, and she was disappointed when she looked out the window and saw that a fresh layer of snow covered the ground. "We can't shoot," she said to her mother. "There's snow everywhere." They waited for the call to come in about canceling the filming for the day. Instead, a wardrobe woman, carrying a pair of jeans and a sweater, knocked on the door. "Mr. Stevens told me to deliver these to you," she stated when the door opened. "Put these clothes on over your bathing suit. We'll be shooting the scene in an hour. The makeup man is on his way."

"But there's snow all over!" Sara exclaimed.

"Mr. Stevens is having an area hosed down where we'll be shooting. And he is putting smudge pots around where the actors will be sitting off camera."

An hour later Elizabeth arrived at the location, wearing the oversize sweater and jeans over her bathing suit. Her hair and body would have to be sprayed down with water to give the appearance that she had just emerged from swimming in the lake. They would be shooting the conversation between Angela and George lakeside after her quick dip in the water. In this key scene, as George and Angela sit by Loon Lake, Angela tells the story of a man and a woman who drowned in the lake and reveals that the man's body was never found. Stevens directed Monty to lay his head in Elizabeth's lap, as George is lost in thought. He has been planning to kill his pregnant girlfriend and is completely conflicted between murdering his darkness and embracing his new life in the sun. "And I used to think I was complicated," Angela says, picking up on his silent intensity.

Elizabeth was transfixed when she was acting with Monty. In front of the cameras, he seemed to split open, allowing all his longings and fears to spill out. She forgot about the cold air. She realized Monty was sweating. Elizabeth was awestruck as he trembled and sweated—not Montgomery Clift, the actor, but George Eastman, the sensitive but driven social climber. Observing him, she thought, *Wait a minute, what's he doing? What's he up to?* she recalled years later.

Elizabeth wanted to know how he managed to shiver and sweat from real emotion, and Monty explained that when the body was really feeling something, it didn't know you were acting. It responded to the feelings. "It sweats and makes adrenaline, just as though your emotions are real." That's an indication of how deeply Monty delved into his characters, how much he became his character when in front of the cameras. He admitted that he was baffled by his inability to bring reality to a situation he did not feel in his heart. "I simply go dead," he explained.

"I thought, *My God, it isn't all about just having fun,*" Elizabeth later commented. "I think that's when I first looked at him and saw how involved he was, his whole being. When I saw how involved he was, I thought, *I've just been playing with toys.*" Up until this moment, acting in a movie for Elizabeth had been little more than memorizing the script and following the director's blocking. The idea of actually creating a character was fascinating to her. At MGM she had been treated like a beautiful prop. Elizabeth would always acknowledge that working with Monty made her a better actress.

Shelley Winters arrived on the set to watch. She, like everyone else, noted the palpable chemistry between Elizabeth and Monty. It was just there. They simply clicked. Shelley would later admit she had felt some jealousy. While Elizabeth's beauty was being accentuated, Shelley's worst characteristics were what was being highlighted. Later during production, Elizabeth sympathized with Shelley over her insecurity about appearing in the film with almost no makeup. She instructed her in how to use an eyelash curler, a makeup tool that curls the lashes upward and makes the eyes appear bigger. Shelley noted that "Elizabeth had such long eyelashes, she had to curl them up and away from her eyes."

But when Stevens caught Shelley on the set using the device, he reprimanded her, reminding her that she had agreed to be photographed without any of the usual glamour trappings. "I know," Shelley replied solemnly. "But does Elizabeth have to look quite so beautiful?"

Intrigued and excited, one day Elizabeth pleaded with Monty to rehearse with her at the end of the day. She wanted Monty to help her understand her character better. Because Angela is a rich girl who represents the American dream of wealth, beauty, and success, it would have been easy to fall into the trap of playing her as a vacuous rich bitch. Had the movie been made with a lesser director and costar, Elizabeth may have played the character that way.

Later that night, when they got together to rehearse, Monty encouraged her to display her vulnerability in the role. Angela, he explained, was a girl who was eager to take a risk, to experience something passionate, something real, and when it came, she was totally open and receptive to it—although it frightened her.

Every night after shooting, they continued to get together to go over the following day's scenes. Mostly, Monty and Elizabeth would work together alone, but sometimes he would ask Mira to come in and watch. "It turned out that Monty coached Elizabeth more than the director did," Mira stated. And she couldn't help but notice that Elizabeth was completely smitten with Monty. "Although, at first, Monty kept up a completely professional demeanor with her. He was aware that she was falling for him and he didn't want to encourage it and he kept his walls up."

After they ran through a scene, Monty would take notes on the ways he thought Elizabeth might improve her performance. Elizabeth would suggest that perhaps they could have a drink and listen to some music while they talked. Instead, Monty would share his notes with her, and then they would go through the scene again.

Sometimes Monty would demonstrate what he meant by acting the part of Angela for her, while Elizabeth read George's lines. There wasn't anything camp or effeminate in his playing, but when he was acting her part, he was able to conjure up believably the essence of a woman. The way Marlene Dietrich performed a song, the way Vivien Leigh held a teacup.

In later years, Elizabeth would recall that the role of Angela Vickers was "my first real chance to prove myself, and Monty helped me . . . [A]t first, I was absolutely terrified, because Monty was this New York stage actor, and I felt very much the inadequate teenage Hollywood sort of puppet. I only wore pretty clothes and hadn't really acted except with horses and dogs . . . For the first time in my life, I took acting seriously. This was my first leading man and my first real actor. And I started to listen and realize it was more than saying some lines. I had learned the night before about hitting my mark. It was more than that. It was something that could make this man shake from head to toe with emotion. And I thought, *I've got to find out what it is inside him that moves him so completely, emotionally, to get him to that state as his character, George Eastman, not Montgomery Clift. To make the sweat, literally, come out of his body. To make his eyes fill with tears.* And I began to think about acting. That's when I first began to act."

Because Elizabeth was working for a new studio, it was the first time many behind-the-scenes people encountered her on a set. In between shots, it became obvious to everyone on *A Place in the Sun* that Elizabeth was not leading her own life. Her mother was leading it for her. Monty would watch from the sidelines while Sara commandeered Elizabeth's on-set interviews, instructing Elizabeth about what to do and when to speak, like one would coach a trained parrot.

Once Ivan Moffat, the producer of the picture, passed by and asked Elizabeth how she was doing. "Oh, hello, Mr. Moffat," Sara chirped. "Elizabeth is fine. She's having a wonderful time." George

Stevens recalled that "Elizabeth was never allowed to speak for herself. When we had lunch in the studio commissary, Mrs. Taylor would preface most of her remarks with 'Elizabeth thinks' or 'Elizabeth says,' until I felt like shouting, 'Why don't you let Elizabeth say it for herself?'"

Understandably, Elizabeth resented her mother's nosiness, her orders. But her feelings about her mother were mixed, because Elizabeth loved her, and parts of her still needed Sara, would always need her. The love/hate ambiguity of the relationship caused her to resent Sara all the more.

Every so often, Monty would catch Elizabeth rolling her eyes before smiling in a tight, plastic way at her mother, but he also noticed how sometimes she would cling to Sara, wanting to please her. He felt a pang of recognition—this was how he used to be with Sunny—and his affection for Elizabeth swelled. Monty would smile with delight when she strode onto the set, plopped herself down in a chair next to him, and huffed, "My goddam mother is a giant pain in the ass!"

Monty's dependence on his coach was just as obvious. It was impossible not to notice Mira Rostova. She was a constant presence on the set, hovering over Monty, scrutinizing his every nuance in front of the camera, intimately whispering to him between takes. "Can you imagine having a coach when you were being directed by George Stevens?" Shelley Winters asked incredulously. At the time, she didn't understand that Monty needed Mira Rostova for the confidence she gave him more than anything she could actually add to his performance.

More than that, even off camera, Mira's role in Monty's life was that of confidante and nutritionist. She reminded Monty when he hadn't eaten and suggested what he should have. Of course, there was no romance between Monty and Mira—just a codependence.

At first, Elizabeth wondered about Mira. Could this solemn, mysterious older woman be Monty's lover? Everyone wondered about them. It was unusual for a man to be so close to a woman without there being a romantic connection. Elizabeth didn't dare ask him about her, but she felt jealous about the relationship.

After long shooting days, she started bringing a cup of tea to Monty's room in the evenings. Then she would ask to rehearse one of their scenes—which she knew he was always up for—and would stay late into the night. As they spent more time together, Elizabeth became more and more enamored with her leading man. She would take three baths a day. "To calm my nerves," she'd explain. She started inviting Monty to join her in the bathroom— to talk—while she bathed. And Monty would sit on the edge of the tub, and to her astonishment, they would actually *talk*—and joke and laugh. Monty didn't seem to be distracted at all by Elizabeth's naked body. (Although he wasn't completely oblivious. He did notice her breasts, later rhapsodizing to a friend about her "magnificent tits.")

For the most part, Monty seemed to be doing the very thing she silently implored everyone to do: He ignored her beauty and sensuality and paid attention to the person inside the gorgeous body. This was new for Elizabeth, and it had a profound effect on her. No one else had taken her seriously before. For the first time, a man had noticed her talent, her humor, her interests—as a result, she acknowledged those things in herself.

The difference was, when they weren't together or rehearsing, Monty didn't really seek out Elizabeth. He liked her, enjoyed working with her, but she was a kid. After working, he shut himself up in his room with Mira. They went over the script, every nuance that was right for his character. Or he would make notes, scribbling in the margins of his script, suggesting reactions and other bits of business. But Monty did feel something for her. Elizabeth felt it. If only she could put a crack in his protective walls.

7

WHO IS BESSIE MAE?

You know how it is when you love somebody terribly, but you can't describe why? That's how I love Bessie Mae.
—**Montgomery Clift**

WHEN THEY ARRIVED BACK IN LOS ANGELES TO SHOOT THE REST of the film, Paramount wanted Monty to attend the premiere of *The Heiress*. Monty dreaded these kinds of razzmatazz events and told the studio's publicity man, Max Youngstein, that he had no intention of attending. When he went out in public, crowds of women surrounded him, pulling at his clothes. He complained that the wives of older studio executives would lean in to kiss him and would stick their tongues in his mouth. Youngstein told him he had to go—it was important publicity for the movie, and besides, the studio was promoting him as a romantic lead. They wanted him to be seen at the opening, wearing a tuxedo, with a beautiful girl on his arm.

Monty countered that he didn't own a tuxedo, and he most certainly didn't have a beautiful girl to latch onto his arm. That had all been settled, Youngstein explained. A tuxedo had already been rented for him, and his date for the evening would be Elizabeth Taylor.

"Oh, no, no, no," Monty said. "She's seventeen! I'll look like her father." Monty knew all about these studio setup dates for their single male stars, the secretly gay stars, who were developing a romantic leading man image. He thought it was absurd to put on a fake show for photographers and the gossip columns. Monty flopped into a chair, lit a cigarette, rubbed a hand through his hair, blew smoke, and declared, "I'm not going."

"Look," Youngstein countered. "Everyone knows the two of you are making a movie together. It's perfectly natural for you to be spending time together—and it gives the movie thousands of dollars in free publicity."

Finally, Monty's agent convinced him to go with Elizabeth as his date. But Monty insisted that Mira accompany them on the charade, so it was arranged that a press agent assistant, Harvey Zim, would accompany Mira as her escort.

That night the dusk sky had an eerie red hue. The limo ride to Elizabeth's house to pick her up was deadly silent. Monty was morose. Mira and Harvey didn't know each other and had nothing in common. They all sat stiffly in the limo, Mira serious and grim faced, Monty uncomfortable in his rented tux.

They pulled up in front of Elizabeth's house, and the seventeen-year-old star emerged—a vision in a white strapless gown with a full skirt—escorted by Sara, who wanted to sneak a peek into the car. Elizabeth broke away from her mother and swiftly breezed into the limo like a breath of fresh air, indifferent to her beauty. She tossed her fur wrap on the seat, merrily complaining about her "nosy bitch of a mother."

Attending a splashy movie premiere was second nature to Elizabeth. She wasn't rattled or uncomfortable—she certainly wasn't stiff. When she went on to gripe about her mother acting like a "cunt," everyone's eyes widened in astonishment—Monty's, in delight. He had used the "c" word on occasion when describing his mother. "She looked ravishing," Harvey Zim remembered. "And she was so foulmouthed and so unconcerned about going to the premiere that everybody else relaxed in the limousine, too."

Elizabeth's earthy energy was contagious. "Why, you look absolutely lovely, Bessie Mae," Monty exclaimed and then suggested they stop for a burger before they made their grand entrance.

The absurd idea of eating a take-out burger in their evening clothes delighted Elizabeth, and Monty instructed the driver where to go.

In the backseat of the limo, they ate take-out burgers with paper napkins spread across their laps. Monty became hyper now, jumping around in his seat and throwing pickles out the window. "Hey, Bessie Mae," he exclaimed, "do you want a french fry?" And, "Can I have a sip of your soda, Bessie Mae?"

"Why do you keep calling me Bessie Mae?" she asked.

"The whole world knows you as Elizabeth Taylor," he said. "Only I can call you Bessie Mae. Elizabeth belongs to the public. Bessie Mae is mine." She was charmed. The great New York actor she had been so intimidated by had turned out to be down to earth and humorous.

Mira and Harvey were dropped off a few blocks away from the theater so Elizabeth and Monty could arrive alone. When they emerged from the limo, their positive energy and good humor spilled out into the street with them. Smiling and waving, they sauntered past the lines of roped-off, applauding fans, right up to the microphone of a radio announcer who was covering the festive event. Elizabeth paused to straighten Monty's tie in front of a photographer.

"I see your escort is the very beautiful Elizabeth Taylor," he said to Monty.

"Is she beautiful?" Monty asked in mock surprise. Elizabeth cracked up. They seemed very at home with each other, very at ease—and they were.

Once they had been seated and the movie had started, Monty's mood shifted again. Watching himself perform on the screen mortified him. He had already seen the film, and his uncomfortable reactions to it had been recorded by a *Life* magazine photographer. However, the previous screening had done nothing to prepare him for his second viewing with an audience. Almost immediately after his first appearance on-screen, he began twisting and squirming in his seat.

Sensing his discomfort, Elizabeth whispered to him, "You're great! You really are!"

"Oh, Bessie Mae," he groaned. "I'm awful. I'm so awful."

"No. You're wonderful," Elizabeth assured him. He grabbed her hand.

When the movie ended, a crowd formed around them, everyone gushing and congratulating Monty for his performance.

"Let's get out of here," he whispered to Elizabeth.

Seeing himself on the screen had unnerved him, but he was also elated at the audience's positive response to the motion picture. Monty had planned on going home directly after the screening. Instead, he agreed to escort Elizabeth to the lavish party William Wyler was throwing at his Hollywood home.

When they entered the party, this striking couple really did seem to be lovers. They were two deities with an intimate camaraderie between them. The backdrop of the party certainly added to the romanticism of their youthful splendor. Wyler had decorated the apartment with fresh-cut flowers and hundreds of lit candles. Waiters in tuxedos walked around with trays of champagne. The guests at the party were the cream of the Hollywood crop, yet all eyes were on Monty and Elizabeth.

For the first time, Monty experienced what it was like to be a movie star. The adoration, the beauty, the lavishness, all illuminated by candlelight. It was impressive and pleasant, but not enough to entice him into wanting this as a lifestyle. It was enough for him to dip his toe in it.

Elizabeth basked in it. Among the crème of Hollywood, she was the youngest, the most beautiful, and her escort was the best looking and most talented. She glided through the crowd of guests with ease and savoir faire, understanding exactly the kind of party small talk that was expected. Monty admired her aplomb at handling people she didn't remember meeting before.

Monty would tell Mira how expert Elizabeth was at being a movie star, marveling at how well she played the game. But when she asked him to dance, Monty had to decline. "You know it's the funniest thing," he told her, "but I can only dance when I'm in character for a part. I have two left feet when I'm not acting."

A barrier between them was broken down that night.

Paramount recognized that a love affair between Monty and Elizabeth could be a publicity bonanza for the movie. They immediately started thinking of ways to capitalize on the headlines and seriously considered changing the name of the movie to *The Lovers.*

There was no doubt left in Elizabeth's mind that she had fallen in love with Monty. She couldn't help it. She still had one foot in helpless childhood, but she was tentatively stepping into voluptuous womanhood. Monty was like no one she had ever known. He was more than just a star; he was an artist. More than handsome, he was beautiful. And more than thoughtful, he was soulful. Monty represented a wonderful adulthood—one that was creative and fulfilling.

Between the work they were doing on the movie and the fun they had socially, she was meeting Monty at a place that combined lust, art, intelligence, and romance. It seemed silly now that she had ever considered anyone else for a husband. Now she was certain she really knew what love was. It was Monty who made her feel important and safe. It was Monty who was her escape from childhood, her family, the studio.

Before long Elizabeth's feelings for Monty became obvious to almost everyone. Luigi Luraschi, a Paramount executive, went to lunch with Elizabeth around this time. "I remember it was pouring and she drove," he recalled. As the rain beat down on the roof and hood of the car, "she couldn't stop talking about Montgomery Clift. I had the distinct and unmistakable impression that she had fallen in love."

She was ready for a big romance, a sexual experience, a husband, and Monty seemed ideally made—he was incredibly beautiful, talented, complex, and he was interested in her. "I'm so lonely," she confided to him. She had no one she could be herself with.

It was, of course, extremely flattering to Monty to have a young woman—one so beautiful and internationally famous—fall in love with him, and he often flirted back with her. Since he gave Elizabeth every indication that he was interested in her, she went on a full-out campaign to seduce him—completely unaware of the turmoil the situation was causing him.

Monty fulfilled himself emotionally with his female friends; he released himself sexually with men. "He wanted to love women," actress Deborah Kerr noted, "but he was attracted to men. And he crucified himself for it." He himself couldn't completely understand his feelings. "I love men in bed," he'd say, "but I really love women." And in that way, he came to love Elizabeth—more so than any other woman in his life.

What astonished him most was the deep level on which he was able to communicate with Elizabeth. It wasn't on a level of education or worldliness. It was a basic affinity they shared, born out of their common experiences and a similar nature. Both had been born preternaturally beautiful. Each of them knew what it was like to be a worshipped celebrity. Both had domineering mothers who lived vicariously through their child star. They both had a raunchy sense of fun. And they could make each other laugh like no one else.

In contrast, Elizabeth sometimes became protective of Monty, solicitous, comforting. Monty's surrogate mothers—Mira and Libby—were older women. Elizabeth was almost a child, yet she had these nurturing qualities. Woman, seductress, child lover— she excited him with her mere presence. With Elizabeth, he didn't have to live up to anyone's expectations—he was completely himself. "I found my other half!" he would exclaim.

For Elizabeth, Monty blurred the emotions of platonic love and sexual attraction. He led her to believe they were heading toward a romantic relationship. They were even seen kissing passionately in the back of limousines. "For three days Monty played the ardent male with me, and we became close," Elizabeth revealed. In that sense, the relationship was certainly sensual, if not sexual. Elizabeth was ready to lose her virginity, she wanted to lose it to Monty, and she let him know she was available. "But just when he overcame all his inhibitions about making love, he'd panic and pull away," she confessed.

Monty realized that he was leading her on and getting in too deep. The time was coming for him to put out or shut up. Still, he couldn't yet bring himself to come right out and tell Elizabeth he was gay. He was too secretive, too afraid, too ambivalent as to how this young woman might take the news to come right out and tell her directly. Instead, he started showing up on the movie set with a series of young men he had picked up the night before, making it obvious that they had been intimate. Elizabeth would describe these men as "obvious."

In his own way, by flirting with men in front of her, he was trying to convey the impossibility of their relationship going any further. "All I could do was sit by helplessly and watch while he threw this in my face," she lamented.

Monty would observe Elizabeth watching him with his latest pickup. But the next day he'd do an about-face. "Then all the young men would be gone," Elizabeth observed, "and Monty would act as if he were trying to make something up to me, affectionate all over again. I felt he was trying to fight it, but I didn't know what I was supposed to do."

Sometimes she got up the courage to face him and have it out. "What are we building here? If anything?" she would demand to know. "Are your feelings for me so tenuous? So fragile? So undefined . . . that you can shut them off?"

Monty would gulp, start to say something, think better of it, and reach for her and just hold her.

Of course, she picked up on these signals he was sending by flaunting men—how could she not?—but her knowledge of homosexual behavior was limited. (She knew her close friend Roddy McDowall was gay, but they hadn't yet discussed his sexuality at length.) Bewildered by Monty's seemingly wavering interest, she decided to press on.

For Elizabeth, if Monty preferred males, that was fine with her. They were merely competition. Like many women before her, Elizabeth was convinced that she was the one woman who could turn the gay man she desired straight. After all, she was considered one of the most desirable women in the world. She was adored by men and women alike. It never occurred to her that she wouldn't get him. Her recent experience with men had proven that she was irresistible. She would continue to try to seduce Monty.

"Doubt played no part in her psyche," actor Frank Langella, who knew her later, would say. "She had a divine arrogance and would not take no for an answer, even if the words were spoken right to her face. She hears it only as 'Not at the moment.'"

Yet more time passed, and Monty still didn't go to bed with her. When Monty brushed Elizabeth aside, it wasn't done lightly or cruelly. He admired her, enjoyed his connection with her, even loved her. It troubled him greatly that these feelings didn't transform into sexual ones—and in his confusion, he kept putting up shields. While he could have experimented with her sexually—Elizabeth excited him enough to perform—this probably wouldn't be enjoyable and could likely end up embarrassing. His ambiguous way of handling this inner conflict was to flaunt men or close himself off completely. But then he would find himself being drawn to her again by her many irresistible qualities.

Elizabeth started wanting Monty with all the passion one feels only for the unattainable. She would plead with him to marry her, and he would gently reply, "No. It wouldn't be right, Bessie."

"When I'm with you, I'm the woman everyone else sees," she told Monty.

Sometimes he tried to diffuse her passion by making light of it. "No. No, Bessie," he'd say. "I'm too old for you, beautiful. I'm an old man, Bessie."

She tried to break down his reserve by becoming more open. "I told him everything—even things I'm most ashamed of," she said. She started writing him letters in which she poured out her feelings of love. "I need you, darling Monty," one said. "I never found any real meaning in my life until I found you."

These letters simultaneously disturbed and flattered him. His conflict led Monty to do irrational things. He gave Elizabeth's letters to a male lover—which would have hurt her terribly if she found out.

The real tragedy of the relationship was that Monty wanted to love Elizabeth—and in a meaningful way, he *was* deeply in love with her. He certainly loved and trusted her more than he had any other woman he had known. Later he would say that she was the only woman he was ever truly attracted to. But he was incapable of a continuing sexual relationship with any woman. Despite his strong, multilayered feelings for her, he wasn't able to stir up enough sexual passion in order to love Elizabeth the way she wanted most.

With Elizabeth, he couldn't have the kind of weird, unconventional, inebriated half-sexual encounters he had with the jaded bisexual Libby Holman—a grope, a drink, and a French kiss. Elizabeth was too inexperienced, too straight, too romantic to understand the many mysterious and private directions sex could go in. She wanted to be swept off her feet in a first-time romantic fantasy. Monty was fearful of humiliating himself. An attempt at an erotic encounter with her might bring up mixed-up feelings of inadequacy and regret, complicating or destroying a relationship that had the potential to be a long-term friendship, a real connection—something that was rare, indeed.

8

THE BEAUTIFUL
COMMITTED MOMENT

In the love scene between Taylor and Clift, physical desire seems palpable.
—**Pauline Kael, the** *New Yorker*

*A*S THEIR RELATIONSHIP GREW CLOSER AND MORE COMPLICATED, something thrilling was happening on the set, too. The emotional chemistry reverberating between Monty and Elizabeth was electric. No one was more exhilarated by this new erotic connection than George Stevens. He studied and used it when rewriting the script. "I love you," George says to Angela in the final version. "I've loved you since the first moment I saw you. I guess maybe I've even loved you before I saw you."

In the evenings, after filming, Stevens ran the rushes for the cast, and a ripple of excitement would run through the screening room. As the footage screened, the director would narrate each take, explaining why one was better than the other, and what was working for the scene, what wasn't, and why he favored particular takes. Elizabeth sat in rapt attention. She was learning that acting in movies wasn't just a job—it was an art form. For the first time in her career, she wanted to be an artist.

Late at night, invigorated by what he had seen up on the screen, Stevens began writing new lines to mirror the chemistry of the

stars. Monty's brooding intensity. Elizabeth's exuberant infatuation and earthiness. In the mornings he would hand them pages
with the new dialogue. Not only was he making a dynamic movie,
but he was also, in essence, documenting a relationship. Stevens
bestowed Monty's character George with qualities the public saw
in Montgomery Clift and that Stevens himself also saw in him. He
envisioned George as an outsider, a person not at home in the
world.

In the scene where George enters the swank party given by his
uncle, who also happens to be his boss, he is the outsider, the one
who does not fit in. The lonely one. This is what defined Montgomery Clift. In this scene, George is not greeted. As he walks
past the Roman columns in the grand house and into the main
room to join the other guests, he is ignored. All around him people are chatting and laughing. George might as well be invisible.
He smiles awkwardly as he slowly strolls past small clusters of
guests, longing for connection, thinking someone will surely
greet him. No one does. He is utterly alone—this affluent world
doesn't belong to him.

In a few screen seconds, Monty's own mixture of awkwardness,
eagerness, and ultimately defeat movingly convey George's feeling of not being at home in the world. Conspicuously isolated
amid the gaiety, all he can do is hide. He wanders into a room
with a pool table, devoid of people. Here Stevens set up a perfect
moment to bring his lovers together, for George and Angela to
meet for the first time. The scene had to be intricately timed.
George, feeling intimidated by the well-heeled guests at the party
at the Eastman estate, begins shooting a game of pool by himself.
Just after George takes a shot, Angela happens to pass the doorway and glance in, and she sees the cue ball ricochet and then
sink the eight ball into a corner pocket.

"Wow," she gasps.

Their eyes meet, and Monty takes a deep drag on his cigarette.
In that moment we see that they're both smitten.

"I see you had a misspent youth," Angela jokes as she lan-
guorously drifts in.

"Why all alone?" she asks, circling the pool table in the masterfully staged scene. She heads toward him slowly, her strapless white satin flowing gracefully around her. "Being exclusive?" she asks softly. "Being dramatic?" She picks up a pretzel from a tray and nibbles. Finally, when face-to-face with him, she asks, "Being blue?"

"I'm just fooling around," he answers nervously.

As played, we see a young woman who is comfortable in the world and a young man who is sensitive, tense, trying to please. Elizabeth is a dreamy vision in the scene, dressed in that billowy white gown of satin and tulle, the bodice highlighted by clusters of velvet flowers (to cover her breasts fully), the absence of straps drawing attention to her lovely bare shoulders.* Wearing this Edith Head design, Elizabeth is the very picture of virginal youth and beauty.

As he delved further and further into the story, Stevens became more serious, more intent, more fanatical about perfection, and more creative in his ways of achieving it. While working, he wanted a very quiet set so as not to break the concentration of the actors. Rather than the usual bustle between takes, the crew tiptoed around, setting things up.

When it came time to shoot intimate scenes, Stevens cleared the set of everyone except the most important crew members. "Everyone had to get off the set, and if you were caught peeking, you'd really get it from Stevens," recalled Marjorie Dillon, Elizabeth's tutor. "He kept all of us away so that Liz and Monty could say what they wanted to say, and he could make suggestions and not humiliate them in front of anyone." He filmed the same scenes again and again—sometimes making minor adjustments—hoping that in the editing room, he would find just the right inflection, expression, or nuance.

*The Academy Award–winning gown was copied by manufacturers throughout the country and was worn to the prom by young ladies for years to come.

Ecstatic over the way his two stars were working with each other, Stevens became even more obsessed with perfection. Sometimes before shooting, he would play music—as he did on silent film sets—to create the mood and help the actors get into character. Most often he'd play the haunting soundtrack to *A Place in the Sun*, written and composed for the picture by Franz Waxman. Other times, during a rehearsal, Stevens might have the actors play the entire scene without dialogue, feeling their way through the scene with emotion. They had to express themselves through body language, especially with their eyes.

One of the most important scenes in the movie is when, at their second party together, George and Angela declare their love for each other during an intimate dance. For the scene, Elizabeth wore a strapless black gown, the bodice adorned with white appliqués. When shooting this dance scene, Elizabeth was surprised to discover how graceful Monty could be. "I told you, I can only dance when I'm acting," he said.

Now was Stevens's chance to try to catch on film the sensual glow generated by the connection between Monty and Elizabeth. For much of this encounter, Stevens decided to fill the entire screen with their faces. Stevens edited the film so that as they slow dance, one ravishing close-up dissolves into the other. For this scene, Stevens again wrote dialogue for them that seems to mirror their real-life relationship.

"You seem so strange," Angela tells George. "So deep and far away. As though you were holding something back."

"I am," George replies.

"Don't," she says, urging him to tell her his secret.

When he blurts out, "I love you," you can see Elizabeth's eyes light up. "I loved you from the first moment I saw you. I guess I loved you even before I saw you."

Here Stevens highlighted Angela's growing panic and excitement at her surging sexual feelings for George. She is just about to declare, "I love you, too," when she turns abruptly and gasps, "Are they watching us!"

The director had Elizabeth look directly into the camera at this moment, implicating the audience as voyeurs. Angela, leading, rushes George out to the balcony. "She took him out there, where they could be alone," Stevens explained. "That set something loose, and he was impassioned." This is the key scene: in a rush of feelings, they just express their passion for each other. It's the first time they each know how the other feels, and together, they rapidly explore their emotions. "I wanted the words to be rushed—staccato," Stevens revealed. "He was so enormously moved by her. Elizabeth must be compelled to tell him how wonderful and exciting and interesting he is all in the space of a few seconds . . . Anyway, it had to be like nothing they had ever said to anybody before."

Stevens stayed up until 2:00 a.m., writing, then rewriting this scene. When he handed Elizabeth the new pages, she read them over. She was aghast. She went directly over to Stevens. "Forgive me," she blurted. "But what the hell is this?"

The lines that baffled her were the ones after George declares, "Oh, Angela, if I could only tell you how much I love you. If I could only tell you all."

To which she replies, "Tell Mama. Tell Mama all."

"This is what you have to say when you pull Monty toward you," Stevens replied.

Stevens wanted to illustrate the nurturing nature in Elizabeth, a quality that she didn't even know she possessed yet, but that she displayed with Monty. And he also wanted to underline Monty's need to be mothered. "Elizabeth dissolved when she had to say, 'Tell Mama,'" Stevens later remarked. "She thought it was outrageous that she had to say that—she was jumping into a sophistication beyond her time." As usual, his instincts with Elizabeth were right. With the cameras rolling, Monty's urgency inspired her not only to say the lines but also to convey believably her mothering instinct. They are overwhelmed by each other's presence. He felt so moved by this girl that it turned her loose. She was just revelatory.

Stevens wanted the lines to pour out of them: fast, staccato, urgent. "I went from one side of the face to the other and then created a tempo with the thing, in which as fast as it could be said, it was said. I explained that I'd like to get the lines into their heads and then get them in there and throw them at one another and move twice as fast, compulsively, one on top of the other."

When it came to editing the scene, Stevens set up two projectors and screens and ran Elizabeth and Monty's close-ups side by side at the same time. This way he could see what the other was reacting to. He then edited the scene to convey the hunger Angela and George have for each other by focusing on the sound of their voices and the need in their eyes. When they kiss, the audience doesn't even see their mouths, yet their lust is tangible. (Stevens would take a year to edit the entire film before it was ready for release.)

The passion in Elizabeth's close-ups is the real thing. She wasn't a method actress, and she didn't yet have the skill as a performer to create passion out of thin air. By observing their developing relationship off-camera, Stevens was clever enough to utilize her erotic longing for Monty and his reactions to it. As a result, the scene transcends generations, because the emotions are eternal. Sixty-five years after the movie was released, Richard Gere, a top star of his own generation, pinpointed this moment as his favorite love/sex scene in movie history. The actor's complete reply is worth repeating:

> The first one that comes to me is *A Place in the Sun*, the dancing kiss. It's not a lovemaking scene, but it's just the most unbelievably beautiful, committed moment of a man and a woman connecting—Montgomery Clift and Elizabeth Taylor. Wow! Incredible scene. I saw it again fairly recently, and it's still the biggest close-ups in the history of cinema. You're seeing into these two souls, and they obviously loved each other. Those two actors loved each other, and they're wide open with each other. They obviously were friends and connected on a deep soul level. Not necessarily on a sexual level, but a deep soul level. I think that's what you were seeing in the eyes. It transcended a sexual surface to it. It was deeper than that.

* * *

Word was getting around that Elizabeth Taylor was giving the performance of her career in *A Place in the Sun*. Sara, always on the lookout for good publicity for her daughter, called her old friend Hedda Hopper and told her about Elizabeth's marvelous work. Sensing a story, Hopper plopped on one of her elaborate hats and rushed over to the set to see for herself what exactly was going on in *A Place in the Sun*.

Spotting Hopper on the sidelines, Monty clearly was not happy to have the snooping gossip columnist on the set—he called her "an old gobbler"—but when Elizabeth appeared in the strapless black velvet gown Edith Head had designed, things grew serious. A hush fell over the soundstage as the director talked softly to the actors.

When the scene started, Hopper stood behind the camera with the rest of the crew and watched—in rapt attention—as Elizabeth and Monty performed. Hopper was so amazed and impressed (and probably a little more than a little envious) by the adult sensuality emanating from Elizabeth, she approached her as soon as the scene was over. "Elizabeth," she asked the seventeen-year-old, "where on earth did you ever learn how to make love like that?"

Elizabeth shrugged off the question, as if her skills as a seductress were inevitable.

Hopper hurried back to her office and dashed off a column, gushingly informing her readers about Elizabeth's budding sexuality. "Liz did the old Garbo trick. She took him. Not a carpenter, electrician, prop man, or laborer left the set. Some even sat on ladders to get a better look. That Liz gets them all—from 15 to 50. What a dish!"

On the other hand, Hopper knew Monty was gay. As a leading columnist with power and contacts, she had an organized network of "spies" mingling in the show-business community and reporting any tidbit of gossip back to her. She had heard about his arrests for homosexual behavior—and about the cover-ups that followed. Most entertainment journalists stuck by the unspoken rule about not reporting on homosexuality, and in return, they were given access to movie premieres, exclusive celebrity interviews, invitations to Hollywood parties, and other perks.* Even so, without coming right out and saying it, Hopper had called Monty a "pantywaist" in print, the equivalent to winking at her more sophisticated readers.

But for now, though, the story of a love affair between Monty and Elizabeth made a great copy. "Those magnificent lovebirds are very soon going to be married," she wrote. Even though she was aware Monty was gay, a marriage might have happened. Lavender marriages were commonplace.

The show-business media took a cue from Hopper and duly reported on the supposed romance. Soon the daily headlines were announcing that Montgomery Clift was to marry Elizabeth Taylor. The news reached Elizabeth in her dressing room at the end of the day, when she came across a newspaper. She reacted to the headlines with panic. "Oh no!" she cried. "Monty will think I did this!" Furious, she threw the paper across the room.

"Come on, Mother," she said to Sara. "I'll take my makeup off at home."

When Elizabeth and her mother arrived home, they discovered the phone had been ringing nonstop all day. Sara immediately began fielding the calls. "My daughter and Mr. Clift are making a fine picture together," she chided. "There is absolutely nothing to the rumor of a marriage!"

In between her mother adamantly denying marriage plans for her daughter, Elizabeth tried to call Monty. It took a while. Monty's phone had also been ringing nonstop throughout the day—the press was looking for a comment from him. When Elizabeth got through at last, she pleaded with Monty to believe that she had nothing to do with this latest stream of gossip.

"I know, I know, Bessie," he assured her. "It was all started by the old gobbler Hopper." He relayed that he had been saying to reporters, "Elizabeth and I are just good friends." And then he

---

*It was not until *Confidential* magazine started outing gay celebrities in the mid-1950s—although the word *outing* hadn't been coined yet and wouldn't be for some years.

howled with laughter at the thought of actually uttering such a
hokey line.

Elizabeth was relieved to hear him laugh—it meant he really
didn't blame her, after all. When Elizabeth hung up with Monty,
she began giggling. The giggles soon grew into laughter, which
soon turned into hysterical guffaws.

"What's so funny?" Sara asked, with a perturbed look.

Next, Elizabeth's guffaws turned into loud, boisterous sobs.

"What's wrong with you, Elizabeth?" Sara almost demanded.
"Why are you crying?"

Elizabeth couldn't answer. She just shook her head and ran to
her room.

Sara realized that her daughter had fallen for Monty, and it
worried her. His homosexuality was accompanied by his drinking
and his tendency toward self-destructive behavior, which was beginning to be whispered about in Hollywood. She warned Elizabeth against a romance with him as she recalled her own
troublesome experiences with her husband. No one understood
what Monty's secret was better than Sara. "He's a disaster," she
blurted out to her daughter. This only made Elizabeth want him
more—she longed to separate from her mother and start her own
life. More than ever, it felt like she and Monty were soul mates,
and she saw him as a romantic escape.

She was hoping something would happen with Monty that
would change his mind about her before the filming of *A Place in
the Sun* ended, but her days with him on a set were numbered.
MGM already wanted her back to shoot *Father of the Bride*. The
script for that film only made her longing more palpable.
Spencer Tracy and Joan Bennett would play her parents in a story
about the trials and tribulations of planning their young daughter's dream wedding to the man she loves.

Toward the end of shooting *A Place in the Sun*, Monty's attention turned fully back to Mira. He would shut Elizabeth out of his
dressing room while he studied the script with his coach. Thinking he had had enough of her and was completely shutting her
out, Elizabeth was hurt. She didn't know that he was preparing

himself for his last big scene, when—isolated and numb—he walks to the electric chair.

But she and Monty still had one last scene to film. The rumors of a marriage between Monty and Elizabeth were still swirling around Hollywood on the day they shot the scene where Angela comes to see George one last time on death row. But there was no talk of that gossip. The set was grim; the mood somber.

The scene took on an even more solemn meaning for Elizabeth because it was the last day she and Monty would be working together on the film. When she entered the jail cell, she dissolved in tears. She wasn't seeing Montgomery Clift. She saw a condemned man on his way to the electric chair. For one moment, Monty broke his concentration to console her, putting his arm around her. "Now, Bessie," he said. "Save those tears. You're going to need them for the scene."

The mixture of Elizabeth's fear of never seeing Monty after the movie was complete and Monty's tenderness with her set up a parallel dynamic scene. Stevens started filming during this emotional upheaval. In the scene, Angela tells George goodbye. "I'll go on loving you for as long as I live," she whispers. The line could also have been said from Elizabeth to Monty.

"Love me for the time I have left. Then forget me," he murmurs back.

On the last day they worked together on *A Place in the Sun*, Elizabeth asked Monty what his future plans were. It was understood long before she started the movie that she would be back at MGM to make *Father of the Bride*. Monty told her that he would probably be spending time with Libby Holman.

Elizabeth had fallen in love with him in an intense romantic way and would never completely stop loving him that way. She realized that Monty could never return her love sexually—and the impossible always keeps us yearning. She learned to love him as a friend, and that love was very deep. Yet, even throughout their brother-sister relationship, there would always be a part of her that wanted Monty in "that way."

Showing maturity and wisdom, Elizabeth finally said to him, "Look, Monty, whatever you want from me, I'm always here for you." They were both young. The most important thing was to remain in each other's lives. Time would tell what developed from that.

Elizabeth emerged from the movie a better actress, with a new respect for the art of filmmaking. Monty would give what would turn out to be one of the most indelible performances of his career. With each other, they had formed a soul mate–like connection without being physically intimate. They could have fun and be affectionate with each other without bringing it into bed. In fact, the bond they formed may very well have been ruined if it had become sexual.

Their connection lasted through many other intimate relationships for both of them, many tragedies and triumphs. And they both knew they would be there for each other for their entire lives. But Monty's wouldn't be very long.

9

MARRIAGE NUMBER ONE

I left home as soon as I could, when I was 18. I thought I was in love and got married—the press called it Prince Charming and Cinderella. He was a Hilton, so I was the poor little Cinderella. And when I got a divorce nine months later, I never told the court why, but he was cruel.
—**Elizabeth Taylor**

*E*LIZABETH'S NEXT FILM, *FATHER OF THE BRIDE*, TOOK ONLY MONTHS to shoot, and as it was being readied for release, MGM was eager to have the public view Elizabeth as an average, all-American girl. Elizabeth had reached the age to graduate from high school, but with no real school for her to graduate from, the studio arranged for her to sit in on the graduation ceremony at University High in West Los Angeles. In an auditorium, among a group of strangers, Elizabeth, wearing a traditional white cap and gown, walked onstage to collect her diploma.

But the thing the high school graduate most wanted to collect was a husband. It was the only out she saw for herself. With a string of broken romances and engagements being played out in the press, MGM executives and her parents worried about Elizabeth's reputation. In that puritanical era, the passionate teenager couldn't have an affair, so the easiest solution was to get her married. "Nothing comes off until the ring goes on," she primly told Louella Parsons when asked about her latest boyfriend. Years later she would reflect, "When I kicked myself out of the nest and got married, I realized I had been a virgin not only physically but mentally."

Conrad "Nicky" Hilton Jr., an heir to the Hilton Hotels fortune, was an example of the exact right person presenting himself at the exact right time. At eighteen, Elizabeth was desperate to marry her way into freedom, and a string of potential grooms hadn't worked out. Monty was still on her mind—she was feeling the unbearable heartbreak of unrequited love. And she needed something to blot it out. Nicky Hilton was the antidote to Monty.

In 1976 Truman Capote asked Elizabeth about her marriages, scoffing at some of her choices. Elizabeth's answer clearly alluded to Monty. "Well, one doesn't always fry the fish one wants to fry," she said. "Some of the men I've really liked really didn't like women." But in 1949 Nicky checked all the boxes for potential husband material. He was twenty-three, boyishly handsome, rich, and claimed he was willing to put up with her career.

The courtship consisted of dining, dancing, and necking. Caught up in a romance with a potential Prince Charming, Elizabeth felt as if she were floating on a "pink cloud" toward an everlasting fairy-tale love. MGM had a movie about a bride to promote, and what better way than to promote it with a real wedding? They encouraged Elizabeth to set the wedding date with Hilton as close to the movie's premiere as possible.

Elizabeth immediately called Monty in New York to gush about the new man she had met, who, she claimed, was "just perfect." Monty wasn't thrilled with the news. He sensed that the main reason for the engagement was so Elizabeth could get away from her mother. That would have been okay if Nicky Hilton were a suitable escape, but he knew of Nicky's reputation as a playboy and a bully and a mean drunk. From other things he had heard, he also thought that Nicky was a racist. But he didn't want to overstep. Having recently broken Elizabeth's heart, he realized that he was in no position to give her romantic advice—and that being eighteen, she wasn't likely to take it, anyway.

"Bessie Mae," he said evenly, "I don't think Nicky is the right guy for you."

Elizabeth's voice leapt forward. "Oh, don't worry, Monty. You'll

grow to love him just as I do, once you get to know him better."
Then she added, "You'll come to the wedding, won't you?"

He couldn't bring himself to lie. "I don't think I will."

"Damn you, Monty!" she retorted angrily. "You said you would
always be close with me! That you'd always be my best friend!"
With that, she slammed down the phone.

Of course, Monty's disapproval did not stop the wedding. The
studio stepped in and paid for everything, including the gown,
the reception for over seven hundred guests, and a new wardrobe
for the bride. For them, the lavishness of it all was a small investment for the amount of publicity the wedding would generate for
Father of the Bride.

On May 5, 1950, wearing a wedding gown of shell-white satin
adorned with bugle beads and seed pearls, one designed by studio costume designer Helen Rose, and a four-carat diamond on
her finger, Elizabeth walked down the aisle while four thousand
fans waited outside, hoping to get a glimpse of the young newly-
wed. Later, at the Bel-Air Country Club, there was a reception
attended by seven hundred guests, including Gene Kelly, Gin-
ger Rogers, Fred Astaire, Van Johnson, and Spencer Tracy.
Monty did not attend.

For a honeymoon set to last three months, Elizabeth and Nicky
sailed for Europe on the *Queen Mary*. For most couples of the day,
the honeymoon period was a time for them to explore their new
relationship as man and wife—emotionally and sexually—and it
entailed a combination of awkwardness and passion.

But the circus-like atmosphere surrounding Elizabeth didn't
allow for that. The Hilton honeymoon was a chaos of reporters,
curious travelers, and overzealous fans. Not exactly looking to
blend in, Elizabeth traveled with seventeen trunks and a small entourage, including a personal maid and a poodle dyed to match
her eyes. It didn't help matters when busboys and waiters called
Nicky "Mr. Taylor."

The Duke and Duchess of Windsor were on the ship (occupy-
ing the grand bridal suite), but even they were ignored—all eyes
were glued to Nicky and Elizabeth. The press was allowed to travel

with them, and they trailed the couple, cameras in hand. Passengers craned their necks to watch the couple's every move and approached Elizabeth for a word or an autograph at every chance.

The passion in their relationship faded quickly. For Elizabeth, the excitement of the wedding, along with her romantic imagination, did nothing to prepare her for the realities of marriage. The sexually sophisticated Nicky found Elizabeth boring in bed (Nicky's's stepmother, Hungarian actress Zsa Zsa Gabor, claimed that she and Nicky had had an affair in 1944, when he was eighteen) and her celebrity quickly grew tiresome to him.

Fed up, he'd stay at the ship's bar, drinking late into the night. When he'd return to their cabin, they'd argue so loudly, guests could hear them. In the mornings Elizabeth, beautiful and melancholy, was spied walking alone on the upper deck, lost in thought.

Very early on the couple realized they had made a mistake, and she grew confused and he became resentful. "I didn't marry a girl. I married an institution," he commented bitterly.

In Paris Nicky would go out gambling all night, and Elizabeth— too young to be allowed in the casinos—was again left alone in the room, brooding and chain-smoking. Next to the stimulating complexity of Monty, Nicky seemed shallow. "The honeymoon in Europe lasted two weeks," Elizabeth wrote in her 1965 memoir. "I should say the marriage lasted for two weeks. Then came, yours sincerely, disillusionment rude and brutal."

A few weeks into the honeymoon, Nicky, frustrated, angry, and drunk most of the time, started physically abusing Elizabeth. On their return to the United States, Elizabeth's friends noticed bruises on her arms. It wasn't until years later that Elizabeth confessed that she left Hilton when one of his beatings caused her to miscarry. "He was drunk. I thought, *This is not why I was put on Earth. God did not put me here to have a baby kicked out of my stomach.*"

Elizabeth called Monty and told him that he had been right— Nicky was a brute. A short time later she announced their divorce (it was finalized in 1952). The reason she gave was "mental cruelty," and she refused Hilton's alimony and instead raced forward with her life, putting the whole thing behind her. The union had lasted thirty weeks. The fairy tale of marriage turned out to be sordid and ugly. "I fell off my pink cloud with a thud," she lamented. But she was a naïve young lady of only nineteen, and it was difficult to blame her for giving marriage another go in the future from time to time.

10

FRIENDS AND LOVERS

People who aren't fit to open the door for him sneer at his ho-
mosexuality. What do they know about it? Labels—people love
putting labels on each other.
—**Marilyn Monroe**

*B*Y 1950, MONTY HAD MADE FIVE GRUELING FILMS IN FOUR YEARS.
Emotionally drained, he put his movie career on hold for a while
and concentrated on his relationships, friends, and lovers. In Los
Angeles Elizabeth had introduced him to her old friend Roddy
McDowall, who fell in love with Monty and followed him back to
New York.

Monty also focused on the friendships he had made during the
filming of *Mexican Mural* a decade before. Everyone knew he was
spending much of his free time with Libby Holman—he took an
apartment in Manhattan on the same block as hers and spent
many weekends with her at Treetops, her Connecticut estate.
When people describe Monty as bisexual, they point to his relationship with Libby as proof, in spite of the fact that the notion of
a young homosexual's codependent relationship with an older
woman has almost become a cliché today.

Although Monty stated emphatically that Elizabeth Taylor was
the only woman that ever turned him on, there is evidence that
an experimental part of Monty's sexuality had to do with being
subservient to strong, domineering older women with a lesbian

past, whom he would kiss and worship. He enjoyed "necking."
MONTY CLIFT'S STRANGE YEN FOR OLDER WOMEN declared a cover
headline on an issue of *Inside Story* magazine, without really getting to the root of his "strange yen." Jean Green remembered sitting in the living room once with Monty when Libby walked in,
her arms filled with flowers. "Monty crawled over to her on his
hands and knees and started telling her how gorgeous and wonderful she was. It was a frightening image."

Others would recall him doing a similar act with the intellectu-
ally stimulating Salka Viertel, an Austrian writer who had penned
some of Greta Garbo's movies and was reportedly her lover. Physically, Salka was a plain woman, thirty years Monty's senior. Shelley Winters had an explicit memory regarding leaving a party one
evening and encountering them. "I noticed in a dark convertible
two people necking in a rather sexual manner. When I peeked, I
realized it was Montgomery Clift and Salka Viertel, Garbo's writer
and a very important person in the Hollywood firmament. She
was about sixty years old."* Other guests of Salka's remember
Monty "being drunk, crawling across the floor on his hands and
knees and kissing her feet."

Still, even among his close-knit group, Kevin McCarthy was
never 100 percent sure of exactly what the relationship was between Monty and Libby. The two gave the impression that they
were in a passionate affair, and friend Jack Larson thought they
were. "He liked younger men and older women," Larson once
stated. Both Libby and Monty liked to create a sexual atmosphere. But were they lovers? They both preferred to leave the
question trailing behind them, like the heavy scent of Libby's Jungle Gardenia perfume.

People were fascinated and appalled that the young movie star
with the face of an angel would be romantically involved with a
mature, hardened woman. To capitalize on the public's fascination with the unlikely romance, Richard Kayne wrote a play, *Single*

---

*Monty was also fascinated with Greta Garbo and took her on several
dates, one of which ended with them kissing. Monty would comment only
that her lips were chapped.

Man at a Party, based on the relationship. Ruth Warrick was cast as the Libby character, and Ron McNeil, a young Monty look-alike, was cast opposite her.

Monty's relationship with Libby wasn't the only one speculated about. In 1950 he also traveled through Europe with Kevin McCarthy and his wife, Augusta Dabney. He remained extremely close with the couple, especially with Kevin, and some tongues did wag from New York to Los Angeles about the two men. Kevin recalled going on an audition for Henry Hathaway and the director telling him that there was a feeling in Hollywood that "there was a hint of a homosexual relationship" between Kevin and Monty. "People are talking about you," Hathaway warned. "They're saying that you're shacking up with your buddy, Monty Clift."

"Jesus!" Kevin replied. "Where did that come from?"

"I don't know where it came from," Hathaway said, "but you've got to listen to it . . . Lose that guy . . . [H]e's killing your career."

More jaded show-business people did know Monty was gay, but they understood why he tried to keep it under wraps. In his unfinished novel *Answered Prayers*, Truman Capote reimagines a scene at a dinner party between Monty, Dorothy Parker, and Tallulah Bankhead, one that humorously conveys sophisticates' ambivalence about Monty:

> "He's so beautiful," murmured Miss Parker. "Sensitive. So finely made. The most beautiful young man I've ever seen. What a pity he's a cocksucker." Then, sweetly, wide eyed with little girl naïveté, she said, "Oh. Oh dear. Have I said something *wrong*? I mean, he is a cocksucker, isn't he, Tallulah?"
>
> Miss Bankhead said: "Well, d-d-darling, I r-r-really wouldn't know. He's never sucked my cock."

Those close to him knew that Monty could become extraordinarily intimate with someone, a man or a woman, and would often overtly display affection, including kissing the person on the lips, groping, hugging, even plopping himself down in the person's lap, without it ever becoming sexual.

In the mid-1950s, Monty became close to a talented young black actor named Bill Gunn. He was twenty, and Monty was thirty-five. For a while, Gunn was one of Monty's closest friends. He would come over to Monty's apartment, pour himself several stiff drinks (to catch up to Monty), and spend many hours talking and laughing with Monty, trying desperately to keep up with the frantic pace of Monty's conversation. "Here was a guy who was completely drunk," Bill Gunn recalled, "and yet every word, every movement caught you. He was so full of wit . . . [T]he drinking seemed to sharpen it."

Often, they would hang out together until Monty passed out. Gunn would help the movie star into the bedroom, would undress him, and then would put him to bed. Because he was also drunk, Gunn would strip down and lie in bed next to Monty and fall asleep. But Gunn maintained that they never had sex. Monty drew a line. This was a nurturing friendship of a teacher and pupil.

Each morning Monty's secretary would discreetly enter the actor's bedroom, pick up Monty's clothes and hang them in the closet, and then tiptoe out. One can only guess what she assumed about the relationship between Monty and the young man habitually sleeping next to him. Gunn often felt that something sexual was on the brink of happening between them, but Monty wouldn't let it.

Almost always, Monty preferred to be mysterious about his partners and to keep his friends guessing about his sex life. Complicating the issue was that Monty liked people to assume he was in a sexual relationship with people who were just friends— particularly women friends. But his sexual relationships continued to be with men.

Throughout 1950, Monty and Kevin were adapting the play *You Touched Me!*, by Tennessee Williams and Donald Windham, into a screenplay. Monty would have three-way sex with Windham and his lover, actor Sandy Campbell. Monty also had lovers over the course of years who rarely, if ever, interacted with his friends. One was Rick, a boyfriend who lived in New Jersey and who saw Monty for over a decade but never became a part of his social set, even though back in those days, many friends within homosexual circles often interacted.

The inexplicable attraction Monty had for Elizabeth still had a hold on him. The bottom line was, if he was going to be with a woman—and he said this himself—it was going to be Elizabeth. While having a drink in his room once with Italian journalist Giuseppe Perrone, Monty confided that he had strong feelings for Elizabeth. "Monty called Taylor his 'ideal woman,'" Perrone recollected. "He spoke of her as his 'twin.' 'We are so much alike, it's fantastic!' he said. They'd both been child actors; they'd never really been kids, he said—no fantasy life, no games or fun . . . He seemed upset about Taylor's marriage to Nicky Hilton, but he didn't think it would last." On impulse Monty brought out some letters Elizabeth had written him and let Perrone read them. He also showed the young writer one he was writing to Elizabeth. "They both sounded childlike and innocent," Perrone noted.

In the early 1950s Monty was at the peak of his beauty, fame, and ability to seduce and perplex. But those close to him noticed a negative change in the Monty they knew before he went into the movies. The change was behavioral, and all the more surprising because it seemed to overtake Monty suddenly and then progressively get worse. "Very slowly, he was really going downhill," Kevin McCarthy observed. "It was like the disintegration of a great structure." Yes, he was still mercurial, and he continued to excite friends when talking about his ideas and his plans for his future career, but there were some deeply disturbing qualities in Monty now.

Sometime in the years he was making films, he went from someone who drank a lot to an alcoholic, from a heavy smoker to someone who was never without a cigarette. And from a man who took pills to a man who had a floor-to-ceiling medicine cabinet specially built in his bathroom to contain his wide collection of pharmaceuticals. Now, he was so out of it at times, he would fall down when walking down the street.

On top of that, he sometimes acted rudely. He would become childlike and imperious with friends. They wondered if it was the alcohol and the pills that were adversely affecting him. "There's something wrong with him. His behavior is so infantile," Kevin's sister, the writer Mary McCarthy, stated about Monty. And it was true. Monty would at times regress to the state of a child. When Monty rented Mary McCarthy's house in Cape Cod, for instance, he trashed the place, leaving cigarette burns all over the place and doing things like grilling a steak in the fireplace, hacking it apart on the white shag rug, and serving it from the floor. Another time he drove his car over a neighbor's newly planted herb garden.

His behavior at the dinner table had become shockingly absurd and offensive, and he had developed a disgusting way of relating to food—his own food and that of his tablemates. He would stick his fingers in the food and eat off other people's plates with his hands. Or he might drop his steak onto the floor, cut it up there, and eat it off the floor. On the rare occasion he could get away with it because he was a movie star. Famous and beautiful, Monty had always felt he had to test people. Some friends awkwardly ignored his table antics; others called him on it.

It was almost as if he thought that acting like a pig made him more human. Monty was exceptionally handsome and talented, everyone knew that. Bad table manners brought him down to earth, and he wanted to see if he was accepted like that. But then it became a habit, and he acted that way all the time.

When having dinner on one occasion with Merv Griffin, then a struggling actor and musician, Monty stuck his finger in the younger man's lemon meringue pie, declaring, "I just want a taste." Clearly appalled, Merv glared at him. His annoyance only egged Monty on, and he leaned over and began darting his tongue into the pie and licking off the meringue. Merv pushed the pie into Monty's face. He looked up and languidly wiped the pie off his face, muttering "Yeah, that's good pie, Merv. You're right. It's real good pie." Merv would say that he and Monty went on to be friends, although Monty never really warmed up to the young singer.

His appalling table manners even made the gossip columns, like the time he was spotted picking his teeth with Libby Holman at the swank 21 Club in New York City.

Eventually, Monty's drinking and drug taking put a wedge in his friendship with Kevin, and they weren't so close anymore. One evening, Monty was visiting Kevin and Augusta, and while he was holding their year-old daughter, he blacked out. Kevin sprung forward and caught her before her head hit the floor. After that incident, they still saw each other—but much less often. Monty never mentioned it, but he never forgave the couple. "He was trying not to see too much of me, because he felt uncomfortable," Kevin commented. "He'd be drinking a little too much and fell down a little too often. He always talked about himself and never asked you what you were doing . . . That kind of personality was emerging, so I felt uncomfortable too."

Monty continued to blur his mind with drugs and alcohol. At dinner one time, Maureen Stapleton did a double take when Monty ordered a "triple." Friends would try to talk to him, would take him aside and tell him that he was destroying his wonderful talent. Monty would give some of his best performances, sighing to the friend, "Oh, thank you. Thank you for letting me know. It takes a real friend to tell me when you really need to pull himself together." Then, the next time they were together, it was obvious to those friends that Monty's life was still heading down the same treacherous road. It was very difficult to watch it. Some, like Kevin and Augusta, continued to distance themselves, in their case until the mutual codependence lessened.

Monty's judgment became impaired by alcohol, and he became careless about his image. Late at night he would cruise Third Avenue in Manhattan, a discreet gay area. "He'd pick up guys and bring them to the duplex," Billy LeMassena said. He was well aware that there was the danger of being recognized now, and that scared him, but the fear added an extra layer of thrill to the hunt.

The threat of a scandal always hung over Monty, with the potential of ruining his career. Gossip and rumors began to spread around that he had been spotted in various gay bars and bathhouses in different cities, and his lawyers had to handle several would-be blackmailers.

Hedda Hopper utilized a system of spies who lived all over the country, forever on the lookout for a celebrity scandal. On one occasion, she was informed that Monty was arrested in New Orleans for picking up a young man, and she discovered that the charge was drunkenness. She called Monty's agent at the time, Herman Citron, with the news, and he managed to keep it quiet. In New York Monty was arrested when trying to pick up a man in Times Square, and his lawyer once again was employed to hush up a scandal.

"He hated that public knowledge of it [Monty's homosexuality] might so easily end his career," said poet Rod McKuen. There is evidence that, when sober, Monty was very concerned indeed about his public image. Once he demanded that his agent meet with him face-to-face about the matter. Monty showed up at Herman Citron's office and wanted to know if he had told anyone that Monty was "a fag." He was greatly relieved when the agent assured him that he had not. Thinly veiled articles attempted to expose Monty's gay lifestyle by highlighting his single status, his fondness for older women, his desire for privacy. A team of publicity people was even hired to document his closeness with Elizabeth and later with Marilyn Monroe.

Monty's behavior became so alarming, his friends convinced him that he should get help. For a while he saw a psychiatrist, Dr. Ruth Fox, who specialized in alcoholism, and Monty attended a few AA meetings, but ultimately, he decided it was not for him. Fox was at a loss on how to treat him and recommended him to esteemed Dr. William Silverberg. However, friends and family came to view Silverberg as one of the most sinister and mysterious characters in Monty's life.

Perhaps there wasn't anything ominous in Dr. Silverberg's clinical treatment of Monty, but the two of them together had a toxic energy that was bad for the actor. Silverberg was a fifty-three-year-old, divorced, closeted gay man. He lived with a lover, Ed Shipley (Silverberg called him his "secretary"), in his spacious Central Park West apartment, which doubled as his office. Monty was at a stage in his life where he wanted answers, and he put all his hopes and trust in Silverberg to solve the mysteries of his life. But Silverberg became an answer man with no real answers.

Silverberg convinced Monty that he had been too passive and encouraged him to be aggressive in all his dealings. "You can achieve anything in spite of obstacles," Silverberg would often say. He more or less encouraged Monty to do what he liked, following a treatment he called "effective aggression."

At the same time, Monty moved into an expensive townhouse at 209 East Sixty-first Street and hired a cook. He also moved in a new lover, "Dino," an unemployed airline pilot who worked as a waiter and was separated from his wife. "He was an absolute moron," Truman Capote observed.

The doctor/patient relationship became a codependent one and crossed all sorts of lines: the two men socialized together and even vacationed together. The doctor gave Monty a copy of a book he had authored, with the inscription *For Monty, my hero. Billy.* In return, Monty called Silverberg "my Mephisto," after the demon in German folklore.

Monty rented a house near Silverberg's in Ogunquit, Maine, a gay enclave by the sea. There Monty picked up young guys on the beach and attended gay house parties, usually stoned. Yet the doctor refused even to acknowledge that Monty had a drinking problem. Monty's friend Billy LeMassena observed, "It was clear to everyone that Silverberg was actually encouraging Monty into excesses rather than preventing them." If it was suggested to

Monty that maybe he should find another doctor, he responded that it was out of the question.

Monty continued seeing the doctor until the end of his life, and he even paid for his appointments when he was traveling or out of town, making a movie. Monty's explanation for this extravagance was that Dr. Silverberg kept Monty's missed appointment times open in case the actor had a crisis and flew in for the appointment.

11

MARRIAGE NUMBER TWO

He married that English tart, Elizabeth Taylor!! Why? Can you tell me why? It must be those huge breasts of hers—he likes them to dangle in his face.
—**Marlene Dietrich**

AFTER HER BREAKUP WITH NICKY HILTON, ELIZABETH WOULD come and spend time with Monty in New York when she was in between films. Although it was reported that she was staying at the Waldorf, most of the time she was with him at his townhouse. She confessed that she felt it was her fault the marriage to Hilton broke up, saying that she had been a disappointment, that she hadn't been mature enough, that she hadn't been sexually experienced enough. Monty assured her that she was perfect the way she was, that the blame was completely on Hilton. He would bring her to all his favorite haunts, like Gregory's, a dingy bar at Forty-fourth and Lexington, and Camillo's Restaurant, a favorite Italian place of Monty's.

There was little doubt among observers that her feelings for him had changed. Singer Eddie Fisher recalled meeting Elizabeth at a party given by Roddy McDowall and Merv Griffin in the apartment they shared at the Dakota apartment building in Manhattan. She was sitting in a corner with Monty, and they were engaged in such intense conversation that they didn't notice the other guests.

Once while dining at Camillo's restaurant, Monty and Elizabeth lingered long after all the other customers had left. The owner, Lawton Carver, wanted to close up—he had plans to paint the place. He told them they were welcome to stay while he painted. To his total surprise, Elizabeth and Monty decided to help him paint. They took off their shoes and painted with Carver throughout the night, talking and laughing.

"She was very much in love with Monty—she wanted to marry him," said Blaine Waller, a photographer who was friendly with Monty. "He would bring her into Gregory's and introduce her as Bessie Mae. She wore an awful lot of makeup, she smoked like a fiend and used more four-letter words than any of us put together, and, boy, was she gorgeous. I have never seen anybody as beautiful . . . [S]he was actually staying at Monty's place. He didn't bring her into Gregory's too much. Mostly, they were by themselves—they were very private."

Monty was a safe haven for Elizabeth. He also brought her to dinner to meet his parents, something he rarely did with the people in his life anymore. "Elizabeth was very sweet," Sunny recalled. "And very much in love with Monty." Elizabeth would send Sunny flowers for a long time—for many years after Monty's death.

He acted decently in front of his parents with Elizabeth, but in adulthood Monty's communications with Sunny bore the scars of his childhood. "It had been a life of coded behavior, impeccable manners, politeness, and clean living," Billy LeMassena commented. Now Monty rebelled. His relationship with his mother deteriorated—all the anger he had pent up rushed out at her when they were together. "He would say, 'Mother, you're such a cunt,'" LeMessana recalled.

Part of Sunny's personality was her obsessive need to control her family's lives, most of all Monty's. She tried to guilt him into behaving more civil towards her. "Monty dear, why are you doing this to me?" she'd exclaim. She still tried to have some influence on him. She detested Libby, for example, and told him so, but that only made Monty flaunt his relationship all the more. "He flaunted all of his bad manners in front of her," Jack Larson noted. "It was a sort of trophy that he had overcome her influence."

With Monty no closer to asking her to marry him, Elizabeth was still on the lookout for a steady relationship, a marriage, when MGM shipped her off to the United Kingdom to star in the 1952 medieval melodrama *Ivanhoe*, again teamed with Robert Taylor. If Nicky Hilton was an experiment in being a grown-up that failed, she wasn't about to give up. Now she knew what she *didn't* want, and she changed her search to a mature, sophisticated man. As if on cue, in London she ran into lean, lanky British film star Michael Wilding at the studio commissary.

She had had a mild crush on him a few years earlier, when she had met him in London while filming *Conspirator*. Now, after her relationship with a boyish playboy, she found Wilding—who was twice her age—sophisticated and classy, and she was very attracted to the thirty-nine-year-old. His twelve-year marriage to Kay Young was coming to an end, and Elizabeth moved in for the kill.

Like everyone else in the world, Wilding had read about her short-lived marriage, and his heart went out to the fragile-looking young woman. He decided to invite her to dinner, correctly assuming that she wasn't being asked out, because everyone in London was under the impression that people would be clamoring to get to her. They weren't. When Wilding called Elizabeth, she picked up the phone herself and said she'd be delighted to go out with him. There was a genuine spark between them, and after that first dinner they started spending a lot of time together. In her loneliness, Elizabeth's attraction turned to full-blown desire.

It could very well be that Elizabeth saw in Michael Wilding a less handsome, less complicated facsimile of Montgomery Clift. Wilding was sensitive, sexually ambiguous, and he preferred relationships with older women. He was a true bisexual and was then in the middle of an intense love affair with the bisexual Marlene Dietrich, ten years his senior. He had also been one of Noël Coward's "boys" in the 1930s and was rumored to be a longtime lover of Stewart Granger.

After her experiences with Monty, Elizabeth was up to the challenge, and she didn't plan to lose this time. She directed her full charm and sensuality on Wilding. His reaction to Elizabeth in many ways mirrored Monty's: he'd be very receptive to her advances and then push her away. One reason for his hesitation was that Wilding was skeptical of their age difference, and he also "dreaded hurting Marlene." Just as Monty had, Wilding protested that he was too old for Elizabeth. He told her he was afraid she would change her mind.

"No," Elizabeth assured him.

"Don't you think we should wait?" he asked.

She didn't. Elizabeth was young and lovely and vulnerable, which are some of the reasons Wilding waffled. If nothing else, Elizabeth was straight-out straight. One of the things she had discovered with Nicky Hilton was that she enjoyed sex. She didn't have an androgynous quality, the sexual ambivalence or the maturity of a Marlene Dietrich, which Wilding found so alluring.

When *Ivanhoe* finished filming, Wilding escorted her to the airport. His hesitation in committing prompted her to nickname him "Mr. Shilly-Shally," and she teasingly told him, "Let's pretend we never met, shall we?"

She had no such intention of forgetting him, but while she waited for him to make up his mind, she made another play for Monty. After landing in New York, she checked into the Plaza Hotel, with the intention of spending some time with him. The management asked Elizabeth how long she planned on staying.

"Five days," she replied.

When shown to a sumptuous suite, Elizabeth balked at the cost.

"It's on the house," they informed the movie star.

Later that night, sitting across from Monty at Voisin, the swanky midtown French restaurant, she showed him a massive sapphire ring surrounded with diamonds, which she was wearing on her marriage finger. She informed him it was an engagement ring from Wilding. Monty doubted it, assuming that it was another trick to make him jealous and lure him into marriage. He suspected that Elizabeth had bought the engagement ring for herself.*

The friendship between Elizabeth and Monty had become sentimental and dramatic, and they enjoyed acting it out like storylines in a soap opera—emotional and exciting. A friend remembered Elizabeth calling Monty from her hotel, begging him to marry her before she committed to Michael Wilding. One drunken evening at an Upper West Side eatery, Monty shouted at Elizabeth, "You are the only woman I will ever love!" Staring into his eyes, Elizabeth slouched down in her chair, whispering, "Baby, oh, baby."

At the same time, she was calling Michael Wilding daily, and she finally convinced him to fly across the continent and rendezvous with her in Los Angeles. Gleefully, she called the front desk at the Plaza and inquired about checking out the next day. The management reminded her that they had offered to comp her for five days. Elizabeth had lost track of time and had been there for a month and was being charged the full day rate.

Elizabeth was furious. She called Monty and explained the situation, and he joined in her anger. "No one's going to treat my friend that way," he huffed. A little while later he showed up at her suite, with Roddy McDowall in tow.

They mixed up a pitcher of martinis, and after they had imbibed sufficiently, their spirits soared. Now they were ready to exact revenge on the hotel. After pulling some long-stemmed chrysanthemums out of a vase, the trio got into an impromptu fencing match, and the room was showered with leaves, petals, and stems. Then the three of them ran around the room, turning pictures upside down and unscrewing bathroom fixtures and cabinet handles.

A few days later, back in Los Angeles with Wilding, Elizabeth announced their engagement. His maturity, she felt, would give

---

*Wilding later confirmed that he had given it to her, but not as an engagement ring.

her "the calm and quiet and security of friendship" she sought. Michael Wilding was the antidote for Nicky Hilton. Whereas Nicky was wild, aggressive, and abusive, Wilding was serene and kind—a real gentleman.

On hearing the news, gossip queen Hedda Hopper summoned them to her home for a chat. As usual, the meeting was about control. First, Hopper warned Elizabeth about marrying him, because of his age. He wore a hairpiece to appear younger, she said. Both Elizabeth and Wilding braved the insults silently. Then Hopper played her trump card.

"How could you think of marrying a homosexual?" she asked Elizabeth.

Elizabeth said nothing.

Hopper went on, "The rumor around town is that he and Stewart Granger are very, very close."

Still there was silence.

"Are you going to deny it, Michael?" Hopper asked.

There was no response from Wilding, either. He just sat there with his eyes downcast.

"Oh, Mikey, don't worry about it," Elizabeth said softly.

"Are you going to marry a man like that?" Hopper asked, incredulous. "Do you know what kind of life you'll have?"

Wilding was a kind and dignified man. He didn't want to damage Elizabeth's career, or her life, for that matter. They wanted to be together, and they didn't see how this biddy's permission had anything to do with it. Still, recognizing her power, they both remained silent. Then, not swayed by Hopper's demands, the couple left with their dignity intact.*

"Even before Hedda Hopper chose to make it public, rumors about Michael Wilding must have reached Elizabeth's ears," her costar June Allyson observed. "On the other hand, why should

---

*Years later, Wilding sued Hopper for three million dollars when she implied that he was gay in her biography, "The Whole Truth and Nothing But the Truth." Unable to prove her assertion, she had to pay a hefty settlement.

she have fled a bisexual fiancé if he was nice and comforting? Her mother had married a nice gay man." In February 1951, just shy of her twentieth birthday, Elizabeth married Michael in London's Caxton Hall Registry Office. In stark contrast to her first wedding, the ceremony was low key and took place in front of fourteen people. She was serious about this marriage being anti-Hollywood, pro-family.

Elizabeth biographer William Mann observed, "Given the fact that gay men were so much a part of her life and she loved gay men, the idea of marrying a gay man would probably seem terrific to her after that horrible first marriage, because she knew her gay friends treated her well."

Back in Los Angeles, Elizabeth threw herself into the role of young wife. When visiting the newlyweds, friends noticed that in contrast to her glamorous screen image, Elizabeth was "a caretaking housewife," very down to earth. When not headed to the studio, she wouldn't get all dressed up—she'd slob around, cooking bacon and eggs, the only thing she knew how to make. She became pregnant several months into the marriage.

12

CAREER AND LIFE ADVANCEMENTS

I don't want to be labeled as either a pansy or a heterosexual. Labeling is so self-limiting. We are what we do, not what we say we are.
—**Montgomery Clift**

ALFRED HITCHCOCK DIDN'T GET MONTY TO PLAY THE HOMOSEXUAL murderer in *Rope,* but he did sign him to play the troubled priest who takes a murderer's holy confession in the 1953 thriller *I Confess.* Working on the film was not a happy experience for Monty. First, he was incensed that the script was changed so that the priest isn't wrongly convicted for the crime and hanged at the end—he felt that ending had dramatic punch. He also was put off by Hitchcock's directing style. Monty felt the legendary director was more interested in the mechanics of filming than exploring the hidden feelings in his characters. "Actors should be treated like cattle," Hitchcock famously once said.

While making *I Confess,* Monty met a young actor named Jack Larson, who was already known for playing Jimmy Olsen in the television series *Adventures of Superman.* He first noticed Larson on the Warner lot. Larson looked boyishly handsome dressed as a sailor for his part in *Three Sailors and a Girl.* Monty, in stark contrast, was dressed as a priest. Monty asked Merv Griffin, who was doing some dubbing for *I Confess* and knew Larson, to introduce them.

Later Merv and Larson visited Monty at his suite at the Roosevelt Hotel. Larson noticed Monty preferred his company. "He liked me right off," Larson recalled. "We just had a very easy, relaxed way with each other." When Merv excused himself to go to the bathroom, Monty grabbed Larson by the back of the neck and kissed the young actor passionately. It took Larson by surprise. Up until that moment, Monty hadn't given him any indication he was interested in a romantic way—Larson hadn't even been certain if Monty was gay. Monty suggested they cut out of there, leaving Merv behind. "I can't stand him," Monty said. He wanted to go look for a mouthpiece for a trumpet he'd be using in his next film, *From Here to Eternity*.

Larson told his friend Ken Storer that on their first date, at a restaurant in Beverly Hills, Monty ordered a martini, took a sip, leaned over to kiss Larson and let the sip of martini drain into his mouth. "That's the first time I ever had a martini," Larson said. It is interesting is that Monty had no problem kissing his male friend in full view in a public restaurant in 1953 Los Angeles.

After that Monty rented a bungalow at the Bel-Air Hotel, where the two could hide out. Larson was at once drawn to Monty in the way most people who met him at the time were. "I never met anyone like him," he said. He disliked the legend of Monty as a tortured, self-loathing drunk. "He was full of ideas and jokes and pranks—enormously lively and fun to be around." Larson went so far as to say that Monty's off-screen personality was close to that of Jerry Lewis, that he was nothing like the image people got from his movies, of a brooding and introspective man. Often Monty's humor was the thing that kept him from despair; he once argued with an interviewer that he wasn't self-destructive, because "I enjoy jokes too much."

Monty was one of the two great loves of Larson's's life. "We became deeply involved for the next two years—it was difficult, because I spent most of my time in Los Angeles, and he was in New

York, but Monty remained a close friend for life. I had a room in his townhouse," Jack Larson would later say.

Over time the relationship became difficult because of Monty's alcoholism, which became severe. For all his magic—and Monty had a lot—there were times when his drinking made him hard to bear. Larson remembered such situations. One time he and Monty were at a restaurant with Farley Granger and Shelley Winters, and Monty was inebriated. Farley was a big star, having done *Rope* and *Strangers on a Train* for Hitchcock, and there was a big push from the studio for him to marry Shelley. The discussion got heated. Monty was against it. Shelley was open to the idea. In the end, they didn't marry, but remaining a bachelor really hurt Farley's career.

Monty introduced Larson to Elizabeth Taylor at the same time he was just getting to know Michael Wilding. "Monty always spent a lot of time with Elizabeth when he was in Hollywood, making a movie," Larson said. "Monty really liked Michael Wilding, too, and that was important to her." While he was in Los Angeles, Monty learned that Elizabeth was having a baby, and he spent as much time with her as his schedule allowed. "There was this enormous closeness between them," Jack Larson recalled.

Elizabeth talked about the unconventional love she had for Monty. Like the time she became furious when the name Libby Holman came up as a possible romantic interest of Monty's. "They're just friends," she asserted angrily. "It's strange because I never get angry or jealous when I hear of Monty with boyfriends," she explained. "But when I hear of him with a woman, I just go to pieces . . . because he's mine. I always consider Monty *my* friend. We go out in public together and he is . . . mine! He's just so mine!"

Jack Larson remembered a time when Elizabeth came to his rescue. He recalled to his friend Ken Storer that at the time, he was sharing a house in the Hollywood Hills with the choreographer Roland Petit, who was in the middle of choreographing the film *The Glass Slipper*, starring Michael Wilding. At a concert with

Larson at the Hollywood Bowl, Petit spotted two hot guys a few seats away. Against Larson's protestations, he invited the guys to sit with them, saying, "This is Jack Larson. You know, Jimmy Olsen from *Superman?*"

After the concert Petit invited them back to the house for a swim. Again, Larson warned Petit that he didn't think it was a good idea, since the guys were acting straight and were slightly menacing. But they accepted the invite, and Petit joined them for a swim at the house. A short time later Petit came rushing inside and said, "Oh my God, Jack. You've got to help me! I made a pass at one of the guys, and he's really angry! He wants to know where the girls are!"

Larson shook his head. "This is your mess, not mine." But he was worried. Who knew what the two irate guys in the pool were capable of?

Petit was freaking out when the doorbell rang. Larson answered the door. It was Elizabeth Taylor and Michael Wilding. Elizabeth said, "We were driving by. We saw your light on. We thought we'd stop by."

"Oh my," Petit gushed. "Come in! Come in!"

As Larson, Elizabeth, and Wilding made themselves comfortable, Petit went out to the pool and announced to the guys, "Come in! There's someone I want you to meet."

When they came in and saw Elizabeth Taylor, they went crazy. Elizabeth understood the situation and spent the next hour charming the two guys, acting flirtatious, gossiping about Hollywood, and telling jokes. By the time she and Wilding left, the two young men were completely smitten.

MGM cast Elizabeth in *The Girl Who Had Everything*, a mediocre film they rushed her into in order to get every cent out of her contract before her pregnancy showed. They added two hours a day to her work schedule so that filming could progress quickly. They also informed their star that her contract stipulated that she would not be paid for maternity leave.

Monty disapproved of Elizabeth starring in what he considered a B movie. Elizabeth confessed that she had agreed to it because she was broke. Wilding's divorce from his wife, along with taxes, had left him penniless. In addition, the contract she had negotiated for him at MGM wasn't all that lucrative, and he had turned down some of the lackluster roles they offered him and so had been placed on suspension. With a baby on the way, it was up to her to support the family.

"I've never felt so important in all my life. I've never felt so beautiful," twenty-year-old Elizabeth declared in early January 1953, after the birth of her son Michael Howard Wilding Jr. For a few weeks during her pregnancy, Elizabeth had enjoyed a short time away from motion picture making, and for a while, she had experienced the kind of blissful married home life she had fantasized about.

MGM, of course, was eager for their important star to get back to work. The studio had been angry when she refused to do the 1953 film *All the Brothers Were Valiant.* (But she had given Audrey Hepburn a great break when she turned down *Roman Holiday.*) A crisis at Paramount studio would bring Elizabeth back to work after only several weeks of motherhood. Vivien Leigh had suffered a nervous breakdown while filming *Elephant Walk* in Ceylon.

This is a dramatic film about a beautiful young woman who marries a rich tea planter and moves with him to an isolated mansion in the jungle. Paramount had already sunk a huge investment into the movie, and the studio needed to cast an actress with a face and figure similar to those of Vivien Leigh, so they wouldn't have to reshoot some of the more expensive long shots in which she appears. Elizabeth fit the bill perfectly.

After that movie wrapped, MGM quickly cast Elizabeth in the 1954 musical drama *Rhapsody,* about a spoiled young woman who falls in love with a talented violinist her father disapproves of. She was then rushed into another costume drama, *Beau Brummel,* a film she thought ridiculous. These movies capitalized on her beauty, kept her working, and did absolutely nothing to excite the public or further Elizabeth's career—as if dressing her in pretty clothes and having her look lovely and tempting was enough to stir up excitement. It wasn't. She sensed that audiences were getting bored with her.

After his disappointment working with Hitchcock, Monty was excited to work with director Vittorio De Sica in Italy on a film that was originally titled *Stazione Termini*, but producer David O. Selznick made the production unpleasant for everyone concerned. The film costarred Selznick's new wife, Jennifer Jones, and he hounded the set with demanding telegrams and fifty-page letters, instructing everyone how things should be done.

The film would depict the end of an adulterous affair on the day the unfaithful married woman plans to return to America. The story unfolds at an Italian train station, and the movie was shot at an actual railroad station in Rome. Because the station was still active during the day, the entire movie had to be shot in freezing weather and between the hours of midnight and 5:00 a.m.

When Selznick had a final print of the movie, he butchered it and reduced it to a one-hour running time, changing the name to *Indiscretion of an American Wife* for the American market. The film flopped, receiving almost unanimously bad reviews, but it still holds an interest for film aficionados. *Indiscretion of an American Wife* isn't a masterpiece, but it gives great Montgomery Clift. There are many revealing close-ups, more than in any of Monty's other movies. Everything that made him devastating to mid-century audiences is here—a messy bundle of vulnerability, sensitivity, anger, and passion. There aren't many faces that could break a heart simply by being looked at. Monty had that.

Though the making of his last two films had brought him disappointment, Monty was excited about his next project. James Jones had sent him his novel *From Here to Eternity*, the story of American soldiers stationed in Hawaii before and after the bombing of Pearl Harbor on December 7, 1941.

Fred Zinnemann, who had worked with Monty so successfully in *The Search*, was already set to direct the film version of Jones's novel. Both Zinnemann and Jones thought Monty was perfect for the character Private Robert E. Lee Prewitt, a champion middle-weight boxer and an expert trumpet player. Prewitt's new captain wants him to box on the company team so they can win the title, but Prewitt refuses to fight since he blinded a friend in a practice match. The captain tries to bully him into the ring by doling out a grueling series of punishments carried out by his subordinates.

"Monty had a special kind of pain—a pain he could not re-lease," Jones observed. "He had a tragedy hanging over him like a big black cloud." Monty had always been drawn to Christ fig-ures—he wanted to release his special kind of pain by displaying it on the screen. With his struggles and suffering, Prewitt is as Christlike as you can get in a modern film—a sensitive, principled outsider with good intentions who is cruelly tormented by both his superior and his peers in the military. He is ultimately shot dead when he is mistaken for an invader.

At first, studio head Harry Cohn objected to casting Monty in the role. "He's no soldier and no boxer, and [is] probably a ho-mosexual," Cohn ranted. He wanted Prewitt to be played by Aldo Ray, a burly and gruff contract player—Ray would cost consider-ably less than Monty's $150,000 salary. Zinnemann argued for Montgomery Clift, citing that the "story was not about a fellow who didn't want to box: it was about the human spirit refusing to be broken." When Cohn held out, Zinnemann threatened to back out of the project and got his way. The decision was right; Monty's Prewitt became the heart and soul of the film.

In preparing for the role of Prewitt, Monty took boxing lessons and learned to play the bugle. He worked out daily and jogged to keep his body lean and muscular. He would be baring his torso in a shirtless scene for the first time on-screen, and in preparation, Monty shaved his chest.

Also, in the cast was Frank Sinatra, whose acting career was on the skids at that time. Nervous tension brought on by his tumul-tuous marriage to Ava Gardner was affecting his voice, and conse-quently, his record sales were down and nightclub offers were drying up. The singer campaigned for the part of Private Angelo Maggio, but Cohn, like most of the film industry, thought Sinatra was washed up. Sinatra had read the novel and felt this was a role that could be his comeback and take his career in a new direction. Ava Gardner, a huge star at the time, intervened on Sinatra's behalf. Cohn finally gave Sinatra the part when he agreed to do it for the paltry salary of eight thousand dollars, a savvy pay cut that revitalized his career.

Clift, Sinatra, and author James Jones became buddies during the filming of *From Here to Eternity* and shared all-night drinking binges. Sometimes Monty talked Sinatra out of suicide when he was in despair over his troubled marriage with Ava Gardner. Sinatra was nervous in his first big dramatic role—it meant life or death to his career—and when they weren't out drinking, Monty coached him on how to play Maggio. It was a kindness Sinatra never forgot. "I must say, the best help I ever had was from Monty Clift," he said years after Monty's death. "We became very close on the picture . . . He was so good. He helped me tremendously."

Monty also helped Donna Reed, who played against type as the hooker Prewitt falls for in *From Here to Eternity*. Having recognized the positive impact Monty had on the cast, Zinnemann said, "Clift forced the other actors to be much better than they really were. That's the only way I can put it. He got reactions from the other actors that were totally genuine." After the release of *From Here to Eternity*, both Sinatra and Reed were rewarded with some of the best reviews of their careers.

At the time, Jack Larson, while visiting Monty, would watch him fill up his flask with martinis in the afternoons and then go out for a couple of hours. On one such occasion, Larson—concerned that Monty was going out somewhere to drink alone—asked what he was up to. Monty explained that he was going to visit Frank Sinatra at Mount Sinai Hospital.

Sinatra had been found in the elevator of his New York apartment building with a slashed left wrist, the result of a botched suicide attempt, made at a rash moment when he was overcome with despair over his marriage to the beautiful and volatile Ava Gardner coming to an end. The suicide attempt was all very hush-hush at the time, as Sinatra's press agents and lawyers did their best to keep it a secret. Monty visited his friend daily in the hospital, sneaking in his flask and sharing afternoon martinis with Sinatra in an attempt to raise his spirits. A short while later, Sinatra presented Monty with a solid gold cigarette lighter. Monty was grateful and moved, but he gave the gift to Jack Larson. Monty loved to give his friends and lovers beautiful things much more than to receive them.

From Here to Eternity received thirteen Academy Award nominations, including one for Monty for Best Actor. Ironically, both Frank Sinatra and Donna Reed won Best Supporting Oscars, while—in one of those shocking Oscar moments—Monty lost. (William Holden won Best Actor for *Stalag 17.*) Everyone connected to the film thought Monty was the dramatic center, and both Sinatra and Reed credited him in their acceptance speeches. Zinnemann, presented with his Oscar for Best Director, told the audience, "I couldn't have won this without Monty."

Once again, Monty needed to take a break from the movies. In yet another attempt to straighten out his life, Monty hired a secretary named Marge Stengel, who would become an assistant, nurse, accountant, and friend, and whose main mission was to help keep his life as organized as possible. She read scripts, made appointments, screened phone calls and visitors, and scrutinized bills before paying them to make sure merchants hadn't inflated them. She fiercely protected Monty's privacy but also learned whom he was always available to—friends, like Roddy McDowall, Billy LeMassena, Jack Larson, and especially Elizabeth.

Monty returned to the stage in 1954, at the height of his popularity, to star in an Off-Broadway production of Anton Chekhov's *The Seagull.* Part of the reason Monty did it was to work with and showcase his actor friends Kevin McCarthy (as Trigorin) and Mira Rostova (as Nina). It was a troubled production, one lacking good direction, which resulted in a multitude of acting styles that didn't mesh well together. Ultimately, Monty was the only one in the cast that really came out looking well.

The great acting coach Mira Rostova, who assisted Monty on all his movies, was met with particularly scathing reviews for her performance in *The Seagull*. It didn't help that she was a forty-five-year-old woman playing Nina, who in the play is nineteen. Dramatic critic Brooks Atkinson in the *New York Times* noted that "Rostova as Nina is handicapped by a heavy accent; she is further handicapped by a florid style alien to the whole spirit of Chekhov." He, however, called Clift's performance as Konstantin "beautifully expressed, without any foolish pathology."

During the two-month run of the play, Monty's behavior became more erratic and self-destructive—due mostly to his alcohol and drug abuse. People began to wonder where the downward spiral would end.

13

JAMES DEAN

I'm going to tell you something, but it's off the record until I die. OK?
—**Elizabeth Taylor**

IN 1954 ELIZABETH WAS PREGNANT AGAIN. BUT RATHER THAN ALLOW her to take time off, the studio cast her in *The Last Time I Saw Paris*, based on an F. Scott Fitzgerald short story, but watered down and glossed up for MGM. It had some undertones of Fitzgerald's own marriage, with Elizabeth being a representation of Zelda—restless, reckless, and beautiful—and Van Johnson of the struggling American writer. She was overworked, tired, and afraid she'd miscarry, but Elizabeth worked hard, trying to add dimensions to a character that was underwritten. For the second time, she played a character named Helen who dies (the first time being in *Jane Eyre*).

Monty was still in town, and he inspired her. She wanted to act, and she wanted to be an artist, but since *A Place in the Sun* she hadn't been given any meaty dramatic roles. MGM thought it was enough to dress her in lovely clothes, and sometimes that rubbed off on her. The director of *The Last Time I Saw Paris*, Richard Brooks, was furious when Elizabeth showed up on the set to film her death scene in full face makeup. "You look like you're ready for a premiere," he yelled. "Your mouth looks like a bloody cunt."

Elizabeth was furious, and she started wiping off all her makeup and did the scene that way.

Later that night she showed up with Monty at a dinner party at the estate of the choreographer Roland Petit. He had happened to be on the set that day, and he commented on how beautiful Elizabeth looked without makeup.

Around this time Monty was spending a great deal of time with Elizabeth and Wilding, again almost becoming a part of their marriage, their family. He was staying with them at their house in the Hollywood Hills. It was Monty who escorted Elizabeth to the November premiere of *The Last Time I Saw Paris*, he in a tuxedo and she covering her pregnancy with emerald-green satin and a velvet coat. They posed, beaming, for photographers, both of them looking very beautiful, and very much alike in male and female form.

There were still some good times. But the bad times with Monty were happening more and more often. Drinking and pill popping would turn Monty from a charming, dignified man into a childlike monster. And everyone who knew him had anecdotes regarding his maddening, sometimes disgusting drunken behavior.

One night, Monty was going to dinner with Elizabeth and Wilding, and he invited his old friends Fred and Jean Green, who were now living in Los Angeles, to come along. Monty was still staying at the Wildings' house, and he asked Fred and Jean to meet him there. When Fred and Jean arrived at the house, Monty had already started drinking. Elizabeth and Wilding were in the middle of a heated argument, and Elizabeth—in tears and late in her pregnancy—retreated to the bedroom.

"Monty was very drunk and ugly," Jean recalled. "Really ugly in a way that's difficult to describe—he became like an animal. We knew we couldn't go out to dinner. No way were we going to allow him to be seen in public. So, we just said, 'Well, let's just fix dinner here.' Fred and I were both good cooks. Wilding said, 'Go into the kitchen. Help yourself to whatever is in there.' We went into the kitchen, and all we could find were eggs and some mushrooms. We decided to make an omelet.

"Monty was furious. [H]e was enraged. He wanted to go out. Fred said, 'No, we are not going out. We're going to eat here.' Monty finally said, 'All right, but if we're going to eat here, *I'll* make the eggs.' He took the eggs away from Fred and he started beating them and he spit into them over and over again. I thought, *This is crazy. What are we doing here? What is this about?* So, I said to Fred, 'Let's get out of here. This is insane. This is no life. You can't be with him. It's not possible to be with him.'"

Apparently, there were more incidents like that while Monty was staying with the Wildings. Elizabeth began calling the Greens, begging them to help her with Monty. Finally, in exasperation, Jean said, "Look, Elizabeth, if you can't handle Monty, why don't you let him move in with us? We love him, and we know how to handle him."

Elizabeth got defensive. "Well, I love him, too!" she snapped, then slammed down the phone. Soon after, the Greens had had enough of Monty's behavior and made the decision to stop seeing him so much. His circle was getting smaller.

Wilding's career never took off in America, Elizabeth's was in the doldrums, and their marriage was starting to fail. She was on the lookout for a vehicle that would resurrect her career when she heard that George Stevens was set to direct the motion picture *Giant*, based on Edna Ferber's novel about a powerful Texas rancher and his wife who are challenged by the changing times with the arrival of big oil. The epic movie would detail the family's jealousies and rivalries over the course of twenty-five years.

This was a movie that had Hollywood excited. With Rock Hudson set to play wealthy Bick Benedict, and Hollywood's newest and hottest property, James Dean, slated for his nemesis, Jett Rink, *Giant* was destined to be the biggest film of the year. Stevens initially didn't even consider Elizabeth for the role of Bick's wife, Leslie, feeling that at the age of twenty-three, Elizabeth was too young to play a character who goes from a young bride to a pretty grandmother in the course of the three-hour epic.

He had originally wanted Audrey Hepburn, who turned the role down. After that, every agent in town started calling the director, offering their clients. Stevens's next choice was Grace Kelly. Before casting her, though, he asked Rock whom he would prefer as a leading lady, Elizabeth Taylor or Grace Kelly. "Rock had already met Elizabeth through Monty and knew she was simpatico with gays," biographer Ellis Amburn said. So, Rock expressed his preference for Elizabeth Taylor. Stevens cast her.

Elizabeth was due to have her baby, but she assured Stevens she would be ready to work soon after. On February 27, 1955, Elizabeth's twenty-third birthday, Christopher Edward Wilding was born by cesarean section. His middle name was in honor of Monty—Edward was Monty's first name. True to her word, she immediately went on a liquid diet consisting of ice water and fruit juice, lost thirty-five pounds and regained her figure in a few months, and was ready to begin work on the new film.

Monty felt a degree of jealousy and resentment that James Dean would be appearing opposite his Bessie Mae in *Giant*. Dean was now being touted as the brooding rebel hero of movies, as Monty had been seven years before. When Monty broke out on the scene, James Dean decided he wanted to be like him. Dean also idolized Marlon Brando, but it was Monty he became obsessed with.

In his ambition and passion to be a great actor, he considered Monty to be the ultimate in screen acting. He would watch Monty's performances over and over again, so he could incorporate into his own acting the way Monty reacted, moved, smoked. After he got Monty's phone number, Dean would call Monty so he could study the sound of his voice, the rhythm of his speech. As far as Monty was concerned, Dean was a nuisance. Now he would be acting opposite Monty's most celebrated leading lady.

With his scrutiny of Marlon Brando and Monty Clift, Dean metamorphized into his own kind of genius. But his personality was even more self-destructive than Monty's. They both aspired to be brave and reckless in their performances, so they felt they should live that way in real life. Their performances are riveting, but the price they paid is very great.

Giant would be yet another turning point in Elizabeth's career. Along with recharging her career, she would make two good friends during the filming—although one of those friendships would be short lived when it ended in tragedy.

Filming took place in Marfa, Texas, and when the outdoor scenes were shot, bystanders gathered to watch.

A Place in the Sun, starring his idol Montgomery Clift, was James Dean's favorite movie at the time. Now he was appearing opposite Elizabeth, Monty's leading lady, in a scene, and he was really rattled. A method actor, he used his past experiences, his feelings, and his surroundings to motivate him for the scene. But nothing was working. He flubbed line after line. After several takes, he turned around, walked one hundred feet away from Elizabeth, unzipped himself, and peed in front of a thousand gawking onlookers. Then he zipped up, walked back to his mark, and shot the scene.

Later costar Dennis Hopper asked him why he had done it. "It was Elizabeth Taylor," Dean explained. "I can't get over my farmboy upbringing. I had to pee, and I tried to use that, but it wasn't working. I was so nervous that I couldn't speak. So, I thought if I could pee in front of all those people, I could work with her."

At first, both Rock Hudson and Elizabeth were put off by antics like this. Then it became clear that Dean—with his mumbling, fumbling, and stumbling around—was trying to throw his costars off and steal every scene. He would pull his hat down low or do tricks with his rope, anything to distract and bring attention to himself. When Rock tried to complain to Stevens about this, Dean called him "a fairy."

Dean told a friend that the friction between him and Rock Hudson arose on the first day on the set, when Rock started hitting on him and then played straight in front of everybody. When hanging out with the local cowboys, Dean would mock Rock, calling him "Rack." The two did their best to avoid each other on the set.

It wasn't long before Elizabeth warmed up to Dean. The young actor's "little boy lost" quality reached Elizabeth and moved her. Dean had lost his mother to uterine cancer when he was nine, and when she heard about this, Elizabeth's nurturing nature again took over. One of her gifts was listening and responding to sensitive souls, like James Dean—and he found himself revealing things to her he seldom talked about.

"Jimmy had been hurt very early on in his life," Elizabeth recalled. "He was full of pain. When we were on location, sometimes he'd talk to me about it. We were very close. We'd talk about things in the middle of the night." Sometimes they would stay up together until 3:00 a.m. Dean talked about his past lives, the grief and unhappiness in his life, and his loves and tragedies.

Eventually, Elizabeth revealed to journalist Kevin Sessums what she and Dean had talked about. "When Jimmy was eleven, after his mother passed away, he began to be molested by his minister," Elizabeth revealed. "I think that haunted him the rest of his life. In fact, I know it did. We talked about it a lot."

The morning following their intimate talk, Elizabeth called out, "Hi, Jimmy!" when he appeared on the set. But he barely acknowledged her with a cursory nod of the head. He couldn't bear that he had revealed so much of himself to her. It would be several days before he relaxed around her and they were friends again.

The oppressive heat at the *Giant* location in Marfa also acted as a catalyst that brought Elizabeth and Rock Hudson together. They would form a close friendship, a lasting relationship that would continue throughout his lifetime, greatly influence the last two decades of her life, and add to her legacy. As he had with *A Place in the Sun*, George Stevens filmed at a painstakingly slow pace. Production on *Giant* dragged on in the oppressive heat. "We had to bolster our spirits any way we could," Elizabeth would say.

To relieve the tension after shooting all day, Elizabeth and Rock would dine together. They discovered their drink of choice was a martini. When she wrote her memoir about weight loss (with some reminiscences), Elizabeth remembered that she and Rock invented the "chocolate martini" by mixing vodka with Hershey's Syrup and Kahlúa.

When there was a hailstorm during filming, Elizabeth and Rock ran outside together and got conked on the head with hail the size of golf balls. "We wanted to get a bucketful so we could make

Bloody Marys," she recalled with a laugh. "We were really just kids. We could eat and drink anything, and we never needed sleep," Rock recalled.

Eventually, even Dean and Rock became friends during the shooting of *Giant*. Elizabeth said they all became like a tight-knit family. "Marfa, Texas, had a population of about two thousand, and we were like the real margins, and we had to stick together. We'd go to the movies and go to the diner and have dinner together. We all had tiny little houses across the road from each other." They were so much like a family that when Dean wrapped his role first, Elizabeth presented him with a Siamese kitten, which he promptly named Marcus, after a cousin.

The night Dean died in a car accident, Elizabeth was in the projection room in Los Angeles with the cast and crew, watching rushes. George Stevens turned on the lights and said, "Ladies and gentlemen, I have an announcement to make. Jimmy Dean is dead." There was a collective gasp in the room—nobody could believe it. Elizabeth found herself wandering around the studio with the young Texas man who had taught Dean his dialect, both shocked and dazed, calling every morgue, hospital, and newspaper, trying to find out if it was true. At nine o'clock that night, she heard the official announcement of his death.

That following morning Monty was in his bedroom at Libby Holman's place. As he lay in the opulent bed covered in white satin sheets, Libby brought him a cup of coffee and the morning newspapers, chattering, "Isn't it terrible what happened to James Dean? He was killed in an automobile race on Highway 66 ... [H]is neck was broken. [H]is chest [was] crushed when it smashed into the steering wheel ... " Before she could say any more, Monty threw up all over the white satin sheets. Later he told his friend Bill Gunn, "James Dean's death had a profound effect on me. The instant I heard about it, I vomited. I don't know why."

14

RAINTREE COUNTY

When MGM released its big-budget Civil War epic Raintree County, *the studio expected the picture to become the* Gone with the Wind *of the 1950s. It didn't. It was nearly a disaster. And yet a mystique has grown up around the picture and something of a cult around that mystique.*
—*The Washington Post*

*B*Y 1956 ELIZABETH'S MARRIAGE WITH WILDING HAD RUN ITS COURSE. Later she would sum it up this way: "We had a lovely, easy life, very simple, very quiet. Two babies were born. We had friends. We didn't do much." She felt bad, but she had outgrown him, and she wanted to do more. Everything he had symbolized when she was twenty-two—comfort, nurturance, family—she was tiring of now. As she came into her own as a woman, it was passion and adventure her heart was hungering for—and that would never stop with her. The rest of her life would be a nonstop roller coaster of adventures.

Elizabeth needed to feel romantically intense about someone again; more than that, she longed to be sexually fulfilled. She thought a powerful man would see the empty space in her and fill it somehow. She searched for that man like a metal detector searching for silver.

Suddenly, she fell into affairs. "She was a woman who loved men as much as they loved her," Eddie Fisher said of her. "She told me that she'd had an affair with Frank Sinatra while she was married to Wilding—and had gotten pregnant with Sinatra's child. According to Elizabeth, she wanted to divorce Wilding and marry Sinatra, so she called him and asked him to marry her, but he didn't want any part of that . . . Frank's manager put her in a limousine and drove her to Mexico—she described it as some dirty place in Mexico—where she had an abortion."

After Sinatra, she met Kevin McClory, then an assistant to the colorful and successful producer Mike Todd. McClory, a thirty-something, handsome, blue-eyed Irishman, was enraptured with Elizabeth, and she fell in a big way for him. A major part of their connection was sex. McClory described their intimate relationship as "totally pornographic." But at the time he was still working his way up the Hollywood ladder. He worried that his salary wouldn't live up to the expectations of a star of Elizabeth's stature.

With her private life in chaos, Elizabeth wanted Monty near her. When she was assigned by MGM to appear in *Raintree County,* a Civil War epic that the studio hoped would rival *Gone with the Wind,* the leading man had yet to be cast. Elizabeth called Monty and said that she would love for him to appear opposite her. Monty was intrigued. He asked that the script be sent to him, and in the meantime, he picked up the book, with the same name, from which the script was being adapted.

MGM owned the rights to the novel, written by Ross Lockridge, Jr. But the thousand-page book proved to be difficult to adapt into a screenplay. It had been sitting in the studio archives for eight years when producer Dore Schary, who was scouting for a major project, picked it up. After reading *Raintree County,* Schary became convinced that this was the book that could be another *Gone with the Wind.* The adaptation from novel to screenplay was done by Millard Kaufman, who ran into trouble when trying to pare down the massive novel and concentrate its focus for the screen.

Raintree County tells the story of a young writer (Monty), his love for a blond girl (Eva Marie Saint), and the bad, unstable, dark Southern belle (Elizabeth) who steals him away and then descends into madness during the Civil War. Poignantly, Elizabeth and Monty would play a married couple who eventually have a son together.

Monty admired the book, but after reading the screenplay, he wavered on whether or not to star in the film version. It was overstuffed with dialogue, characters, and superfluous situations, which may have worked in the novel but wouldn't be effective onscreen. He instinctively started crossing out large portions of the script so that the story would move along. Monty also recognized that underneath all the writer's attempts to make *Raintree County* an epic, the story was little more than a glossy soap opera. "A soap opera with *elephantiasis*," he called it. But soap operas are often very successful, and being involved with another hit was something very much on his mind.

Weighing into his decision was the fact that Monty hadn't made a movie in three years. He was still a valuable commodity, but he had borrowed thirty thousand dollars from MCA, his agency. Still, Monty didn't have to do *Raintree County* purely for financial reasons—it was also time to get on with his career.

With his long absence from the screen, he had already lost some momentum. In the past few years, James Dean had come along and blazed triumphantly, and now he was gone. Brando had come out with *The Wild One, On the Waterfront, Désirée,* and *Guys and Dolls.* Leading men like William Holden, Kirk Douglas, Burt Lancaster, and Rock Hudson had been very productive and successful during Monty's hiatus. Many of the roles that were hits for these actors had been turned down by Monty.

In many ways, *Raintree County* seemed like the kind of movie that would be a perfect vehicle for his return to the screen. The prestige of the project was confirmed when it was announced that MGM had given it a budget of five million dollars, which would make *Raintree County* the most expensive film the studio had ever made. The script may have not lived up to his artistic standards, but it appeared to have huge commercial potential. And in this sweeping, colorful historical epic, Monty would indisputably be the lead, surrounded by a talented and popular cast that included Eva Marie Saint, Lee Marvin, Rod Taylor and, most enticingly, Elizabeth Taylor.

The past few years he had been messy for Monty. Although he hadn't been on the screen, stories had been going around about his slide into alcoholism. After his long absence it was important for him to carry a popular hit. "He wanted to reform himself," Kevin McCarthy explained. This movie would be filmed in color, Monty's first, and he thought that the intense chemistry between him and Elizabeth could create magic again. He called Elizabeth and told her he would do it. Then he called his agent and told him to negotiate the deal. Next, he called Jack Larson in Hollywood.

"Jack," he said, "I'm coming out to Los Angeles. I'm going to do *Raintree County*."

"Is it good?" Larson asked.

"No, it's not good. But it's good enough," Monty replied. "And I'd be a coward not to do it. And it means I'll be working with Bessie Mae again. I love her."

In 1956 Monty was still considered the bigger star of the two. And so Elizabeth was being paid $150,000, but Monty was offered $300,000 for starring in *Raintree County*. He, however, told MGM that he would happy to play the part of John Shawnessy for $250,000 and that the studio should use the rest of the money to "make the picture better."

The director chosen for the project was Edward Dmytryk, who had scored a huge hit in 1954 with *The Caine Mutiny*. Before production started, Monty became good friends with scenarist Millard Kaufman. For one thing, Monty liked and respected writers. For another thing, he wanted an ally when it came to incorporating his editing and rewrites for the script.

Regardless of his dissatisfaction with the screenplay, Monty flew out to Los Angeles in March of 1956, two months before shooting was to begin, to prepare for the film. Before arriving, he decided that he no longer wanted to drive. Therefore, the studio rented him a house on Dawnridge Drive in Beverly Hills that came with a houseboy, Florian, who would serve as Monty's driver.

As her marriage had unraveled, Elizabeth was particularly happy to have Monty close at hand. She was looking for fulfillment outside the marriage, was having affairs, and she wanted a confidant to whom she could state her case, someone who understood her. She knew Monty would never judge her. All day he would listen to Elizabeth's version of the marital problems, her gripes, and yearnings.

Then, in separate conversations in the evenings, Monty had to hear Wilding get out his side. The two men had grown fond of each other, and in the evenings, Wilding often visited Monty's house to give his version. Of course, Monty's allegiance was with Elizabeth, but he was fond of Wilding, too, and he tried to be diplomatic. Wilding called him "an interpreter for two people who no longer spoke the same language." Wilding told him that he was still in love with Elizabeth, but that there was now a barrier between them. "Once, I thought I could influence this trembling little creature and guide her along life's stony path," he said floridly. "Lately, I'm simply told to shut up."

When Monty strolled across the elaborate sets constructed on many soundstages across the studio's back lots, he was awestruck by the detail and the grandeur—the expertise and the expense that was put into the production was mind boggling. In that moment he saw the film's potential. "It's going to be an epic movie!" he exclaimed to producer Dore Schary.

To capture the splendor of the sets and the beauty of the cast, the movie was being filmed in a new 65mm process called "Windows of the World." MGM announced it would give audiences the most crystal-clear, sharpest image they had ever seen. With this new filming process, the camera would pick up every detail, including every flaw and blemish.

For *Raintree County*, Monty wanted to get his mind and body back into shape. For the first time before beginning a movie, the actor was really worried about how he would look on-screen. In the early part of the film, he would play a young man just graduating from school. He had been off the screen for three years. Time and substance abuse were just beginning to show around the edges of his handsome face. In addition, years of chain smoking had damaged his voice. It sometimes sounded phlegmy, and sometimes it was a hoarse, raspy squeak, making him sound years older than he was.

He was particularly concerned about the scene in which he was to be given a bath by local townsmen in order to sober him up to run a footrace against Lee Marvin. Monty objected strongly to the scene, since he would have to appear bare chested. In *From Here to Eternity*, Monty's body is buff and shaved, and he had consented to being filmed shirtless. He was now very thin, and his slight chest was covered with a thick carpet of hair. (The studio heads liked hair on the chest of a man; in that era it signified masculinity and virility.) Monty requested that the scene be removed from the script. The producers refused to cut it.

On the other hand, at twenty-four, Elizabeth had many more years left at the pinnacle of her beauty, which kept evolving. But in between making films, she had a tendency to put on weight. Before filming on *Raintree* began, she went on a high-protein crash diet, enabling her to lose fifteen pounds in two weeks. Next, she began the long, complicated costume fittings for her 1856 wardrobe. At the same time, she was studying with a dialogue coach, Marguerite Littman, to fine-tune a Southern accent. It would come in handy for several movies in the coming years.

In spite of his resolution to clean up for the movie, Monty couldn't or wouldn't control his drinking, even in front of colleagues. Dmytryk had scheduled a read-through of the script by the entire *Raintree County* cast. On the day of the reading, the director was surprised to see that Elizabeth was on time, while Monty was nowhere to be found. Elizabeth settled in with the rest of the actors at a long library table. *Raintree* producer Dore Schary would read for all the actors who couldn't make the reading because of scheduling conflicts. Schary was getting ready to read Monty's part just as he strolled in, very drunk, and took his place at the table. Everyone held their breath.

"The script reading started moving along," Dmytryk recalled. "At Monty's first line it all came to a halt. He stared long at his script, then started to speak, haltingly and awkwardly, like a four-year-old trying to read Daddy's newspaper." Schary waited until Monty wrestled with his next line, then politely excused himself. "When he was out of the room, there was a long sigh at the table, and we all looked at Monty," Dmytryk said. "He sat there, hunched over and looking perplexed. Was this one of his best performances?"

Soon after, Dore Schary called Monty into his office for a serious talk. The producer explained that he was counting on Monty to "behave" during production. "Absolutely no drinking during work hours," he said. *Raintree* had a massive five-million-dollar budget, the highest of any MGM film up to that time, and the studio couldn't take any chances.

As a backup, Schary called on Elizabeth to keep an eye on Monty, to use their closeness as a way of keeping him in control, keeping him from drinking too much. Elizabeth, more than anyone, was aware of Monty's decline. The childish habit of eating off other people's plates at dinner. The excessive drinking, to the point of incoherence. "Elizabeth saw it, but she never talked about it much with me," Michael Wilding stated. "She didn't like speaking of Monty behind his back; she was much too protective of him."

Of course, Elizabeth hoped that Monty would rein in his drinking while working on the movie—but in the long run, she realized she had little influence over him. But in her mind, he was still an artistic genius and a loving person—and her attitude was to let Monty be Monty. She was sure he would come through.

Schary wasn't so sure, and when Monty continued to appear drunk at rehearsals, the producer took a step that he'd never done before. He took out an insurance policy on the movie. He would later say that it was a "funny premonition" that led him to that decision. The policy was for five hundred thousand dollars, which would be paid if, for any reason, the filming of the movie was halted. It was with these concerns, but with still a shaky optimism, that production started on April 2, 1956.

* * *

Most of the scenes that took place indoors were scheduled to be shot at the studio in Los Angeles. Then the production would move to southern locations to film the majority of the outdoor scenes. When shooting started, Monty seemed to make a definite effort to curb his drinking, although he did close himself off from the rest of the cast—with the exception of Elizabeth. At first, he didn't drink excessively on the set, but he did sometimes show up in the mornings with a hangover, which made it difficult for the cameraman to shoot his eyes, which would be bloodshot. Monty walked around the set with cold compresses on his eyes to keep the swelling down.

Eva Marie Saint, the method actress who had won the Academy Award for Best Supporting Actress the previous year for her performance playing opposite Brando in *On the Waterfront*, was cast to play Monty's youthful love, Nell. She admired Monty's great talent, but found his protective walls impossible to penetrate. "He was so beautiful. I felt a little self-conscious in his presence," the actress admitted. "He was just a very private person."

As shooting progressed, the talk of the set became the thermos Monty carried around on the set, along with a gray leather bag. It was surmised that the thermos contained alcohol. (It did. It had a mixture of orange juice and vodka.) The cast and crew soon found out that the leather bag contained a vast quantity of different medications.

15

WRECKED

The wreck obviously had an effect on his looks. What it did was take away the delicacy of his features. Not the beauty, but the delicacy.
—**Elizabeth Taylor**

WHILE MONTY WAS WORKING ON *RAINTREE COUNTY*, JACK LARSON was living in Los Angeles, shooting the *Superman* television show, playing cub reporter Jimmy Olsen. The two men hadn't seen each other in a while and took this as an opportunity to spend some time together. Right away Larson was startled by the change in Monty. For one thing, he was drinking too much, even for him. "I always knew Monty drank—in the same way everyone drank in those days—but I never saw it as a problem before." Now he saw that Monty's drinking was continuous, out of control.

Although Monty had always been casual in his appearance, Larson discovered that he had become sloppy and unkempt, and he seemed agitated. He also noticed that Monty was physically frail, that "his body had lost muscle." Monty was still handsome, but he had aged.

However, there was nothing dark or foreboding early on Saturday, May 12, 1956, the day of Monty's ultimate tragedy. Jack Larson came by for a visit, and they sat around Monty's rented house, talking. Half of *Raintree County* had been completed. Now filming would be moved to the South to add some authentic locations to the story. One thing that Monty did feel troubled by was that Elizabeth might steal the film. Her mad Southern belle role was so showy, so colorful. But, he said, it was "worth it to be working with Bessie again."

Throughout that afternoon, Elizabeth kept calling. She was having a small dinner party and desperately wanted Monty to come. It was a sort of going-away party, since the *Raintree County* location work would be starting the following week. But Monty was exhausted and kept telling Bessie that he didn't feel up to socializing. Monty confided to Larson that the weariness of being in almost every scene of a big-budget epic, mixed with the exhaustion of being caught in between the arguments of two good friends in a relationship, was draining him. He feared the dinner party would be more of the same, and he couldn't deal with any more.

Elizabeth called again. She wanted her best friend at the party. In an attempt to make the gathering more enticing, Elizabeth had invited a cool young priest, Father George Long, who, she hinted suggestively, would be fun for Monty to meet. "It's okay," she explained. "He's a modern priest. He says 'fuck.'" The priest, who was a cousin of one of Elizabeth's friends, had seen Monty in *I Confess* and was a big fan. Monty still begged off.

At one point, Wilding got on the other extension and pleaded with Monty to come. Monty had an inkling of what the night would be. He'd be acting as buffer between Elizabeth and Wilding as they engaged in arguments. He again declined. After they hung up, Monty turned to Larson and told him about the hip young priest who cursed. They thought it was hilarious, the idea of Elizabeth fixing Monty up with a priest. But Monty wasn't tempted. "I don't care how cool he is—I'm tired. I want to stay here." The two friends talked some more. "Just as I was leaving," Larson said, "the phone rang, and once again it was Elizabeth."

On this call, something Elizabeth said—or perhaps it was just her insistence—touched the soft spot Monty had for her, and he decided to make an appearance at the party, after all. Or so he told her. Shortly after he agreed to come to the dinner, he fell asleep.

"That evening, Miss Taylor was a busy young woman, trying to keep dinner from growing cold while awaiting a missing guest," Eddie Dymtryk recalled. "Monty was late." The small group of guests sat around the living room, lingering over their drinks (warm rosé), waiting for Monty. Finally, Elizabeth called him again, and this time roused him from a deep sleep. He promised he'd be right over.

Florian had the night off, and Monty no longer felt comfortable driving. He dreaded making the trip to Elizabeth's mountaintop place in the dark. It was a foggy night, too. To get to the Wildings' house, high in the Hollywood Hills, you had to drive up a very narrow winding canyon road. Back in those days, this road was secluded—there was only a scattering of houses on the way up to Benedict Canyon, and most of them were still under construction—and the lighting was terrible.

He managed the tricky road just fine, and shortly after Elizabeth's call, he arrived at the Wilding house, disheveled, sleepy eyed, and unshaven, but willing to at least take a stab at being pleasant and social. Elizabeth, in contrast, was magnificently attired in a white satin cocktail dress and sparkling gems.

Monty stepped into the living room and said hello to the other guests: Edward Dymtryk and his wife, the actress Jean Porter; and Rock Hudson and his new wife, Phyllis Gates, who, everyone at the party knew, was acting as Rock's Hollywood beard. (The previous year the scandal rag *Confidential* intended to out Rock, and his agent, Henry Willson, knew there was only one way to silence the homosexual rumors: marry Rock off as quickly as possible.)

Also at the dinner was Monty's old friend Kevin McCarthy. They hadn't been close in recent years, but they greeted each other warmly and fell into the routine of old friends. Monty immediately made an agreement with Kevin that the two of them wouldn't drink too much.

The priest who had been mentioned to entice Monty to come to the party didn't show up at all.*

As the guests ate and sipped warm wine, the dinner conversation was the kind that is common in Hollywood—it revolved around their latest projects. Kevin McCarthy chatted brightly about his second film, the science fiction horror movie *Invasion of the Body Snatchers*, which was a surprise hit of 1956 and was still playing in theaters. Phyllis Gates remembered Kevin as "bright and intelligent." She noted, "He kept the conversation alive, meanwhile eying Monty to make sure he didn't consume too many drinks."

Rock Hudson was working on a "Technicolor noir" entitled *Written on the Wind*, with Lauren Bacall. Ironically, the script was a thinly disguised retelling of the Libby Holman scandal involving the death of her first husband. Monty must have been aware of this, although nobody mentioned it.

Elizabeth chattered about the beautiful costumes that had been designed for her for *Raintree County*. No expense was being spared, she said. Even her petticoats were being created from the finest material, despite the fact they would hardly be seen on the screen. Monty remarked that no one would be looking at her petticoats, anyway. "All they'll see is your tits, darling," he said dryly. Everyone laughed.

And then Monty and Elizabeth joked about how young and gorgeous the film's cinematographer, Robert Surtees, was making them look—observations that would soon have a tragic irony. Elizabeth's delicate beauty—her oval face, big eyes, and tiny waist—was well suited to the costumes of a Southern belle. Monty, although beginning to look more mature than he had in his earlier films, could still be photographed to appear startlingly hand-

---

*A few years after the devastating drama of this evening, Monty would meet this priest at a dinner party given by Elizabeth and her then husband Eddie Fisher. At this gathering the priest would get the chance to display his infatuation with Monty. "By dessert the priest was playing with Monty under the table," Eddie Fisher recalled.

some. In this film the crystal blueness of his eyes would be seen for the first time by audiences.

After dinner the party took on a more somber tone. The one career that was not going well was Michael Wilding's. He hadn't been offered any movie roles recently, and he lay sullenly on the couch, zonked on pain medication. He was having back problems. Elizabeth was playing Sinatra records on the hi-fi. Phyllis Gates recalled that Elizabeth and Monty sat very close together on the couch and "conversed almost in whispers."

It would have been an unmemorable occasion in every respect if Monty had left his car there for the evening and asked Kevin McCarthy to drive him home. Which he did not do—and no one seemed to think he was inebriated and shouldn't drive, anyway.

Monty, of course, could be a discreet drinker. On this night, the guests generally agreed that Monty seemed to drink very little, comparatively speaking. Kevin McCarthy always spoke of the pact not to get drunk that he and Monty had made earlier in the evening, and maintained that his friend had one glass of wine. Elizabeth Taylor told interviewer Larry King that Monty had "two glasses of wine." Rock Hudson saw him drink "several glasses." Monty later told Jack Larson that he had a glass of sherry at the dinner party. However little (or much) Monty had to drink, shortly before midnight he went into the bathroom and swallowed a couple of downers. He planned to leave the party soon and hoped that by the time he arrived home, the tranquilizers would have relaxed him enough to fall asleep right away.

This time the mix of pills and drink had a quick effect on him. When he came out of the bathroom, Monty was glassy eyed and swaying. Wilding roused himself from the couch and made his way over to him.

"How are you feeling?" he asked.

"None too gorgeous," Monty murmured.

To Elizabeth, that meant that he was falling under one of his sudden waves of depression. She tried to press another drink into his hand. "Don't look so sad," she said. "I want everyone, most of all you, to be happy with me."

"I'm always happy with you, Bessie," Monty mumbled as he lumbered past her. "You'll have to excuse me, sweetie. Not feeling too gorgeous, you understand."

The Dmytryks had already left the party. Monty made his way over to Kevin McCarthy, who was getting ready to leave himself. Monty said, "Why don't I go with you? I'm afraid I won't find my way down that road. I'll follow you in my car."

Outside, in the parking area in front of the house, Monty and Kevin leaned against their cars and chatted. It had been a while since they were friendly. It was clear to Kevin that Monty was depressed. Monty revealed how disappointed he was with how the movie was going. The complex characters and situations of the book were becoming cliché and plodding in the film adaptation. He talked of how much he hated Hollywood and acting in films. The filmmaking establishment didn't seem to understand acting—everything seemed mechanical and fake, with no regard for art.

After saying their goodbyes, they got in their cars, and Kevin started leading Monty down the steep canyon road. This area, called Beverly Estates Drive, was not built up at the time. It was a dark road, with a number of sharp turns on the way down. McCarthy later recalled their descent down the road: "He was following me, and he'd come up behind me very fast and very close to my bumper—and these roads were treacherous. His lights were coming up awfully close. At first, I thought that he was pulling a prank, trying to bump into my car. It was the kind of thing he would do. Dangerous pranks were Monty's thing. But this time it was life and death. I was afraid for him, but I was afraid for myself, too. If he were to bump me, my car could easily tumble off the road.

"All I could see in front of me was what the car lights showed. Blackness on either side of me and his headlights in my rearview mirror coming closer and closer. I sped up to distance myself from him as much as I could while I kept an eye on his car in the rearview mirror. I made the first turn very quickly. I thought, *Whew . . . Made it!* The second turn was a real hairpin turn, treacherous. Before turning, I checked the rearview mirror again. I saw his headlights were swerving from one side of the road to the other. Dust was flying. I thought, maybe, he passed out behind the wheel and the car was driving itself."

After he made the sharp turn, Kevin put on his brakes and waited for Monty to catch up. "Suddenly, I heard a crash. Monty's lights were no longer in my rearview mirror, but I could see a cloud of dust. I turned my car around and drove back one hundred yards or more, where he was." Monty's car had veered off the road and smashed into a telephone pole.

The road was so dark, Kevin could barely see anything else. There was no sign of Monty in the car. Yet the sound of the motor revving up resounded weirdly through the canyon. The smell of gas was everywhere. Afraid that the car might catch fire and blow up, Kevin reached in through the broken window and turned off the ignition. There was still no sign of Monty. He went back to his car and drove it closer to the accident so he could shine his headlights into Monty's car. Now when he approached the wreck, Kevin could see inside the battered car.

"Monty," Kevin gasped. Monty's body was scrunched up under the dashboard. "I realized the motor had been running because Monty's body was crumpled on the gas pedal," Kevin observed. "I could see what looked like a face—all ripped up. Blood everywhere. No sounds coming from him. I was terrified he might be dead. I reached and tried to open the door, and I couldn't."

Kevin got back in his car and drove frantically back to the Wildings' house. He banged on the door. Wilding opened it, looking bemused.

"Monty's dead!" Kevin screamed out. "Monty's dead!"

Wilding thought he was joking. "Oh, come on now, Kevin . . .

Elizabeth came to the door. It was immediately apparent to her that this was no joke. Kevin's face was ashen; he was trembling all over. "What's happened? What's happened?" she screamed.

"There's been an accident! I think Monty's dead!"

Rock and Phyllis joined them at the door, someone ran back to call an ambulance and Monty's private physician, Dr. Rex Kennamer, Kevin, Rock, and Wilding stood together, having decided to drive down to the accident scene. They tried to convince Elizabeth to stay behind and wait.

"No! I'm going to Monty! I'm going to Monty!" she screamed.

Phyllis joined her, and they all set out in two cars and drove to the scene. They parked as close to Monty's car as possible, so that their headlights shone on the wreckage, which looked like an "accordion-pleated mess." They got out of the cars and, in disbelief, approached the smashed-in heap of metal and shattered glass. It was impossible to imagine Monty alive somewhere in that mess. But when they looked in, they could see him still curled up under the dashboard. Now he was moving a little.

"We can't get to him. The doors jammed," Kevin informed them.

Rock attempted to open the driver's door, but it wouldn't give. Elizabeth tried a back door and found that it, too, was stuck. She used all her strength and pulled and pulled until she wedged it open. "Adrenaline does something to you," she would later explain. Kevin would never forget Elizabeth's heroic strength that night. He told biographer Patricia Bosworth that she "was like Mother Courage." She was determined to get to Monty. She was fierce. "She climbed over the seat and somehow got down into the car and was able to somehow cradle Monty's broken, battered head," Kevin McCarthy said.

Already it was apparent that Monty's beauty would not, could not, ever be the same. His face appeared to be torn in half. But what mattered now was Monty's living or dying. "I was just holding him like a baby and rocking him," Elizabeth remembered. "He opened his eyes and saw me. His eyes looked the color of a bright red rose."

On seeing Elizabeth, Monty mumbled, "My teeth . . . are . . ." and then he started choking. He pantomimed that something was in his throat.

Unbeknownst to the others, he was suffocating. "His front teeth were knocked out, and they were stuck in his throat," Kevin explained later. "And she reached into his mouth and pulled those broken teeth out of his throat."

As they looked on, it was apparent to the others that Elizabeth had saved Monty's life. His warm blood continued to flow rapidly from his wounds, dying Elizabeth's white satin dress crimson and pooling in her skirt, where it formed a puddle around Monty's head in her lap. The smell of it wafted up to her nose, but she continued to talk to him. "I'm here. I'm with you, baby," she said.

"I remained totally calm," Elizabeth explained later. "Did what I was supposed to do. I didn't cry until later on that night."*

Dr. Rex Kennamer arrived on the scene. Monty was in and out of consciousness, but he managed to say weakly, "Dr. Kennamer, meet Elizabeth Taylor." Kennamer had known Elizabeth as a child star when he was the physician for MGM, but he became reacquainted with her now, and after this night he became her personal physician, too.

With the help of Rock Hudson, Dr. Kennamer managed to pull the driver's-side door open. The two men gingerly moved Monty out of the car and laid him on the road. Again, Elizabeth tenderly cradled him in her arms like a pietà. They were open and exposed on an eerily silent road—spotlighted by the glow of headlights. After retrieving it from his emergency bag, the doctor quickly gave Monty some pain medication and then assessed the damage. The most immediate concern was the loss of blood. "He was bleeding so much, he was in danger of dying from blood loss alone," Kennamer said.

The scene was surreal and terrible. "It was so unbelievable, yet there we were, breathing the night air, with this horrible tableau in front of us," Kevin remembered. In the dark, in the stillness,

---

*When Elizabeth told the story through the years, the details sometimes changed. No doubt she was in various stages of shock throughout the ordeal, and her body was working on automatic pilot, her emotions deactivated. All the witnesses, however, saw her pull the teeth from Monty's throat.

they realized this was something that would change all their lives forever, most of all Monty's.

There was no sign of the police or an ambulance, but as if on cue, a horde of photographers arrived on the scene. Not yet termed "paparazzi," these Hollywood shutterbugs made their living selling pictures of celebrities at various show-business parties and events. But they also maintained contacts with hospitals, police stations, and mortuaries, hoping to get a scoop on a tragedy involving a famous name.

This scene could have been a bonanza for the photographers. A bloody accident site involving Kevin McCarthy, a known actor, along with three of the world's biggest and most glamorous stars: Rock Hudson, Elizabeth Taylor, and Montgomery Clift. Monty torn up and bleeding, possibly dying—wrapped in Elizabeth's arms.

As the photographers descended on the scene with cameras raised, Elizabeth once again sprang ferociously into action. When it came to Monty, she felt tender and protective, but she could be a tigress. "You son of a bitch," Elizabeth screamed. "I'll kick you in the nuts! If any of you dare take a picture of him like this, I'll never let you near me again! Get out of here, you fucking bastards!" Rock Hudson recalled, "She prevented the photographers from taking Monty's picture by using the foulest language I ever heard. She shocked them out of taking it."

Everyone was too stunned to act quickly or decisively. "Miss Taylor, you shouldn't be talking like that," one of the photographers meekly ventured. She stared him down with a furious look. The photographers stood around gawking, but they lowered their cameras. These photographers knew that in the long run, photos of Elizabeth Taylor taken along the path of her career would be priceless. They couldn't gamble on the possibility of her shutting them out.

Wilding, Rock, Kevin, and Dr. Kennamer formed a human wall—standing side by side, arms folded—to block Monty and Elizabeth and further ensure no photographs would be taken.

"Take a picture of us," Rock chided. "We'll smile for you." He grinned for the photographers.

After an awkward pause, the road grew silent and ghostly, the only light coming from the parked cars' headlights. The photographers stood around with their cameras lowered. No one said a word, except to occasionally mutter, "Where the hell is the ambulance?" They didn't yet know that the ambulance had thus far been unable to locate the unfamiliar road.

After forty-five minutes the ambulance arrived, the attendants full of apologies. They had gotten lost. They darted into action and efficiency and placed Monty onto a stretcher, then lifted him into the ambulance. "Oh God, it was horrible," Elizabeth recalled. "He was squirting blood all over his face. He never once complained." She rode with him in the ambulance, afraid that he might die on the way to the hospital. "By the time we reached the hospital, his head was so swollen that it was almost as wide as his shoulders," she later noted.

Reporters rushed to the hospital, where a hysterical Elizabeth was being sedated. She had been stoic throughout the ordeal, but when Monty was wheeled into the emergency room, suppressed emotions rushed over her like a tidal wave. She looked down and saw her white silk cocktail dress dyed crimson with Monty's blood. "The sick, sweet smell of it made me want to vomit," Elizabeth said. She collapsed in a sobbing heap into the arms of Phyllis Gates. From then on, dreams of Monty's bloody, ruined face would haunt Elizabeth. "It would come up in front of me like a balloon in the night," she said.

In the emergency room the doctors were getting a sense of the damage to Monty—now a grotesquely swollen head on a slender body. "I don't think anybody knows how brutal the accident was," Jack Larson later observed. His face had been completely smashed in. His nose was broken in two places. His right cheekbone was shattered. His upper gum was crushed, four of his teeth had been knocked out, and his nasal cavity had been squashed. His upper lip was torn in half. His jaw was broken in four places and snapped off at both joints. A nerve had been severed on the left side of his face, which would render that side nearly immobile. Writer Robert LaGuardia described the damage this way: "a face had been painted on a hard-boiled egg, and then the egg dropped [and] cracks rippled through his facial skeleton."

The doctors would perform no plastic surgery; the lacerations on his face would heal on their own. But there was a lot of reconstruction work to be done on the bones, under the skin, to the structure of his face. Monty's jaw had to be wired shut so the broken bones could mend correctly. His broken nose was snapped back into place. And a bridge had to be created for his knocked-out teeth.

News of the accident was soon reported on the radio. Any of his friends giving a statement was out of the question—the only news the media could report was that Monty Clift had been in an accident and had been taken to the hospital.

As Monty lay in sedated slumber with a severe concussion, Libby Holman arrived from New York. Libby—coarsened by tragedy and booze—stormed around the hospital room, barking orders disguised as advice with the authority of someone who has been through enough in life to not give a damn anymore. She realized the doctors were under tremendous pressure from the MGM execs to get the famous movie star healed and functioning so he could finish the picture he was starring in. They injected him with cortisone and other "stuff" to quicken the healing process. As a result, he would develop scar tissue that otherwise wouldn't have formed.

Usually, Libby's abrupt tone stopped doctors and nurses dead in their tracks. But one person who didn't cower before Libby was Elizabeth. Libby was still jealous of Monty's special relationship with her, and when Elizabeth walked into Monty's hospital room while Libby was visiting with him, Libby immediately started to lay the blame for the accident on Elizabeth.

"It must have been obvious Monty was drunk when he left the party . . ."

"Screw off!" Elizabeth snarled in a tone that stunned even the brassy Broadway diva into silence.

But that was far from the end of it. Libby started in on Elizabeth whenever the two of them found themselves in Monty's room together, and a shouting match would ensue—much to the shock and delight of the hospital staff. Libby described Elizabeth as "sensuous and silly—like a heifer in heat. There's no telling where her lust will lead her next." She was seemingly unaware that she could have been describing herself.

To better keep an eye on Monty's recovery and assert her power, Libby moved into his hospital room, where she slept on a couch at the foot of the bed. In the coming days, Libby sneered at the parade of movie executives who filed into Monty's room. They appeared to be empathetic, but she knew their real goal was to assess the damage and try to convince Monty to return to the movie as soon as possible. They cared about their financial investment, not about Monty's well-being.

As far as Libby was concerned, nobody cared for Monty like she did.

The cast and crew of *Raintree County* took up a collection and sent a large floral arrangement to Monty's room. He was so moved that he told second assistant director Hank Moonjean through his wired, clenched teeth that he would keep the flowers in his sight "until they rot." Meanwhile, Monty's problems continued. His broken jaw had been set wrong, and it had to be broken again and reset. His mouth was wired shut, and he could take nourishment only through a straw.

Friends filed in and out of his room—like guests on a somber talk show—wanting desperately to give him comfort. But there was very little they could do in the face of things. What Monty needed was time to heal, and time was something he didn't have. Hanging over him was always a sense of urgency for his face to repair quickly. So his friends smuggled in liquor—the only comfort they could give him that was attainable. When Kevin came for a visit one afternoon, he found Monty sitting up in bed, sipping vodka through a straw.

"For nourishment," Monty said.

"Monty being Monty, within a few days, he was already straining to move his mouth, even though the wired teeth were there to preserve whatever healing might take place," Kevin recalled. "If he'd gone through with the treatment, he probably would have looked much better than he did when he finally got out of the hospital."

The reason for Monty's accident that was released to the press was that he simply fell asleep at the wheel. Or, as he quipped, "I had one blink too many." That seemed plausible to anyone who knew him. Jack Larson commented that "Monty would be so tired, he'd fall asleep talking to you."

In an attempt not to scar the reputation of the film, the studio continued to downplay Monty's injuries to the press, so that the public was led to believe that he had just been banged up a little. And Monty, without being sure of anything, would echo their assertions that he was fine. "I'm exactly the same as I was before," he would repeat over and over. "They didn't have to do plastic surgery—which I was very lucky for." But saying it didn't make it so. It was immediately apparent to almost everyone that his face was not exactly as it was—and probably never would be.

While he was recovering in his hospital room, he was not given a mirror, and he did not ask for one. He was, however, shown newspapers with photos of his wrecked car that had appeared the following day. He was shocked that he had survived such an accident.

When friends like Jack Larson came by, they were not ready for the sight of their beautiful friend's swollen-looking and distorted face. "When I saw him for the first time after the accident, I was in shock," Larson stated. Monty tried to gloss over his friend's reaction.

"I don't look too different, do I, *mon vieux*?" he implored.

"No, no!" Larson assured him. He realized Monty wanted honesty, but he was afraid the truth would shatter him. "Of course, he looked completely different," Larson later admitted.

Because Monty was in so many scenes in *Raintree*, there really was very little the studio could shoot without him. They had no choice but to close down production until, they hoped, he was ready to return. Of course, there was some talk about replacing him. But half of the movie had already been shot, at a cost of well over two million dollars. It would be a tremendous loss to the studio if the footage was scrapped and the production started all over again with a different leading man.

Nevertheless, there were some meetings held to discuss whether it would be financially feasible to wait for Monty to be well. Some executives absolutely wanted to replace him, feeling that his altered appearance would never match the existing footage. Once again, Elizabeth was called in to confer about the dilemma. She pleaded with Schary to wait for Monty to heal. She said she feared he would kill himself if he was fired.

After two weeks in the hospital, Monty was sent home to rest at his rented house. His father flew in from New York to spend some time with him. As did Marge Stengel. Monty, however, forbade his mother to visit. He was convinced Sunny would find the exact right moment to say the exact wrong thing—somehow blaming him for the accident and making him feel even more horrible. As cantankerous as their meetings were, Monty really didn't want to fight with his mother. She simply had a way of egging him on as no one else could.

During the period of his recuperation, the rented house overflowed with anxiety. Monty's pain was excruciating, but on top of that, he spent every moment worrying if he'd heal enough, and in time, to return to finish *Raintree*. Friends visited him daily, Elizabeth Taylor, Kevin McCarthy, Jack Larson. But no one ever mentioned his face, and Monty couldn't bring himself to look at it closely. Studio executives continued to visit Monty at the house to check on his progress.

Although Monty did his best to hide his agony, at times he was overcome. One evening, when having dinner with Libby and Larson (for Monty, "dinner" meant pureed food through a straw), Monty excused himself from the table. After a while they went to see what was wrong, and they found Monty shaking in pain from head to toe.

Libby once again attempted to convince Monty to leave the "meaningless" movie. "Let the insurance cover it," she implored.

"That's what it's for." She reasoned that pushing himself would do only more damage, that he needed many months—if not years—to heal both physically and emotionally. He should have plastic surgery slowly, carefully, bit by bit, to restore his face. She implored him to return East with her, to be in the care of New York specialists, not Hollywood doctors.

Monty made it seem as if he were on the fence about returning, that it was possible he might just walk away from the movie for good. In reality, he had always planned on finishing it, if they would have him back. When Monty finally vocalized his decision to return to the studio to complete *Raintree County*, Libby was beside herself with rage. She threw up her hands and resigned to return to New York. Jack Larson pleaded with her to stay, to help usher Monty through the completion of the movie. But Libby was having none of it. Her compassion for Monty had reached the limit. "As long as I could help him, I'll do it," she stated. "But he is acting foolishly." She said it as vehemently as she could to make it clear how frustrated she was. Monty couldn't see what was best for him—while she could see it so clearly.

16

MIKE TODD

Every woman should have a Mike Todd in her life. God, I loved him.
—**Elizabeth Taylor**

*E*LIZABETH WAS FOREVER CHANGED BY MONTY'S ACCIDENT. IMAGES of blood haunted her in her dreams. Now she was terrified to drive down the winding road from her home. She said she couldn't pass by the spot where the accident happened without seeing Monty's battered face. The ordeal had left her completely shattered emotionally and had added strain to her already very troubled marriage.

While the movie was on hold, there was little for Elizabeth to do but visit Monty when he was feeling up to it. In truth, Elizabeth did feel responsible for his accident. Clearly, he hadn't wanted to come out that dreadful night, and he wouldn't have if she hadn't pressed him.

On May 22, Elizabeth was at the hospital when Monty was released, and she accompanied him back to his rented house to settle him in. Elizabeth wrote to a friend, *We brought Monty home from the hospital today, and he is remarkably improved. Because of a fracture just above his upper teeth, it will be at least two and a half weeks before he'll be completely well.* Like the studio, Elizabeth seemed to be overly optimistic. In reality it would be two and a half months before Monty could return to the set, and even then he had a lot of healing to do.

In her boredom and unsettledness, she intensified the affair she had started with Kevin McClory, and there was even talk that they would marry once she was divorced. Michael Wilding tried to give her some freedom, thinking that maybe if she played the field awhile, she would get the excitement of new romances out of her system and ease back into a settled married life with him. But as far as Elizabeth was concerned, their marriage was over. She was simply waiting for the right moment—or the right man— to make the announcement. That month she was certain Mc- Clory was the man for her. McClory's friends warned him that Elizabeth would expect him to provide her with a lifestyle, and gifts, he simply couldn't afford.

However, Elizabeth, still in the throes of girlish romanticism, said she didn't care if McClory didn't earn an enormous salary; she could live contentedly with him in a small beach house in Malibu. She was desperate for a new life—McClory was there. In strong contrast to Michael Wilding, he was dominant and as- sertive. When he informed her that he would expect his wife to be at home and to "iron his shirts," Elizabeth was able to rapidly brush that absurd notion aside, too.

McClory's boss, Mike Todd, was at the time producing the star- studded big-screen epic *Around the World in 80 Days*. The film was being shot on a four-million-dollar budget quite literally all over the world, from London to Spain, from Japan to China, from Paris to California. Its bigger-than-life producer, forty-eight-year- old Mike Todd, was short, compact, and muscular, not conven- tionally handsome, but with dark hair, piercing eyes, and a confident swagger that some women found dazzling—and that gained the admiration of many men. He was only five feet five, but he carried his solid body as if he were over six feet tall. Some people compared his looks to those of a middleweight prize- fighter; others said he had the dynamism of Napoleon.

Todd was intrigued that his assistant had so quickly become in- volved with a prize like Elizabeth Taylor. Todd was a man used to getting what he wanted. He was currently engaged to Evelyn

Keyes, an attractive, sophisticated actress best known for playing Scarlett O'Hara's younger sister in *Gone with the Wind*. At the time Evelyn wore a 29.4-carat diamond ring that Todd had presented to her. Todd didn't do anything small.

Todd's colorful personality was reflected in his colorful life. He was born Avrom Hirsch Goldbogen to Polish immigrants. Clawing his way out of the Chicago slums, he became an entrepreneur at an early age, at first selling kitchen appliances and gadgets on the street. While still in his twenties, he had made and lost over two million dollars. Eventually, he built his fortune again: he became a theatrical producer and got a number of hits under his belt. Throughout his life he would make and lose millions of dollars. A big gambler, Todd liked to say, "I've never been poor, only broke. Being poor is a frame of mind. Being broke is only a temporary situation."

Todd had been married twice before. His first wife, Bertha Freshman, died after she cut herself with a knife during an argument with Todd, though the actual cause of death was an allergic reaction to the anesthesia used while she was being treated. After that he was married to actress Joan Blondell, who divorced Todd after he had gone through her fortune. His other romances included one entered into with Marlene Dietrich and another with Gypsy Rose Lee.

Now he decided that the next big thing he wanted was to know Elizabeth Taylor, and his mind began spinning a plot to meet and seduce her. He slyly told McClory to invite Elizabeth to a weekend party he was giving on his yacht on June 29, 1956—the better to meet the star in a relaxed setting on his own lavish turf.

Elizabeth didn't exactly take the bait to be seduced: she showed up on the yacht with Michael Wilding in tow. But she found herself in the unique and flattering position of being at a party on a yacht with her husband, her lover, and a would-be suitor. Todd had thought that he might have to compete with McClory for Elizabeth's affections; the last thing he had expected was to have to contend with her husband.

In spite of that, Todd plunged ahead in his slow, calculated seduction of Elizabeth. His plan was to send her mixed signals, paying a lot of attention to her one moment and ignoring her the next. While Wilding and McClory did their best to avoid each other by staying clear of Elizabeth, she found herself transfixed by Todd's intense bright-eyed stare, which he would maintain for several seconds before he then would turn away and chat with another guest. She was intrigued as, sipping glass after glass of expensive champagne, she watched him pay an enormous amount of attention to Evelyn Keyes.

At one point, Elizabeth became seasick. Her remedy for that was to have another glass of champagne. Todd crossed over to her as she poured. "Go ahead," he told her merrily. "It's your stomach." And then he was off again.

McClory and Wilding evaporated in the background. Later Todd approached her again and commented, "You know, honey, I think you are a latent intellectual." Elizabeth froze for a moment. Did he mean it as an insult? That she had no intelligence that could be discerned? Or was he complimenting her? Concluding that underneath her image as a decorative beauty, she really seemed quite smart? She was confused but curious, and a little spark of attraction ignited in her.

When, a few days later, Todd invited the Wildings to a barbecue, Elizabeth showed up looking stylish and racy in skintight capri pants and a yellow-and-white checked blouse, unbuttoned halfway down. She openly flirted with Todd. Two people who observed the growing attraction between Elizabeth and Mike Todd were the popular crooner Eddie Fisher and his movie star wife Debbie Reynolds. Fisher was Todd's best friend, and he looked to him as a mentor/father figure.

A few days later Todd invited the Wildings to a dinner party he was having for Edward R. Murrow, who was making a special appearance in *Around the World in 80 Days*. There were over a hundred guests, including the French singer Édith Piaf. Someone who was expressly not invited was Kevin McClory.

Elizabeth's appearance was certainly calculated. Todd's fiancée, Evelyn Keyes, wearing a simple Spanish peasant blouse and skirt, paled in comparison to Elizabeth, who was dazzling in a formfitting white satin gown. She was an expert at stealing the show—and steal it she did. Every eye in the room was on her—with lust, admiration, or envy. At one point in the evening Todd and Elizabeth found themselves sitting on opposite ends of a divan, their shoulders touching, amid an atmosphere of music and party chatter. "It was as though my spine was tingling," she said. Although they were talking with other guests, Elizabeth felt a sexual current, like electric shockwaves, every time their shoulders or backs touched.

For a gambling man, Elizabeth Taylor was the biggest jackpot Mike Todd was ever going to get. And he knew it. By the end of the evening, he was absolutely sure. He wanted Elizabeth at any cost, and—as he would find out—Elizabeth could be very expensive.

Kevin McClory evaporated from her memory as fast as Evelyn Keyes faded from Todd's. To clear the way for his continuing seduction, Todd sent McClory to Mexico to oversee the shooting of a bullfighting scene for *Around the World in 80 Days*. At the same time he sent Evelyn Keyes to Caracas, Venezuela, ostensibly to scout for movie theaters that would be suitable for screening the film. Afterward, she was to go to Paris and London to meet with actors from the film. She was unaware that he was simply getting her out of the way.

Before Evelyn left, he asked her for the 29.4-carat diamond engagement ring he had given her. He convinced his soon-to-be ex-fiancée that the ring was too big for her finger and explained that he would have it resized while she was gone. That wasn't exactly his plan, but Evelyn had no way of knowing that. Now Todd's path to Elizabeth was clear.

To the relief of MGM executives, the doctors proclaimed Monty well enough to resume filming on Monday, July 23. That meant that he and Elizabeth would be leaving for location work in a few days. Monty wrote to his old friend William LeMessana, *You may be interested to know that after what seems like months in the dentist chair, I have dentures now, which, if you were to anger me, I would pop right into your face.**

With no time to lose, Todd made his move. He asked Elizabeth to meet him at the MGM commissary. When he found Elizabeth there, sipping a Coke as she waited for him, Todd took her by the arm and led her through a complex system of hallways and elevators to an empty office. He plunked Elizabeth down, and while pacing the room, he—in a ninety-minute monologue declared his love for her. He asserted that he knew her marriage to Wilding was over, and stated bluntly, "Now, understand one thing and hear me good, kid. Don't start looking around for someone to latch on to. You are going to marry only one guy, see, and his name is me."

When she tried to protest (albeit weakly) that she was in love with Kevin McClory, Todd would hear none of it. He looked directly into her eyes and barked, "Elizabeth, I love you, and I'm going to marry you, and from now on, you'll fuck nobody but me."†

Elizabeth sat there "like a rabbit hypnotized by a mongoose." Then she walked out of the office in a daze. They had known each other for less than a month.

*Monty would have to wear the dentures through shooting until permanent teeth could be put in.
†When gossip columnist Hedda Hopper wrote about this, she quoted him as saying, "You'll know nobody but me." And then she added coyly, "But he didn't say 'know.'"

17

NATCHEZ

Elizabeth helped to keep Monty on track. . . . Dore (Schary) realized Liz was the only member of the cast who could adequately control Monty, and he implored her to keep an eye on Clift.
—**Edward Dmytryk**

ON JULY 23, 1956, APPROXIMATELY NINE WEEKS AFTER THE CAR crash, Monty was deemed ready to return to *Raintree County*, although he was still in the early stages of healing from his substantial wounds. The swelling hadn't completely gone down, and his bones were still mending. But he had felt the pressure of being responsible for holding up filming.

The first of the location shooting was scheduled to take place in the small town of Natchez, Mississippi. On his flight there Monty became a source of tension when he discovered that assistant director Reggie Callow had been given the task of keeping an eye on him. Monty liked Callow, but he resented being assigned a babysitter. He proceeded to get completely bombed on the plane. The flight landed in New Orleans, where they were to switch planes. Unfortunately, there was a gaggle of reporters waiting for them when they disembarked. Monty reacted by bolting.

The gang of excitable reporters took off after him, and Callow joined the pursuit. It was an amusing sight for onlookers. Monty seemed to be playing a game of cat and mouse, weaving in and out through the crowd of travelers, closely followed by photographers and his "handler." Eventually, he evaded them when he ducked into a bar for a couple vodkas. The reporters later found him there—by then he was too oblivious to care. Photos of a drunk and disoriented Monty were splashed across newspapers the next day.

Even though the citizens of Natchez read about Montgomery Clift acting like a "lunatic" in the morning papers, the town was giddy with excitement at the thought of being involved with the production of a major movie and being amid important stars. Everyone was on high alert for an Elizabeth or Monty sighting.

Dmytryk liked filming outdoor scenes on an open set. This allowed inquisitive spectators to mull around the location and watch the filming, much to the annoyance of Monty and Elizabeth. Flocks of young girls, who remembered Monty from *A Place in the Sun* and *The Heiress*, descended on the location, hoping to get a glimpse of him. If they encountered him, they discovered he was a far cry from the handsome leading man they remembered. Always thin, he now seemed emaciated. As far as anyone could tell, he was existing on a liquid concoction of raw eggs and milk. Monty explained that it kept him "starved but focused." Fans particularly wanted to see Elizabeth Taylor, who was a constant on magazine covers and an ever-present name in the gossip columns.

To protect themselves from curious fans and the prying press, both Monty and Elizabeth—each going through personal dramas—stopped making themselves available to autograph seekers and ducked out of sight whenever they weren't filming. In the evenings they ate dinner together in one or the other's hotel room, and sometimes Monty slept in Elizabeth's bed. Neither wanted to be alone.

Studio executives, concerned only with getting their expensive picture completed, showed no empathy for Monty's condition, no consideration. In fact, he was infuriated when the producers allowed photographers and journalists to roam freely on the film's location to generate audience anticipation. There reporters witnessed behavior by a major Hollywood star that they had never quite seen before. "There was an enormous difference in his behavior after the accident," Millard Kaufman observed.

Monty was in a tremendous amount of pain—his back had been injured in the accident, and it would torment him for the rest of his life. In addition, he was under a great deal of pressure to look passable and to perform. His suffering was extreme, and he had to struggle simply to move around, let alone to give a performance. Before the crash, he had been considered a risk because of his drinking. Now he had added the dangerous habit of mixing potent painkillers with alcohol. He had also added liquid codeine and syringes to the already overstuffed gray leather pharmaceutical bag he carried around with him. The cast and crew were aware of this bag but didn't dare mention it. While he continued to drink from his thermos of vodka and grapefruit juice, Monty would also escape inside his trailer and inject himself with codeine before filming his scenes.

Monty's altered face and his substance abuse also caused a myriad of problems for director of photography Robert Surtees. "The question of what to do about Monty's face came up a lot when we saw the rushes," he said. "But Monty was never told we were worrying." Along with Monty's altered facial features, the cameraman was having a problem with "the dead quality" in Monty's eyes—caused by his alcohol and drug intake. "They were always slightly bloodshot and veiny. We had a hell of a time trying to compensate. All we could do was give him a little softness and photograph him so that the camera never saw two eyes at the same time." It was decided that Surtees should shoot Monty primarily from the right. That side of his face had been less damaged.

After makeup, Monty walked around the set in a daze—the excruciating pain not completely numbed by the massive doses of alcohol and painkillers he was taking in an attempt to squelch it. "Monty did not tell us that he was in constant pain," Dmytryk said. He'd mope around the set, forgetting the lit cigarette in his hand—a cigarette was such a constant with Monty, it was like an extra part of him by now. When he brushed by people, he'd unknowingly burn them on the hand or some part of their clothes.

Along with his hidden physical pain, no one could imagine the inner anguish he was feeling—the fear of a future without beauty and therefore without a movie career.

To add to his agony, they were working in difficult environmental conditions. It was an extremely hot and humid summer, and they were shooting outdoors. In heavy makeup and heavier period costumes, Elizabeth and Monty sweated and cursed in the blazing summer sunlight, waiting for the setup to be complete so they could get their scenes done. Often they sat with cool, wet towels on their heads as they waited. Worse than the onlooking fans were the insects that swarmed and swooped on the cast and crew.

Both Monty and Elizabeth were lost in private dramas. Elizabeth herself was unwell. The pressure of worrying about Monty and the queasy excitement of a new relationship with Mike Todd while her marriage was breaking up made her sensitive and edgy, and she was unable to sleep. Drugged, Monty was trying to focus his concentration enough to act coherently in front of the cameras when the time came.

"Another day of this hell," Elizabeth would murmur as they sat side by side. But she acted like a total professional. She would call the script supervisor over and ask, "What are we shooting today?" He'd hand her five or six pages. Elizabeth would look them over and be letter perfect by the time the cameras were rolling.

With Dmytryk leaving his actors to their own devices when it came to their performance, Elizabeth had been hoping for some of the student/teacher relationship she had shared with Monty on the set of *A Place in the Sun*. There she had observed his introspective style of acting and had absorbed it, resulting in the understated intensity of her finest performance up to that time. This time Monty was not well enough to coach her very often between scenes—and his own performance was lacking the intensity of their first film together.

With no one reining her in, Elizabeth had a tendency to overact. Since her character was mad, the extremity in her voice and the stuttering delivery of some lines pleased Dmytryk. As a result, sometimes she was quite good, but at other times she overacted her little heart out. Dmytryk liked her flamboyance. It was after shooting the scenes in Natchez that Dmytryk had an epiphany: "It was Elizabeth who was carrying the weight of the picture—she was the real star." This realization came as a relief to him. Up until the shooting in Natchez, the director had felt the movie was lagging. Although he would never say it at the time, he had put some of the blame on Monty's bland performance.

To compensate for Monty's lackluster portrayal, he let the supporting actors play their roles larger than life, actors like Nigel Patrick and Lee Marvin, who played the professor and "Flash," respectively. But he especially encouraged Elizabeth to let loose. As he watched the rushes, he decided that although Monty's character was in almost every scene, it was Elizabeth's character, Susanna, who put meat on the bones of the story. "She was the center of attention and dramatic movement," he observed. The shift of the director's focus to Elizabeth came at precisely the right moment, as the scenes of Susanna's descent into madness were forthcoming.

In contrast, Monty's character seemed lifeless. Under better circumstances, Monty could have brought more to his characterization of John Shawnessy. However, due to the degree of pain he was in and the amount of drugs he was taking, his performance comes across as colorless and unmemorable. To some degree, this was also due to the character as written. "John Shawnessy of the novel sees lots of life but in a strictly dramatic sense doesn't do much of anything," observed Larry Lockridge, the son of the author of *Raintree County*.

The main reason for shooting on location in Mississippi was the spectacular Windsor Ruins, which are located forty-three miles from Natchez. The ruins are all that remain of a Greek Revival mansion that stood on the site from 1861 to 1890, when it was destroyed by a fire. Twenty-three imposing columns that supported the roof of the mansion were left standing, each forty-four feet tall; five partial columns survived; and at the time of filming, a cast-iron stairway that led to a scorched veranda still remained.

In *Raintree* the site would double as Susanna's childhood home, which burned to the ground when she was a child, killing her parents and her beloved black governess. In the scene, Susanna brings John to look over what remains of the mansion as she talks about her childhood and the fire. In her monologue, which was several pages long, Elizabeth had to convey that behind Susanna's grace and charm lay an emotionally damaged young woman with deeply buried psychotic secrets.

As usual, Elizabeth was costumed in heavy period regalia, including a hat, a tight corset, slips, petticoats, and a hoopskirt gown with long frilly sleeves. It was a particularly scorching day. Despite the heat, Dmytryk felt Elizabeth gave a startling performance, incorporating all the psychological nuances the director had been hoping for. "She was forceful enough to make us believe her and to be deeply concerned for Susanna," he said. Even the crew was impressed—until Elizabeth uttered her last line. The stifling heat, the intensity of the monologue, and the constriction of her costume had overwhelmed her. Elizabeth collapsed.

Pandemonium broke out at first, and crew members scurried around, fetching water and cold compresses. But there was a doctor somewhere on location at all times. As someone ran off to find him, they gently lay Elizabeth down on a patch of grass. She was breathing spasmodically, and it was at first assumed she was suffering from hyperventilation. But the doctor arrived, and a quick examination revealed a more serious condition—tachycardia. For this condition, "strong medicine" is needed, but the company doctor didn't have a license to practice medicine in Mississippi and thus could not procure it. The nearest resident doctor was miles away in Natchez.

When Monty heard the word *tachycardia*, he knew at once what Elizabeth needed. Although Monty's gray pharmaceutical bag was an open secret on the set, he did his best to be discreet about the contents. "He was the most secretive of addicts," Dmytryk stated. "He never overtly sipped a drink or took a shot." Now Monty had to make a quick decision: keep his drug use merely speculation and gossip or bring it out into the open in order to help his stricken friend. He didn't think long—Elizabeth's welfare came first. Monty retreated to his trailer and quickly emerged with his leather case.

When the doctor opened it, he saw that it contained two vials of Demerol and several shiny syringes, everything neatly stored in the appropriate compartments. This was the medication that Elizabeth needed, and the doctor was able to administer it. "Monty had exposed himself courageously, and without a moment's hesitation, to help a friend in trouble," Dmytryk observed.

Elizabeth was put to bed, and the doctor arranged for an intravenous relaxant to be pumped into her arm. The doctor decided she couldn't film again until she was completely recovered. To make her feel less claustrophobic and to keep her spirits up, Monty, Dmytryk, and screenwriter Millard Kaufman agreed to have dinner in her room every evening.

Because rest was vital to Elizabeth's recovery, the doctor also prescribed the fast-acting sedative chloral hydrate so she could sleep soundly through the night. When Monty found out about the prescription, he, with his vast pharmaceutical knowledge, gave Elizabeth a lively lecture regarding the effects of the drug. "Basically, it's a fantastically strong Mickey Finn, Bessie," he explained. Then, when she wasn't looking, he proceeded to steal half of her twenty-four-pill supply to add to his already expansive pill collection.

Later that evening, Monty didn't show up on time for dinner, and when Monty was late, alarm bells went off. Dmytryk and Kaufman began to worry. They waited a little longer, then started calling his room. No answer. Elizabeth grew concerned, too—then she remembered the chloral hydrate and Monty's enthusiasm when talking about the drug. She checked the supply and noticed some half of the pills were missing.

Kaufman and Dmytryk ran to Monty's room. They found Monty fully clothed but passed out on the bed. It was obvious to them that he had fallen asleep while smoking. The cigarette in his hand had smoldered all the way down, badly burning the flesh of the two fingers holding it. Dmytryk found a pencil and pried the cigarette butt out of the actor's burned fingers. Monty continued to sleep soundly. They quietly slipped out of the room and rejoined Elizabeth to confer on what they should do. While they were talking, Monty strolled in, wide awake, smiling, his fingers freshly bandaged. If they hadn't just been in his room, they never would have guessed that he had been out cold minutes before.

When he sat down to join Elizabeth for dinner, Kaufman and Dmytryk excused themselves, explaining they needed to work on the script. In reality, they went back to Monty's room to see if they could locate what was left of Elizabeth's prescription. They found the door to his room unlocked and immediately began rummaging through drawers, checking suitcases, opening cabinets. As they searched meticulously, Dmytryk recalled later, they found "vials full of powders, liquids, small cases of syringes, and a couple of bottles of whiskey, but no chloral hydrate." They kept on. And in a drawer in the nightstand, they found a plastic pill bottle that contained a white powder. Dmytryk poured the contents into his hand and discovered football-shaped pills hidden amid the powder. When he brushed the pills off, he saw their colors were yellow and blue. He had discovered the chloral hydrate. There were ten pills. That meant Monty had taken two.

They realized they had to get the remaining sedatives away from him. The problem was how. They couldn't very well steal the pills back. That might infuriate Monty and cause a volatile situation. Then Millard had a brainstorm. Perhaps he could find a pharmacist who would be able to replace the chloral hydrate with a placebo of some kind. Dmytryk decided it was worth a try.

Millard set out on his mission, and he did indeed find a pharmacist who was able to closely match the chloral hydrate, and he returned to the room with ten almost identical-looking vitamin tablets. They put the duplicates in the plastic pill bottle and returned the bottle to the drawer. They doubted Monty would fail to notice the difference, but they gambled that he wouldn't confront them about the switch. They were correct—he never mentioned it.

* * *

Although Elizabeth was consumed with her affair with Michael Todd, many on the *Raintree County* production team were sure that she and Monty were in love. Crew members would gossip about the fact that hotel maids found their towels all over each other's hotel rooms. The truth was that they were so close, they often exhibited the behavior of two people engaged in a heated affair. They spent hours in each other's hotel rooms, sometimes sleeping in the same bed. On some nights, Monty showed up at Elizabeth's door, drunk and naked. She would let him in, shower him, towel him dry, and tuck him into bed.

Sometimes the intensity of Monty's emotional suffering was just too much for Elizabeth to take, and she wanted to be by herself. She would gently ask him to leave her hotel room, but he would not go quietly into that good night. If he wasn't in the mood to be alone, he'd put up a fight until Elizabeth insisted he leave. After one such scene, Elizabeth went to check on Monty a few hours after throwing him out of her room. Checking the bathroom, she found the glass shower door shattered and the tiled floor covered with shards of glass and what looked like blood.

Elizabeth ran from the room screaming. She found Dymytrk and hysterically told him that Monty had somehow been horribly hurt. They returned to his room together, only to find Monty giggling. He had intentionally broken the glass shower door and sprinkled the scene with orange-red Mercurochrome. It was his idea of a joke to get back at Elizabeth for banishing him. Understandably, she was not amused after having gone through Monty's tragic car accident just a few months before.

Initially, Monty didn't exactly approve of Michael Todd—he considered him vulgar and boorish, especially when compared to the gentlemanly Michael Wilding. But he loved Elizabeth and understood her need for passion. In addition, he welcomed any distraction from his suffering. The two friends conspired together and giggled over the harebrained schemes they concocted to get Elizabeth and Todd time alone together.

In fact, Monty spent so much time in Elizabeth's hotel room, the local gossip columns began reporting that they were not only having an affair but were also flaunting it. When Elizabeth was well enough to resume filming, teenagers gathered in front of their hotel, hoping to catch a glimpse of the couple interacting in person. But when the stars emerged, they rushed past the crowds into their waiting cars.

The fans were disgruntled. They felt as if they were being snubbed by their heroes. After filming was completed in Natchez, the press reported the two actors were "booed out of town." It was reported that they breezed past a crowd of townspeople who had come to see them off at the airport. The fans, fenced off from the runway, booed as Monty and Elizabeth rushed by, with their heads down, and went up the ramp to the private jet. The crowd grew impatient and then angry, and their anger emboldened them. "Liz! Liz!" they shouted. "Come out so we can get a look at you!"

Fans didn't like it when their icons turned out to be snobs. And this wouldn't be good publicity. It wouldn't be good for the actors' images, and it could hurt the reception of the film. After talking it over in the plane, Elizabeth and Monty sauntered back down the ramp to take pictures with fans and sign autographs— which they did in a perfunctory manner before hurrying back to the plane. The media was not appeased and dubbed them the "deep freeze stars." They blamed Monty for this aloof behavior. "Elizabeth seems to have caught some of Clift's aloofness," the media groused.

18

DANVILLE

Stretch pants had just been invented, and we'd never seen them before. They looked like you'd just melt and pour yourself into them. Elizabeth Taylor was wearing them, and I thought my husband would fall off the back porch when he saw her. Oh, she was pretty.
—**Eleanor McDonald (Danville resident)**

To put it on the line, he looks like hell and feels like hell. He's been through hell and still stares it in the face. He does not look like himself, because he is not himself.
—*Motion Picture Magazine,* **June 1958**

AS IT HAD IN NATCHEZ, THE FILM GENERATED INTENSE EXCITEMENT throughout the community of Danville, Kentucky. The town was "electric" with excitement, and for years to come, people would recall the "mythic" summer that the production of *Raintree County* came to town. Meanwhile, Mike Todd was determined to remain relevant to Elizabeth.

Elizabeth and Monty stayed in rented houses in Danville that were almost directly across from one another. Upon her arrival, Elizabeth's house, from the foyer to the sitting room to the old-fashioned bedroom, was already filled with bouquets of flowers—all from Mike Todd. He would not allow her to forget him. Todd was on the phone with her from almost the moment she arrived at the house, and he proceeded to entrance her on the phone for two hours, until he looked at the clock. "Hey, it's time for you to eat. Don't eat alone. Go with Clift or Dmytryk. Eating alone is torture. Go right now. I'll call you back at your bedtime."

He would continue with the long phone conversations almost every minute she wasn't on the set. He had befriended a production assistant, and he would call ahead to get Elizabeth's schedule. Thus, Todd knew exactly the right time to call her. He even had a shooting script sent to him, and the assistant kept him informed of what scenes would be shot on what day, and Todd would call Elizabeth to discuss the scenes with her. Elizabeth was captivated by his strong, take-charge attitude.

Across the street, Monty had a rack built in his rented house specifically to hold his liquor bottles. That started the town buzzing. Outside the privacy of their rented houses, Monty and Elizabeth remained tense, as the buzzing didn't stop. *Life* magazine was there, always snapping pictures, documenting every move. At the Danville gala parade the town threw for the production, Charlotte Henson noted that Elizabeth looked like a caged animal in her limousine as townspeople surrounded it and banged on the glass. "She looked frightened, confused, and angry all at the same time," Henson recalled. Meanwhile, the press reported that Monty "stumbled and mumbled through a ceremony wherein the governor's wife made him an honorary colonel."

Eben Henson and his wife, Charlotte, owned and operated the Pioneer Playhouse in Danville. Eben loved show business, and it was he who had convinced MGM to come to Danville and scout locations for *Raintree*.

Ron Chilton, a young local actor, was first selected to be an extra for the film, but then he was upgraded to being Monty's stand-in for the duration of the location work. "I was introduced to him as his stand-in, and he nodded and said, 'Hello,' but that was about the extent of his conversation with me or with any other crew member," Chilton recalled. The young actor couldn't help but notice Monty's physique. "Physically . . . Monty was extremely thin," Ron Chilton noted. "He walked with an unsteady gait and even seemed to be unbalanced at times."

The first time Chilton stood in for Monty, he faced Elizabeth's stand-in, another young local actor, named Liz Kernen. Suddenly Liz Kernen backed away, and Chilton found himself "toes to toes and almost nose to nose with the most beautiful queen in Hollywood. I felt as if I were going to faint; my knees buckled, but then Monty tapped me on the shoulder, and the spell was broken." Chilton stepped away, and Monty stepped in.

On the set, Chilton found Elizabeth to be courteous, kind, cooperative, and pleasant. When he asked her to pose for a picture, she readily agreed. Monty, on the other hand, wanted as little association with his coworkers as possible. In the mornings Chilton would witness Monty drinking from his container. Later, he "would see him sitting with Liz, quietly chatting or perhaps rehearsing lines, but he had very little contact with other cast members."

Sixteen-year-old Liz Kernen, who doubled for Elizabeth during the Kentucky shoot, also got a chance to observe Monty up close. In one scene, Monty had his head in her lap while they were shooting his close-up. Even at her young age, she could sense there was something special about him. But she sensed his pain, his aloneness. "He had a lot of things working against him," she observed. The crew attempted to cheer him up by feeding him the wrong lines. Liz also noted that they were very careful to film him from his good side.

Most of the gossip around town about Monty concerned his getting drunk every night—alone. After filming hours, townspeople spotted Monty drinking whiskey out of a teacup in local restaurants like Anna & Pierre's on Herrington Lake or the Townhouse on Main Street. The crew came up with code words to signal to each other the level of Monty's inebriation. *Bad* was "Georgia," *very bad* was "Florida," and *worst of all* was "Zanzibar."

One day, when the crew was filming an outdoor scene in which Monty was supposed to jump into a horse-drawn open buggy, followed by Elizabeth hopping in through the opposite door, and then drive away, a group of local townspeople gathered to watch. "Action," called Dmytryk. Monty, obviously in "Zanzibar" that day, jumped into one side of the buggy and toppled out the other. Dmytryk called for another take, and once again Monty lunged into one side of the buggy and fell straight out on the opposite side. This time the spectators broke out laughing. Monty was embarrassed and feeling dopey, so he grinned and bowed. Elizabeth suggested she get in the buggy first, to block Monty from falling off on that side of the buggy.

That worked. Monty hopped in, and blocked by Elizabeth, he didn't topple out. But when the buggy moved forward, Monty was thrust back, and he tumbled out again. The crowd was now delirious with laughter. Monty was coming across like a rodeo clown. Ultimately, Dmytryk broke the scene down to two shots so they could shoot Monty getting into the buggy, cut, tie him to the seat of the buggy, and then film the buggy driving away. By this time, Monty seemed oblivious.

Even though she had not yet announced plans for a divorce from Michael Wilding, the infatuation between Elizabeth and Mike Todd was already being written about in Hollywood gossip columns, and a few of Danville's telephone operators confirmed to a hungry press that there had been many calls from Todd to Elizabeth.

Monty still enjoyed the distraction of being a participant in Elizabeth's fairy tale. He often acted as a cover, or a conspirator, in her covert shenanigans with Todd. Elizabeth would fly off on weekends to be with her lover, and upon her return, Monty would pick her up at the airport in a battered car—an old blue sedan—so that they wouldn't be spotted. After one such trip, in the car, Monty presented Elizabeth with a fancily wrapped gift from Todd. She tore into the package to find a thirty-thousand-dollar black pearl ring. Todd had entrusted the jewelry to Monty, instructing him to give it to Elizabeth, along with a card that read: *This is for weekdays. Can't get your engagement ring to you until Sunday.*

Even Monty was impressed with the size of the ring. "Take the month off," he joked. "That ring is equal to a month's pay."

"More," Elizabeth sighed.

Soon enough, Todd made good on his promise and presented Elizabeth with the engagement ring he had originally bought for Evelyn Keyes. He never had it resized for Evelyn's finger, as he had promised. He had never intended to. Instead, he had it sized for Elizabeth's finger. The 29.4-carat diamond was, indeed, spectacular. Evelyn never saw the ring again. It now belonged to Elizabeth—and so did Todd.

Later, when Elizabeth and Todd needed a place to rendezvous on the East Coast, Monty convinced Libby Holman to let them meet at her estate in Connecticut. As a favor to Monty, Libby put her hostility toward Elizabeth aside and allowed the couple to meet there—and they arrived with Monty in tow. Libby watched Elizabeth with amusement as she showed off her gigantic diamond engagement ring. Even the jaded Libby was impressed. As they were leaving, Elizabeth was unable to fit her dainty white kid glove over the huge rock. In annoyance, Elizabeth tossed the gloves on the floor and headed out with Todd and Monty. For a moment, Libby turned into another starstruck fan, scooping up Elizabeth's gloves and placing them in an envelope, which she labeled ELIZABETH TAYLOR GLOVES—1956.

In her excitement, Elizabeth started to overeat again—causing her weight to yo-yo. Elizabeth would call the production chef in charge of meals at all hours of the night and order rich desserts. The film's producers started worrying about her fitting into her costumes. Mindful of the tiny waistlines on her costumes, Dmytryk instructed the chef not to make the desserts for her.

Elizabeth's dialogue coach, Marguerite Littman, recalled that when she was having lunch on the set, an assistant director would "wander over to look at Elizabeth's plate to see what she was eating." But Littman noted that crash dieting allowed Elizabeth to keep her svelte figure. "She could lose more weight between a Friday and a Tuesday than anyone I ever met," Littman said.

Late at night, from a mixture of alcohol, nightmares, and medication, Monty would dash out naked into the darkness and go down Main Street. His nude nocturnal escapades were quite something to the little town. As stories about this started to circulate, some elaborated that one evening Lee Marvin and Rod Taylor disrobed and joined Monty in the bare carousing.

One night, at a late hour, while wandering around the town's relatively empty streets in the nude, Monty was spotted by a shocked night-duty policeman. Upon recognizing him, the cop escorted Monty—naked and disoriented—back to his house. After that, the production hired a bodyguard—an off-duty policeman—to stand watch in front of Monty's house in case he wandered out again. Eventually, Dmytryk asked the cop if he enjoyed his late-night duty.

"Oh," the officer replied, "it was quite interesting. I had to stop Mr. Clift a number of times, but he didn't seem to mind. We would sit down and talk until he was ready to go back to bed. A wonderful talker! Although it wasn't clear what he was talking about. But he was always friendly and seemed to enjoy our chats."

"By the way," he added, "Your drunks are a lot less belligerent than ours."

Although the gossip mags hinted at something perverse, Monty tried to explain away these episodes in a straightforward manner, injecting the story with some of his trademark honesty. "I slept so fitfully because of worry of the next day's scenes that I'd leave the lights on all night. If I didn't and then woke up in the middle of the night, I'd think I was in my New York apartment and get up and crash into a wall."

As the painful production inched its way toward its conclusion, Monty's drinking continued on and off the set. Dmytryk liked Monty and never disparaged him during his lifetime. But after the actor's death, he would admit that he did everything in his power to try to get Monty back on the wagon, but that all his efforts failed. After attempting to shoot a scene when Monty could scarcely talk, the director had had enough. Not wanting to face the star alone, Dmytryk asked his production assistant to accompany him to Monty's trailer. He wanted a witness.

When the two entered the trailer, Monty smiled warmly—as

was his custom when greeting people. But Dmytryk was determined not to be charmed. He was angry, but he kept his voice polite yet firm, ready for an argument. "You are incapable of giving a good performance for the rest of the day," he admonished. "I suggest you go back into town." Monty's face froze. Even after displaying his medical stash in order to help Elizabeth, he had been under the impression that he had been deceiving his director. He was so stunned, he didn't attempt to disprove Dmytryk's claim— or even to defend himself. Several minutes later Monty called for his car and left the location.

Within an hour Monty called the set and asked for the doctor. Monty was so upset, he spent the rest of the afternoon punishing himself. He kicked a tree and broke a toe. Then he "banged the injured foot into the floor until the broken toe was a mass of shredded flesh," Dmytryk recalled. "According to the doctor, he was even contemplating suicide. But a strong sedative put him to sleep for the rest of the day and night."

After sending Monty home, Dmytryk worried about when, if ever, Monty would return to the set, but "the next morning Monty was on the set, on time and apparently in fine fettle," Dmytryk said. "He showed no signs of a limp, and there was not mention of physical or mental discomfort."

All the behind-the-scenes drama was making it into the press, which didn't bode well for Monty's leading-man status for future motion pictures, the reason he had decided to finish the film in the first place. The once gorgeous prince of the movie industry was now described as a mysterious mess.

Visiting the *Raintree County* set, gossip columnist Hedda Hopper walked into Monty's trailer unannounced and discovered the star injecting himself. "Just some vitamins," a startled Monty told the reporter. He explained that the long period of having his mouth wired shut had left him malnourished. Still unable to chew solid food, he was living on the same concoction of two raw eggs mixed into skim milk. Always slender, Monty was now emaciated from his liquid diet. Hopper wasn't swayed.

Of course, the actor was well aware of how he was perceived. "I particularly liked Hedda Hopper telling the world I'm a drug addict," Monty fumed when a studio executive asked him how he was doing. At other times he was downright furious about the studio allowing the press to roam freely on the set in the first place. "Jesus Christ," he called out in frustration. "I'm at my absolute worst! Everyone thinks I've gone round the bend!"

And indeed they did. In future movie magazines, journalists would inform readers of his decline. One stated, "Monty Clift is out to destroy himself—deliberately—if not consciously."

And *Motion Picture Magazine* asked, "What's the matter?" An extra on the set revealed, "We all thought he should be at home in bed. Women usually feel motherly toward him . . . I felt that, and pity, too." A sardonic anonymous friend described Monty in this way: "[I]n some ways he's infantile. He's a poor little self-destructive stray who makes two hundred thousand dollars a picture [. . .] an undernourished St. Bernard, full of friendliness. If he likes you, he leans on you, steps on your feet, and gives you not-so-playful punches."

After the location work was finished, *Raintree* still had two weeks of filming, to be completed in Los Angeles, on MGM's back lot, where swampy terrain had been re-created. Monty had to film a scene where he gets trapped in quicksand after a treacherous run through the swamp.

The deterioration Monty had suffered since the accident was apparent to everyone he encountered. He joined novelist Christopher Isherwood for dinner, along with voice coach Marguerite Lamkin. Isherwood wrote in his diary: "He arrived drunk, crumpled somewhat during supper, but didn't spill anything and left soon after. I was really shocked by the change in his appearance since I last saw him. Nearly all of his looks have gone. He has a ghostly, shattered expression. Monty is touching, and very anxious to be friendly, but, oh dear, how sorry he is for himself."

Filming ended on October 17, which also happened to be Monty's thirty-sixth birthday. Unable to face going back to New York, Monty rented a new house in LA, on Kenter Avenue. It was closer to Jack Larson. He spent most days with the shades pulled down and the curtains drawn. He wandered around in the gloom, drink in hand, blasting Sinatra and Ella Fitzgerald records while ignoring the constantly ringing phone.

Occasionally, to change up the scenery and get some sun, he'd sit out in the back, by the pool. Jack Larson would sometimes join him there to keep him company. There wasn't much Larson could do; Monty never felt like talking much. They'd sit quietly, Monty taking long pulls on his cigarette and staring out over the pool.

One day, Marlon Brando, still in his costume and makeup for his role as a Japanese interpreter in Okinawa in 1946 in the film *The Teahouse of the August Moon,* showed up at the door. He had come directly from the studio. In spite of his appearance, Marlon's talk was serious. He had been hearing all kinds of things about Monty's self-destructive behavior: his drinking, his drug taking, and now his shutting himself away.

Marlon said he was sympathetic. It was impossible to imagine having to deal suddenly with such severe damage to one's face, the most important thing an actor has. The thought of losing one's looks was unfathomable. Yes, said Marlon, the accident had been a horrible, tough break. The worst. But the world needed Montgomery Clift to be a working, functioning artist. And Marlon needed him, too. They needed each other. They fed off each other. They competed with each other, and that made them better.

Marlon admitted, "When we were both nominated for the Oscar in fifty-one, I went to see you in *A Place in the Sun.* I was hoping you wouldn't be as good as everyone was saying. And then I saw it, and you were even better. I was so jealous! I was sure you were gonna win it."

"I thought the same thing about you!" Monty replied, admitting he had been blown away by *A Streetcar Named Desire.*

Then Marlon brought up the main reason for the visit. He wanted Monty to go to AA. The path Monty was going down was clear to Marlon. Getting off the alcohol would be the most important step in recovering himself. "I'll go with you!" Marlon abruptly shouted. "I'll go to every single meeting with you! We'll sweat it out together . . . I'll hold your hand all the way through it!"

Monty, who had been silent, replied that he was really grateful, but, really, he was just fine. "Fantastic," Monty assured him. "Everything's going to be okay."

Later, Marlon would tell Maureen Stapleton that he had tried with Monty, but that he had insisted he didn't have a problem. "All the while we were talking, Monty was pouring vodka into a tumbler and downing it like water," Marlon told Maureen. He had left Monty's house feeling that he was "a lost cause."

A few days later, when he and Larson were sitting out by the pool again, Monty excused himself and went back into the house. A long time passed, and Monty still hadn't returned to the yard. After waiting a while longer, Larson went to check in the house to see if Monty was okay. A few steps in, he heard loud sobbing coming from the bathroom. Feeling that Monty might be embarrassed to be seen like that, but concerned for Monty's well-being, Larson gingerly approached. He stood by the bathroom doorway and saw Monty then, staring in the mirror, wailing. Everything Monty had been holding in came pouring out of him in a torrent of tears: fear, dread, anger, pain, and shame—shame because it was embarrassing to him to have lost his beauty.

"Monty, are you all right?" Larson asked softly.

Monty just continued crying.

Crushed to see him like that, Larson turned around and went back out to the yard. A while later Monty, composed now, joined him. After some time, he spoke.

"Jack, I know you saw me," he said. "I heard you call my name. I was crying because . . . for the first time since the accident, I got up the . . . guts to really . . . look . . . at myself. And I think . . . I still have a career. I still have a career!"

Until that moment, Monty had been too terrified to look closely at his face. He knew his looks were different, and he had come to accept that *Raintree County* would be his last movie. He had truly thought he'd never work again. Now, although it would almost be like starting over, he tentatively believed he could move on with his career and life.

Monty predicted that *Raintree County* would make money only because audiences wanted to see what his face looked like after the accident. About this, he was correct. When the film was released the following year, critics called *Raintree County* a monumental bore, but curious audiences flocked to see it.

Later Janet Maslin noted that the movie "alternates scenes of a young, vital Clift with a stiffly sad faced, deeper voiced man . . . [T]here are moments when the actor attempts his old coquettishness with his new face, with agonizing results." The *New York Times* mentioned "[t]he strange appearance and the aging, husky voice of Mr. Clift."

Another thing that attracted audiences to the film was Elizabeth's florid, over-the-top performance, which many critics admired. "Elizabeth Taylor as the frightened and pathetic wife is the best of the actors," the *New York Herald Tribune* declared. For her work in the film, she was nominated for an Academy Award, her first.

19

MARRIAGE NUMBER THREE

Mike Todd gave me the tools to understand love.
—**Elizabeth Taylor**

MIKE TODD WAS THE ANTIDOTE TO MICHAEL WILDING. WHILE Wilding was a sweet, sensitive gentleman, Todd was passionate and strong and domineering. But while the new couple was vacationing in the Bahamas in early December, the fast pace of the Todd-Taylor romance stopped abruptly when Elizabeth slipped and landed on her tailbone when the yacht they were cruising on suddenly lurched forward as she was going below deck. Or, as she later put it, "I fell six steps and landed on my fat ass."

Her earlier back injuries, starting with the one sustained during the making of *National Velvet*, were exacerbated by the fall. When she tried to get up, she found that she couldn't—the pain was excruciating. Todd had her rushed to Columbia-Presbyterian Hospital in New York. Upon examination, doctors discovered two things: Elizabeth had crushed three spinal disks and she was pregnant.

After further tests, orthopedic specialists determined that her spinal column would have to be partially reconstructed in a very delicate operation. During the four-hour surgery, doctors first had to cut away all the damaged bone right down to the spinal cord's nerve center. Then using bone from her hip, pelvis, and a bone bank, the surgeons constructed "little matchsticks" to take the place of the damaged disks. Eventually, the newly formed clusters would fuse together and calcify, becoming "one long column approximately six inches long."

When Elizabeth came out of the anesthesia after the operation, Todd was waiting for her. The first words she said to him were "Where's my diamond?" which he gleefully reported to journalists.

As she recuperated, Todd went one better than bestowing upon her another piece of jewelry. Deciding that her drab green hospital room needed cheering up, he went out and bought a series of paintings to enliven the room. The wall decorations included a Renoir, a Pissarro, a Van Gogh, and *Portrait of a Man*, by Frans Hals.

Monty was one of the few people allowed to visit her in the hospital during her recovery. She confided that after the fall, she was unable to take a single step, and now her biggest fear was that she would never be able to walk again. Monty did his best to reassure her. He reminded Elizabeth how strong she was. He admired her, he said, not only because she got everything she wanted, but because she actually *knew* what she wanted. Even if it was something very small in the moment, she was very clear on her desires. When she was ready to walk, she would walk, he promised. A few crushed disks in her back weren't going to stop her.

He commented on the paintings hanging on the walls, and Elizabeth's mood brightened. Giggling, she told Monty that Todd had damaged the Van Gogh. While talking excitedly with a pencil in his hand, he had punctured the canvas, leaving a tiny hole. Luckily, Elizabeth's family had experts in the art world, and they planned on having the tiny hole repaired.

While Monty appreciated that Todd was attentive to Elizabeth and spoiled her, he was put off by what he called Todd's "vulgarity." He resented the way Todd exploited his generosity toward Elizabeth by turning it into self-promotion—Todd always made sure his lifestyle and his gifts were well publicized.

* * *

In an era when an out-of-wedlock pregnancy could end a career, Mike Todd and Elizabeth had to do some fancy footwork involving the calendar. Shortly after her release from the hospital, they set their wedding date for February 3. They would marry in Acapulco. "That's Atlantic City with a Spanish accent," Todd quipped. Elizabeth's back had still not completely healed, and she was in a great deal of pain. She often wore a back brace under her designer clothes. But the wedding was on.

Singer Eddie Fisher would be the best man and his wife, Debbie Reynolds, would be matron of honor. Eddie looked at Todd as a mentor and considered him his best friend. Elizabeth and Debbie had known each other for years; they both had been child stars at MGM. Nearly the same age, the two stars had even gone to the famous Little Red Schoolhouse on the MGM lot together. Often the two of them had been the only pupils in the class.

For the third time in seven years, Helen Rose designed Elizabeth's wedding gown. The night before the wedding, Debbie Reynolds washed and set Elizabeth's hair. "And I helped her get dressed for the wedding," Debbie recalled.

Eddie Fisher would remember that the morning after the wedding, Todd escorted him into the bedroom he shared with Elizabeth "like a sultan bringing me into his tent." Elizabeth was still on the bed, barely covered by a flimsy nightgown. "Mike wanted me to see her," Eddie reported. "He was just showing his best friend his greatest treasure." Elizbeth, he said, didn't seem to mind.

A few weeks after the ceremony, Elizabeth and Todd attended the Academy Awards. *Around the World in 80 Days* beat her film *Giant* for best picture. Considering that she now owned a percentage of Todd's film, it's unlikely that she minded. With Elizabeth at his side, wearing the tiara he had given her, Todd said after the ceremony, "I won the two biggest prizes you can get. The Academy Award and Elizabeth Taylor. That's not bad for luck."

Elizabeth announced that the only thing that was more exciting than this was that she and Todd were expecting their first child. At the time, the couple seemed so lucky to onlookers, and

Hedda Hopper sent them a note that read, *You must know that most people in Hollywood are so jealous of you, they could cut your throat.*

Their daughter, Elizabeth Frances Todd—thereafter to be called Liza—was born in August 1957. Reporters and the public counted the months since their February honeymoon, and the proud parents made sure the public was aware that little Liza had been born premature at just slightly over five pounds. "The baby is so beautiful, she makes her mother look like Frankenstein," Todd crowed.

The arrival of Liza didn't slow them down. Determined to keep *Around the World in 80 Days* gushing money, Todd and Elizabeth traveled around the world, publicizing the movie as a phenomenon and themselves as a couple. They spent much of that year turning a publicity tour for the movie into an extended belated honeymoon. They travelled to Britain, Japan, Australia, and even the Soviet Union. Sometimes they were accompanied by Eddie Fisher and Debbie Reynolds. "We went to the racetrack, nightclubs, to shows, dinners," Fisher recalled.

Part of Todd and Elizabeth's bigger-than-life image as a couple was their over-the-top fighting. "This kid's been looking for trouble all her life. Now she's got it," Todd bragged. "When she flies into a rage, I fly into a bigger one. We also happen to love each other very much." A famous photo shows them together at a London airport. Todd's face has a snarl and a grimace, and he is making a gesture of frustration toward her; while her face is contorted with anger. It was published all over the world.

Mike Todd showed her that she didn't want just a protector—she wanted a combatant. It seemed everyone in Hollywood had a story about witnessing a brawl between Elizabeth and Todd. To them, open displays of arguing, screaming, fighting only underlined their passion for each other. "We have more fun scrapping than most people do making love," Elizabeth declared. And she meant that literally. Brawling opened an erotic door in Elizabeth that she had never experienced before. She came to view their noisy arguments as foreplay—a slap would usually end with a steamy session in the bedroom.

More than just liking it rough, there seems to be an exhibition-ist element in the couple's startling actions, since they did much of their fighting in front of people. Their brawls became as much a part of the public's image of them as their extravagances were. Eddie Fisher recalled that he and Debbie Reynolds once wit-nessed the couple arguing at a dinner at the Fisher home. "All of a sudden," Fisher recalled, "Mike leaned toward Elizabeth and whacked her, knocking her to the floor. He really belted her!"

Debbie also remembered the incident and recounted the shock of seeing Elizabeth knocked off the chair. "I almost fainted," she stated. "I had never seen anything like that! I mean, that [whack] hurt *me*!" Her knee-jerk response was to jump on Todd's back in an attempt to pull him off Elizabeth.

"Hey! Knock it off, will you?" Todd screamed.

Debbie demanded that he get out of her house. On hearing that, a rumpled, wild-haired Elizabeth stood up, smoothed out her dress, and sighed, "Oh, Debbie. We're just playing."

"I think you two need to go somewhere else and slug it out," Debbie replied.

"Don't be such a Girl Scout," Elizabeth retorted. "Really, Deb-bie, you're so square."

There does seem to be some correlation between Elizabeth's view on being manhandled and her notion of power. Aware that her husband could intimidate people, she viewed Todd as a wall of protection. Everyone always seemed to want something from her. Now, to get to Elizabeth, you had to go through her husband. Under his "loving care," her sense of self-worth soared. With her contract with MGM coming to an end after two more films for the studio, she would be free for the first time in her adult life. Todd convinced her she would do better as a freelance artist. He wanted to produce her next film, and he was planning on doing *Don Quixote* sometime in the near future. Of course he wanted Elizabeth Taylor to be the star.

20

A NEW FACE

I had to try to master myself, find the real me outside my looks,
which people were hung up on, and so was I.
—Montgomery Clift

ONCE HE WAS BACK IN NEW YORK, THE FIRST THING MONTY DID
was have all the mirrors removed from his apartment. One of the
deceptive charms in some extremely beautiful people is that it appears as if their physical appeal is unimportant to them. They ignore it completely and go about their business, letting their looks
do the talking for them. But once those looks start to fade—or
are taken away suddenly—they begin to feel how much a part of
them their beauty really was. To lose it can feel like the amputa-
tion of a vital limb.

It was that way with Monty. Before the accident he often shrugged
off his beauty, giving the impression that it was of no importance
to him. But those who knew him very well, like Bill Gunn, were
aware that he was quite vain. "I've never seen anyone who liked
being in front of a camera as much as Monty," Gunn recalled. "He
was the same way in front of a mirror—never ashamed. [H]e
enjoyed looking at his reflection. He was like a woman in this regard. He could stare for minutes on end at his image, unself-
conscious—totally relaxed."

When the swelling was gone and the bones in his face had

healed, it was apparent that Monty's face was not completely ruined. Yes, it was less dazzling, but it was still attractive. He looked like the older, less handsome brother of an extremely gorgeous man. It was a face he could not hide behind. With his new face, he had to show who he was, and in that regard, Monty seemed to want to confirm the worst.

In his first weeks back in the city, wearing a trench coat and a wide-brimmed hat pulled low to his eyes, he would show up on friends' doorsteps unannounced and wait for a response. Merv Griffin remembered swinging open his door to see a man whom he did not recognize standing wordlessly in the shadows. "You don't know me, do you?" Monty growled after a pause. And Merv suddenly knew who it was, but before there was an answer, Monty turned around and quickly walked away.

At the end of an expensive dinner with the writer Robert Thom at Trader Vic's, the tiki restaurant in the Savoy-Plaza, the waiter presented Monty with the bill. Monty had an expense account there and in his usual fashion, he scribbled his name, leaving an indecipherable scrawl. The waiter stared at it, bewildered. After a moment he took the bill to the back. Shortly, he returned to the table and asked Monty if he had any identification. Monty was obviously shaken. He whipped off the horn-rimmed glasses he was wearing and stared openly at the waiter. "Only my face," he announced grandly.

The waiter became more confused. He simply didn't know who Monty was. He brought the signed bill over to the manager, and they both conferred over it, looking over at Monty. The manager didn't know who it was, either. Monty refused to intervene. He could not, would not, accept the fact that he wasn't recognizable. At last, Thom leaned over to Monty and whispered, "You're a son of a bitch. Don't embarrass the poor bastard. Tell him who you are, or let *me* pay the check with cash." Before that could happen, someone from the restaurant recognized Monty. Apologies were made to the actor, and he and Thom finally left.

Monty complained bitterly to Kevin McCarthy that some people seemed to be pleased by the sudden diminishment of his looks. "People always thought I had everything," Monty said in his husky voice. "And they resented it. But I never felt like I had so much. Now the same people are so gratified when they see me. They have this little smile. 'He's not so pretty anymore.'"

One person who didn't bristle upon seeing him was his old costar Shelley Winters. "I saw Monty at the Actors Studio," Shelley remembered. "He had come to watch a friend who was performing in a scene. I recognized him right away—and from a distance. I spent so much time staring into his mesmerizing eyes when we were making *A Place in the Sun,* I would have recognized him with a ski mask. I gave him a hug, and he was so skinny, it was like hugging myself. I said, 'Monty, you need a good home-cooked meal.' He told me he was losing weight for a picture."

Monty had been hired to appear in *The Young Lions,* another film directed by Eddie Dmytryk. Monty would play Noah, an outcast Jewish soldier. The role was similar to that of Prewitt in *From Here to Eternity,* in that his character is an outsider who doesn't fit in with the other men in the platoon—this time because of anti-Semitism. The men steal his money and bully him. His only friend in the platoon is Mike Whiteacre, a drafted Broadway singer who would do anything not to have to fight in the war. Mike was to be played by Dean Martin. The private also has a love interest, but unlike in *From Here to Eternity,* where obsession is a "bad" girl, here the character falls for a "good" girl, played by Hope Lange.

Outcasts, drifters, loners, rebels, misfits—these were the kinds of characters Monty was always drawn to, but more so now than ever. There was something about himself in the part of Noah that he could latch on to and connect with. But he was fearful of facing the cameras again. For better or worse, his face had healed, and this was the way he looked now. There would be no special lighting, makeup, or camera angles to camouflage his appearance. In fact, Monty announced he was going to make Noah more unattractive than need be. He said he would use putty to change the shape of his nose and would also use it behind his ears to make them stick out. Perhaps this was a tactic to trick audiences into thinking that his altered face was intentional.

Monty was intrigued by the role, but what was even more interesting was the news that Marlon Brando had been cast as Christian Diestl, a German Nazi soldier. Marlon was also changing his appearance for the role—he would dye his hair blond.

Unfortunately, Monty and Marlon have no scenes together in the nearly three-hour film. *The Young Lions* tells the stories of three men, with Monty and Dean Martin's story line running parallel to that of Marlon, a German Nazi who is growing increasingly remorseful and confused. Monty would have more interaction with Dean Martin acting in the second story line. Only in the last scene would Monty and Marlon be on-screen together for one brief moment, when Christian dies. They have no lines with each other.

As with Sinatra, Monty connected in friendship with Dean Martin, and it shows on the screen. Part of the movie is the story of their friendship. They had a number of important scenes together, and Monty, as he had done with other actors, coached the suave Italian crooner in what was his first dramatic role.

Conversely, Monty didn't spend all that much time socializing with Marlon. One evening Dmytryk took his two stars to dinner. Having observed Monty barking at the waiters and eating food off everyone's plates, Marlon suggested that Monty should see a psychiatrist. Even though Monty already saw Dr. Silverberg regularly, Marlon's insinuation did not go over well.

Monty was more irritable than usual in those days. No one knew better than he did that his once expressive face was now limited. The left side was now paralyzed—he couldn't move it at all—and he didn't yet know how to work around that. So, he had to learn how to act in a different way. "One of Monty's greatest assets is his eyes," George Stevens had observed during the making of *A Place in the Sun*. "It is an intangible quality which brings an audience to him." Now Monty had to learn how to utilize his eyes to greater effect. He would also use his body more. All of this would be learned and put into practice during the making of *The Young Lions*.

21

RUNNING FROM A NIGHTMARE

They said the wreck happened about two in the morning. It was awful. I picked up a shoe from the ground, and there was part of a foot in it.
—Dave Candelaria

*T*ODD WAS NOW MAKING DECISIONS FOR ELIZABETH'S CAREER, AND A role he approved for Elizabeth was in the 1958 movie version of Tennessee Williams's smash Broadway play *Cat on a Hot Tin Roof*. She would play Maggie "the Cat," a Southern woman desperately trying to get her alcoholic, homosexual husband to sleep with her so she can produce an heir in the family and therefore get a bigger place in Big Daddy's will.

Cat on a Hot Tin Roof, starring Elizabeth opposite Paul Newman, began shooting on March 2, 1958. Todd often dropped by the set to watch her work. It turned him on to watch his wife slink around in a white slip and satin pumps, trying to seduce Paul Newman as her brooding, closeted husband.

The weekend of March 14, Todd started making arrangements to fly out to New York on the private jet he had named the *Lucky Liz* to receive an award at the Friars Club for showman of the year the following Sunday. Todd and Elizabeth were scheduled to be the guests of honor at the event.

On Wednesday Elizabeth started feeling sick. Her private doctor, Dr. Rex Kennamer—Monty's physician, whom she met on the night of his accident—found that she had bronchitis and was running a fever. She was sent to bed immediately and was also out sick on Thursday. By Friday it was clear that she was still too ill to fly to New York—her fever was 102 degrees. Although she begged Dr. Kennamar to let her go to New York, he ordered her to stay in bed, arguing that the trip would be too much for her. In those days Los Angeles to New York was a ten-hour flight.

Without his wife for company, Todd started calling friends to invite them along on the trip. He figured a long poker game would make the time on the flight go by faster, and he tried to put together a small party. The plane's interior was suitable for a party, decorated like a plush living room—there was thick carpeting, a deep foam-rubber couch, drapes, a buffet bar, an oak conference table, and bronze ashtrays. The toiletries were engraved LIZ and HIS.

He tried Kirk Douglas, the comedian Joe E. Brown, and film director Joseph Mankiewicz. All of them had other plans and couldn't make the trip. (In the case of Kirk Douglas, his wife, Anne, had a funny feeling about Kirk flying in that small plane.)

Finally, writer Art Cohn, who had just ghostwritten Todd's autobiography, jumped at the chance to accompany Todd to New York for the gala.

It was raining on Friday, March 21. Before leaving for the airport, Todd ran upstairs five times to hug and kiss his feverish wife, who was propped up in bed. This would be the first time they were separated during their marriage, and he dreaded it, and so did she.

Elizabeth begged him not to go. "Please, baby. Get someone to accept the award for you," she pleaded. Todd told her she was being silly. Everything would be fine. He regretted only that she wouldn't be with him. "Without you, honey," he said, with his last embrace, "I feel like half a pair of scissors." She recalled that when he descended the stairs for the final time, they were both weeping.

Todd called Elizabeth from the airport in Burbank and promised he would call again at about six in the morning, when the plane landed in Albuquerque to refuel. It was still pouring rain, and Elizabeth felt uneasy. Again, she tried to talk him out of taking off in that weather. "Don't worry, honey," he assured her. "I can fly above any storm."

Elizabeth tossed and turned while waiting for Todd to call. "When Mike left, I didn't sleep all night. Something was wrong, something I couldn't explain." Todd didn't call at six, as he had promised, and she began to tremble with fear. Like Anne Douglas, Elizabeth was having a weird premonition of disaster. During the early morning hours of March 22, 1958, her entire body was filled with the same foreboding, the same feeling of dread.

At approximately two o'clock in the morning, while cruising at eleven thousand feet over Zuni, New Mexico, Todd's pilot reported "moderate icing." The pilot was radioed back permission to climb thirteen thousand feet. At this dangerously high altitude, the right engine failed. The plane had already been overloaded, the icing increased the load, and the remaining engine couldn't handle it. The pilot lost control, and the plane crashed, killing everyone on board instantly.

Dick Hanley, Todd's personal secretary, who was now working for Elizabeth, as well, received the news before Elizabeth. He had already received a call from Elizabeth earlier that morning. She was worried that she hadn't yet heard from Todd. Now, knowing the terrible news of the fatal crash, Hanley was fearful of what might happen when Elizabeth heard that Todd was dead. He called her physician, Rex Kennamer, and he and Hanley went together to the house in Coldwater Canyon to break the news. They rushed to get there before she started receiving phone calls or heard the news on the radio.

As soon as she saw the two men entering her bedroom, Elizabeth screamed. She instinctively knew why they were there. "Nooo!" she howled. She put her hands over her ears. Before they could grab her, she bolted out of bed. "Her first instinct was not to listen," Hanley later said. "Like, if she didn't hear it, it didn't happen. Keeping reality at bay. Running from your own nightmare while you're still in it."

She ran down the stairs in her transparent nightgown. The two men ran after her as she ran down the staircase, screaming. She pulled open the front door and ran into the street and fell to her knees, still screaming. "No, not Mike! Not Mike! Dear God, please, not Mike!"

Her screams could be heard all over the neighborhood, and people began to gather in front of her house. The two men lifted her up and carried the screaming, struggling Elizabeth back into the house up the stairs, and to her bed. They had to say the words "The *Lucky Liz* has crashed. Everyone on board is dead. Mike is dead."

Debbie Reynolds, who had just heard the news, rushed to take Elizabeth's sons, Christopher and Michael Jr., and her daughter, Liza, not yet eight months old. As Debbie pulled up to the house, the only thing she could hear was Elizabeth still screaming. She took the children, along with their nurse, and brought them back to her house.

Hanley and Dr. Kennamer were terrified Elizabeth would do something crazy, like jump out a window. The doctor sedated her, but no amount of tranquilizers could totally knock her out. She lay in bed, in semiconscious confusion, her head turning from side to side as she muttered incoherently. By now a crowd of neighbors, the media, and curiosity seekers had gathered in front of the house, as the news of the plane crash was widely reported on the wire services. Police and police cars were called to guard the premises.

A few people who were very close to her were allowed to visit Elizabeth, and they attempted to comfort her, to reach her through the haze of tranquilizers she was taking. Early on it was decided she could not be left alone. Elizabeth always felt everything to the tenth power, so she probably did feel suicidal, and that was a real danger. Until the next big emotion took over to push the thought of suicide away.

Elizabeth at age two. In her face you can already see the otherworldly beauty of the woman she would become. *(Everett Collection)*

Long before he was a movie star, Monty's delicate good looks and sensitive, naturalistic acting style made him a popular actor on Broadway. Here he is at twenty in *There Shall Be No Night* with costar Elisabeth Fraser in 1940. *(Everett Collection)*

At first, studio executives thought eleven-year-old Elizabeth looked too young for the lead role in *National Velvet*. But over a period of three months—she would say— she willed herself to grow three inches in time to be cast. The part made her a star in 1944. *(Everett Collection)*

The making of *The Heiress* (1949) was not a pleasant experience for Monty. He felt that director William Wyler favored Olivia De Havilland *(Everett Collection)*

In the late 1940s, audiences discovered a new kind of leading man in Montgomery Clift. His combination of beauty, vulnerability, and sensitivity excited a generation of moviegoers. *(Everett Collection)*

Elizabeth, Monty, and Shelley Winters in a publicity photo for *A Place in the Sun*. The movie was filmed in 1949 but wasn't released until 1951. *(Everett Collection)*

During the filming of *A Place in the Sun*, the electric chemistry between Monty and Elizabeth inspired director George Stevens to write new scenes that incorporated the mood of their unfolding, real-life relationship. *(Everett Collection)*

Elizabeth was Monty's "date" for the premiere of his film *The Heiress* in 1949. It was set up for publicity, but a genuine love and affection had started between them. *(Everett Collection)*

Monty and Elizabeth in one of the most famous love scenes in film history. Critic Peter Bradshaw wrote, "They are almost like reflections of each other; when they kiss, something incestuous and thrillingly forbidden throbs out of the screen." *(Everett Collection)*

Elizabeth with her mother, Sara, and first husband, hotel heir Nicky Hilton, in 1950. At eighteen she saw marriage as the only way to escape her mother and transition into adulthood. "I had been a virgin not only physically but mentally," she would confess. *(Everett Collection)*

The lasting bond between Monty and Elizabeth kept the media guessing about the nature of their relationship. Here they are attending Judy Garland's concert at the Palace Theater in NYC in 1951. *(Everett Collection)*

Although he often shrugged off his good looks, those close to Monty knew he could come across as vain. "I've never seen anyone who liked being in front of a camera as much as Monty," a friend observed.
(Everett Collection)

After her disastrous first marriage, Elizabeth quickly married British actor Michael Wilding in 1952. Their two sons, Michael, Jr. and Christopher, were born in 1953 and 1955.
(Everett Collection)

Marlon Brando visiting Monty on the set of *From Here to Eternity* in 1953. Considered the greatest actors of their generation, they had a friendly competition that kept them both at the top of their game.
(Everett Collection)

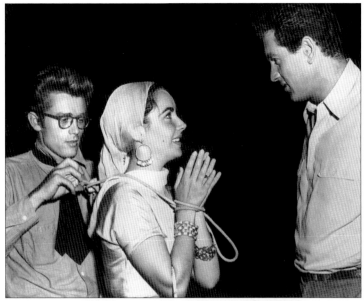

James Dean, Elizabeth, and Rock Hudson on the set of *Giant* in 1956. She became great friends with both actors, although rivalry and jealousy kept Dean and Hudson from becoming close. *(Everett Collection)*

In the summer of 1956, after nine weeks, Monty returned to work on *Raintree County* following the accident that severely damaged his face. He was still in the process of healing. The cameraman tried to photograph him from his right side as much as possible since it was less damaged. *(Everett Collection)*

Cast and crew members noticed that Monty would only speak to Elizabeth on the set, usually in whispers. He was in agony, and his drinking and drug taking increased dramatically. "We all love him so, but he needs help," co-star Eva Marie Saint told the press.
(Everett Collection)

Publicity still for *Raintree County*. Monty felt the movie was a bore, but predicted audiences would come to assess the damage to his face. Elizabeth was nominated for her first Academy Award.
(Everett Collection)

Elizabeth with her third husband, Mike Todd, standing in front of the private plane he named after her. On March 22, 1958, he would die when the plane suffered engine trouble and crashed.
(Everett Collection)

It was difficult for Monty to adjust to his altered appearance after the accident. The left side of his face was left partially paralyzed, and he had to learn new ways to express emotions in his acting.
(Everett Collection)

When Eddie Fisher left his wife Debbie Reynolds for the newly widowed Elizabeth, the scandal sent shockwaves throughout the world. Here they are attending the Academy Awards in 1961. Elizabeth had won Best Actress for *BUtterfield 8*. *(Everett Collection)*

In 1959, Elizabeth insisted that Monty be cast as her leading man in *Suddenly, Last Summer* By that time, she had become the bigger star while his career was on the wane. *(Everett Collection)*

Monty, Elizabeth, and her son, Michael Wilding, Jr. are visited on the set of *Suddenly, Last Summer* by actor Burl Ives. He had costarred with Elizabeth in *Cat on a Hot Tin Roof*. *(Everett Collection)*

Unsure of how to advertise a movie as strange and unnerving as *Suddenly, Last Summer*, the marketing department created posters of an alluring Elizabeth in a bathing suit from the film. *(Everett Collection)*

Monty attending the premiere of *The Misfits* with close friend Marilyn Monroe in 1961. Marilyn would say, "He's the only person I know who's in worse shape than I am." *(Author's Collection)*

Richard Burton playing Antony to Elizabeth's Cleopatra. Their overwhelming passion for each other destroyed both their marriages and enthralled the public for years to come. *(Everett Collection)*

Elizabeth and Monty attend the premiere of *The Night of the Iguana* in New York in 1964. When she realized how desperately he needed to get back to work, she became determined to find a new movie for them to costar in. *(Everett Collection)*

Ravaged and ill, Monty completed the low-budget spy thriller *The Defector* in 1966 to prove that he was fit to film *Reflections in a Golden Eye* with Elizabeth. But he died before filming began. *(Everett Collection)*

In her later years, Elizabeth devoted much of her life to raising money
for AIDS research. Here she is attending a benefit with Elton John in 1991.
(Everett Collection)

Of course, her family came to see her. Francis, Sara, and her brother, Howard—grim-faced, eyes downcast—would make their way through the curious mob as reporters shouted questions. Designer Helen Rose visited for a while. MGM hairdresser Sydney Guilaroff, who was a close friend of many MGM female stars, Elizabeth included, spent a night sleeping on a couch at the edge of her bed. Even Greta Garbo made an unexpected visit, beelining to Elizabeth, putting her hand on her shoulder, stating, "You must be brave," and then turning on her flats and exiting.

A shocked Eddie Fisher, one of Todd's closest friends, was in New York, in business meetings about his television variety show, when he heard the news. He flew back to Los Angeles and headed straight to Elizabeth's house. He needed to grieve with someone who loved Todd as much as he did.

Eddie started spending a lot of time at Elizabeth's house. "[I]t seemed natural we should try to comfort each other," Elizabeth explained. Debbie felt the same way. "I actually sent him over there," she admitted. She continued to care for Elizabeth's children.

To Eddie, Mike Todd had been a king, and Elizabeth was his queen. He didn't dare think of Elizabeth as anything more than a grieving friend. In an attempt to console her, Eddie would read aloud passages from the thousands of condolence cables and letters that were pouring in from around the world. She stored them in shoe boxes around the bed.

"I remember being in the middle of a perfectly lucid conversation with Elizabeth, and an instant later she would be crying hysterically," Eddie Fisher recalled. "I remember her alternating between blaming herself for allowing him to go and screaming she should have been on the plane with him, that she should be dead, and she wanted to be dead."

In the midst of her grief, funeral arrangements had to be made. Of course, as Mike's widow, Elizabeth had to be consulted. Todd's son, Mike Todd Jr., thought that it would be best if the few remains that had been identified be cremated. He felt a public funeral would be too much of an emotional strain on her and might also present a physical risk. No doubt such a funeral would attract enormous crowds to Jewish Waldheim Cemetery in Chicago, which was to be Mike Todd's final resting place. But Elizabeth and Todd had discussed death, and she remembered that he had once told her he was against cremation, so that plan was vetoed.

Of course, it would have to be a closed casket. "I knew it was more for show than anything else," Eddie Fisher said. "The plane had exploded on impact." There wasn't much of Mike Todd left to bury. When officials combed through the charred wreckage, searching for remains, they found Todd's 's wedding ring, which was given to Elizabeth. (She would have it melted down to fit her finger and would wear it for years to come.) The only other remains were a few bone fragments, a handful of ashes, some burned clothes, and a piece of nylon seat belt. Nothing more. All of this was scooped into a rubber bag and placed in a glass case, which was laid in the bronze casket.

Friends tried to talk Elizabeth out of attending the funeral, but she insisted she had to be there. Howard Hughes stepped in and offered Elizabeth the service of one of his private TWA jets to fly to Chicago. Joining her on the trip were Dr. Kennamer, Dick Hanley, Eddie Fisher, her brother, Howard, and Helen Rose. (Rose, who had designed Elizabeth's wedding dress for her marriage to Mike Todd, now designed the black suit she would wear to his funeral.) Once again, Debbie stayed home to look after Elizabeth's children.

Elizabeth did not return any of Monty's messages, but he rationalized away her silence. She was overcome with grief, and her agony was beyond words—even between the two of them. He wasn't invited to the funeral, either, but he flew to Chicago, anyway, feeling that his presence would anchor her.

Elizabeth was staying at the Drake Hotel with her entourage, and Monty took a room at a hotel down the street, expecting to, at the very least, see her briefly. He called her suite and was greeted by Dr. Kennamer. Monty told the doctor that it was okay if Elizabeth felt too overwhelmed to see him, but he wanted her to know that he was nearby if she needed him. He was also going to the funeral, and he would be in the crowd if she wanted his support. When Kennamer told Elizabeth that Monty was on the line, she shook her head. Kennamer knew how this would affect Monty, and after they hung up, he took off to visit him at his hotel so they could spend some time together before the service.

He found Monty pacing around the room, chain-smoking, expecting Elizabeth to call back. Kennamer could see that Monty was "deeply hurt" that she seemed to be shutting him out. "Monty seemed unaware of the burden he put on some people," Kennamar said. "Elizabeth didn't feel up to it." His excess drinking, his intermittent childlike behavior could be draining.

Elizabeth was one of his friends who loved him unconditionally, but she was in no condition to put up with him at this time. Monty always provoked a feeling of protectiveness in his closest friends, but now, in the midst of her worst tragedy, Elizabeth wanted to be the one who was protected. "With Monty, part of the relationship was that you always assumed certain responsibility for him," Kennamer stated. "It happened that way with many others—like Elizabeth. They just didn't have the time to assume the responsibility."

Even though the March day was cold, more than twenty thousand fans lined the route to the funeral to watch the funerary procession pass by, and hundreds more waited at the cemetery. Hordes of photographers roamed the graveyard grounds to document the event. The festive atmosphere surrounding such a somber occasion added a macabre "carnival of souls" vibe to the proceedings. Fans sat on tombstones, drinking Coca-Cola and eating snacks, while some groups of people were having full-on picnics in the chilly air.

At the cemetery Elizabeth emerged from the car, her black gloved hand shielding her veiled face, and was escorted by Dr. Kennamer, Mike Todd Jr., and Howard as the policemen tried to hold the onlookers back. Even in mourning she looked every inch a movie star, wearing dangling diamond earrings, a black suit, and hat along with the veil that covered half her face. Only her scarlet lips were visible. A black mink coat was slung over one arm. Parents held up their babies so they could get a look at one of the world's biggest movie stars.

Barricades had been put up to keep the crowd at bay, and a tent had been erected over the grave site to shield the mourners from the loud, cheery gawkers during the service. Monty, wearing an oversize raincoat, still extremely gaunt from his weight loss for *The Young Lions*, stood, unnoticed, in the crowd.

He watched Elizabeth, being led by Kennamer and her brother, slowly make her way to the tent. She seemed to be dazed, but when she first entered the tent, she cried out, "Oh God!" And when her eyes focused on the bronze casket, she attempted to embrace it as she cried, "I love you, Mike. I love you." She was led away from the casket by Kennamer.

Throughout the brief ceremony, as the Jewish prayer for the dead was recited, the crowd chanted, "Liz! Liz!" When the service was over, Elizabeth asked to be left alone to spend a few private moments in mourning. Still, the crowd chanted. Chaos broke out when she emerged from the tent. The shouting crowd, now a mob, stormed through the barricades and surrounded her, then clawed at her, pulled the veil from her face, and tore clumps of hair out of her head—desperate for some kind of association with a star. "I became totally hysterical," Elizabeth recalled, "[from] the grief and the fact that it felt like my brains and body were being clawed by birds. I came undone."

"Get back! Get back!" her brother shouted at the mob. He, along with Kennamer, Mike Todd Jr., and Eddie Fisher, tried to form a protective wall around Elizabeth, and they slowly fought their way to the car. Policemen helped them into the limousine.

Once they were back inside the car, relentless fans jumped up on the hood with cameras in an attempt to see the beautiful widow and snap her photo. People rocked the car, called her name, and pressed their faces up against the windows, leaving greasy palm prints and lipstick smears on the glass. They seemed to feel Elizabeth owed them something, and they were demanding payment in the form of her acknowledgment.

The chauffeur was afraid to drive on, until Elizabeth leaned forward and shouted, "For God's sake, get this thing moving!" The car jerked forward, and the frenzied mob parted. Looking back at the pack of fans, Eddie Fisher said that he felt "hate" for them. "It was bizarre, unbelievable," he recalled. And watching from within the mob, Monty, too, was appalled by the spectacle. "It was noisy, vengeful," he told Elizabeth weeks later. "I saw envy in their faces, envy and hatred and bleakness." He was disgusted to observe that many of the grotesque figures were munching on potato chips. Elizabeth remembered that detail, too.

22

THE YOUNG LIONS

The person he most admires is himself. The trouble is, he is also
the person he hates.
—*Motion Picture Magazine*

*T*HE YOUNG LIONS WAS SET TO PREMIERE ON APRIL 2, 1958, IN NEW
York City. Monty was filled with fear and anticipation. He was always critical of his work, but one thing he knew for sure: he had
worked on the performance as hard as he could and had given it
everything he had in him.

He was so proud of his work in the film, he sat down for a rare
interview with *Newsweek*, his first since the accident. "I always expect the worst when I go to see any performance of mine," Monty
admitted. "But I'm genuinely proud of Noah, the character I play
in *The Young Lions*. I've done some really good things in the picture . . . I think I've erred less than I have in any of the other nine
pictures I've made. I feel a great affinity for the character—a shy,
sensitive, introspective man of the people. I'm thirty-seven and
Noah is twenty-five, but our characters met in this movie. Strange,
isn't it? It's impossible to explain, but I couldn't have played
Noah ten years ago."

But even though he was feeling that optimism, Monty knew
this was a turning point. *Raintree County* had been a success be-

cause a gruesomely curious public had flocked to see it. *The Young Lions* would be the test that determined if he was still a movie star or was now a mere curiosity. Libby Holman was to be his date that for the premiere and his press agent, John Springer, was going to accompany them to keep Monty calm and reassured. Up until the last minute, Monty threatened not to go. "I can't go," he grumbled. "I can't face it." He was visibly trembling. Finally, Springer got him into his tuxedo—always a chore, as Monty hated evening clothes—and to the Paramount Theater.

Of course, the teaming of Monty and Marlon Brando in the same motion picture generated tremendous excitement. The night of the New York City premiere was star studded. That the film was being screened as a benefit for the Actors Studio only added to the luster of the event.

The screening got off to a disconcerting start. When Monty's face appeared on the screen for the first time, a scream rang out from the audience. A woman sitting in the balcony had shrieked and then fainted, apparently from the shock of seeing her idol's changed face magnified on the screen. The scream unleashed a current of uneasiness that rippled through the theater. There were gasps of "Is that him?" because others, too, were shocked by Monty's altered appearance. Monty didn't visibly react at all. He sat stone still and stared stoically at the screen.

Later in *The Young Lions*, after a fight scene, there's a shot of Noah's injured face being patched up by a medic, and this once again sent an agonized shudder through the theater. Monty does look odd in the opening scenes. Stooped and injured and old. The weight he took off for the role was unnecessary. Monty exuded vulnerability effortlessly; he didn't need to make his body more delicate to indicate emotional fragility. The emaciated look of his body made him appear ill rather than fragile.

But as the film moves on, Monty seems to grow more assured in the role. In Monty's performance there is, of course, his characteristic vulnerability, but there is also a quiet dignity and strength. Because he makes Noah so endearing, you stop noticing his appearance. He looks better as the movie goes on. By the end of the film, a new mood had overtaken the audience at the Paramount. It was a triumphant one. The filmgoers were floored by Monty's performance and cheered in their seats. The message was clear: Monty didn't need his exceptional beauty to continue to be a powerful actor.

That night many of the industry's biggest names, including Paul Newman and Marilyn Monroe, rushed up to congratulate him. Maureen Stapleton remembered her first reaction to his performance was noticing "that poor, ruined face." Later she would elaborate, saying, "The physical change in him was so startling . . . Because he had been supremely beautiful, and while he was still terribly moving and good as an actor, I had to get used to the change."

The premiere's guests ventured to an after-party at the Plaza, where the positive feedback continued. Monty and Libby sat at a table with Hope Lange and her husband, Don Murray, and publicist John Springer. As was tradition on a movie premiere night, everyone was waiting for the morning papers to come out, so they could read what the critics had to say.

In that era the most important review for any movie was the one that appeared in the *New York Times*. A review in that publication could make or break a film—and set the tone for many to follow. This was something that was understood by everyone in show business, and on opening nights, everyone held their breath until the *Times* review came out. When the papers, hot off the presses, hit the newsstands that night, Springer and Murray got ahold of the *New York Times* out of sight of the rest of the guests.

Bosley Crowther, the number one movie critic at the publication, did not like *The Young Lions*, and his harshest criticism went to Monty. He wrote, "Mr. Clift is strangely hollow and lackluster as the sensitive Jew." Springer and Murray were crestfallen. They knew what this review would do to Monty, how much he had riding on this role. Hope Lange came over and read it, and she cried. Actors know what critical reviews can do to other actors.

Meanwhile, guests kept approaching Monty, heaping on compliments. Seeing that he was high with praise and anticipation,

Springer and Murray decided to keep the *Times* review away from him for as long as possible. They dreaded hurting him. It was a struggle, because, naturally, he was eager to see how his performance was viewed by the critics.

As Monty waited and waited for the notices, there was a mounting tension, and they could feel his anxiety, which only made them want to put off the inevitable a little longer. He was having such a good time, and that happened so rarely lately. Whenever he started wondering out loud where the papers were, they would change the subject and call attention to something else.

In the early morning hours, when most of the guests had gone home, Springer suggested they drift over to Reuben's to continue the celebration, which was really a way of keeping Monty distracted. They were joined by Hope Lange and Don Murray. Other newspapers had started coming out, and the reviews for the film were fine. In a number of them, Monty was singled out for praise.

Still, he kept asking to see the *Times*. When he got up to go the men's room, he came across a stack of papers. He brought one of the *New York Times* back to the table, braced himself, and began to read the review out loud. He came to the part where Crowther had written, "Mr. Brando makes the German much more vital and interesting than Montgomery Clift and Dean Martin make the Americans." Then the ax dropped. "[Mr. Clift] . . . acts throughout the picture as if he were in a glassy-eyed daze."

Monty's face registered pain only for a moment. He had become expert at covering up his emotions. Hope Lange, however, burst into tears again. Monty comforted her, insisting that the review didn't matter. Like an animal that had been shot, he just kept on running, ignoring the bullet, chattering on about how some critics just didn't understand. He didn't want them to see how the review had wounded him.

Even though other newspapers with excellent reviews for Monty were brought out, they did nothing to lift his spirits. He could focus only on the bad one, which happened to be the most important one. Libby and John Springer could sense that Monty wasn't ready to go home. Libby suggested they all go back to her apartment for a nightcap. There was nothing left to say. They were all too drained to keep up the pretense. They all sat around, silently staring at their drinks. Then Monty's dam burst. "Oh my God! Oh my God!" he wailed. "Noah was the best performance of my life. I couldn't have given more of myself. I'll never be able to do it again. Never."

Monty was vindicated in the coming weeks when the magazine reviews for *The Young Lions* came out. *Newsweek* considered him "virtually flawless," while *Time* found aspects of his performance "wonderfully funny and touching." But Monty ignored them. Only the negative critique mattered. When he wasn't nominated for an Academy Award, it only further convinced him that his performance was a failure.

In late 1957, Monty continued to attract new people, make new friends, who were simply drawn in by his energy. With the diminishment of his looks, he made a new discovery—his appeal wasn't exclusively physical. Like a number of big stars from that era, Monty had been blessed with more than external beauty. He had that inscrutable X factor that drew people to him, a star quality that fascinated and beguiled but also exasperated. So even when he was no longer achingly handsome, people were still powerfully attracted. He would organize dinner parties at his apartment— and no matter what his behavior (and sometimes his behavior got very outlandish)—successful, talented people showed up and stayed. The writer Robert Thom commented, "He actually had wit, intelligence—dulled, thrown out of whack by alcohol—but nonetheless genuine."

Around this time Maureen Stapleton was in rehearsal for a television production of *For Whom the Bell Tolls*. She introduced Monty to the talented cast, including actress Maria Schell, Christopher Plummer, and Jason Robards. For a while, Monty's dinner parties included this group. Maria Schell later stated, "[Monty] never stopped. Never stopped talking or drinking. He was always in motion, performing little jigs, mimicking, curling his body around a chair. He seemed alternately charming, ludicrous, disagreeable, shifting, teetering into his own private abyss."

There were those who were fascinated and were happy to peer down the abyss with him. All the endearing qualities Monty possessed that had always drawn people to him earlier were still evident. There was something thrilling in his presence—inexplicable but there. "He had a vast knowledge of literature and a great command of language, and yet it was part of his approach to go out of his way to simplify his words," Bill Gunn observed. "[A]nd if he did use the big words he knew, he would say them in a funny way, almost mispronouncing them, so that he wasn't calling attention to the fact that he was using them."

But friendship with Monty could be trying. Bill Gunn was appearing in the play *A Member of the Wedding* with Ethel Waters in Massachusetts when Monty reached him at the theater long distance. Monty had obviously been drinking—he told Gunn that he had been out to dinner with Libby Holman. As was the norm, he had had too much to drink, and on the way home, he sat down on the curb.

A man approached him and said, "I know who you are. Let me walk you home." It wasn't unusual to see Monty stumbling around Manhattan late at night. Comedian Skip E. Lowe—who later became a Hollywood talk show host—once saw Monty slouched against a building in Times Square.

"Are you lost?" Lowe asked.

"I'm always lost," Monty muttered.

He allowed Lowe to escort him home. Lowe said that when they reached the town-house doorway, Monty took off his coat and gave it to him in gratitude. "I don't think he knew what he was doing," Lowe observed. "He was just grateful and wanted to say thank you, and it was the only way he could think of. I tried to refuse it, but he insisted. It seemed important to him that I take it."

On the evening he called Gunn, Monty had allowed the stranger to accompany him inside the town house, but the rest of the night was a blur. Now he was hearing noises in the house—

and he was terrified. Since Monty sometimes picked up hustlers and then passed out while they roamed freely through the apartment, it was plausible that the guy could still be there.

But, as Gunn explained, he was over two hundred miles away, in the middle of a performance. There was nothing he could do. "Call the police," he urged and then rushed off for his next scene in the play. But Monty kept calling the theater.

"You've got to come, Bill," he pleaded. And then he explained in detail how he would have a car pick him up and take him to the airport, and then a charter flight would bring him back to Manhattan. It was a ludicrous notion, but Gunn agreed to fly to New York to help Monty deal with the situation.

Shortly after his curtain call at the end of the performance, a car picked Gunn up and drove him to the airport. Then a plane flew him to New Jersey, where a limousine was waiting to drive him to Monty's place in Manhattan. It was 3:00 a.m. by the time Gunn arrived at Monty's house, but there was no answer when he knocked and rang the bell. Gunn was well acquainted with Monty's drug-induced slumber, so he went to a pay phone at a bar on the corner and called. He had to remain on the line for many rings before Monty at last picked up—groggy and confused. "I thought you were in Massachusetts with the play," he exclaimed when he recognized Gunn's voice.

Gunn reminded him of the panicked phone call, the fear that someone was lurking in the house. Monty was baffled. He had no recollection of hearing anything unusual, let alone summoning Gunn and making the extensive arrangements to have him flown in.

Gunn's next dilemma was that he had to make it back to Massachusetts in time for the evening performance. Monty hired a private helicopter to get him to the theater on time. That evening he was onstage, acting opposite Ethel Waters. The twenty-four-hour experience had been maddening, but it was the kind of adventure that certainly made life interesting to a young actor.

Others weren't so willing to put up with Monty's drunken eccentricities. He was still spending a lot of time with Libby at Tree-tops. Composer Ned Rorem encountered Monty one weekend there. He described Monty as a "spoiled, cantankerous drunk" and found that physically, he had "a kind of translucence to his skin, a sickly sheen. The former pretty boy looked like a sexage-narian."

23

ELIZABETH THE CAT

I almost lost my mind with grief.
—**Elizabeth Taylor**

*E*LIZABETH HAD NEVER FELT SUCH A LOSS BEFORE, AND IN THE FIRST weeks after Mike Todd's death, it felt like she would never work her way through her grief. She slept with Todd's pajamas under her pillow. When the maids tried to change her sheets, she wouldn't let them. She said she wanted the sheets on the bed as long as possible, as long as Mike Todd's smell remained on them.

A sense of extreme loss and disbelief kept cutting through the heavy sedation, and she felt the deep, piercing pain. Mike Todd Jr. spent some time at the house with her and witnessed Elizabeth in mourning. On several occasions "she relapsed into a state of near hysteria," Mike Todd Jr. observed. She was crying and fighting against the fact of his death. When she'd pull herself together, she would say, "Mike can't be dead. I don't believe it."

"I dream of Mike almost every night, dream that he is still alive," she told Mike Jr. "In the dream, I'm in his apartment on Park Avenue . . . He comes into the room. 'You thought I was dead, didn't you? But I was just laying low until things got straightened out.'"

She tried everything to numb her pain. Mike Jr. even felt that the two of them might fall into an affair as a way of consoling each other, a notion his wife also considered possible, so she put her foot down and had him return home.

Monty telephoned her often, and eventually, she began taking his calls. She rediscovered their unique camaraderie, and she leaned into his support. She began phoning him, too, and he always made himself available to take her calls. But most of the time, she was climbing the walls, unable to sleep except when drugged. "I could not bear the loneliness of being without the man I really loved," Elizabeth recalled. "I could not sleep, and as the weeks went by, my insomnia grew worse. As a result, I began to take sleeping pills."

Slowly, tentatively, she started to think about getting back to work—partially because she did need to get her mind off of Todd's death, and partially because he liked her in the movie she was doing at the time. He had seen some of the early rushes and thought she was a delicious Maggie "the Cat." It was because of him that the motion picture was being made in color, and finishing it would be a kind of tribute to him. One day she pulled up to the studio in a black limousine and sent word that she wanted to see director Richard Brooks. He immediately left the set and joined Elizabeth in the back of the limo.

"Mike said I look wonderful in the rushes," she said. "I think I should come back. I owe it to him."

"When?" the delighted director asked.

"How about now?" she replied.

She went directly to wardrobe and makeup and shot a scene there and then. "And it was the worst possible one," Brooks remarked, recalling the similarities in her lines and what had happened in her life. "The one where Big Mama tells her Big Daddy has cancer and is going to die. One of the lines she had to speak was, 'I know what it's like to lose someone you love.' She did it on the first take perfectly." In her grief she had lost twelve pounds and looked more beautiful than ever.

Soon she was working full days. Typically, she found escaping into the world of make-believe, being someone else, extremely therapeutic. "When I was Maggie, I could function," she explained. "The rest of the time I was a robot." But the shooting on *Cat* concluded in May, and once again Elizabeth had to deal with the day-to-day emptiness and loss. She was twenty-six years old and was no longer thinking of suicide, but she had yet to find something that made her feel alive again.

By the summer of 1958, Elizabeth's pain had dulled enough for her to take little steps, to venture out in public. In June she flew out to spend a few days with Monty, and the friendship picked up as if there had never been a hiatus. She told Monty the worst part of her days now was the loneliness, something that he understood all too well. Todd had been dead for only three months, and she couldn't imagine finding someone who could ever take his place, but she hated being alone.

In Los Angeles Elizabeth started seeing men. She didn't consider them dates, actually, but she wanted to be in their company. Soon she was being romantically linked to Arthur Loew Jr., the theater-chain heir and movie producer, who was paying her an inordinate amount of attention and seemed to have fallen in love with her. He took her children, along with their nurse, to live in his house for a while to relieve Elizabeth of some of the pressure. Yes, some eyebrows were raised from the surprise of a romance for the young widow beginning so soon. But no one judged her too harshly. She was young and hurting, and they really couldn't blame her for indulging in a distracting flirtation. For Loew, it was more than a flirtation, yet he realized that Elizabeth was still in mourning, and rather than push for a relationship, he presented himself as a caring friend.

But Eddie Fisher felt uneasy about Elizabeth spending time with men. He couldn't explain his reasons for feeling possessive of her, but he justified it by telling himself he was simply being protective "like a brother or a father." At the time, Eddie didn't dare admit to himself that his true feelings toward Elizabeth were more than brotherly. He was falling in love with her. She made her first public appearance when she joined Debbie for Eddie's opening night in Las Vegas. Eddie announced her presence from the stage, and the audience gave her an enthusiastic round of applause. They felt real affection for her; she was a survivor of a terrible tragedy.

Soon after, she dined with Paul Newman and Joanne Woodward and also socialized with Robert Wagner and Natalie Wood. Next—gowned in red and dripping with jewels given to her by Mike Todd—Elizabeth attended a party at Romanoff's in Beverly Hills with Hedda Hopper. There was an immediate rush of warmth toward Elizabeth. The biggest stars surrounded her, embraced her, offered the beautiful young widow and mother sympathy and encouraging words. She chatted with friends about her immediate plans: she was making arrangements to go on a long trip to Europe with her children.

It wasn't just chatter; Elizabeth really was planning on going to Europe. She sent eight large suitcases on to Paris to arrive ahead of her, but then she discovered that her passport bore the joint names of Mr. and Mrs. Todd. She would have to await a new one. During that wait, something would happen that would cause her to forget about the European trip altogether.

That "something" was named Eddie Fisher.

24

GOOD MONTY/
BAD MONTY

One put up with Monty—not just because of his extraordinary talent, but because he liked, loved enormously.
—Robert Thom

*L*IKE MOST FASCINATING, ARTISTIC PEOPLE, MONTY WAS A DI-chotomy. Yes, there were times when he was demanding and infantile. But there were many times when Monty could still be charming, intelligent, creative, and kind. It was these qualities, along with the memory of what he had been, that drew new friends and kept the old ones in his life.

Monty showed various sides of himself to different people. He saved his charm and warmth for a few close friends or new sexual interests—he grew impatient and indifferent with everyone else. He didn't care how he came across or what people thought of him anymore. Still, he was an original. There was no one like him. It made people want to know him, do things for him, be a part of his life.

At a time when Elizabeth was preoccupied with her own grief, and Libby was attempting to distance herself from illness and depression, a bright spot in this darkening period for Monty happened when he reconnected with Nancy Walker, a woman who would become a close lifetime friend. Monty had met the comedienne ten years before, when he had helped her find a pay phone in a darkened bar.

In the 1970s Nancy would become a beloved television legend, playing Ida Morgenstern, Rhoda's mother, on the hit TV show *The Mary Tyler Moore Show* and then reprising the role in the spin-off *Rhoda*. But in the fifties she was simply a promising stage actress, appearing occasionally to good reviews on Broadway and Off Broadway. Her short stature—she was four feet eleven—her large head, prominent facial features, perpetual sardonic expression, and a honking voice made her ideal for musical comedy roles.

In 1957 Monty connected with Nancy again when he paid a visit to her backstage while she was performing in a play. Their rapport fell into place with ease. Nothing was off-limits; they would talk about anything. And at the time they were both going through a difficult period. Before long, Nancy and Monty were meeting several times a week for lunch or dinner—sometimes she'd bring along her husband, David Craig. They began talking on the phone every day, at times for up to two hours. They'd talk about everything, from their fear of aging to whether or not a skit they had seen on television the night before was funny.

Although Monty's friendship with Elizabeth remained strong, she, in many ways, had come to mother him. And Libby enabled, even encouraged, his vices. Nancy filled a different place in his friendship arena. Nancy was more available to Monty and also more needy, which allowed him to bring out more of his nurturing instincts. She was raw and open about her need, she was unfulfilled, and her career wasn't moving. He was a good and understanding soul to his friends. Nancy would assert that "he needed to be needed."

It wasn't long, however, before Monty put Nancy through one of his endurance tests. It happened while Monty and Roddy McDowall were having dinner with Nancy and her husband, David. The two couples were chatting pleasantly when Monty started eating off the plates of everyone at the table, as was his habit, and targeted Nancy's in particular.

Nancy wasn't yet used to Monty's grotesque table manners, and as he grabbed at her food, she quietly asked him to please not eat off her dinner plate. In his typical fashion, Monty ignored her and continued snatching morsels from her plate.

"Please, Monty," she said. "It makes me very nervous when you do that."

He ignored her plea, reached over to her plate, and announced, "But, oh, Nancy, I just love your anchovies."

Nancy had had enough. She took the plate and dumped the contents into his lap.

Monty burst into tears, but she wasn't sympathetic. She stormed out of the restaurant and called for a cab, her husband hot on her heels, trying to calm her. But Nancy had been pushed too far, and she was really furious. Monty called her for days after, profusely apologizing. He was always pushing friends; it was almost as if he put them on trial, or forced them through boot camp to see how much they could take. Most of them decided simply to ignore Monty's antics, look the other way, and try to get out of the situation with the least amount of embarrassment. Not Nancy. She loved Monty, but she drew a line.

Eventually, Nancy decided to forgive him. The experience established one important boundary. Monty never ate off her plate again. "The amazing thing is that Monty lost very few friends," Robert Thom said. "[E]ven when his day was past, his behavior abominable, his future unthinkable. He meant something to us." Thom attempted to convey Monty's hold on the people in his life by explaining that "when you were with Monty, he made you feel you were the most important person in the world, that your talents were limitless."

When Robert Thom referred to Monty's behavior as "abominable," one of the things he was talking about was Monty's conduct at the small dinner parties he held at his apartment. Drinking unleashed the disturbed demon in him, a child demon. Sometimes when very drunk, but before passing out, he would sit at the table, choose one of the guests, and hurl insults at them, as if he were throwing bricks at their protective walls, breaking them down, trying to get them to reveal themselves. For example, on any given night, he might start making fun of Nancy Walker's looks. "When Monty chose to be cruel, he was devastating— particularly so because his most evil lines were delivered with saintliness, compassion," Thom observed.

On one occasion, Christopher Isherwood was visiting with Monty when Isherwood's young lover, Don Bachardy, joined them. "Nobody invited you," Monty sneered. And when Don was leaving, Monty blurted, "Goodbye, shit face." Isherwood wrote, "Clift certainly is, even at his best, a dismal kind of degenerate, with a degenerate's ugly, unfunny, aggressive attempts at humor."

On such occasions, Monty's closest friends made allowances for him, because they knew he was drunk, and they understood that he was half-crazed with frustration and rage, and that he wanted people to see it. If he needed someone to suffer along with him for a while, they loved him enough to endure the pain with him.

So, while Nancy would not tolerate Monty picking food off her plate, she found that she could stand him picking on her over her physical appearance. Everyone would sit silently, staring at their plates, while Monty delivered his long, ugly speech. Then he might pass out, his head in his dish, and Roddy McDowall would lift Monty's head off the plate and lay him down on the carpet while the dinner party continued.

He really didn't want to hurt the people he loved, but he couldn't feel too terrible about it, since he never remembered any of it the next day. If someone ventured to tell Monty what had happened, he would respond sadly, "I don't remember." Regardless of that, he apologized and apologized.

One evening, when Robert Thom was visiting with his girl-friend, Janice Rule, Monty unleashed the drunken demon. At the time Janice was a beautiful actress whose career was faltering. As the couple was leaving the town house, Monty took her face in his hands very tenderly, as if he was about to pay her a penetrating compliment. Looking tearfully into her eyes, he said, with much emotion, "I don't understand it . . . How can you act . . . when you don't have any feelings?"

Janice took in a sharp breath, which indicated a sudden blow. Thom was furious, as well he should be. They both left the town house, bewildered and angry. What had prompted Monty to say such a thing? How could he be so cruel? Afterward, Monty made many apologetic phone calls to the couple. For once, Thom was the one delivering the tirade, chewing Monty out with a lot of anger and foul language. Monty took it. Agreed with it. Then asked for forgiveness. It took some time, but eventually, Thom and Janice were once again seeing Monty.

To an outsider, it's difficult to imagine why so many friends stuck by Monty when he was at his most difficult—and how he managed to keep attracting people to him. For all his difficulty, at his best, he still had the ability to turn on an extraordinary seducing quality, one that had to be experienced to be understood.

By now, Monty had more or less given up on meeting the love of his life, but he did still crave male companionship. Late in 1958 he met Claude Perrin, a young Frenchmen who had come to America to try to get into the fashion business. Claude was handsome, with well-groomed dark, wavy hair and almond-shaped eyes. He was a masculine man, but he had a high-strung dramatic style that was often made more amusing by his heavy French accent.

Seduced by the aura of Monty's celebrity and glamour, Claude decided he wanted him right away—and he set out to get him. The previous year Claude had been "kept" by a rich fur manufacturer. Now he went on an all-out campaign to win Monty's affection—writing ardent love letters, telling Monty he couldn't live without him, and threatening to kill himself if he couldn't win his affection. All that aside, if not an intellectual equal, Claude was pleasant to be around—and a good drinking companion. And Monty was lonely.

Not long after Claude began his campaign, they became a couple. Although the young Frenchman gave off a Continental savoir faire, with his stylish clothes, French accent, and expensive colognes, he belonged to the world of kept boys, sex parties, and drugs. If his presence led Monty a step down into the depths, he seemed happy to follow.

Certainly, the handsome young man had no means of support, and Monty began giving him money, although it never seemed to be enough. But it seemed a small price to pay for the distraction of being included in Claude's debauched milieu—Monty was now on a constant search for ways to get himself away from himself. So Monty also turned a blind eye to the jewelry and silverware that started disappearing from the town house after Claude's visits. Although he tried to keep his new boyfriend separate from his friends, Claude hung around a lot.

Mostly, Claude hung around Monty's place, drinking, doing drugs, or bringing hustlers around. Monty didn't object to any of it and participated in most of it. Claude was spending so much time at the town house, Monty gave up and allowed him to move in. He eventually gave Claude the title of "assistant," and over time those in his circle came to know Claude.

25

A VERY UN-PRIVATE AFFAIR

Sexually, she was every man's dream. She had the face of an angel and the morals of a truck driver.
—**Eddie Fisher**

"**I**T WAS DURING THIS VULNERABLE PERIOD THAT I HAD BEGUN MY relationship with Eddie Fisher," Elizabeth would explain years later. Although there was a mutual attraction between the two, at first, the relationship was the simple comfort they felt in being with each other. There was nothing sexual, not even anything romantic, between the two of them in their meetings, although Eddie had begun to fantasize what it would be like to have Elizabeth.

Even though only several months had passed since Todd's death, Debbie still thought it was perfectly natural for Elizabeth and Eddie to continue to spend time together, each easing the other into an acceptance of a life without the strong presence of Mike Todd in it. Meanwhile, Debbie was planning a big party in Las Vegas to celebrate Eddie's thirtieth birthday. Of course, Elizabeth was invited to the bash—Debbie even reserved the seat next to Eddie for her—but she didn't show up.

She was sorry she couldn't be there to wish Eddie luck on his birthday, and she called him a few days later to tell him so. She explained that she had wanted to be there with him, but that she had had her period and couldn't go. From her slurred voice, Eddie thought she was either on pills or was drinking—or both. Prescription pills were getting to be a serious habit with her. But, even with her thick speech, Eddie was glad to hear her voice. Without mentioning Debbie or the children, Eddie confided that he was feeling lonely. "I know the feeling," Elizabeth said. "Isn't it awful to be lonely?" She asked Eddie to come over the following day, explaining that she had something of Mike's she wanted to give him for his birthday.

Eddie would always maintain that what happened that day was meticulously planned by Elizabeth. When he arrived, he found the front door open. He walked through the house, calling her name, but there was no answer. He continued out to the back-yard. Then he saw her sitting by the pool, playing with baby Liza and drinking a glass of white wine. The way she looked certainly seemed calculated; she was absolutely fetching in a flesh-colored bathing suit.

It was the moment that Elizabeth turned to him and their eyes met that he knew for certain he was in love. Electricity crackled between them. "Not a word was spoken," Eddie recalled, "but I knew I just started the rest of my life. One look, our eyes met, and the feeling that ran through my body . . . I never felt anything like it before, but somehow I knew, this is what love feels like."

She handed the birthday present to Eddie. It was the solid-gold money clip she had given Mike, engraved with one of his favorite sayings: BEING POOR IS A STATE OF MIND. I'VE BEEN BROKE LOTS OF TIMES BUT I'VE NEVER BEEN POOR. "He'd want you to have it," she said. "I hope it brings you a lot of luck and happiness."

He was very moved, but the atmosphere all around them was heavy and melancholy. Mike Todd was in the air. But it was Eddie who was there with her now. Although she would always maintain that she was never in love with Eddie Fisher, whatever it was she was feeling was very strong. And the heat of her desire was better than nothing. "My intense loneliness, combined with the near-ness of someone who had been so close to my beloved, made me susceptible," Elizabeth explained. "In hindsight, I know I wasn't thinking straight. At the time I thought he needed me and I needed him."

Of course, Eddie recognized her neediness. "Elizabeth's eyes," he said, "I can't ever forget how they burned into my heart that day. I felt her need for me to the depths of my soul. My feelings were identical to hers."

Eddie suggested they take a ride to the beach. They ventured to his car, bringing little Liza with them. It seemed perfectly natural that during the drive to Malibu, Eddie reached over and took Elizabeth's hand. He held it as he drove. When they reached the beach, Eddie spread out a blanket on the sand. The passionate kissing that followed also seemed very natural, with Liza playing near them in the sand.

Taking a page from his best friend and mentor's book, he declared, "I'm going to marry you, Elizabeth."

"When?" she asked breathlessly.

"Soon," he responded. "As soon as possible."

After that afternoon, they spent every minute they could together. Eddie Fisher was the antidote to Mike Todd. They started to make excuses to get together for lunches and dinners and meetings. He told Elizabeth that his marriage to Debbie was a sham. "I never loved her," he confided. Insiders felt that when he married Debbie Reynolds, the very ambitious Eddie Fisher was hoping to move his singing career into movie stardom, like Sinatra had.

The Fisher/Reynolds marriage had gone on the rocks relatively early. On Debbie's suggestion, they had tried marriage counseling, but it hadn't worked. For Eddie, the passion just wasn't there. They had planned on calling it quits the year before, but Debbie had found out she was pregnant again, and Eddie had agreed to give the union another go. In the irony of ironies, they had named their newborn son Todd, after Eddie's friend and mentor Mike Todd.

Now, with Mike dead only a few months, Eddie would come to Elizabeth's house to see her. "We sat and drank and talked about Mike for hours," she recalled. Sometimes they would go for long drives and wind up at the beach, and they'd stroll along the water. On other occasions, they had to bring Debbie along. Keeping their passion for each other under wraps made it all the more thrilling. Elizabeth would hold Eddie's hand under the table, or provocatively guide his hand up her dress, while Debbie chattered, oblivious, on the other side of the table. Eddie felt like Elizabeth didn't care if they were caught. "Elizabeth lives by her own rule," he remarked. "She wants what she wants when she wants it."

But they kept the physical side of their romance to kissing and holding hands. "The passion inside of us was growing and growing and growing," Eddie remembered.

Eddie realized intuitively that Elizabeth was out of his league. That after Mike Todd, she was attracted to strong, domineering types, which Eddie wasn't. He also understood her restless nature, her insatiable passion for expensive gifts, her need to be the center of attention. He knew she was confused, lonely, and still hurting, but he was happy to brush that aside and continue down a romantic road with her. "I knew what it was to have my greatest fantasy come true," he said.

No longer able to contain their passion, Elizabeth and Eddie arranged to rendezvous in New York. Eddie told Debbie he had some business to take care of with the sponsors of his television show. Elizabeth said she was going to New York to "spend some time with Montgomery Clift." Elizabeth didn't think she was doing anything wrong. Hollywood was filled with unhappy marriages, extramarital affairs, couples on the cusp of breaking up. She had been through two divorces herself. In addition, she believed it when Eddie told her his marriage to Debbie had long been over and was now nothing but a sham.

Elizabeth checked into a suite at the Plaza. Eddie checked into the Essex House, making a fuss about being in town for meetings regarding his television show. There was no business other than Elizabeth, and he walked over to the Plaza to visit her in her suite. The moment they were together, she fell into his arms.

"When are we going to make love?" she whispered.

"Tonight," he answered.

Life was in the here and now. They had waited long enough. They undressed each other, then fell onto the bed—and so began a sexual marathon that lasted for hours, that lasted for months to come. After the blandness of being married to America's girl next door, Debbie Reynolds, sex with sultry Elizabeth Taylor was cat- nip to Eddie. Her lushness, her greediness consumed him. He simply could not get enough of her not being able to get enough. "We'd make love three, four, five times a day," he said.

Eddie's lovers, past and in the future, talked about his sexual prowess, his staying power. Some girlfriends would claim he could have sex up to a dozen times a night—soon after orgasm, he was ready again. His addiction to methamphetamine likely had a lot to do for his insatiable sexual appetite. The size of his penis was also reportedly impressive; although years later Debbie Reynolds would—perhaps bitterly—refute this. (Elizabeth would not.)

What especially thrilled and enflamed Elizabeth was Eddie's passion for her. He was the first man she had had near her own age in a long time. His seemingly endless desire for her made her appetite surge and match his. "She was uninhibited, wild, so to- tally free with her body. We couldn't get enough of each other," he gushed. Elizabeth was a sex goddess who really enjoyed sex.

When Eddie and Elizabeth came up for air, they began being spotted together socially around Manhattan. At first, they at- tempted to make it appear as if they had run into each other in Manhattan purely by coincidence. When they started to be seen together here and there, no one thought too much of it. After all, he was the best friend of her dead husband. But when they were spotted dancing closely at the Blue Angel club, a few eyebrows were raised.

Eddie went back to his room at the Essex House only to shower and shave, so the staff would see him coming and going. He was actually staying in Elizabeth's room. Debbie was confused when she wasn't able to reach him. She started calling Elizabeth's room "just to chat," but she was really trying to pump her friend for in- formation.

The first real rumbling of the earthquake of a scandal that was to follow was printed in New York writer Earl Wilson's column on August 28, 1958. "Elizabeth Taylor and Eddie Fisher were dancing it up at the Harwyn nightclub this morning. Eddie, having been Mike Todd's close friend, is now sort of an escort service for Liz." Wilson went on to report that Elizabeth and Eddie had seen the William Gibson play *Two for the Seesaw* on Broadway the night before. (Elizabeth would later be offered the movie version.)

Word of their affair was leaking out, and that seemed to embolden them. They were giddy in love, and it seemed to them that the world would understand and be on their side. "Look, we felt we could get away with anything," Eddie explained, looking back on the affair years later. "After all, we had climbed to the top of our professions and achieved more than we dreamed possible, so we felt invincible. We did whatever we wanted to do and then waited for the consequences."

They were spotted kissing on Fifth Avenue in broad daylight—they even went to the Central Park Zoo. That weekend they took off for Grossinger's, a romantic getaway hotel resort in the Catskills, in upstate New York, that was known to cater to honeymooning couples. Fisher had a history with the resort—he had started his singing career there, and it was the very place where he had married Debbie Reynolds. For three days, Elizabeth and Eddie would show up in the resort's dining room first thing in the morning and order a champagne breakfast.

On their return to Manhattan, when Elizabeth shopped with Monty in the afternoons, she told him that she and Eddie had fallen in love. "I've known for months that Eddie was in love with me," Elizabeth admitted. "Even Mike knew that, but he dismissed it as a harmless flirtation."

In the evenings Elizabeth dined with Eddie. Now photographers and reporters were hot on the trail, and the chase was on. Sensing that something hot and steamy was brewing, the press decided to stir the pot. They called Debbie in California to find out what Mrs. Eddie Fisher thought of her husband wining and dining the widow Todd in New York. "Why shouldn't Eddie go out with Elizabeth?" Debbie told the press. "We're all such close friends. My, how Mike Todd would laugh over all of this."

But in reality, Debbie wasn't laughing. She knew something was up and continued attempting to reach Eddie at his hotel. Each time she called, she was informed he was not in. Finally, at two thirty in the morning, she decided to call Elizabeth's room. She wanted to catch Eddie there off his guard, so she cooked up a scheme, telling the hotel operator that there was a call from Dean Martin for Eddie Fisher. The operator put the call through to Elizabeth's room.

Eddie, who had been in a dead sleep, picked up the phone, and he was informed he had a call from Dean Martin.

"Dean? What's up?" Eddie asked, sleepy voiced.

"It's not Dean, Eddie. It's Debbie."

"Oh shit!" he barked, suddenly wide awake. "What the hell do you think you're doing, calling me here at this time of the night? Goddamnit! You have no business calling me here!"

"Roll over," Debbie said with a steely calm, "and let me speak to Elizabeth."

Eddie refused to put her on the line. "Look, this is ridiculous. We're just talking. I just stopped by."

"Eddie, it's getting close to three in the morning. You didn't just stop by. I woke you up."

Eddie kept insisting that they weren't in bed. They were just talking. Then, suddenly, the attempt at holding in his passion for Elizabeth seemed ludicrous. He stopped mid-conversation and abruptly announced, "Elizabeth and I are here, and we're both very much in love. I'll fly back to California tomorrow."

"Well, you don't have to bother," cried Debbie and slammed down the phone.

Newspapermen now had three people on their radar: Elizabeth, Debbie, and Eddie. Once the collective wind of the gossip columnists caught on to the story, it spread like a wildfire through the front headlines of early morning newspaper editions. In the eye of the brewing media storm, the knee-jerk reaction of the three major players in the unfolding melodrama was to deny, deny, deny any romance. Elizabeth said, "It's much too soon to forget all Mike meant to me. You know Eddie and I are friends. I can't help what people are saying."

Eddie and Debbie gave a joint statement to Louella Parsons, insisting that the whole thing had been a "misunderstanding." On September 9, the *Los Angeles Examiner* ran the headline EDDIE FISHER ROMANCE WITH LIZ TAYLOR DENIED.

But in a matter of twenty-four hours all these quotes denying the romance seemed silly. The truth was going to come out sooner or later, and the longer they lied about it, the worse it would seem. The gossip columns steamrolled ahead with news stories of the affair, and soon such headlines as EDDIE FISHER IS DATING LIZ TAYLOR were running simultaneously with the denials.

Now Debbie's mind went into overdrive. She realized a major scandal was about to explode, and she needed to construct how her role was perceived in it. Immediately, she began planting the seeds of the sweet and innocent wronged wife. When a bunch of reporters came to her door to deliver the newspapers bearing the headlines that Eddie and Elizabeth were dating, she answered the door, clad in white pajamas and a robe. "I have never heard of such a thing," Debbie said as she grabbed the papers and stalked indignantly back into the house. Later she issued a statement through a studio press agent: "I am deeply shocked from what I have read in the papers, and there is nothing further to say at this time."

Knowing full well that Eddie wasn't flying home that day, Debbie went to the airport, anyway. She rightly assumed reporters would be there waiting to get some quotes from him, and she wanted to make her presence known. As the reporters waited for the plane to arrive, all eyes were on Debbie. She was wearing blue jeans, her face was scrubbed of makeup, and her hair was pulled back in a simple ponytail—the very image of the dutiful young wife. The gaggle of reporters watched her as she waited for all the passengers to depart from the plane. When it was clear Eddie was not on it, she put her chin up and walked bravely away. The reporters rushed back to file the story: Eddie didn't come home.

When Eddie did arrive the following day, hoping to head off the scandal, he found a mob of reporters gathered in front of his house. Once inside, he confronted Debbie, admitting, "I love her and I never loved you and I want a divorce."

"You go off and be with her," she retorted. "She'll throw you out within a year and a half. She doesn't love you, Eddie. She'll never love you. You're not her type," she said, spitting out the words like poison. Then she added, "She'll be through with you within eighteen months. And then we'll see if we could work it out, because I'll never give you a divorce."

Eddie moved out of his and Debbie's home.

When Elizabeth's plane arrived in Los Angeles, a mob of photographers and reporters was there waiting for her. They rushed toward the plane as Elizabeth emerged and regally made her way down the steps, decked out in a bejeweled blue turban and clutching a Yorkshire terrier to her chest. She kept her eyes lowered as the media mob called out questions. One of her assistants, Dick Hanley, had flown out East to escort her back, and he was beside her. At the bottom of the plane stairs, her agent, Kurt Frings, was waiting for her.

The three of them got into a TWA station wagon that was stationed there to transport them across the tarmac, and the media mob was in hot pursuit. They were still shouting questions at her as she changed cars, getting into Frings's Cadillac. Elizabeth rolled down the window but kept her eyes downcast. The reporters fired off questions in rapid succession, overlapping, outshouting each other.

"Do you know if Debbie and Eddie are breaking up?"

"Will you see them?"

"Why did you come back to the coast?"

Elizabeth remained somber and silent.

"Miss Taylor," one reporter called out above the other voices. "Won't you say anything?"

At last she raised her blazing blue eyes. "Hello," she said softly.

Then the car pulled away.

26

A LONELY HEART

There was a touch of madness in his genius.
—Vernon Scott

IN 1958 THERE WAS A SHIFT IN MONTY'S RELATIONSHIP WITH HOLLY-wood. Whereas he had always had the upper hand in picking and choosing projects, now he was no longer thought of first for sensitive leading man roles.

Oh, scripts continued to arrive at Monty's apartment, but there was a change in the quality of the material he was offered. Although he was coming off two high-profile productions, now much of what he was being offered was lower-budget melodramas, horror movies, and spy thrillers.

He had a reputation for substance abuse, which was high-risk behavior on film sets, plus, it enabled him to work only half days, and no one wanted to insure him anymore. Friends' diaries had entries like this one in Christopher Isherwood's: "Don has taken Marguerite's red Dior dress to the cleaner's because Monty Clift vomited [all] over it." On top of that—let's face it—he no longer looked the part of a leading man. He had lost his perfect face, his most powerful protection. His most effective weapon. His most valuable bargaining tool.

Monty was willing to lower his sights, but he wouldn't consider anything too far below his standards. He took to saying that he had made some movies that didn't turn out as well as he would have liked, but he had never made a movie that he was ashamed of—and he intended to keep it that way.

There was another reason Monty was no longer receiving top-notch material. One of Monty's agents was one of the most respected and influential players in the industry. At one point, Monty had been the crown jewel in his stable of stars—one friend described their relationship almost as "father and son." Now, the agent/father began warning producers not to use Monty, his own client. "He's too much trouble," the agent would say. He'd add, "He's a loser. Not worth the risk."

Later in the year, Monty was offered a script that he felt enthusiastic about. Producer Dore Schary, who had worked with Monty on *Raintree County*, was now an independent producer, and he wanted to do a film adaptation of the respected novel *Miss Lonelyhearts*, by Nathaniel West. The studio agreed to the production if Schary could do the film for under a million dollars. The offer was by no means of the same caliber as those Monty was used to getting, but he was drawn to it.

West's book is a savage satire set during the Depression. In the story an unnamed journalist at a New York newspaper is assigned to handle an advice column called "Miss Lonelyhearts" (like the column "Dear Abby"), where lonely readers write in, asking for solutions to their misery (for example, a teenage girl who was born without a nose). The anguished letters from his readers begin to affect the journalist. Miss Lonelyhearts begins to view himself as a Christ figure, and he truly wants to help the readers of his column.

Monty was attracted to the material since the troubled Miss Lonelyhearts sacrifices his own well-being, and ultimately his life, for the salvation of his readers. West's world is ugly and angry—and Monty often had the same worldview at the time. Unfortunately, producer/writer Dore Schary wrote an adaptation that had little to do with the source material, particularly the mood.

Wanting to make the story more palpable to a mid-century audience, Schary gutted the book, removing all the bite and cynicism and replacing it with a sappy soap opera. The unnamed protagonist to be played by Monty was even given a name as bland and unimaginative as the rest of the movie: Adam White. Schary made up for the lack of intensity in the script by casting the movie with popular movie stars, most of whom were friends of his, and like Monty, they agreed to work for much less than their usual salaries. Stars like Robert Ryan and Myrna Loy signed on, and the film would introduce respected stage actress Maureen Stapleton to movie audiences.

Toward the end of the novel, Miss Lonelyhearts has sex with Mrs. Doyle, a reader who wrote to his column regularly. She is a sexually frustrated woman whose husband is a cripple. When he refuses to sleep with Mrs. Doyle again, she tells her husband that Miss Lonelyhearts tried to rape her. At the end, Mr. Doyle shoots Miss Lonelyhearts, and the two men tumble down the stairs. Schary further diluted the novel by reworking the ending so that Miss Lonelyhearts is not killed.

When Nancy Walker read Schary's screenplay, she pronounced it "crap" and begged Monty not to do it. Even Maureen Stapleton, playing Mrs. Doyle, expressed disappointment in the finished script.

"Your character can't live in the end," she cried. "Oh, Monty, I'm so disappointed."

"Oh, I don't know." Monty shrugged. "I'm used to being disappointed."

Monty flew to Los Angeles for production and checked into a cottage at the Bel-Air Hotel. By then Jack Larson had become involved with a talented young writer named James Bridges. Monty became involved sexually with both of them. "The three of them slept together as a throuple when Monty came to visit in the late 1950s," producer Neal Baer said. "They were living this life sort of under the radar but very boldly."

Jack Larson was around to assist Monty again, and he would visit him at his bungalow. Larson noticed the actor's restlessness, his nervousness. Once again, he would run lines with Monty, but the script would be a jumble of pages, wrinkled and out of order. Sometimes, when Monty was drinking and taking pills, he would pass out, and Jack would put him to bed. "He weighed almost nothing," Larson recalled. It was also sad to note that Monty had darkened the windows of his bungalow so that he wouldn't have to look at himself in the light—and that explained at least part of his anxiety.

In *Lonelyhearts* Monty would be playing the idealistic cub reporter, Adam White. He pointed out to Larson that there were lines in the script that referred to Adam's innocence and youthfulness. Of course, Monty had always been cast as the young rebel fighting his way through a corrupt world. But he no longer looked the part, and he knew it. Monty was thirty-eight and looked at least a decade older. Would audiences accept him as the youthful hero? he asked again and again.

He worried obsessively about what he would look like acting opposite sweet-faced Dolores Hart, a twenty-year-old ingenue, who had been cast as his love interest. In *The Young Lions* he looked a bit long in the tooth to be courting twenty-five-year-old Hope Lange, and it was made more awkward when she kept calling him a "young man." Now his leading lady was being played by an actress who looked like Hope Lange's younger sister.

His friend Robert Thom privately scoffed at the idea of Monty in the role. "Youthful?" Thom asked. "But the hands shook, and the face was old and battered, far beyond repair . . . trapped in a body that was without hope, a fretting cadaver . . . He had not been able to grow up, and he had not been able to remain young."

Costar Robert Ryan revealed, "Monty was very ill, extremely ill, looking almost like a dying man. There was something terrible in him. I never knew what tortured him, but he could not work in the morning and I did not know what he was doing. He just tormented himself. [I]t was already a dead man, a dead man in waiting."

Once filming started, Monty's troubling, erratic behavior surfaced again. Dore Schary invited Monty and reporter Vernon Scott out for a steak lunch at the studio commissary. After Schary placed an order for three New York steaks, the three men noticed that diners at neighboring tables had recognized Monty and were staring and whispering. Monty decided that they were chattering about how different the movie star now looked. Schary and Scott did their best to ignore it, but Monty grew more and more uncomfortable.

"The more they talked, the worse he got," Scott observed. "He began slumping down in his chair."

"Let's get out of here," Monty said.

Schary attempted to appease him. "Just relax, Monty. Everything will be fine."

By the time the steak dinner was placed in front of him, Monty was in a state of extreme anxiety and the diners were still gawking. He decided to really give them something to look at. First, he lathered the steak with pats of butter until the meat was coated with a thick layer. Next, he topped that off with a mountain of salt, and then he blackened it with a shaker of pepper.

Schary and Scott watched in horror as he grabbed the steak with both hands and ducked under the table.

"Then we heard what sounded like an infuriated dog growling and barking," Scott recounted. The two men lifted the tablecloth and looked under the table. Monty had taken the steak and wrung it out with his hands and put it on top of his head, so that all the steak juice and butter were running down his face. In front of the shocked patrons, they lifted Monty to his feet and took him to the men's room to clean him up. By that time Monty was weeping loudly.

This was part of Monty's behavior now—he didn't even try to change it. He had developed a "take it or leave it" attitude about his drunken behavior. And a surprising number of friends took it, although they were hard pressed to explain why. "Sometimes one wondered why anyone put up with Monty; his behavior, public and private, was frequently painful, embarrassing, monstrous," Robert Thom remarked. Then, further considering what it was like to know the actor, Thom concluded, "One put up with Monty—not just because of his extraordinary talent, but because he liked, loved enormously."

Despite all the noisy, off-putting theatrics that characterized Monty's social behavior, there were aspects of him that remained so dear, so sensitive, friends were willing to overlook the worsening faults. Friends like Nancy Walker. Nancy recalled that during this period, she was nearly out of her mind with anxiety. She had had periods of success, which whetted her appetite for fame, then long periods of nothingness. There was no one in the world except Monty whom she felt she could explain her turmoil to. "I just have to talk to Monty," she told her husband on one occasion. And she reached out to him long distance, in Los Angeles. Monty understood something was seriously wrong.

"What plane will you be flying in on tonight?" he asked.

Later that evening, after she had arrived in Los Angeles, Nancy and Monty talked until the early morning hours at a quiet Italian restaurant. Monty explained that she had to step away from her ambition from time to time, learn to savor the other things in life, her husband, her daughter, her friends . . . the sky. He calmed her, as she knew he would, and Nancy decided to stay with him for the duration of the shooting.

Another woman who fell under Monty's spell during *Lonelyhearts* was costar Myrna Loy. Once referred to as "the Queen of Hollywood," Myrna, at fifty-three, was still a very attractive woman, with hooded gray-blue eyes and delicate features. His irresistible qualities affected her. Although her bigger scenes in the movie were with Robert Ryan, most of her attention went to Monty. "He was so vulnerable under his social veneer," she observed. Myrna fell, if not in love with him, into a deep infatuation—as many women did. He seemed to be parts son, lover, and friend rolled into one.

Maureen Stapleton remembered Monty sometimes falling asleep in her arms between filming. The disintegration of one who was once so exceptional—even fleetingly—added something poignant and poetic to him. As he napped, she would focus on things like his delicate bare feet, with blue veins showing through the skin—a metaphor for a broken and fallen hero. The all-around fragility of Monty pierced her, and tears would stream down her face as she held him.

The filming of *Lonelyhearts* took fifty-four shooting days, with the cast and crew alternating between adoring and coddling Monty to being annoyed by his childish tactics, like stomping around the set in oversize boots when he was shooting to call attention to himself. Or jumping in Dore Schary's lap while they were watching the rushes.

Three months later, when *Lonelyhearts* was released nationwide, it was greeted with apathetic reviews. The critics didn't lambast it—they seemed to respect the effort of the actors—but they disliked the film. It seems ironic that Bosley Crowther of the *New York Times* went out of his way to praise Monty's performance in this film. Perhaps the critic felt remorse at the swipe he had taken at the actor's (much better) performance in *The Young Lions.* The observation that Monty seemed to be acting in "a glassy-eyed daze" is much more fitting to *Lonelyhearts.* For this film, however, Crowther wrote, "Mr. Clift is remarkably affecting as the troubled, young, lovelorn columnist whose internal battles and soul-searchings get him into some terrible sweats."

When he was not working, Monty's assistant, Marge Stengel, seemed to be the only one around him that was keeping some semblance of order to his life. She would faithfully report to the town house daily to answer the phone, deal with the mail, and try to hinder the stream of unsavory leeches that attempted entry into Monty's life—men that Monty had picked up in bars or met on the street but whose names he didn't remember.

Marge also did her best to limit Monty's drug intake. Since Monty was able to get prescriptions for virtually any medication he wanted from any number of doctors, Marge would call the drugstores and threaten them if they dared fill them. Sometimes it worked. She could be very stern in her protectiveness of Monty.

Monty was still seeing Dr. Silverberg daily, but all his friends agreed no good was coming from it. Knowing the influence the doctor had on Monty, Marge called him again and again to convince him to persuade Monty to go into a hospital to dry out. The psychiatrist refused, stating that Monty was not an alcoholic.

Dr. Silverberg still had a stranglehold on Monty, even though he wasn't being analyzed much anymore. The most important thing that Monty's visits to Dr. Silverberg achieved was adding structure to his day. Most days Monty had no other reason to leave the townhouse. Much of the office hour was more like a discussion between two friends having lunch than analysis. By now, Silverberg would talk more about himself than Monty did.

Jack Larson also telephoned Dr. Silverberg and suggested he commit Monty to Silver Hill Sanatorium to detox, but the psychiatrist cut him off, telling him not to interfere. "Here was this doctor taking Monty's money, his time, fucking him over, and letting him kill himself by inches. [I]t was criminal," Larson stated. To prove the severity of Monty's condition, Larson brought Monty, passed out drunk, to the psychiatrist's office at ten in the morning one day and deposited him on the doorstep, but it did no good. Silverberg still refused to acknowledge that Monty had any drinking problem.

Ultimately, Larson, Marge, and Roddy McDowall devised a scheme to get Monty hospitalized for two weeks. They had his medical doctor tell Monty that he had hepatitis. Monty was promiscuous, so it was something he would believe, and he did. Monty agreed to be admitted to the hospital. But it didn't work in drying him out. Monty convinced friends to sneak alcohol into his hospital room, and he drank continuously throughout his two-week stay. Nothing was accomplished by the ruse.

27

DEBBIE, EDDIE, AND THE WIDOW TODD

No one could equal Elizabeth's beauty. Women liked her, and men adored her. I know because my husband left me for her.
—**Debbie Reynolds**

*I*T WAS A SHOCKING THING.

It wasn't that people didn't have affairs in 1958. Or didn't wait the proper time of grieving before having an affair. Or even didn't steal the maid of honor's husband. It's just that it wasn't out in the open.

Today, in a culture where scandals are cooked up and dished out on a daily basis—mostly by the people who are involved in them—the Elizabeth Taylor/Eddie Fisher/Debbie Reynolds scandal might not seem like much. But in its day, the romance between Elizabeth Taylor and Eddie Fisher really infuriated the country. And fascinated it.

Hedda Hopper, the queen of gossip, wanted to be the first reporter to remove all doubts and confirm that Elizabeth Taylor was indeed having an affair with the very married Eddie Fisher. Although she felt that her crown and her power in the industry were slipping, Hopper still wielded enormous influence, with a combined readership somewhere around thirty-five million people. Aware that some stars were terrified of getting on her bad side, she dubbed her Beverly Hills mansion "the house that fear built." When the English actress Merle Oberon asked her why she reported such terrible things about people, Hopper smiled demurely and replied, "Bitchery, dear, sheer bitchery."

Now she would prove to her millions of readers just what a bitch she could be. Hopper discovered that Elizabeth was staying with Eddie in the home of her agent, Kurt Frings. Hopper called her there for a woman-to-woman talk, although it turned into more of a gossip columnist–to–movie star interview. When Hopper got Elizabeth on the phone, she frantically waved to her assistant sitting across the office, indicating for him to pick up the extension and start writing down the conversation in shorthand.

Elizabeth realized she would have to admit to her affair, and she figured that Hedda Hopper was the best choice to get the scoop. After all, Elizabeth had known the columnist since childhood, and in spite of Hopper's infamous reputation for breaking scandals, Elizabeth felt she could trust her to report on the affair sympathetically, as a friend rather than a columnist. She didn't.

"Elizabeth, you've got to level with me," Hopper began. "For I shall find out, anyway. What's all this business between you and Eddie Fisher?"

At first, Elizabeth tried to brush it off flippantly. "The last time I looked," she retorted, "Eddie was still married to Debbie Reynolds."

"Obviously," Hopper continued. "But they're breaking up, and everyone is saying you're the cause of it."

"That's a lot of bull," Elizabeth blurted. "I don't go breaking up marriages. Besides, you can't break up a happy marriage, and theirs never has been."

Hopper knew she had angered Elizabeth, and moved in for the kill. She was canny enough to know that she could get more out of a provoked Elizabeth Taylor.

If only Elizabeth had parsed her words a little more carefully. If only she hadn't come off as quite so defensive and gloating. If only she had shown a tad of vulnerability—as the brokenhearted widow who fell in love again—she may have defused the eruption of the scandal that followed. But that wasn't her style. She was defensive. Assertive. Combative. Truthful. Even by today's standards, Elizabeth's comments in print came across as callous and shocking. In 1958 they were downright explosive.

"You can't hurt Debbie like this without hurting yourself more," Hopper scolded. "People love her very much because she's an honest and wonderful girl."

"Eddie is not in love with her, and he never has been," Elizabeth snapped. "Only a year ago they were about to get a divorce but stopped it when they found out she was going to have another baby . . . I'm not really taking anything from her, because she never really had it."

"What do you suppose Mike would say?" Hopper asked, aghast. "He and Eddie loved each other."

"No, you're wrong. Mike loved Eddie," Hopper asserted. "In my opinion, Eddie never loved anyone but himself."

"Well, Mike's dead and I'm alive," was Elizabeth's response.

Hopper almost dropped the phone. What Elizabeth said next—Hopper wrote—was unprintable. Years later the famous columnist printed the unprintable in her autobiography. What Elizabeth had said was, "What do you expect me to do? Sleep alone?"

That didn't make it into the 1958 column. But what did was enough to cause a firestorm, leaving millions of readers wondering what Elizabeth could have replied that was so obscene.

After Hopper hung up, she knew what she had—the scandal of the decade—and she rushed to her typewriter to unleash it. When Hopper wrote up the conversation for the column, she started off by declaring her authority. "I've known Elizabeth Taylor since she was nine years old—always liked her, always defended her. She never wanted to be an actress. [T]hat was her mother's project. I've seen her through her marriages to Nicky Hilton, Michael Wilding, and Mike Todd. But I can't take this present episode with Eddie Fisher."

Hopper concluded the column in the way of a disapproving parent. "Well, Liz, you'll probably hate me for the rest of your life for this, but I can't help it. I'm afraid you've lost all control over reason. Remember the nights you used to call me at two and three in the morning because you were having nightmares and had to talk to somebody, and I let you talk your heart out? What you just said to me bears not the slightest resemblance to that girl. Where, oh where has she gone?"

Hedda Hopper's column, which ran on the front page of the *Los Angeles Times* on September 11, 1958, and was syndicated all over the world, became a mission accomplished. Millions of readers were absolutely mortified as they read Hopper's column. What had been rumors and gossip was now fact. The newly widowed Elizabeth Taylor was having an adulterous affair with Eddie Fisher, her late husband's best friend—whose wife had served as matron of honor at her wedding.

Hopper, who feared that her style of gossip was becoming passé, was elated to find herself once again the breaker of big entertainment news, and the moral high priestess of celebrity behavior. Cables and letters started arriving at her office at once, some from celebrity couples, some from other journalists, congratulating her for a fine piece of writing that worked a higher-ground message into a salacious scoop.

The public also wrote to Hopper. Particularly in those days, fans considered movie stars as family. They followed their lives avidly and cheered and booed at their behavior as it evolved.

For weeks to come, thousands of angry, venting letters arrived at the gossip columnist's office, addressed only to "Hedda Hopper, Hollywood." Some included newspaper clippings about the Eddie Fisher/Elizabeth Taylor affair, in case Hopper had somehow missed them. Many decried Elizabeth's behavior and expressed sympathy for "sweet little Debbie and her two wonderful children." All of this Hopper read, filed and, in some cases, answered.

"Dear Hedda Hopper," one letter began, "I would like to nominate Miss Elizabeth Taylor for the biggest bitch of the year." It was signed "A disgusted moviegoer."

Some of the letters were mournful, the letter writers having been longtime Elizabeth Taylor fans, who now found themselves brokenhearted that "she has made herself sickening and disgusting." Another letter writer offered, "She is nothing but an alley cat with a pretty face."

The public simply couldn't get the affair off their minds—it was everywhere. As one fan put it, "There is so much feeling about this wherever we go." What astonished some fans was the degree to which the affair consumed their lives. "I am so disgusted with myself because I have let the Fisher-Taylor scandal upset me, but one hears about it everywhere," one housewife lamented.

Elizabeth had played her cards wrong. Before she gave the interview to Hopper, she was still riding the crest of love and sympathy the public bestowed on her when Mike died. As far as she was concerned, her fans were on her side. They wanted her to be happy. They would understand. She was wrong about that. The public wanted her to suffer a little longer, but they didn't exactly reject her, either.

The press went absolutely wild. Celebrity journalists were delighted to have enough juicy behavior on the part of Elizabeth and Eddie to keep them in headlines for months. It appeared that they were indulging in a public and private erotic sideshow of lewdness. The moralistic public was horrified and fascinated.

Although Elizabeth, Eddie, and Debbie all would have preferred to live without the scandal, now that they were in it, they did what stars try to do. They tried to manipulate the scandal into useful publicity for themselves. Each of them battled out the narrative through quotes in the headlines.

Behind all their real emotions, these were, after all, movie stars; and a movie star's career is always on the top of his or her priority list. So, if Debbie was going to be cast as the wronged wife, she decided to play the part to the hilt. Actually, she truly was heartbroken and hurt. "It was a very public humiliation, and she wanted to die," daughter Carrie Fisher remarked years later.

"And she had two small children, and you cannot have the luxury of being depressed." It was less painful to hide true feelings behind a constructed image.

To keep her part of the story alive, Debbie appeared in front of reporters with her hair in pigtails and diaper pins clipped on her blouse—some say that her agent suggested that little touch. Her son, Todd, was still in diapers. The sight of a young mother abandoned by her husband touched the public, and suddenly the "sugary girl next door" musical star was big news.

Whenever "caught" in public, Debbie did not look like a movie star. Her hair was in curlers or in a mousy ponytail. She never wore makeup. And she was usually ready with something quotable for page one. "It seems unbelievable to say that you can live happily with a man and not know that he doesn't love you," she said with a quivering voice. But she maintained she would not give Eddie a divorce.

In one of their "Elizabethan" phone calls, Elizabeth told Monty that Debbie wasn't the delicate flower she appeared to be on-screen. Elizabeth scoffed at Debbie's victimhood, referring to her behavior as "antics." She believed Debbie's victim status was contrived for sympathy and maximum publicity, and Elizabeth refused to feed into Debbie's image as the long-suffering, wronged wife. "She's in show business and didn't get to the top of her profession by being weak-kneed," she fumed. "She must have some inherent strength, like every other dame in this goddamn business."

If Debbie was the victim of the melodrama, Elizabeth was the vixen. On September 28, in the midst of this brouhaha, MGM released *Cat on a Hot Tin Roof.* The movie showcased Elizabeth as Maggie "the Cat," a sexy seductress who slinks around in a satin white slip, trying to get her incredibly hot (and homosexual) husband to sleep with her so she can get pregnant and nab a chunk of the family fortune.

Naturally, the advertising for the movie revolved around Elizabeth, and now—in addition to nonstop coverage in the newspapers and magazines—everywhere the public went, they were treated to a poster or a billboard of a sultry Elizabeth Taylor lounging on a bed in a tight white slip.

In the film she shouts at her gay husband, who is lamenting the death of his best friend, "Skipper is dead and I'm alive," which is strikingly similar to her words quoted by Hopper, "Mike is dead and I'm alive!" It was becoming impossible to tell where fictional Liz ended and real-life Elizabeth began.

As the public speculated, gossiped, and raged, Elizabeth kept staring down at them from billboards with a disarming come-hither look—brazen, defiant, sexy, proud. The outrage didn't stop audiences from seeing the movie. The film was a smash hit and was number one at the US box office for five weeks in a row. For her performance, Elizabeth received her second Academy Award nomination.

The only one who seemed not to benefit from the scandal was Eddie Fisher. He didn't have the suave sex appeal to pull off being a lady killer, and audiences tired of him. Record stores stopped carrying Eddie Fisher records, and some radio stations refused to play his music. After initial curiosity in the beginning of the season of his show, viewership dropped, and the show was canceled. He tried to take it in stride. He did, after all, have Elizabeth.

Elizabeth was truly shocked at the intensity of the red-hot hatred the public felt for her. She did not just read about it in virtually every newspaper and magazine. She also experienced it out in public. Groups of people would stop her and Eddie in traffic, not to get a look at her, as they had in previous times, but to hurl insults at them. Even many of Elizabeth's Hollywood friends dropped her. The couple was shunned everywhere.

The two walked out of the Hollywood eatery Musso & Frank Grill one evening to find a rowdy crowd of press and public waiting. Walking past wildly flashing cameras, Elizabeth could distinctly hear a sound that was new to her—the roar of an angry, disapproving public.

"Shame on you," someone called out.

"Whore!" yelled another.

Eddie recalled that the two of them huddled in the back of their black sedan. As the driver pulled away, Elizabeth looked back at the angry mob.

"Oh, dear Lord," she gasped. "What the hell have we done?"

On March 3, 1959, Elizabeth was converted to the Jewish faith. After taking the Jewish name Elisheba, she said, "This is something I've been wanting to do for a long time. It had nothing to do with any future marriage plans."

A new mass of scathing letters was sent to the columnists, this time by anti-Semites. Refusing to hide from the attacks, Elizabeth made the decision to hold her head high at the Academy Awards, with Eddie Fisher as her date. About her nominated performance in *Cat on a Hot Tin Roof*, she had already made a prediction. "I won't win. There is too much sentiment against me," she said.

On April 6, 1959, Elizabeth strode up to the stage with Dirk Bogarde and Van Heflin to announce that *The Defiant Ones* (an ironic title if there ever was one) had won the Academy Awards for Cinematography and Screenplay. While most of Hollywood would have liked to have seen her with a scarlet *A* emblazoned across her chest, she instead held her back straight and her head high, sheathed in a plunging black gown, with dangling chandelier earrings and a diamond brooch at her waist. When the Best Actress award was announced, Susan Hayward won for *I Want to Live!* But Elizabeth felt triumphant, having managed to maintain her dignity in a crowd of her sneering peers.

Shortly after the awards ceremony, Eddie received an offer to appear in Las Vegas. He and Elizabeth were both thrilled; this was a chance for Eddie Fisher to make a comeback. With her parents in tow, Elizabeth rented a ranch house near the Strip. At a ringside table at one of his performances, she sat erect and proud, stoically smoking cigarettes from a diamond-encrusted holder. Fisher sang the entire show while looking at Elizabeth, but the audience didn't mind one bit—they were absolutely giddy about being a part of the ongoing real-life soap opera that the world was talking about.

During his engagement in Vegas, Debbie finally announced that she would grant Eddie a divorce. On May 12, 1959, a whopping three hours after the Fisher/Reynolds divorce became final, marriage number four took place when Eddie married Elizabeth at the Temple Beth Sholom in Las Vegas. Elizabeth's father, Francis, was there to walk his daughter down the aisle. "Always a bride, never a bridesmaid," one observer quipped.

28

SUDDENLY, LAST SUMMER

A witch's broth of Venus flytraps, frontal lobotomies, massacred baby turtles, loony bins, cannibalism, voyeurism, homosexuality (just a pinch of this, a mere soupçon), near rape by lunatics, a dowager who is sinister even by Tennessee Williams's standards, and a mother who is willing to have her perfectly sane daughter lobotomized in order to get her hands on $100,000 cash.
—Dwight Macdonald, Esquire

*F*OR HER FIRST FILM AS A FREELANCE TALENT, ELIZABETH COULD HAVE her pick among any number of first-rate scripts, such as *Two for the Seesaw* or *Irma La Douce*. Both had been Broadway successes. Instead, she chose Tennessee Williams's one-act play *Suddenly, Last Summer,* which was being adapted for the screen by Gore Vidal and produced by Columbia Pictures.

This play had been a commercial hit and a much-discussed piece when it played Off Broadway the previous year. With a canny instinct, Elizabeth was attracted to the material because it was complex, controversial, and daring—just as she was at that exact moment in time. Like her own image, she knew that the subject matter would repel some and fascinate others—and the majority would line up to see what all the fuss was about.

The plot revolves around a wealthy Southern widow named Violet Venable, who wants a doctor to perform a frontal lobotomy on her niece, Catherine, who knows the truth about the grue-some way her son, Sebastian, died while they were vacationing in a Spanish town called Cabeza de Lobo the previous summer. Eliz-abeth would play Catherine, the disturbed but desirable young woman whose gay cousin, Sebastian, uses her as bait to attract young boys for him to seduce into homosexual encounters—which leads to his death.

But before she signed on to do it, she told the producer, Sam Spiegel, and the director, Joe Mankiewicz, that she wanted Mont-gomery Clift to play Dr. Cukrowicz, the neurosurgeon who falls in love with her, which would once again cast Monty as her leading man. As a major Hollywood player, Elizabeth knew the industry's current opinion on Monty. She had seen *Lonelyhearts* and thought it beneath him. The least she could do was get him in a first-rate, high-profile Tennessee Williams project. But even more than that, she wanted to work with Monty again. She loved Monty, she knew they'd have chemistry on the set, and she knew if they were near each other, they could each pull the other through whatever trauma was going on in the moment.

On the other hand, Mankiewicz had reservations about casting him. Drinking, drug taking, and odd behavior were now part of Monty's legend, and they could no longer be written off as a tem-porary madness brought on by the horrific accident. But to se-cure Elizabeth as the star, Mankiewicz agreed to cast Monty, under the condition that he passed the physical exam needed to get him insured for the movie.

Once she agreed to it, production of *Suddenly, Last Summer* was scheduled to begin in May 1959 at Shepperton Studios in Surrey, England. Taylor would be paid the enormous sum (by 1959 stan-dards) of five hundred thousand dollars to star in the movie.

When Monty was offered the part, he was intrigued by the idea of being directed by Mankiewicz in a Tennessee Williams work—his reputation could use the boost of a prestigious project. Joseph Mankiewicz was a heavy hitter in Hollywood, a writer, director, and producer known for witty, sophisticated classics like *All About*

Eve and *The Barefoot Contessa.* Monty joked with friends that he was thrilled to be playing a doctor—at last, he could put his bedside manner to good use. But most of all, he was pleased to have the opportunity to work with Elizabeth again.

A physical examination was set up for Monty to see if he would be able to be insured for the film. To be safe, Marge Stengel set up two appointments with different doctors in New York. During both examinations, Monty was so agitated that the doctors were unable to pass him for the insurance. For a third physical, set up in Los Angeles, he showed up at the appointment too sedated to get accurate test results. Wanting to keep Elizabeth satisfied, the producer Sam Spiegel took a huge chance and hired Monty without insurance, anyway, and he was cast as Dr. Cukrowicz (meaning "sugar" in Polish), the young neurosurgeon who helps Catherine remember the events leading up to her cousin's death.

Katharine Hepburn signed up to play Violet Venable, the superrich, über-bitch aunt. However, used to being the likable character in her movies, she was not pleased about playing the villain of the piece. Mrs. Venable is a woman willing to bribe a hospital to perform a lobotomy on her niece in order to save the reputation of her dead son.

When *Suddenly, Last Summer* was announced as Elizabeth Taylor's next vehicle, audiences didn't know what to make of it. Especially when movie magazines like *Picturegoer* warned them that it dealt with "morbid subject matter" that would do its star, Elizabeth Taylor, "no good at all." Or as Eddie Fisher so succinctly described the script: "Your basic mix of homosexuality, cannibalism, and pedophilia, with a lobotomy thrown in for drama."

Set in New Orleans in 1937—back in the days when homosexuality was considered taboo and evil—the story concerns the aftermath of the mysterious death of Sebastian Venable, a gay poet from a wealthy Southern family. Even when the wealthiest of men are cruising for gay sex, everything has to be covert and secretive. And Sebastian likes his men straight and young. Being shy about approaching such men, Sebastian travels each summer with his widowed mother, Violet Venable (Katharine Hepburn), who is wealthy and attractive and outgoing, the perfect person to lure men into Sebastian's circle, making them easier targets for him to choose and seduce. Thus, he uses his own mother as a procuress for gay sex.

But when Violet becomes too old to attract the kind of guys Sebastian desires, he invites his lushly beautiful cousin Catherine (Elizabeth Taylor) to vacation with him in a Spanish town called Cabeza de Lobo and leaves his mother at home, hurt and furious. Now it is his cousin he uses as bait to attract even younger boys, who live, naked and hungry, on the beach. It is on the trip last summer that Sebastian suddenly dies.

That's just the backstory.

Sebastian is actually already dead at the opening of the movie, and the plot concerns how these details of his life led to his premature death. The mystery of what exactly happened to Sebastian unravels through a series of poetic and perverse monologues given by Catherine and Violet. When the movie opens, Catherine is back in America and, having had an emotional breakdown, has been confined to St. Mary's, a mental hospital. The facts behind Sebastian's death remain a mystery, and Violet is grateful for that. She treasures the memory of her son, and she frantically attempts to keep details about his unsavory life and gruesome demise a secret. She promises to donate one million dollars to the state mental hospital, Lyons View, if its prominent surgeon, Dr. Cukrowicz (Montgomery Clift), performs a lobotomy on Catherine, thus silencing her forever.

This was extremely daring stuff for a Hollywood film in 1959, and the combination of big names and shocking subject matter almost guaranteed that it would be a smash hit. That is, if it could get made. To ensure the script would get past the censors, Gore Vidal had to meet with a priest biweekly to show him drafts of the script. After Vidal completed a draft he thought was satisfactory, Sam Spiegel submitted Vidal's adaptation of *Suddenly, Last Sum-*

mer to the Production Code Administration. Although they refused to approve the screenplay, the board suggested that Spiegel
and Mankiewicz make the film and then submit it to the appeals
board.

By the time of the making of *Suddenly, Last Summer* in 1959, a
lot had changed for Elizabeth Taylor and Montgomery Clift—in
both their private and professional lives. At the age of thirty-nine,
after years of being one of the most sought-after actors in Hollywood, Monty's box office appeal had slipped significantly. After
Lonelyhearts came and went in theaters without a ripple, Monty
was no longer considered bankable. It was shocking in Hollywood
circles that this romantic lead of a few years before—with the
power to pick and choose whatever he wanted to do—now had
the reputation of being an alcoholic and could no longer bring
people into a movie house based on his name value alone.

As for Elizabeth, her image had also changed drastically through
the years. First, she was a child star. Then she was the very beautiful and very dull wife of Michael Wilding. Next, she was a widow.
Now, in the public's eye, she was a slut. Not that it was hurting her
career any. Audiences loved her and hated her—and loved to
hate her—but they couldn't get enough of her. Moviegoers condemned her off-screen behavior, all the while eagerly reading
about her latest exploits in fan magazines and flocking to see her
on the screen.

For the first time, Elizabeth would receive top billing in a
movie costarring Monty. By 1959 she had become the bigger star.
For *Suddenly, Last Summer,* Monty would receive third billing after
Elizabeth and Katharine Hepburn.*

Katharine Hepburn arrived in England already in a cantankerous state of mind. Her longtime partner, Spencer Tracy, was ill,

*Although this was the official credit listing of the stars by contract, on the
movie print their names appear side by side, with Elizabeth first from the
left, Monty in the middle, and then Hepburn. This gives the impression
that Monty is the star.

she had been caring for him, and she felt guilty being away. Also, it displeased her that Violet Venable was a supporting character, which was why she had begrudgingly agreed to second billing. It irritated her that Elizabeth would come before her.

When Elizabeth landed in London, she reluctantly agreed to a press conference to announce the start of filming, with the condition that she would be asked only reasonable questions. If she thought the British press might be more kind to her, she was sadly mistaken. Swathed in a white fur coat, she faced the cameras, doing her best to go nose to nose with the media.

"What is your greatest ambition?" a reporter asked.

That was benign enough, and she replied demurely, "To be a good wife and mother."

Suddenly, there was a shift in tone. "But haven't you said all that before?" the reporter asserted. "Didn't you say it just eighteen months before to Mike Todd?"

"Certain things happened, you may remember," she replied in an ice-water tone that contrasted starkly with her sickly-sweet smile.

The press conference was abruptly ended, and Elizabeth was hurriedly escorted away.

To assure that she didn't have to go through any more of that kind of confrontation, Mankiewicz had the *Suddenly, Last Summer* set closed off. That didn't stop the press from regularly reporting on Elizabeth. With her huge appetite and continuously seesawing weight, reporters noted, she had once again gone up a few dress sizes. Although she wasn't yet scheduled to start shooting, the media surmised that Elizabeth's weight gain was holding up production. Elizabeth fumed, declaring that it was simply water retention.

When Mankiewicz first saw Elizabeth in London, however, he was shocked. This was not the svelte beauty in a satin slip from *Cat on a Hot Tin Roof.* She was positively zaftig. "Are you planning on losing any weight?" he asked straight out. She coolly replied that she hadn't thought about it. He reached over and jiggled the fat that had developed on her upper arms and declared it was like "mice in a sack." He suggested that she tone up. Rather than being angry with him, Elizabeth loved it. She could admire a strong man who told it like it was—when she was in the mood for it. And Mankiewicz was the strong, confident, domineering type she normally found herself attracted to. She was attracted.

While she dieted, Mankiewicz defended her in the press. When a gossip columnist suggested that the movie was being delayed because of Elizabeth's weight, Mankiewicz fired off a telegram to her: *If Elizabeth Taylor is overweight, I, for one, am at a loss to suggest what there should be less of.*

29

WHAT'S WRONG
WITH HIM?

It was a hard time for Monty . . . We were assured by Joseph Mankiewicz that as soon as Liz arrived, he would be all right. And he did improve. But it was difficult working with him. We shared a scene, just a half page or so of dialogue, but we did over thirty takes on that one scene alone and then started over again the next morning—he just could not remember his words.
—Pat Marmont

MONTY WAS SCHEDULED TO START SHOOTING BEFORE ELIZABETH. There was contentious debate as to who would travel to England with Monty. Of course, Claude wanted to accompany Monty, to entertain and be entertained. Marge Stengel felt she should be the one to go, to be a steadying hand. It was eventually decided that Marge would be the one to travel with Monty to England, as a sort of security blanket, with the main mission of trying to keep him sober, punctual, and functioning. It would soon prove to be an almost impossible challenge. Monty passed out on the way to London and had to be carried from the plane. He would continue with that line of behavior in limousines on the way to several social functions.

But before principal photography began, Monty went through

great pains to win over his coworkers and start off on the right foot. For Katharine Hepburn, he traveled to every florist shop in town, choosing the most unusual blossoms available at each location. When at last he had accumulated an enormous assortment, he carefully arranged the flowers together in a truly eye-catching bouquet. He then slaved over the wording for the card to be included with the arrangement, which he hand delivered to Hepburn's house. But he was too shy to give the bouquet to her himself; he thrust it at the maid who answered the door, and scurried back to the waiting limo.

He was still adored. What Monty had now was a little boy quality, which still drew people in and made them feel tender toward him. He visited Gary Raymond, who was cast as Elizabeth's brother in the film, at his flat in Westminster. Monty presented them with "Good Monty," and both Raymond and his fiancée, Delena Kidd, were captivated by him. "He was a delight," Raymond recalled. "He had this extraordinary presence. Not dynamic in any way, but you just wanted to nurture him. Tennessee Williams wrote about 'the charm of the defeated,' and Monty Clift had it absolutely."

On the other hand, Mankiewicz only fleetingly fell for Monty's endearing qualities. On hearing that the director wasn't feeling particularly well, Monty paid him a personal visit. Sober, charming, and enthusiastic, he again presented "Good Monty," and Mankiewicz was completely won over. In return for the gesture, he and his wife invited Monty to dinner.

Unfortunately, "Bad Monty" showed up at the restaurant. Mankiewicz was appalled as Monty proceeded to throw his food on the floor and insist on eating it there—all the while calling out slurs to the gawking patrons and insults to the waitstaff, who tried to help him to his feet. "That dinner finished it all," Marge Stengel recalled. Mankiewicz lost all respect for him.

Adding to his irritation, Mankiewicz was suffering from a dermatological condition on his hands, which caused the skin on his fingers to split open. To cover it up, he would wear white film editor gloves throughout most of the production. The painful condition became much worse when he was under stress—which he constantly was during the production—and Monty would continuously try his patience.

Filming got off to a precarious start with Monty's first scene—a lobotomy operation, which would kick off the movie. The crew thought it was particularly ironic that Monty was playing a brain surgeon, when in reality his hands were so shaky in the mornings, he could barely hold a cup of coffee steady. In his first scene in the movie, he is supposed to be performing delicate brain surgery while a small crowd of medical students observes from an upper level. The state hospital he is working in is broken down: the lights flicker on and off, and pieces of the room are crumbling.

As the doctor, Monty is supposed to comment occasionally on what he is doing for the observers, and then he is to furiously address the room regarding the primitive conditions in which he has to perform such a risky operation. Mankiewicz wanted to shoot the action straight through in one long take, which turned out to be impossible. Monty would say one line correctly and then stumble over the next one.

"What's wrong with him?" Mankiewicz would ask in exasperation. "He acts like he doesn't hear me." Mankiewicz surmised that Monty was either smoking or taking dope. He asked the film's editor, William Hornbeck, who knew Monty from *A Place in the Sun*, to sit with him in his dressing room to try to figure out what he was taking to get in such a state. Of course, Monty never did anything in front of his friend. He sat there quietly, sipping his orange juice, leaving Hornbeck and Mankiewicz to wonder what it might be spiked with.

In the end, the director was forced to break up the scene into fourteen segments, each take representing one line of dialogue. It was all for naught. In the finished film, only a few lines remain—the rest ended up on the cutting-room floor.

Monty's other early scenes were with Katharine Hepburn. After first meeting Dr. Cukrowicz, Violet walks the surgeon through the unusual and "unexpected" garden of her late son, Sebastian. The studio set was designed to look more like a jungle than a garden, overgrown with exotic greenery and decorated with primitive-looking statuary. Under the hot lights, the set was described as an "inferno." In the stifling heat on the soundstage, Katharine Hepburn was required to recite long complicated monologues about her relationship with her son and the nature of her niece's mental illness, along with the devouring nature of nature.

Monty mostly had to react to Hepburn's eccentric anecdotes and descriptions, occasionally interrupting to ask a question or make a comment. "He used to have the most peculiar expression on his face," Hepburn remembered. "Whenever we'd shoot a scene, big beads of sweat would pour out of his forehead."

Although she felt uncomfortable with much of the dialogue, Katharine Hepburn spoke Tennessee Williams's lines beautifully and eloquently. But often in the middle of one of her speeches, Monty would stumble over a word or forget his line, and Hepburn would have to start all over. Each time a take was interrupted, Hepburn, too, would be drenched in sweat and would have to take a cold shower and change her costume before they could begin again. It was difficult to get the two actors costumed and on the set, ready to work, at the same time. By the afternoon Monty fell apart and had to be sent home, and the scene was scheduled to continue the following morning.

On the second day of filming this scene, Mankiewicz did his best to guide Monty through the takes to completion. Kenneth L. Geist, a theater student, was a rare visitor granted permission to visit the soundstage. Katharine Hepburn had already arrived as the stagehands were busy moving around plants and trees. Eventually, Monty wandered onto the set, in a condition Geist described as "shattered."

As they prepared to enact the difficult scene, it was apparent that Monty wasn't well. "It was a considerable shock to see this sensitive actor's deplorable condition," remembered Geist. "He was now a mass of tics and spasms, constantly snorting from an ever-handy inhaler . . . My curiosity about how Clift could be photographed, let alone act in this condition, was soon satisfied . . . Mankiewicz grasped Clift by the shoulders and began to impart his directorial suggestions . . . While riveting Clift's attention with a piercing gaze, Mankiewicz surreptitiously started to massage Monty's neck and shoulders. The result was astonishing. Clift's tremors subsided, and despite the annoyance of a malfunctioning mountain, he maintained his composure through a series of repeated takes."

Hepburn was unfazed by Monty's behavior. "She was very good with him," observed Gary Raymond. "She respected Monty as an actor and liked him as a person." Hepburn's nurturing nature took over. Spiegel agreed: "She really spread her mother wings over him."

But the amount of work that was going into getting a few usable minutes of Monty made it seem hopeless. After Spiegel and Mankiewicz screened the rushes from Monty's first few days of work, they both wanted him fired. Together, they decided to bring in Peter O'Toole—then just at the start of his career—to replace him. When the news reached Elizabeth, she would have none of it. "If he goes, I go," she warned. He didn't go.

30

STRANGE ARRANGEMENTS

"Elizabeth was still mourning Mike Todd. Miss Hepburn was suffering through Spencer Tracy's illness . . . Joe Mankiewicz had some kind of skin disease on his hands and he had to wear gloves all through the picture . . . Of course, Monty was in torment. Everybody connected with the film was going through some kind of personal anguish and it showed."
—**Mercedes McCambridge**

AT LAST, ELIZABETH ARRIVED ON THE SET CONSIDERABLY THINNER than she had been at the press conference, but still in a foul mood. The British press continued to give her snarky coverage, but her moodiness derived from more than that. When she allowed her mind to stop racing to keep up with the pace of her career, and she gave herself some quiet time, she was beginning to think that, maybe, Eddie Fisher would have been better off as a fling than a marriage. She had never fully mourned the death of Mike Todd, and she was beginning to see that her rash romance with Eddie had been her way of not dealing with the loss.

On the *Suddenly, Last Summer* set, she buried her confusion with an outward display of passion for her new husband, which was noticeable to everyone, but gave off mixed signals. She openly conveyed her lust for Eddie in front of the entire company—plopping down in his lap on the soundstage and escorting him to her dressing room for some heated hanky-panky between takes.

She seemed to be trying to prove that Eddie really was the great passion of her life. Some even bought it.

Publicist Harold Salemson recalled, "[S]he was crazy about Eddie, who had a lot of influence over her. I could get her to do a lot of things if I went through him first. He'd go to Liz, and then she would do it. Otherwise she wouldn't." The English crew was shocked by her foul language, which she sometimes used as terms of endearment, sometimes in anger. Salemson continued, "Once I had to tell him to tell her to stop using such foul language on the set. It was making a terrible impression on the British crew. She was always hollering, 'Hey, shmuck,' 'Hey, asshole,' and making everyone uncomfortable. So I went to Eddie and asked him to get her to clean up her language, and it worked—for a while."

But to others, Eddie Fisher seemed more like an assistant than a husband. He fetched things for her, relayed messages, and sometimes during filming, he'd stay at the hotel with Elizabeth's children, singing and playing with them. As the relationship with his wife consumed him, Eddie was not blind to his position, writing in his memoir, "My real job was keeping Elizabeth happy. My own career was disappearing. My singing, which had once been the thing I lived for, was becoming more of a well-paid hobby."

The studio had already begun to send out press releases announcing that *Suddenly, Last Summer* would introduce the public to a new Elizabeth Taylor—stripped of glamour, no makeup, limp, tangled hair, and drab hospital clothes. But in her first scene, she informs Dr. Cukrowicz, "I want you to know I can look attractive . . . if I have my hair done." And then she asks if she can wear a pretty dress. The answer is yes. The doctor thinks it would be better for her mental health if she were to wear her own clothes. Soon Catherine has her hair freshly styled and is wearing full makeup and Paris dresses accessorized with a brooch and earrings. And so audiences were treated to an institutionalized Catherine who was as glamorous and beautiful as Elizabeth Taylor at any Hollywood function.

As Mankiewicz predicted, Monty became much more lucid and

capable when Elizabeth began work on the film, and he is at his finest in their first scene together. The chemistry between Monty and Elizabeth was still a powerful current—now more complicated and poignant—and this new chemistry transferred to their characters.

Their first scene together is where Dr. Cukrowicz silently observes Catherine as she interacts with a nun at St. Mary's, then makes his presence known and sets out to find out more about her, to assess the severity of her mental illness. They probe and spar and flirt, feeling each other out.

Cukrowicz: "*Insane* is such a meaningless word."

Catherine: "But *lobotomy* has a precise meaning, hasn't it?"

The doctor attempts to ascertain if she's unbalanced, as he's been led to believe. Catherine tries to see if he is someone who might be able to really help her. From the very moment they meet, her eyes search him out for help, and she clings to him for comfort, support, answers. But she is also sexually attracted to him. She throws herself at him, and as she looks to him as a possible savior, she also emanates a feeling of coddling him, wanting to protect him, too.

As the doctor, Monty has a look of genuine fondness for Catherine in his glazed eyes and goofy half smile—he is bemused, sympathetic, interested. It seems perfectly natural when she kisses him out of the blue. It's almost immediately obvious that these characters have a future together. Which better explains the doctor's trepidation in performing the lobotomy in exchange for Violet's million-dollar donation.

But Elizabeth never plays it in a way that you seriously think Catherine may be mentally ill. From this very first appearance in the film, Elizabeth conveys that Catherine is a sharp, healthy, sane young woman, who really has been unjustly locked away to shut her up. This does drain a certain degree of tension from the proceedings. From the very beginning she is angry, rather than fearful.

Tennessee Williams told *Life* magazine, "It stretched my credulity to believe such a 'hip' doll as our Liz wouldn't know at once in the film that she was 'being used for something evil.' "* Williams elaborated by saying, "I think Liz would have dragged Sebastian home by his ears, and so saved them both from considerable embarrassment that summer."

As the weeks went on, everything on the set became more strained. They would all talk about how the dark themes of the movie seemed to mirror, and add to, conflicts and unhappiness that they were feeling in their own lives—and that put a gloomy fog over the set.

The relationship between Elizabeth and Katharine Hepburn was decidedly chilly. When Elizabeth was a child, newly contracted to MGM, she approached Katharine Hepburn with her autograph book. Katharine signed it, but she was so cold and dismissive, Elizabeth never asked for another autograph in her life. That was a long time before, but Elizabeth held on to a few tiny seeds of hurt feelings and resentment.

On the other hand, Elizabeth was frequently late to filming, which would infuriate Hepburn. Unlike the way she dealt with Monty, Hepburn had no patience with Elizabeth—she grew enraged as she waited for the star. She perceived that Mankiewicz was lavishing more attention on Elizabeth and ignoring her. Katharine Hepburn was usually the focal point on a "Hepburn" film, and she felt threatened that this was turning into an "Elizabeth Taylor" movie.

No doubt some on-set gossip about Elizabeth having an affair with Mankiewicz had reached her and added to her chagrin. It seems difficult to believe that Elizabeth would start an adulterous affair so shortly after putting her career in jeopardy for Eddie. He himself didn't believe it. But a couple of years later, when Mankiewicz was directing Elizabeth in *Cleopatra* in Rome, a reporter asked him if he was having an affair with Elizabeth. "Fuck

---

*The posters for the movie would cry, "Suddenly, last summer, Cathy knew she was being used for something evil."

no," Mankiewicz shouted. "That was during our last picture." Considering *Suddenly, Last Summer* was the film they made before *Cleopatra*, this was virtually an admission to an affair.

For now, Elizabeth kept up a front of complete devotion to Eddie Fisher. But everyone on *Suddenly, Last Summer* was gloomy and concealed. It wasn't a friendly, jovial atmosphere on the set. Most of the time, the main players kept to themselves. "It was a strange arrangement on that film," Pat Marmont observed. "All three principles would go to their caravans and have their lunch, and the rest of us would have lunch in the canteen. It was two distinct camps, and they never mixed. The non-principals formed a little repertory company."

When overcome with depression in the middle of the night, knowing that he couldn't disturb Elizabeth, Monty would start drinking and would slip out of his hotel suite into the night. As in earlier times on other locations, reports of his nocturnal wanderings would reach the producer and director. Like the night he conked out at the fashionable Stork Club and was carried to the manager's office. When the staff couldn't wake Monty up, a doctor was called, but by the time he arrived, Monty was wide awake and ready to order another drink. Management wouldn't allow that and, instead, had two waiters carry him to a taxicab as he sang old sailor songs at the top of his lungs.

Of course, when Elizabeth was on the set, working with Monty, Mankiewicz wouldn't show his anger and instead would be exceptionally patient with Monty. After all, Monty was her best friend, and Elizabeth was the power player in the movie. But when she wasn't around, sometimes he would explode.

The experience of an obnoxious, infantile man eating off the floor in an upscale restaurant had left a bitter taste in his mouth. In addition, he couldn't forgive the amount of time he was wasting with Monty's antics. He was often at the end of his rope with Monty. When all his other tactics failed, he attempted to shout and threaten him into straightening out. "Mankiewicz bullied him," Gary Raymond recalled. Raymond felt that Monty was like a "battered baby." Years later, Sam Spiegel would say, "Mankiewicz is an excellent director, but devoid of a great many human considerations when it comes to weaker beings than himself."

Most of the cast and crew put up with a lot more from Monty than they would from most anyone else. They recognized he was a brilliant artist with a troubled soul. They made allowances. They looked the other way. Katharine Hepburn started inviting Monty to spend the weekends at her country house outside London. She was an old hand at drying out drunks, having seen Spencer Tracy through a number of productions. But nothing seemed to help Monty. "I think he was weak," Hepburn would surmise later. "Sympatico, but weak."

Mercedes McCambridge, who played Catherine's greedy, scatterbrained mother, would sometimes share Monty's car on the way to the set. McCambridge would never forget her impression of Monty: "[He was] milky-eyed, sweating from all his pores the sweetly-sickly odor of vodka, fetid and foul. He was haggard; the once-so-beautiful face scarred and hollowed into deep grooves where the stubble of his beard grew, already gray." En route to Shepperton Studios, they would pass a penitentiary named Wormwood Scrubs Prison. In the misty morning gloom, the establishment lived up to its name. "[A] hulk of gray stone hell," McCambridge called it.

Monty would make the driver stop the Rolls-Royce in front of the building, and through the closed window, he would scream out toward the locked fortress, scream to the "poor locked-in bastards, sons of bloody bitches." One of McCambridge's most vivid memories was of Monty calling out to the prisoners "feebly, drunkenly, this doped-up genius of a man." He wanted the inmates to know that he felt he belonged in there with them; many free men were just as guilty as they were, the criminals weren't always in prison, and the insane weren't always locked away.

"Monty had a cackle laugh," she recalled, "flat and cruel when he wanted it to be. As the driver pulled away from the ugly façade of Wormwood Scrubs, Monty's snide, giddy giggles would diminish until his head fell back against the elegant buff upholstery and he was back into heavy drugged sleep."

The men's prison became a private joke between Monty and McCambridge. Whenever the atmosphere on the set became too heavy or things went wrong or something was out of place (like when a pompous Laurence Harvey visited the set), Monty or McCambridge would call out, "Wormwood Scrubs," and they both would crack up. It put everything in perspective.

At other times she would observe Monty's suffering, his shoulders hunched with tension, sweat pouring out of him. He seemed lax—like a marionette with its strings cut. But his face was wild, and his eyes looked terrified. "I can remember mopping his brow several times, trying not to spoil his makeup," McCambridge recalled. She had battled alcoholism herself, and she understood some of the things that Monty was going through. Sometimes she would stand behind him and place her hands on his shoulders to comfort him with a show of support. "My heart ached for him," she said.

At times Elizabeth would forget her own troubles and focus on Monty. His physical decline distressed her, but she didn't dare be overly solicitous with him—it would only draw attention to his torment and make him more self-conscious. Elizabeth was absolutely right; he didn't want any attention brought to himself. He hated to be asked if he was okay. If anyone approached him and expressed concern, Monty would simply walk away, mumbling, "I'm fine. Fantastic." He wanted them to ignore his tics and tremors—as he ignored them. But sometimes in Elizabeth's dressing room, he would collapse and cry in her arms, until he would distract himself by telling her some funny anecdote.

One day when Monty seemed to be having a particularly hard time, McCambridge approached Elizabeth. "Is there anything you can do for him?" she asked.

"I don't know," Elizabeth replied sadly. "I tried to get through to him. I just can't."

31

THE FLASHBACK SCENE

Suddenly, Last Summer *was the most difficult, most com-plex picture I've ever worked on. It certainly was no musical. Katharine Hepburn, Monty Clift—in fact, everyone—had to concentrate to make it what it was. It is a startling theme, but even the idea of cannibalism is presented, I think, beautifully and artistically.*
—**Elizabeth Taylor**

*T*HE RUMORS OF ON-SET JEALOUSIES, RIVALRIES, FIGHTS, DELAYS, AND troubles began appearing in the papers. It distressed Monty; the last thing he needed was more bad press. He called Elizabeth from his hotel room, wondering if there was anything they could do to squelch the stories.

The accounts of friction on the set were so rampant in Holly-wood that, rather than deny them, they cooked up a scheme to make fun of the gossip and therefore make it seem ridiculous. They had the four main players of the production pose for a photo in which they mocked the rumors. In the foreground of the picture, Katharine Hepburn, with a fiendish grin, looks as if she is about to smack Elizabeth, who stands there with her hands up in mock terror; while in the background, Mankiewicz and Monty are at each other's throats. How could such good-humored artists be at odds with each other? the photograph seemed to ask.

* * *

The use of visual flashbacks was the biggest change in the adaptation of the play into the film—these vignettes would depict the killing of Sebastian, which accompanies Catherine's final monologue. Concluding that the majority of people don't enjoy "talky" movies and wouldn't want to see a twelve-page monologue recited on the screen, Vidal and Mankiewicz decided on the "show, don't tell" theory for the film, incorporating explanatory dreamlike flashbacks, which were filmed in Spain. Mankiewicz incorporated these scenes in a way that would reveal what happened to Sebastian, as witnessed by Catherine.

Sebastian is not a sympathetic character. He uses people to get what he wants; he is a sexual predator and probably a pedophile. Williams felt that no actor could properly portray Sebastian and that not showing him would only add to his mystery and make his presence more strongly felt. Mankiewicz agreed, and so Spanish actor Julián Ugarte was hired to play Sebastian, but he was always shot with his back to the camera, so the audience sees him only from a distance and always from behind in hazy flashbacks.[*]

In contrast, Elizabeth would be featured heavily in the backstory scenes, and the flashbacks resulted in one of the great iconic images of her career—kneeling on the beach in a white one-piece bathing suit. The scene was to be used in one of the sequences that would solve the mystery of what exactly happened last summer.

Sebastian forces Catherine to wear the bathing suit in order to catch the eye of the poor young boys who live on the beach. He drags the reluctant Catherine into the water while the boys gawk at her sexual desirability. She describes the bathing suit as "a scandal to the jaybirds," because the white material became transparent when wet. "I came out looking naked," she cries. Which accomplishes cousin Sebastian's goal of attracting the beach boys to her, so he can meet and get to know them for himself.

The bathing suit worn by Elizabeth Taylor "should not be trans-

---

[*]In some production stills from the filming, Julián Ugarte as Sebastian looks handsome and gaunt, with more than a passing resemblance to Montgomery Clift.

parent," the Production Code had warned in its appraisal of the script. "Furthermore, the children (the young boys on the beach) could not be naked." Ultimately, the suit was a tight white one-piece with a plunging neckline and a "keyhole" cutout beneath the breasts. The scene was filmed in Begur, a resort town in Spain, on the coastline of the Costa Brava. Elizabeth looked voluptuous and ravishing, but the locals—used to tall, lean ladies in bikinis—scoffed at Elizabeth's curves. "Elizabeth's face is her fortune," someone remarked. "Her body belongs to someone else."

The last two days of shooting were to be devoted to Elizabeth's twelve-page monologue, in front of the entire cast. She and the other family members gather on the Venables' garden patio, and she narrates at last exactly what she had witnessed in Cabeza de Lobo the previous summer—how the young boys that Sebastian had used and discarded all summer had taken their revenge by chasing him down and devouring his body. This monologue would share the screen with the impressionistic flashback images already shot. As in their first movie together, Monty helped Elizabeth with this long speech, rehearsing with her for several days before the actual shooting of it. It's filled with hesitations, pauses, stutters.

To begin with, the doctor has given Catherine a sedative to relax her and bring down the walls that she has built to block off the memory of what she had witnessed. The drug (which she calls a "truth serum") opens the floodgate, and she describes how her cousin Sebastian was attacked and killed by the young boys he had seduced that summer.

In the screenplay, Tennessee Williams and Gore Vidal have Catherine often repeat the film's title:

"Suddenly, last summer he wasn't young anymore."

"Suddenly, last summer, he became restless . . ."

"Suddenly, last summer Cousin Sebastian changed to the afternoons and the beach."

As she listens, Mrs. Venable clutches Sebastian's empty journal. Catherine describes how he became restless, older, sicker, and he took Catherine to Cabeza de Lobo to stalk the beaches for erotic encounters, which is where he forces her to wear the immodest white bathing suit in order to attract the young boys. It is all in an attempt to alleviate his agitation and loneliness.

At the start of the second day of shooting, Elizabeth was in a near state of hysteria. This was the climax of the movie, where Catherine would scream in unison with the memory of her cousin Sebastian and would describe how he was overtaken and cannibalized by the boys. Mankiewicz called this portion of the monologue "an aria from a tragic opera of madness and death."

There would be no flashback images with this part of the speech. The camera would focus on her as she walks past the entire cast (who are listening in horror and fascination) and then falls to her knees, sobbing. Mankiewicz had Elizabeth do the scene five times from different angles, but by a midday break he still hadn't gotten exactly what he wanted from her. Doing it over and over left her exhausted and emotionally drained.

"It tore Elizabeth's guts out," was how the director described it. A few minutes into the break, his assistant director approached him and said, "Joe, look at this." Mankiewicz followed the assistant to a secluded spot behind some scenery. Elizabeth was lying flat out on the floor. "I thought at first she had fallen and hurt herself. Then I heard her sobbing."

Since it was nearly five o'clock, Mankiewicz decided to call it quits and extend production another day. "Okay, everyone," he shouted. "Fresh start in the morning."

Suddenly Elizabeth appeared. "Fresh start, my ass," she bellowed. The emotions were with her in the here and now, and she intended on using them.

She marched back onto the set, and they once more began the scene where Catherine, screaming and sobbing in a fevered crescendo, calls up the memory that she had buried deep in her subconscious. "He . . . he was lying naked on the broken stones. And this you won't believe! Nobody, nobody, nobody could believe it . . . ," she sobbed. And then she screeched the reveal. "It looked as if . . . as if they had devoured him!"

Never a method actress, now Elizabeth used her grief over

Mike Todd's gruesome death to demonstrate Catherine in extremis. It is interesting to note that as she called up tragedies from her own past experiences to add shading to her characterization, Monty was also on the set, acting with her. At the end of the scene, she had to remember, "There wasn't a sound anymore. There was nothing but Sebastian . . . Sebastian lying on those stones, torn and crushed." Just as she had cradled the crushed and torn head of her best friend on a dusty, silent road three years before.

When the director called "cut" for the last time in the early evening, Elizabeth lay crumpled on the set. She could not stop crying—the crew was cheering, while simultaneously wiping tears from their eyes. Mankiewicz was already predicting she would win an Oscar, which was something Elizabeth had recently stated was one of her goals. She was still weeping as Eddie Fisher led her off the set, with her head buried in his shoulder—and she continued crying through the night at the hotel. She had been holding a lot in for a long time.

When Truman Capote saw it, he said that Elizabeth's final dramatic monologue was "the best scene she ever performed before and likely again. She should win the Oscar." Tennessee Williams still believed she was miscast as Catherine, but when her monologue was screened for him, he was impressed and went on to proclaim that her performance was a "triumph of miscasting."

One person who was not happy with that final scene was Katharine Hepburn. When she viewed the rushes, she was furious with the way Mankiewicz had had her photographed. To make Violet appear more devastated by the story of her son's death, Mankiewicz had Hepburn filmed without a filter on the camera.

"I wanted her suddenly to look old," Mankiewicz explained. "In other words, the destruction about the legend of Sebastian, her son, destroyed her illusion of youth." Harsh reality showed freckles and lines on Hepburn's face and age spots on veiny hands. She particularly disliked showing her neck. Her appearance was especially unflattering since the shots would be contrasted with Elizabeth's flawless youthful beauty in extreme close-up.

After listening to the horrific tale—even though it is obviously the truth—the aged Violet is unable to accept it. She has gone mad—and in her madness she perversely mistakes Dr. Cukrowicz for her dead son. In spite of Hepburn's objections, it's a powerful moment. The truth of her son's grotesque death now out in the open, Violet retreats into a fantasy. Mankiewicz focuses on Violet's aged hands caressing the empty pages of Sebastian's journal.

Hepburn was angry about other things besides the unflattering shots. Like the way Mankiewicz had treated Monty, and how he favored Elizabeth over her. After the scene was screened, she approached the director and asked him if she had finished her duties on the movie.

Mankiewicz said that she was wrapped. There was no more work for her to be done.

"Are you sure?" she asked.

"Quite sure."

"I just want to leave you with this," she said. And then she spit in his face. Then she marched over to the office of the producer, Sam Spiegel, and spat at him, too.

For days after she filmed the last scene in the movie, Elizabeth was wracked with anxiety and tension. It was during this time that she privately confessed to Monty that her marriage was already in serious trouble. Her connection with him was still like with no one else—not even the men she was sleeping with. She clung to Monty, wanting to be stroked and comforted. Weeping, she told him, "My despair is so black, I can't face waking up in the morning." The whole thing had been a mistake, she said. In marrying Mike Todd's best friend, she confessed, "I thought I could keep Mike's memory alive this way. But I have only his ghost."

And she felt she had been forced into the marriage because of the public hostility against her. Within weeks of their union, she had figured out the strongest bond between her and Eddie was the dead man who had been her husband and his best friend. "My life is a goddamn shambles," she cried. "I made a horrible mistake in marrying Eddie . . . I don't love him. Sometimes I can't even stand him." But she couldn't face a divorce. It would tear her apart. Later, after more consideration, she would state, "I didn't love Eddie, and it wasn't I who needed him. I married him because he needed me."

That was her private life. In her professional life Elizabeth was flying. While she was toiling away at *Suddenly, Last Summer* on the gloomy closed set at Shepperton Studios, unhappily married to Eddie Fisher, two major high-profile movies were taking shape for her in Hollywood. One was *BUtterfield 8*, her last contracted film for MGM. The other was an offer from 20th Century Fox for her to play the most legendary seductress of all time, Cleopatra. That would be the film that would prove to be a turning point in her career and would introduce her to the true love of her life.

As the movie neared its release date, Sam Spiegel worried about how to advertise it. He wasn't completely sure how much the controversial subject matter would affect ticket sales. In addition, the movie was low on action and heavy with dialogue. The solution, of course, was Elizabeth Taylor. The idea was to sell the star, and the publicity department created a poster featuring ravishing Elizabeth kneeling in the sand on the beach, wearing the racy white swimsuit, her tan skin in delicious contrast to the white suit.

"Suddenly Last Summer Cathy knew she was being used for something evil!" the copy on the provocative poster teased. The bait that Sebastian used to lure in the boys for "evil" would be the same bait that the producers used to attract audiences to movie theaters.

Critics were divided as to whether Elizabeth nailed the tricky role of Catherine, who is basically sane but sometimes teeters on the brink of madness. Some thought she overacted at times. Like Bosley Crowther, who wrote, "Elizabeth Taylor is rightly roiled as the niece, but her wallow in agony at the climax is sheer histrionic showing off." *Esquire* openly mocked her by stating, "[Mankiewicz] can score one directorial triumph: he has somehow extracted from Elizabeth Taylor a mediocre performance, which is a definite step up in her dramatic career."

Others thought she brought the many shadings that the char-

acter needed. All agreed that she possessed an explosive combination of beauty and charisma that was nearly impossible to take
your eyes off. "If there were ever any doubts about the ability of
Miss Taylor to express complex and devious emotions, to deliver a
flexible and deep performance, this film ought to remove them,"
the *New York Herald Tribune* stated.

John L. Scott of the *Los Angeles Times* called the movie "an ab-
sorbing, in part, shocking motion picture," in which Hepburn
and Taylor "pull out all the histrionic stops, resulting in performances that will undoubtedly bring plenty of votes come Oscar-
nominating time." (He was correct.)

In spite of Mankiewicz's initial misgivings, Monty is very good
as the sympathetic doctor. Next to the characters of the monstrous mother and the traumatized cousin, the Dr. Cukrowicz role
is relatively thankless. "Clift is little more than straight man to the
two ladies," *Variety* rather wryly observed. His main function in
the piece is to ask questions and react. It is a testament to Monty's
inherent star quality that he makes his character memorable—his
Dr. Cukrowicz is almost necessary to making the film work. He
uses expressive hand gestures to add emphasis to his delivery of
uncomplicated lines. Monty's traumatic history works for him
here. His former beauty peeks through his tired, careworn face,
and his glazed eyes give the sense of a slightly twisted professional
who has seen the dark side of human behavior and is now un-
shockable.

Monty's hidden sexuality and tragic decline would also add another layer to the twisted yet compelling tale. In a way, he mirrored Sebastian Venable: he is talented, sensitive, attractive, but
in the end is devoured by his own demons. The script accentuated the similarities. "Such extraordinary eyes—so like his," notes
Sebastian's devoted mother, Violet, while she is looking at the
doctor.

A number of critics did hint that Monty's lifestyle was creeping
into his characterization. Paul V. Beckley opined in the *New York
Herald Tribune*, "Despite his soft, sympathetic eyes, Clift does not
strike me as a chap I'd want fiddling with my tonsils, let alone cut-

ting a fantail into my skull." And in the *New York Times* Bosley Crowther observed, "Montgomery Clift seems wracked with pain and indifference." *Esquire* lamented that he was "sincere, woebegone and inexpressive, as usual."

Many critics clutched their pearls and decried the perversities in the story and fell over themselves to express how shocked and appalled they were. "I loathe this film. I say so bluntly. To my mind it is a decadent piece of work, sensational, barbarous, and ridiculous," fumed C. A. Lejeune in the *Observer*.

Screenwriter Gore Vidal credited the film's more scathing reviews for boosting the box office. The descriptions of the complex, decadent themes usually forbidden in the 1950s whetted audiences' appetites. Moviegoers wanted to know just what happened last summer that so thoroughly disturbed reviewers, and they turned up in droves to witness just how perverse the perversities could get.

Elizabeth's instincts were 100 percent correct. *Suddenly, Last Summer* proved to be a huge box office hit, one of the top attractions of the year, earning over twelve million dollars worldwide. It catapulted Elizabeth to the list of the top box office attractions in Hollywood and made her the highest paid star in the world. It was also the last smash hit that Montgomery Clift appeared in.

32

TWO DIFFERENT PATHS

The closer we come to the negative, to death, the more we blossom.
—**Montgomery Clift**

If someone's dumb enough to offer me a million dollars to make a picture, I'm certainly not dumb enough to turn it down.
—**Elizabeth Taylor**

WITH THE COMPLETION OF *SUDDENLY, LAST SUMMER*, ELIZABETH'S and Monty's lives would go in opposite directions. It wasn't that they felt less close to each other—by now their connection couldn't be broken—but for the next several years, movie work and personal dramas would keep them both busy and mostly apart. Both started off the decade by playing legendary figures in history. He, Sigmund Freud. She, Cleopatra.

Elizabeth, in particular, was entering into what would turn out to be the busiest and most exciting decade of her life, both professionally and personally. With only one more film to complete on her MGM contract, as a free agent Elizabeth would go on to have the kind of power that Monty had at the beginning of his movie career—and then she would surpass even that. Not only would she be able to choose the projects she wanted and the directors she would work with, but she could also dictate who her costars would be and where the movie would be shot. As it turned out, 20th Century Fox wanted to add her to their list of big box office names and thought that *Cleopatra* would be the ideal vehicle for her.

Before Fox thought of Elizabeth as the lead, *Cleopatra* started as a very different project. Originally, it was to be a moderately budgeted picture that was to be made on the back lot and was to star the alluring Joan Collins, who had a contract with the studio, in the hopes that a sexy costume drama with the green-eyed siren would turn a quick profit. Collins became disgusted, however, when a studio executive guaranteed her the role if she would "be nice" to him.

Fox was in financial distress, and they needed to bring in a quick profit. When producer Walter Wanger became involved, he convinced the studio heads that the picture could be a blockbuster and persuaded them to raise the budget from two million to five million dollars. As the studio heads got more excited, Wanger's thoughts turned to Elizabeth Taylor. If he could get her, they would put more money into the production and turn it into a lavish epic. At first, she had no desire to appear in the movie.

When Wanger contacted Elizabeth at her London hotel during the making of *Suddenly, Last Summer*, Eddie Fisher picked up the phone. The producer made his pitch to have Elizabeth play the Egyptian queen in *Cleopatra*. When Eddie covered the mouthpiece on the phone and relayed the message to Elizabeth, she scoffed at the idea. "Tell him I'll do it for a million dollars," she said sarcastically. Eddie got back on the line and repeated Elizabeth's offer. The couple couldn't be more shocked when the answer came back "yes." Fox would be willing to pay Elizabeth a million dollars, at the time the highest salary ever given to an actor, to play the dark seductress. Then, feeling her power as the first million-dollar star, she stipulated that the film be made outside the United States (for tax purposes.) To please their glamorous new star, the studio agreed.

Unfortunately, she had one more film to do under the kind of "slave contract" she'd been working under since she was a child. Elizabeth was furious. Adding to her rage was that MGM had chosen *BUtterfield 8* as the last film she was obliged to make for them.

The screenplay was based on a novel by John O'Hara about a

Manhattan model/call girl. Elizabeth said she resented the part because the character was nothing more than a call girl, but more to the point was the fact that the million-dollar salary waiting for her at Fox had to be put on hold until she finished this picture for MGM. Actually, it's never been made quite clear exactly what her character, Gloria Wandrous, does. To get her services, you have to call BUtterfield 8. It's a basic story of a man married to a blond good girl who falls in love with a dark bad girl, and through love the bad girl finds redemption and then death.

On September 25, at 209 East Sixty-first Street in Manhattan, billows of thick black smoke could be seen rising out of Monty's townhouse. Libby Holman, who was walking by to her own apartment on that street, rushed over to the crowd of onlookers to see that firemen were already there working on the fire. Monty had already been evacuated. Firemen had broken into the top-floor bedroom to find Monty and Claude in bed, completely oblivious to the fire. The firefighters had led Monty and Claude to the roof of the building and then to an adjoining roof and safety.

One newspaper headline the next day reported MONTGOMERY CLIFT LED TO SAFETY FROM FIRE. The accompanying article stated that actor Montgomery Clift and "an unidentified male friend were escorted out safely by firemen." The article went on to explain that "[s]moke and flames prevent Clift and his friend from getting to the street." The official story that was printed was that the building's lobby was being painted and workers had left inflammable material, which had ignited and caused the fire.

Salacious gossip, not in the papers, spread that Monty had been having a cocaine party with Claude and some hustlers when the fire broke out. Another rumor was that Monty had fallen asleep with a lit cigarette—he had started fires that way before but had always woken up in time to snuff them out before the flames spread.

Whatever the reason for the fire, the surrounding news did Monty no good, adding to his already badly tarnished image. He was already widely considered a high-risk actor, and the story sim-

ply proved his recklessness. The surrounding gossip only confirmed his homosexuality in executives' eyes and underlined his
dangerous substance abuse.

It was another step down the ladder of Monty's reputation.
Friends who had tried to remember the young prince he once
was started to see him as a hopeless cause and distanced themselves from him. Even the ever-loyal Libby was moving away. She
was looking for stability now and had started a relationship with a
straight man her own age, who would not allow her to fraternize
with her gay circle. A few months after the fire, Monty was forced
to move—the damage to the building was too extensive. He
bought a brownstone at 217 East Sixty-first. The new place was an
upgrade—a four-story building with seven rooms, six fireplaces,
six baths, and a huge garden. He lived there until he died.

33

MARILYN

Monty and Marilyn were psychic twins. They recognized disaster in each other's faces and giggled about it. Marilyn herself described him as "the only person I know who is in worse shape than I am."
—**Frank Taylor**

Marilyn Monroe seemed to have a kind of unconscious glow about her physical self that was innocent, like a child. When she posed nude, it was, "Gee, I am kind of, you know, sort of dishy," like she enjoyed it without being egotistical.
—**Elizabeth Taylor**

MONTY WAS NO LONGER A HOLLYWOOD GOLDEN BOY, AND BE-cause of the trouble he had caused on previous productions, his career was now considered a series of second chances (third and fourth). It was close friendships with people that respected his talent that would secure Monty's next two jobs.

The first was *Wild River*, directed by Elia Kazan, who had directed young Monty on Broadway in *The Skin of Our Teeth*. Kazan originally wanted Marlon Brando, but when he refused the part, Kazan offered it to Monty, under the condition that he promise not to touch a drop of alcohol during the production. Excited by the prospect of working with Kazan again, and eager for a chance to redeem himself, Monty agreed. His costar would be Lee Remick. Monty would play a government official sent to a flood-ravaged Tennessee town to order the residents to relocate so that a dam could be built.

Monty lived up to his part of the bargain and remained sober throughout filming, until the very last day of production, when he showed up dead drunk. The director forgave him. "Congratulations, Monty," Kazan said. "Up to now you've done fine. Now lie down." Unfortunately, in spite of the good reviews for Monty, audiences greeted *Wild River* with complete apathy, and it did nothing to boost his box office appeal.

It was Monty's friendship with Arthur Miller and Marilyn Monroe, and their high regard for his talent, that got him cast as Perce, the battered rodeo cowboy, in *The Misfits*. Arthur Miller's script revolves around three aging cowboys in the Nevada desert, each of whom are attracted to a sensitive (if not neurotic) divorcée, to be played by Marilyn. It was the most talked about script of the year for the cast alone: Clark Gable opposite Marilyn Monroe in a role meant to be her big dramatic debut in films, written expressly for her by her Pulitzer Prize–winning husband. Monty would be third billed, although he had less screen time than Eli Wallach. His character, Perce, a lonely drifting rodeo cowboy, was the most fully realized character in Miller's turgid screenplay.

Shooting took place in the blazing hot Nevada desert, and the media was allowed to swarm the set. Magnum Photos had exclusive photographic rights, and a small army of their photographers was sent there to cover the shooting.

Monty surprised everyone by being the polar opposite of his recent image. On the set he appeared sober, punctual, and line-perfect—he had memorized the entire script before shooting began. In reality, he was drinking, but he kept it in moderation, and perhaps because all eyes were on Marilyn, nobody seemed to notice. His introductory scene in the movie is among the greatest of his career—a full page of dialogue, in which the vulnerable cowboy Perce calls his mother on the phone while the rest of the cast, sitting in a car, looks on. Monty described the shot as an "audition in front of the gods and goddesses of the performing arts." The scene was shot in an actual stifling phone booth on the side of the road, and Monty played the entire scene straight through, in one take. "It was scheduled for two days," Monty said. "We shot it in two hours." (When director John Huston yelled cut, the cast and crew burst out in applause.)

"Shall we do it again?" Monty asked.

"No," replied Huston. "It's never going to be better than that."

It was Marilyn Monroe who caused great irritation on *The Misfits* set. She was addicted to sleeping pills and was constantly holding up production. The brutal desert heat, the disintegration of Marilyn and Miller's marriage, and her drug addiction made for a cocktail of misery on the set. She was often late, sometimes not showing up for hours, even days at a time, and the production crawled forward at a snail's pace.

Miller's main concern was finishing the picture, so he tried to appear stoic, presenting himself as the humiliated but supportive husband who was unwaveringly devoted to Marilyn. But it soon became clear to the entire cast and crew that the marriage was in serious trouble. The set soon divided into two camps, one of them sympathetic to Marilyn, the other hostile toward her. Gable and Monty tried to stay above the fray and not take sides. In actuality, Monty was in Marilyn's camp.

The two troubled stars had become close in recent years. Their apartments were several blocks away from each other in Manhattan, and the two would socialize, seeing plays or having quiet dinners together. Also, they were both lifelong insomniacs and became "phone buddies," calling each other in the middle of the night. "Monty and Marilyn were psychic twins," the film's producer, Frank Taylor, said. "They were on the same wavelength. They recognized disaster in each other's faces and giggled about it."

Assistant producer Edward Parone observed, "In between takes Marilyn would wander over to Monty. She'd rest her head on his shoulder or he would rub her back—they'd whisper to each other. Marilyn would ruffle his hair. She didn't often seem happy on the set, but Monty could always make her laugh. I remember one time Marilyn was very late and the crew was studiously ignoring her. She went over to Monty, whose back was to her, and asked how he was doing. He whipped around with a big grin. 'Are you talking to me, darling? I'm fine! How are you, little brat!' They got the giggles. I remember another time they were sitting there talking about the way they'd like to die. Monty said, 'Coming off-stage after giving a marvelous performance in *Hamlet* would be a gorgeous way to go.' "

Once, when Monty was walking behind Marilyn, he playfully grabbed her bottom, and she turned around and gave him a radiant smile. For years after, Monty would come alive when telling that little anecdote to friends.

At one point the production was shut down when Marilyn was sent to a hospital to detox. For a time, there was a genuine concern that the movie would be shut down for good and she'd never work again. After a week, however, she returned to the set, fragile and run down but eager to finish the film.

The first scene to be shot was with Monty. Marilyn was playing Roslyn, a lonely, recently divorced woman who is sympathetic to Perce, who had been "kicked by a bull" earlier at a rodeo. After drinking and dancing at the bar, these two lost souls, drunk and weary, stumble out to the back alley. Monty places his head in Marilyn's lap and spills out the sad story of his life—being physically broken by his life as a rodeo cowboy and emotionally broken by his family, friends, and lovers. It is a well-written scene, and it was beautifully acted, although it is extraneous to the movie. It works as a scene alone because it is two vulnerable artists playing isolated characters—both hurting, yearning, and searching.

As it turned out, the scene had the sparks of greatness and genius and sensitivity that the whole film needed. After shooting this scene, Huston decided that he wanted to pair Marilyn Monroe and Montgomery Clift in his next film, *Freud*, with Clift playing the legendary psychiatrist and Marilyn as his patient Cecily. In spite of all the trouble on *The Misfits* set, he offered them both the roles. Only Monty would accept.

Back in Los Angeles for the last days of shooting, Monty showed up very drunk for dinner with Marilyn at the Beachcomber. At the restaurant he removed his shoes and socks and insisted on feeding her fried shrimp and rumaki with his feet, dipping the hors d'oeuvres in the sauces. Of course, Marilyn was no stranger to bombed behavior, and she would never embarrass him. Monty always treated Marilyn very gently, and she was always so sweet with him. "She even ate it," Jack Larson said with a smile. When together, they were like two babies, taking turns at trying very hard to act like a parent in order to protect the other. This time it had been Marilyn's turn. "He's the only person I know in worse shape than I am," Marilyn would say.

Elizabeth knew about the closeness between Marilyn and Monty, but although she was jealous of the relationship, she never brought it up to him. But she must have cringed when she read Monty's quote about Marilyn: "I would rather work with her than any other actress. I adore her." The two movie goddesses were built up as rivals in the media, but in actuality their images—both publicly and on the screen—couldn't be further apart.

Elizabeth had become acquainted with Marilyn in Las Vegas in 1961, when Frank Sinatra threw a birthday celebration and gave a special performance for Dean Martin at the Sands Hotel. Marilyn was there as Sinatra's date, and she sat ringside with Elizabeth and Eddie at Sinatra's performance. At one point they talked about show business. Jeanne Martin recalled Marilyn joking, "I guess it just wasn't my destiny to play an ingenue."

In Marilyn's last miserable months, when she was fired from her current film, *Something's Got to Give,* by the studio, and trapped in a web of despair over her encroaching age and broken love affairs, Elizabeth called her and offered help. Elizabeth was riding high with the power that her million-dollar salary gave her. "If there is anything you need—anything at all—call me and you will have it within twenty-four hours," she told Marilyn. Elizabeth recognized the pain the media was causing Marilyn, and her heart went out to her sister in celluloid.

* * *

The Misfits, talky and slow, was a box office disappointment, considering all the attention and hoopla surrounding it. Marilyn and Monty attended the premiere together in the winter of 1961, and although they posed for photos in front of the theater before the start, they both rushed out as soon as the screening was over, heads down, did not stop to chat or pose for reporters, and did not attend the after-party.

One of the things that Monty had always said was that he didn't care about the size of a role or the amount of the paycheck; it was the character that was most important to him. After *The Misfits*, Stanley Kramer offered him a supporting role in *Judgment at Nuremberg* as a Jewish man who had been sterilized by the Nazis. "I went to see him in New York," Kramer recalled. "He looked absolutely brutal. I mean, he looked terrible. He looked as though he had one foot in the grave. This beautiful leading man had come to this. He was perfect for the part."

Because the role was small, the producers could not pay Monty his current salary demand per movie. Monty loved the role. "God, I start crying thinking about it," he said, crying. He waived his fee and agreed to do the role for minimal compensation. In character for Monty, he asked that the part be made even smaller to increase its impact. Initially, there was a scene where his character is asked if he would testify about being castrated, but Monty felt it would be much more powerful if he appeared as a surprise witness. No one would have believed someone was actually sterilized by the Nazis until he appeared. Eventually, Kramer agreed. Monty made it a condition on whether or not he would do the part—and the first scene was edited out.

In the movie, Monty has one scene in which he is the haunted victim testifying on the witness stand about being sterilized by the Nazis by force. It had to be done in long takes while the camera circled around him, with the illustrious cast watching. Spencer Tracy is the judge, and Richard Widmark and Maximilian Schell are opposing attorneys. Monty was rattled during the scene and was shaking and sweating, as the character but as himself, too.

For years it's been insinuated that Monty was actually falling apart, that the performance was improvised, and that Spencer Tracy and Kramer suggested he ad-lib—this would add to the character's confusion. Yet Monty's script shows that his performance, even considering the editing done on it, is remarkably close to the script, including his own revisions to it. "Since that day I am half of what I have ever been!" he shouts in his croaky voice during the scene. The cast looks genuinely moved. "He wasn't always close to the script, but whatever he said fitted in perfectly, and he came through with as good a performance as I had hoped," Stanley Kramer remarked. Yet the notes Monty made on his script show that he had carefully worked out the nuances of his performance beforehand.

"I think his performances pleased him once he wasn't so extraordinarily handsome anymore," Jack Larson said. His friend Lorenzo James agreed. "You have to have experience with life in order to give a performance like that," he stated.

The result of Monty's work is a shattering performance. At a screening of the movie, Nancy Walker was walked out of the theater immediately after Monty's one scene as she was so moved by it. "Let's get cheesecake," she suggested to her husband. "Nobody's topping that." The critics agreed, and for his performance, Monty was nominated for his fourth Academy Award, this time in the Best Supporting Actor category. Again, he did not win the Oscar, this time losing out to George Chakiris for *West Side Story*. It would be Monty's last nomination.

34

CLEOPATRA IN LONDON

*Cleopatra was conceived in emergency, shot in hysteria, and
wound up in blind panic.*
—Joseph L. Mankiewicz

*O*THER THAN ELIZABETH'S ENORMOUS SALARY, NOTHING SEEMED
too unusual about the start of filming of the big-budget motion
picture *Cleopatra* in England at the end of September 1960. To direct, the studio had chosen Rouben Mamoulian, who had done
so well with Greta Garbo in *Queen Christina* and with Tyrone
Power and Rita Hayworth in *Blood and Sand.* The sets re-creating
ancient Alexandria—palaces, statues, and temples—had been
built across eight acres in Pinewood Studios at a cost of six hundred thousand dollars. Peter Finch was cast as Julius Caesar, and
Stephen Boyd would portray Mark Antony.

For the first few weeks of filming, Elizabeth called out sick with
a cold and fever. But this was typical Elizabeth; scheduling in
extra time for illnesses seemed par for the course with her. By
now various ailments were part of her image, from frequent colds
and viruses to her serious back problems. The London weather
was damp and chilly. A lot of *Cleopatra* was to be filmed outdoors,
and it wouldn't be worth the risk to have her work a few days, only
to have her symptoms worsen.

Nursing her at their suite at the Dorchester Hotel was Eddie

Fisher. With his career stalled, his main job now was to be at Elizabeth's side and assist in keeping her functioning. Weeks passed, and Elizabeth was still running a fever. She was never well enough to shoot anything other than costume tests. For a couple of days, she was carried to the set, she did a few tests, and then she was rushed home. Dr. Kennamer was once again summoned from Beverly Hills to attend to Elizabeth in England.

The focus of the film, of course, was on Elizabeth as Cleopatra. There was very little Mamoulian could shoot without her. While the production waited for her, enormous sums of money kept bleeding out of the failing studio, which was desperate to get the film finished in order to save itself. Hundreds of extras sat around waiting on the enormous sets. Palm tree fronds were steadily flown to England—to be added to the imported trees around the set, in an attempt to make frosty London look like ancient Egypt—only to die and be replaced by more tree fronds. The production was losing a hundred thousand dollars a day.

At last the root of her illness was determined to be an abscessed tooth, which was removed, and producers were told Elizabeth would be ready for shooting in a few days. A few days later, however, Elizabeth was carried out of the Dorchester Hotel on a stretcher, moaning and clutching her head. Her fever had returned. She was diagnosed with inflammation of the spinal cord and brain. Her symptoms mirrored meningitis. There was nothing left to film without Elizabeth. The studio had no choice. They told her to take a month off to recuperate. By the end of November, Mamoulian had to shut the production down. It remained shut down until January 3, 1961. In the meantime, the script, which none of the actors were satisfied with, would be rewritten.

In January 1961, Elizabeth returned to the set, well enough to start work. Almost immediately, new problems cropped up. Both Elizabeth and Peter Finch still found the script appalling, calling it "unactable." Mamoulian liked the script and, fed up with the continuing problems, threatened to walk out. It was a bluff to get his way, and it backfired on the director.

"Let him walk out," Elizabeth instructed the Fox heads. That's

what they did. They called and accepted Mamoulian's resigna-
tion. To his surprise, after his many months of work and after
spending millions of dollars, Mamoulian was off the film. Exercis-
ing her director's approval clause, Elizabeth announced there
were only two directors she'd be willing to work with, interestingly
both from movies she had made with Monty: George Stevens and
Joseph Mankiewicz.

With seven million dollars already spent, more than the entire
budget of the film, only ten minutes of usable film had been
shot—none of it featuring Elizabeth. *Cleopatra* had started out as a
disaster. The production continued to hemorrhage money at an
alarming rate, so Fox inexplicably thought the best thing to do
was to throw more money at it. Making a deal that would bring
him several million dollars, Mankiewicz accepted an offer to
rewrite and direct *Cleopatra.*

By the time he arrived in England to take up the production,
Elizabeth was again sick in bed, this time with the Asian flu. Production on *Cleopatra* was once again on hold. Things became
much more serious for her when the flu worsened to pneumonia.
She was still being attended to in her room by Eddie and a full-
time nurse when she slipped into a coma. The nurse called the
front desk for help. In a lucky break, a lifesaving break, the
Dorchester was hosting a party at which one of the guests was a
prominent physician. He rushed to her room and began working
on her until the ambulance arrived.

At the hospital Elizabeth slipped in and out of consciousness.
"I was pronounced dead four times," she'd recall. "Once I didn't
breathe for five minutes, which must be a record." Some reports
leaked out that Elizabeth Taylor had died. Then the news was cor-
rected: the star was near death. The world held its breath. Doctors continued working on her—later she would recall an
out-of-body experience in which she floated above the room and
watched them trying to revive her. She had to be given an emergency tracheotomy so she could breathe. When recalling those

moments, she would say, "I went to that tunnel, saw the white light, and Mike [Todd]. I said, 'Oh, Mike, you're where I want to be.' And he said, 'No, baby. You have to turn around and go back, because there is something very important for you to do. You cannot give up now.'" Suddenly, she jolted back to life.

After her near-death experience, Elizabeth was sent back to the United States to recover once more. Her near fatal illness again reversed the public's opinion of her ever-changing image. The star had stopped breathing and had been given a tracheotomy. She had almost died. The woman had suffered enough, they concluded.

Resting in California, she felt well enough to attend the Academy Award ceremonies, where, to everyone's surprise, she won the award for Best Actress for *BUtterfield 8*, a movie she hated and a role she loathed. Insiders agreed that it was a sympathy award. Or a "We love you again" award. Shirley MacLaine, nominated for *The Apartment*, sarcastically stated, "I lost to a tracheotomy."

Even after she received the Oscar, the insurance companies, considering all the costly delays and Elizabeth's still fragile health, demanded she be replaced with another star. They ridiculously suggested that, perhaps, Marilyn Monroe be cast as Cleopatra. Ridiculous because the one person in Hollywood with a worse reputation than Elizabeth Taylor for lateness, sickness, and absenteeism was Marilyn Monroe.

No, Fox would not replace Elizabeth. They had invested so much in her already—and they were counting on her to save the studio. They moved forward, now with Joseph Mankiewicz at the helm.

While preparing to restart production on *Cleopatra* as Elizabeth recuperated, Mankiewicz argued to Fox that London in no way could ever duplicate Rome or Egypt. He convinced the studio to move the entire production to Rome. Everything that had been built at the Pinewood Studios was demolished—more money, more waste. The ten usable minutes of footage from the London production would have to be scrapped. *Cleopatra* would begin from scratch. The cost to the studio so far was twelve million dollars, and the filming had yet to begin.

Not surprisingly, Peter Finch and Stephen Boyd both bowed out of the film. They had waited around for months, pacing around the dressing room in full period costumes, going mad, waiting, waiting, to get in front of the cameras, and now they had other commitments. Rex Harrison was cast as the new Caesar, and for Mark Antony, Mankiewicz cast a handsome Welsh actor named Richard Burton.

35

THE FREUD FEUD

I liked him and detested him. His behavior was just so offensive. Belching and farting and, you know, stinking. He was awful, awful. I couldn't bear him.
—**John Huston**

WHEN HUSTON OFFERED MONTY THE ROLE OF FREUD, IT LOOKED like his career could be on its way to a comeback. In *Judgment at Nuremberg* he had had a small part, but he had been nominated for an Academy Award. *Wild River* and *The Misfits* were not financially successful films, but they were prestigious projects involving some of the most important names in the business. No doubt *Freud* appeared to be the vehicle that would put Monty back on top with a commercial success and important artistic achievement. Unfortunately, the film was neither, and it turned out to be one of the most hellish experiences of his career.

John Huston had been dreaming of making a film about Sigmund Freud for years, and he originally commissioned a biographical screenplay from Jean-Paul Sartre, but the script turned out to be too long—a movie from it would run for over nine hours. Huston then brought in Wolfgang Reinhardt to rewrite the script and pare it down to a filmable length.

Reinhardt's rewrite covered the five-year period of 1885 to 1890 in Freud's life, the years during which he began exploring mental illness in patients who had been diagnosed as "hysterical."

These patients, mostly women, had maladies that could not be diagnosed. In his first years of discovery in the realm of mental illness, Freud used hypnosis—a very controversial technique—to probe the mind for origins of mental trauma so extreme, it caused blindness or the inability to walk.

This was another troubled production. The project was faced with uncertainty from the beginning: the script was never satisfactory, and Monty's health was failing. The dysentery he contracted back in his Broadway days had never left him, and it kept him terribly underweight. In addition, a thyroid condition, along with his drinking and drug taking, was causing him to age prematurely. At the age of forty-one, his eyesight was failing, his hands were gnarled, and his hair was falling out.

Before filming started, Huston invited Monty to visit him in his Georgian-style manor, St. Clerans, in Ireland. Immediately after arriving, Huston walked in on Monty in bed with Claude. It was uncharacteristic for Monty to bring a boyfriend when visiting a professional acquaintance, but perhaps it was a testament to how comfortable Monty felt with Huston in the beginning. It turned out to be a miscalculation on Monty's part.[*]

Huston was shocked and aghast. "I didn't want to touch anything his lips were near," Huston said. The talented filmmaker was homophobic, and Monty's flaunting of his gayness particularly offended him. "Did you know this about Monty?" he asked Wolfgang Reinhardt.

"Yes, of course," the writer responded.

"I think it's disgusting," Huston stated. "Why didn't you tell me?"

Huston was highly offended and felt his house had been polluted. "The incident seemed trashy," he told Patricia Bosworth. "I felt Monty had insulted me. I wish he had considered my family. I can't say I'm able to deal with homosexuals."

Although Huston was not a prude in most matters and was con-

---

[*]Another version of this story claims that Huston found Monty in bed with his assistant. Still another says that it was a journalist.

sidered a sexual adventurer, he felt uneasy in the presence of homosexuals. It seems peculiar that he hadn't heard of Monty's homosexuality by now, but Huston wasn't the type to listen to gossip.

"The funny thing about Clift is he only propositioned men
when he was drunk. There was nothing abnormal about him
when he was sober. I found him a delight to work with, which
is why I offered him *Freud*," the director noted. Huston's use of
the word *abnormal* regarding Monty reflects the opinion of many
Hollywood professionals at the time. Being gay was tolerable as
long as you kept it to yourself.

Huston became fearful that Monty's homosexuality would hinder his work and would generate bad publicity if Monty played
Freud as "gay." He gave Monty a humiliating set of rules: "Monty
was not to behave in a homosexual manner, and to not have any
kind of homosexual relationships while he worked on the film.
He was to behave in a normal manner. He was not to drink or
take pills. He was not to have dependent friendships with older
women."

Huston was now contracted to work with an actor he disliked
and resented, which shattered Monty's confidence. Tense and humiliated, he got drunk on his flight to Munich, where *Freud* would
be shot. Monty refused to fasten his seat belt, and the flight attendants were forced to hold him down the entire trip. When word
of Monty's drunken behavior reached Huston, he was further disgusted. Under these circumstances, *Freud* began filming. Monty
was well aware of Huston's feelings toward him, and his good behavior on their previous film went out the window. All his most
unappealing traits—including drinking on the set—resurfaced,
and Huston did nothing to hide his revulsion.

"I shied away from him," Huston confessed. "He was, or had
been, a wonderful actor, but I got the remnants of him, not the
man himself. He was pretty shredded by the time he came to me.
The troubles I had with him were not his fault. He was just not capable anymore. The accident to his face had done great interior
damage to him. He had been very good in *The Misfits*, but he had
very few lines in it, mostly colloquialisms, and I was taken with his
performance, and I thought he could do *Freud*."

Aware of Huston's feelings, Monty introduced Claude as his secretary and kept him away from the set. During shooting, the tensions between Monty and Huston intensified anyway. Monty was having a problem with the script—he found Huston's rewrites to be too literal. "The lines needed immediacy to keep the audience caring," Monty explained. "Every time there was a break to explain something, the audience would be lost. Many of the lines given me, I couldn't say: they made no sense." Hours would go by, and nothing usable would be filmed.

Huston thought Monty was using his dislike for the script as an excuse for no longer being able to remember lines. Monty countered that the script was constantly being rewritten, so that it was a waste of time to memorize a scene all night, only to be given pages of new dialogue in the morning. "I averaged four hours' sleep a night," Monty said. In an attempt to get something usable on film, Huston posted the new lines all over the set, on the labels of prop bottles, on walls, on the tables, so Monty could read from them. That didn't work, either. Monty's cataracts had worsened, which made it impossible for him to see the lines. He took off to London to have his eyes checked. Now, adding to his troubles, Monty feared he might be going blind.

On his return, Monty was still unable to pick up the pace. Huston would pressure him, bully him, scream at him, and finally, he would simply ignore him, but nothing worked. Monty could not, or would not, learn his lines. Enraged, Huston would have Monty do the scene over and over again, refusing to acknowledge that the actor had the shakes and was sweating profusely. "I think John was relentless," associate producer Doc Erickson observed. "He wouldn't give an inch—would not see that what he was doing was only aggravating the situation. He would not try to modify his behavior . . . He could charm you out of your seat, and he could have used his charm to great advantage, but he chose not to." Monty described Huston as "a sadist who takes delight in needling."

Sometimes Huston didn't bother to watch Monty when he was acting in a scene. Instead, he'd sit with his face buried in a newspaper, secretly raging. "Do it again," he'd murmur without looking up, and Monty would despair and grow more humiliated and therefore more flustered. There were three or four times when he ran off the set sobbing. "In some ways Monty was the male equivalent of Marilyn Monroe," Huston griped. "He put on a little boy act."

Monty's costar, Susannah York, who played one of Freud's sexually repressed patients, Cecily, noted that "the relationship with John Huston was terrible. They were so utterly opposed as people. John Huston was intolerant and impatient and hard and . . . cruel. Monty was totally other. It was two people where there was no point of meeting."

The five-month shoot was a terribly torturous time—not just for Huston and Monty, but for all involved with *Freud*. Many of the delays were due to Huston's extravagance: He kept having the costumes changed. He ordered hundreds of extras, when only a few dozen were needed. Yet he continued to use Monty as a scapegoat.

With a production that dragged on and on, Monty's reputation got more and more trashed. He was already considered a risk by Hollywood, and as news dripped out about his inability to remember lines and his various illnesses, he was just confirming what the industry felt about him. He was a high-risk performer who wasn't worth the trouble.

As had happened with *The Misfits*, the cast and crew took sides. Some were sympathetic to Monty, and others were on Huston's side. Susannah York was mostly on Monty's side. As he had with many of his costars, he would meet with her in the evenings and coach her in her role. But she did understand some of Huston's frustrations. "I liked Monty enormously right away," she said. "He was extremely generous and extremely forthcoming . . . but also a very incredibly difficult person . . . a very difficult, neurotic man to deal with."

Years after Monty died, John Huston's cruelty to him during the making of *Freud* started seeping into part of his legend, and the director attempted to explain his behavior and reverse public opinion. "I was never kinder to anyone than I was to Clift," Huston asserted. "Sometimes I spoke harshly to him, but it was an attempt to awaken something in him. The combination of drugs, drink, and being homosexual was . . . just too much."

Whereas others saw Huston using his power as a director to punish Monty, he saw it in a different light. "I wasn't trying to destroy him," Huston stated. "I wanted to save my movie." When everything else failed, Huston even resorted to the threat of violence. "Finally, I decided I would get rough with him. I went to his dressing room, opened the door and slammed it behind me so hard, a mirror fell off the wall and shattered, showering glass shards all over the room . . . I wanted him to feel my anger . . . I wanted to scare him, thinking that fear would do something." It didn't. Monty continued to show up for work unprepared, which kept Huston attempting new ways to get to his star.

Toward the end of shooting, Huston's sadism and Monty's masochism found perfect expression when the time came for them to shoot a dream sequence in which Monty, as Freud, was to slide down a rope. Spectators maintained that Huston demanded that Monty do take after take without wearing gloves to protect the skin on his palms. Huston had a different explanation. "After each shot, when I called, '*Cut!*' Monty proceeded to slide down the rope, holding tightly. In this way, he burned his hands horribly. Monty's defenders have charged that I did this to him deliberately, going so far as to demand take after take while blood from Monty's hands streamed onto the rope. Unthinkable nonsense."

The making of *Freud* was a harrowing journey for almost everyone concerned, most of all Monty, because the repercussions would tail him for the rest of his life. When the movie wrapped, the production was massively over budget. Huston blamed Monty's inability to memorize lines, along with his illnesses, as the reason for all the costly delays and the bloated final budget.

The result of all the on-set turmoil was a series of drawn-out lawsuits and countersuits between Huston, the film's distributor, and Monty. In addition, Paramount held back the final payments of Monty's salary. While the lawsuits were being litigated, he couldn't work, and for Monty, not working was soul crushing. "That began the terrible years," his brother, Brooks, said. The stories about Monty delaying the production did so much damage to him. Brooks believed the lawsuit was the main reason Monty died when he did.

Monty was furious that the studio executives were further destroying his reputation by putting the blame on him, and he poured out his frustration in a televised interview: "The executives try to sort of hide their tracks by blaming it on the poor fellow who has to act it," Monty fumed. "A set isn't built on time—they blame the actor. The script is not ready—you get a white version, a blue version, a pink version, and a yellow version, and that night you get the final version, and that's what you have to study, because you can't memorize the first version. So the actor doesn't know the lines that morning, he's to blame. Even if he stays up until three o'clock in the morning and has to get up at 5:30."

Because of the beating his reputation was taking while the lawsuits dragged on, Monty very much wanted, needed *Freud* to be a success when it was released—if for nothing else but to repair some of the damage the lawsuits were inflicting on his reputation and to prove his value to Hollywood. He did more press for this movie than usual, including a television interview on *The Merv Griffin Show*, an hour-long discussion with Hy Gardner, and even an appearance on *What's My Line?*

At times, he was still asked about a possible romance with Elizabeth. Monty thought carefully before answering. "You mean romantically, personally?" he asked on one occasion. "No, we were close in the sense of friendship. Period. When they start to say in the magazines, 'Will Monty be Elizabeth's next?' Well, now she's married, but I don't know who her next is going to be, but it's not going to be me."

Still, *Freud* was a flop. Although audiences lined up to see it in the two theaters it was playing in, in Manhattan (Cinema 1 and

2), they stayed away in the rest of the country and in Europe, and, of course, attendance is needed in those places to make a movie a success. But because of the capacity crowds in New York, Monty was able to spin the film in interviews as being a hit.

Monty eventually won the lawsuit, blame was removed from him, and he was paid his remainder salary, but his reputation was so ruined that he could not get insurance for another movie. No producers would touch him.

36

THE CLEOPATRA AFFAIR

Since I was a little girl, I believed I was a child of destiny, and if that is true, Richard Burton was surely my fate.
—**Elizabeth Taylor**

WHEN ELIZABETH LANDED IN ROME TO BEGIN FILMING *CLEOPATRA* again, it was an entirely different project than the one she had started the year before: new script, new director, new sets, new cast. Only she remained.

The studio was determined to keep her satisfied. They rented an entire villa for her and Eddie to live in during the production, and it was filled with servants to ensure she wanted for nothing. Fox paid Eddie a salary, although he never quite figured out what he was being paid for, other than trying to keep Elizabeth functioning.

Since Mankiewicz was shooting the film in sequence, all the scenes involving Cleopatra and Caesar would be shot in the first months. Almost all of Elizabeth's scenes were with Rex Harrison. Mankiewicz would shoot all day and would work on the script in the evenings.

Eddie noticed that Elizabeth was drinking a great deal—she'd start off the day with a Bloody Mary and continue all through lunch. "What's going on?" he asked, confronting Mankiewicz about Elizabeth's boozing. The director was aware she'd been drinking on the set. He took a deep drag on his pipe and replied,

"Eddie, she hasn't the faintest idea what she's doing." The enormity of the production was obviously pressuring Elizabeth. She was, after all, Cleopatra, and the eyes of all Hollywood, all the world, were on her. If the movie failed, it would be her failure, so she boosted her confidence with alcohol.

As the first day of shooting with Richard Burton approached, Elizabeth wasn't expecting anything out of the ordinary to happen. Elizabeth had met Burton years before, and he hadn't made a good impression. "He was rather full of himself," she recalled. "I seem to remember that he never stopped talking, and I had given him the cold-fish eye."

The thirty-six-year-old Welsh actor had a commanding presence. Blue eyed and handsome but with a pockmarked complexion, he was especially known for his mellifluous baritone voice (he could recite long passages of Shakespeare on a whim, particularly when drunk), his drinking, and his reputation for bedding his leading ladies. It was also known that no matter how many affairs he had, Richard always returned to his wife, Sybil. The couple had been married for twelve years.

However, on January 22, 1962, their first day of shooting together, Burton showed up on the set with a brutal hangover. On laying eyes on Elizabeth in her Cleopatra getup, he used his thunderous voice to toss off this vast understatement: "Has anyone ever told you that you're a very pretty girl?" He had the shakes and was trembling so much, he couldn't lift a coffee cup to his lips. When he asked Elizabeth to help him, her mothering instincts kicked in, and she melted. "Our eyes locked and he drank the whole cup and we just kept looking at each other," Elizabeth said.

Journalist Richard Meryman recalled, "She described him as all giggly and boyish and childlike and helpless and needy . . . found it endearing. Here was this titanic actor intellectual—a needy child." Richard found Elizabeth "beautiful beyond the dreams of pornography, making an affair between them inevitable." When Elizabeth and Richard started filming their first scene, producer Walter Wanger noted, "It was quiet, and you could almost feel the electricity between Liz and Burton." From their very first day on the set, they set out to conquer each other. This was all very Cleopatra and Mark Antony, and Elizabeth became the modern embodiment of the Egyptian queen.

In their very first days of acting together, the costars became secret lovers, but gossip spreads fast on a movie set, and soon the secret got out. Richard and Elizabeth were having an affair. In one of their love scenes, Mankiewicz said, "Cut," but their kiss went on and on. They would hole up in their trailers for long afternoons. The passion she felt for him was a violent jolt. When Elizabeth fell for Richard—so full of poetry and fire and sex and booze—she wasn't escaping from anything, and she wasn't trying to re-create anyone. This was the real thing. She was twenty-nine years old and ripe for the great love of her life, and Richard—with his appetite for beauty, great fame, and sex—was ready to give it to her.

As the affair continued and became more intense, Richard no longer tried to hide it. At one point he strode into the men's makeup trailer, announcing triumphantly, "Gentlemen, I've just fucked Elizabeth Taylor in the back of my Cadillac!"

At first Eddie Fisher and Sybil turned a blind eye to the affair, but it soon became apparent this was more than a fling. The latest love almost always feels the most intense and complete, but Elizabeth had a lot of loves in her recent past to compare it to. She had known other kinds of love before, but this was the kind of love you're always waiting for—and it doesn't always come along.

The passion between Richard and Elizabeth was so strong, it couldn't be kept under wraps. It demanded an audience. After a drunken dinner one evening at Eddie and Elizabeth's villa, Richard demanded, "Elizabeth, who do you love? Whooo do you love?"

She glanced at Eddie. Then she fixed her stare on Richard and hesitated a brief moment before answering, "You," while looking into Richard's eyes.

Richard then picked up a framed photo of Elizabeth with Mike Todd. "He didn't know how to use her," he said, indicating the photograph, "and neither do you."

Elizabeth broke down, but she didn't deny it.

Eddie—still passionately in love with Elizabeth—found himself in the humiliating position Debbie Reynolds had been in some three years before—on the losing end of a love triangle with Elizabeth Taylor. He was devastated. He'd wander around the hotel suite, unshaven, unbathed, stunned by his feelings of loss over the woman he had more or less given up his career for. Eddie paid a visit to the Burtons' villa for a heart-to-heart talk with Sybil. "I said, 'You know, they're continuing their affair,'" Eddie recalled. "And she said, 'He's had these affairs, and he always comes home to me.'"

Eventually, Eddie decided there was nothing he could do to stop the torrent of love Elizabeth felt for Richard. As far as she was concerned, there was no going back to Eddie. He decided to go back to New York and hope Burton and Elizabeth's passion would burn itself out. At one point, it seemed like maybe it would—when Richard announced that he would remain with Sybil. This caused Elizabeth to take an overdose of sleeping tablets, and Richard rushed back into her arms. Their illicit romance continued. If Elizabeth felt remorse about the failure of her marriage with Eddie, it was overwhelmed and pushed aside by her great passion for Richard.

It would be difficult, if not impossible, to stun and obsess the nation today in the way that Elizabeth Taylor stunned and obsessed *the world* in the early 1960s.

When word leaked out to the public of Elizabeth's affair with Richard, the public could hardly believe it. Was it only three years before that Elizabeth had scandalized the world by stealing Eddie Fisher from Debbie Reynolds? Could she now be doing the same thing with Richard and Sybil Burton? Some people's rage was reignited, but this time their fascination with her trumped their fury, and they grappled with how they should feel about it. Elizabeth lived her life the way she wanted to, not the way society told her to live. In the changing sixties, some couldn't help but admire her for it. That she was starring as Cleopatra helped them accept it—in many fans' eyes, she had become the embodiment of the dangerous siren, the queen of desire, a conqueror of men.

The crazy, passionate, intense love between "Liz and Dick" made headlines around the world. It became known as *Le Scandale*. A Georgia congresswoman and an Ohio representative tried to bar the stars from returning to the United States on grounds of "undesirability." Even the Vatican denounced Elizabeth, condemning her for "erotic vagrancy." Being condemned by the Vatican was a big deal in 1962, but the term *erotic vagrancy* did have a deliciously sinful and forbidden ring to it.

Le Scandale was the biggest story of the decade—and people ate up every morsel served to them and eagerly waited for the next serving. Paparazzi swarmed the set, desperate for a picture of Elizabeth or, better yet, a picture of Cleopatra with Richard Burton. It was utter madness. They disguised themselves as priests, masqueraded as servants, bribed members of the crew. They climbed trees to look into her compound and directed telephoto lenses at the couple wherever they went.

The affair unfolding before the world did nothing to slow the lovers down, as Elizabeth disclosed. "Even with paparazzi hanging out of the trees and hearing them tramping on the rooftops above us, even with all that going on, we could make love and play Scrabble and spell out naughty words for each other, and the game would never be finished," she said.

Fox couldn't ignore the headlines. At first, they were terrified that an affair between the married costars could sink their epic film. All they could do was hold their breath as the massively expensive and chaotic production inched forward. However, as the scandalous affair continued—and the publicity continued to take on a life of its own—the studio executives began to realize that the scandal might be the very hook that would lure audiences in to see the picture. As the production dragged on and on, the studio maximized the publicity, and *Cleopatra* fever took over popular culture. In fact, Elizabeth's costumes and makeup would set the tone for fashionable women in the mid-1960s.

"It was probably the most chaotic time of my life," Elizabeth revealed to *Vanity Fair* in 2011. "What with *Le Scandale*, the Vatican banning me, people making threats on my life, falling madly in love . . . It was fun, and it was dark—oceans of tears, but some good times, too."

When production was finally complete, the film consisted of many hours of footage that needed to somehow be assembled into a watchable movie. Mankiewicz's cut of the film was eight hours long. His desire was to release it as two movies, *Caesar and Cleopatra* and then *Antony and Cleopatra*. But Fox was eager to get the film into theaters while the public still obsessed about the affair between Elizabeth and Richard. Who knew if they'd still be together after a Cleopatra and Caesar movie premiered? At Fox's insistence that one movie be constructed from all the footage, *Cleopatra* was cut down to four hours for the first screening and finally to three hours for the general public release. Both Elizabeth and Richard would complain that all their best work was edited out of the final cut. Elizabeth admitted she was so upset by the final cut, she walked out of the screening and vomited.

After a three-year buildup and unprecedented publicity for the movie, some of the reviews were snarky, focusing on Elizabeth's histrionics and fluctuating weight throughout the film. Since the movie was filmed over such a long period of time, Elizabeth's weight does go up and down from scene to scene. She looks anywhere from young, slender, and ravishing to positively zaftig. According to Eddie Fisher, she drank throughout the filming, and she would have her favorite chili flown from the restaurant Chasen's in Beverly Hills to Rome.

"Overweight, overbosomed, overpaid, and undertalented, she set the acting profession back a decade," griped critic David Susskind. But some greatly admired Elizabeth's obvious mix of kitten and lioness. Bosley Crowther stated: "Elizabeth Taylor's Cleopatra is a woman of force, of dignity, fired by a fierce ambition to conquer and rule the world."

For years after, the gossip about *Cleopatra* was that it was a huge flop. It was nothing of the kind. *Cleopatra* was the number one grossing movie of the year, bringing in an impressive fifty-seven million dollars. Yet because of the final budget, it would be several years before *Cleopatra* would show a profit.

37

IT'S VERY HARD

Mr. Clift wishes to see no one. Not even himself in the mirror.
—The *Daily Sketch*

*B*ACK IN NEW YORK AFTER FILMING *FREUD*, MONTY SAW THE BAR-
rage of *Cleopatra* headlines. Even he was stunned, and a little impressed, by the intensity of the world's Elizabeth obsession. "I
don't think it's possible to become more famous than Bessie
Mae!" he declared to Jack Larson.

It's true that Elizabeth's face, her violet eyes dramatically kohl
lined in Cleopatra eye makeup, was on many more covers than
any star of that time period. Her antics on the set of *Cleopatra* had
delegated every other show business story to a minor mention in
some corner of the publication.

Still, when the need to confide became so great, it was Monty
whom Elizabeth would call long distance to talk about *Le Scandale*.
"Monty was somebody she could always call no matter where he
was and say, 'Monty, I need some help,'" Eddie Dmytryk said.
"Part of our friendship was our trust in each in other," Elizabeth
observed, "in knowing that the secrets we shared were sacred."

She told Monty that she understood that people would be
hurt—she was particularly concerned about Sybil Burton, whom
she liked—but she had fallen hopelessly in love with Richard, and

there was simply nothing she could do about it. Eddie Fisher had been a rushed affair to anesthetize her terrible mourning after Mike Todd's death. Now she had fallen in love with Richard, and she desperately needed him in order to be happy. "Lots of people have affairs," she said. "I can't help it if the press follows me around and reports everything I do."

Then she asked him if she was being reckless.

"No," Monty replied. "I think you're lucky that you can still feel that way."

Then she revealed that Richard had confessed to her that when he was young and struggling, he had a few homosexual dalliances with two mature, successful actors. He also had a mentor who pressed for "more than friendship" from Richard. As Elizabeth put it, "Richard understood a gay subtext." Elizabeth was aware of how a casting-couch environment worked and said that his past didn't bother her. She just wanted to be sure it remained "all in the past." Still, by being accepting, Elizabeth did make Richard "less ashamed" of his homosexual experiences.

Monty would never judge his Bessie, but he did criticize Richard Burton behind her back. He felt that Burton was using her and that he was the one who was leaking details of their affair to the press, feeding the media stories. "Richard wants to be famous at any cost," he told friends.

His long-standing friendship with Elizabeth and her long-distance calls once again served as a diversion from his own life, which was falling apart. "His body was shot—there was nothing left," Susannah York observed. Monty was physically ill throughout the summer of 1962. He was in and out of the hospital to address a variety of ailments: to remove cataracts, to repair a hernia, and then again to treat the varicose veins in his legs. He feared he was going blind. He was losing his sight. "Honey, I wouldn't know you were my brother," he said in a late-night phone call to Brooks. "Isn't that horrible . . . ? I mean, I wouldn't burden you with it, but do you see how terribly depressing this is?"

The problems he was facing weren't just physical. Monty's personal life was in tatters, too. He was shattered when Marilyn Monroe died that August—one fewer person in the world he felt understood him. Monty and Elizabeth talked about Marilyn's death.

"I don't think Marilyn committed suicide," Elizabeth said. "I don't think Marilyn was murdered. I think it was an accident. But she was playing with fire."

Monty said that Hollywood deaths came in threes. Two of the leads of *The Misfits* were now already dead: Clark Gable and Marilyn. Monty was the third lead of that film.

Monty's relationship with Claude was still hanging on by a thread. They continued to live together at Monty's brownstone, but the relationship had become destructive. In spite of their constant bickering, he and Claude clung to each other, mainly because they had nothing else to cling to. But rather than holding each other up, they dragged each other down in a seedy sea of alcohol, drugs, and hustlers.

Both of them had been heavy drinkers, but Claude claimed it was Monty who introduced him to hard drugs, including heroin, and got him addicted. A notorious drug dealer of the day known as "Bird" recalled the night Monty was scoring heroin in a Harlem bar when a pimp was shot right in front of them.

Friends who saw Claude and Monty together felt that the younger man did love Monty in his own destructive, degenerate way, but he was also dependent on him for money, a place to live, and as a conduit to drugs and men. With Monty Clift as bait, Claude could lure a better class of lowlifes into their lair. "Claude only wants me for my fame," Monty would complain. But if it wasn't for the sinister trade Claude brought around to entertain them, Monty's life would be completely empty.

Monty was far too ill to perform sexually—the alcohol and pills made him impotent—but he wallowed and distracted himself in the sexual atmosphere that Claude was so good at perpetuating. It became commonplace for Monty to be beaten up by hustlers. At clubs and orgies—arranged by Claude—a drunken Monty would pass out and anyone could have him. He became a sort of sexual prop, in that his body would be stripped, licked, and worshipped as a fallen movie idol, sex symbol, icon in the degenerate flesh. A few years before they had seen him and lusted after him in the movies—when he was so marvelous and untouchable—and now he was right in front of them to do with what they pleased. This was all that was left for him. There was nowhere lower to go.

These scenes were also a way for Claude to exact revenge on Monty. He would expose him to the humiliation that followed the revelation that the great leading man was impotent and had inadequate equipment.

One of the strangest stories about Monty during this time was told by the dapper and sophisticated Frank Taylor, who had produced *The Misfits*. Taylor—a married man with children—also had a double life. Several evenings a week, he would visit Monty at his town house after work, and they'd share several martinis in the garden and gossip.

One late afternoon they sat in the garden, lamenting the failure of *The Misfits*. Afterward, with the intention of being dropped off at the train station, Taylor got into a chauffeured limo with Monty and Claude and ended up at Dirty Dick's, a bar on the West Village waterfront—in those days a hidden area, dark, dingy, and dangerous, with no tourism or nightlife.

For the most part, only the police knew about the bar, along with rough trade, leather guys, young hustlers, and the occasional "slumming" celebrity, like Leonard Bernstein, who liked a taste of the wild side. In the gay underground, it was known that bad things happened at Dirty Dick's. After hanging out there, "a number of young men were seen for the last time." Monty and Claude drank there regularly.

Afraid to go in, Taylor remained in the limo, while Monty and Claude went inside. A short time later two policemen tapped on the window. They wanted him to go inside and get Montgomery Clift, explaining that he was there almost every night and there had been trouble in the past. After fortifying himself with a stiff drink at the front of the bar, Taylor went to the back room, located behind a leather curtain. There he saw about thirty people crowded around some kind of table.

After he pushed his way through, he saw Monty passed out on

the pool table, "fully clothed in his grey flannel suit, while butch dykes, transvestites, drag queens, guys in leather jackets crawled all over him, humming like insects. Monty was a drop of honey circled by lurid, swarming bee, Some were kissing his neck. Others were fondling his crotch. I thought I was going to vomit. It was the most debauched scene I've ever witnessed—like some Dionysian rite." Taylor plunged into the orgy, scooped Monty up, and carried him back to the car, while the salivating crowed screamed, "No, no, don't take him away. You can't take him away."

After that night, Taylor never saw Monty again. Most of his solid friends from years before now distanced themselves from the wreckage of Monty. "We didn't see him anymore. It became too painful," Kevin McCarthy explained. Jean and Fred Levy had also stopped seeing him. "It was not possible to have any kind of relationship," Jean said. "We couldn't be his friend . . . We had to give him up and let him go. There was nothing anybody could do. Nobody could help him. He was way beyond help."

Not working was tearing Monty apart. Jack Larson, who was now concentrating on writing, came to stay with Monty for a while. "Monty had to pretend everything: interest in people, interest in life, in the very words he spoke," Larson recalled. He stopped finishing his sentences. "Sometimes, I would pass Monty's bedroom. The television would be on, and Monty would be sitting, scrooched on his sofa, crying, not paying a bit of attention to the television." Monty cried almost all the time now. The very act of living had become painful.

He cried during an interview for the *Daily Sketch*. During the talk, Monty kept interrupting his flow of thought to ask, "Did you see me in *Judgment at Nuremberg*?" Or he would say, "Tell me, did you see me in *The Young Lions*?" And then he began to weep. The reporter was taken aback. It was poignant and painful to see someone who had been revered a mere decade before now almost pleading for recognition of what he once was.

Peter Bogdanovich remembered meeting Monty while working at the New Yorker Theater, before he became a successful director. A revival of *I Confess* was playing, and on a rare venture out of his apartment, Monty went to see it. Bogdanovich approached him.

"I came up and said I worked there," he recalled. "He was polite. I said I liked the picture and asked if he did. The huge image on the screen at that moment of his pre-accident beauty must have seemed to mock him. He turned away and looked at me sadly. 'It's . . . hard, you know.' He said it slowly, hesitantly, a little slurred. 'It's very . . . hard.' "

The theater had a request book where audiences could suggest what they'd like to see. Bogdanovich showed Monty where someone had written down, "Anything with Montgomery Clift!" Bogdanovich watched Monty for a reaction. " 'That's very . . . nice,' he said and continued to look down. I realized he was crying."

On occasion, when speaking to journalists, Monty did his best to reverse the depiction of himself as being on a road to destruction. "I have a rather large capacity for life," he told one journalist, "and I ain't gonna give it up." But as more and more time passed without any movie offers, Monty became scared. When he wasn't working, he barely felt alive, and the few friends that hung around noticed that he seemed to have given up. "All of my triumphs add up to nothing," he told Jack Larson.

After many years of estrangement, Monty was too tired to keep his mother away, and he allowed Sunny to come around for short visits. Bill Clift also started spending more time with Monty. He had come to a begrudging acceptance of Monty's homosexuality, although he still couldn't completely embrace it.

Meanwhile, the relationship between Monty and Claude had disintegrated into a series of vicious arguments and sparring matches in which the goal was to one-up each other out of cruelty. Claude's theatrics culminated in him attempting suicide by taking an overdose of sleeping pills. He nearly died and was rushed to the hospital, where they managed to revive him. Sunny and a few friends convinced Monty that the two of them had to be separated for their own good.

Upon his release from the hospital following his overdose,

Claude agreed to move out of the town house and in with Monty's old friend Billy LeMassena until he could get back on his feet. Now Monty found himself utterly alone, tormented by crippling depression of various origins: No longer being offered quality work. The loss of youth. Not having a partner to love or depend on. The feeling that he had squandered his best years.

"There were many who tried to save Monty," Robert Thom said. "They tried because of his deep talent, because they loved him . . . He both unsettled you, made you reexamine yourself— never had you lived up to your potential—and, also, he made you know that that potential was significant, vast."

But after a while, even his most devoted friends gave up. Marlene Dietrich liked to brag that she could accomplish anything. "If I had to swim the Atlantic with a child on my back, to save the child, I could do it." But when it came to Monty, she admitted she was incapable of helping him. Roddy McDowall confided to Maureen Stapleton that all they could do was hold his hand to the grave.

Monty's strange behavior became stranger, more reckless. He accepted a hustler's dare to run naked down Third Avenue. Using the fire escape, he climbed up to the roof of his brownstone in his pajamas. Blind drunk, he made his way along the parapet—staggering. He had to be carried down and put to bed. When his father came over to check up on him, he found two hustlers trying to cook breakfast in the kitchen. "Pa," Monty exclaimed dramatically, hands outstretched, making a grand entrance down the staircase. "So good to see you!" Appalled, Bill beat it out of the townhouse quickly

It was decided that Monty wasn't able to be left on his own, so the new goal was to find someone to care for him. Billy LeMessena, along with Sunny, consulted with his medical doctor, who recommended Lorenzo James to be a companion and make daily visits. Lorenzo, a handsome, affable black man, had been an actor and was now working as a nurse. It was the right choice: He turned out to be smart, firm, devoted, and trustworthy.

Along with getting Monty to cut back significantly on his drinking and at times to give it up completely, Lorenzo also saw to it that Monty exercised daily. Before long, he was screening visitors and phone calls to keep the seedy element away from him. During the time Monty had been living with Claude, the front door had been broken. Vagrants and hustlers had wandered in and out of the townhouse Lorenzo had the door repaired and changed the locks. Claude would still show up at times and demand to see Monty. Lorenzo stood firm. Claude was effectively shut out—Monty didn't seem to mind at all.

Without Claude's influence, Monty remained sequestered in his darkened townhouse for days, weeks, a recluse, with no differentiation between week and weekend, day and night. Sometimes it seemed a relief that he didn't have to leave the safety of the cocoon-like comfort of his apartment. "No more new people," he emphatically instructed Lorenzo. He admitted that he enjoyed being a recluse, reading, listening to music.

The brownstone became his fortress, and he concentrated on decorating it, having a bar installed, organizing his books in alphabetical order on the extensive bookshelves, having orange awnings put over the windows so that when the afternoon light filtered in, the rooms were bathed in an amber glow.

To break up the monotony, he would venture out to an early movie with Lorenzo. Passing him on a busy Manhattan sidewalk was a macabre sight. People would point him out. "What happened to him?" they would gasp, finding it hard to believe that the bent, skeletal figure was Montgomery Clift, the ravaged movie star.

"His body was rigid. His movements constricted. And the face was a mask; the eyes dull," writer Ralph Zucker, who spotted him on the street, recalled. "He could hardly walk. A friend led him by the elbow. His hands trembled. He stumbled slightly as he moved along. He seemed as if he were in a trance, as if he were no longer with us, as if his overwhelming personal isolation was irredeemable."

One sunny afternoon, on one of his walks, Monty spotted actress Kim Novak, who had a place on the same block. To introduce himself in a joking way, he asked the blond star for her autograph. But the joke backfired when Kim smiled patiently and asked, "Who, sir, shall I make it out to?" She truly didn't have any idea who he was.

Monty was stung, but as always, he did his best to cover his hurt. "Make it out to me, dear. My name is Monty Clift."

38

HAMLETS IN NEW YORK

I can't say I'm just melancholy. Or I'm just sad. Or I'm just anything. It's a part of one's life.
—**Montgomery Clift**

Elizabeth is not only rich and beautiful, [but] she is also very shrewd.
—**Ernest Lehman**

WHEN FILMING ON *CLEOPATRA* WAS FINISHED AT LAST, ELIZABETH emerged from the chaos of production as the most powerful actor in Hollywood; with her overtime, her final fee for the movie was seven million dollars. Richard Burton, too, was richer and more famous than he'd ever been—and more famous than he would ever have been had the affair never happened. The world dubbed them "Liz and Dick."

In spite of all the bad publicity, the moral outrage from the press and the public, Elizabeth's life was more riveting than any soap opera. The public—even the public that hated her—was interested in everything about her life and everyone in it. "Some audiences out there, and don't ask me who they are, but there are millions, like scandal. They like filth," she told TV personality Larry King.

While they waited to be divorced from their respective spouses,

Elizabeth and Richard agreed to costar in another movie together, *The V.I.P.s.* They did so in part to stay near to each other.
Originally, her role was intended for Sophia Loren, but Elizabeth
wasn't about to let Richard be on a set with the Italian beauty for
an extended period of time. She convinced the director, Anthony
Asquith, to cast her instead. "Let Sophia stay in Rome," she declared.

After that shoot completed, rather than pursue more movie
work, Elizabeth chose to devote her life to Richard. Still married
to other people, they couldn't bear to be apart—and Elizabeth
couldn't bear the thought of leaving him alone on the set surrounded by attractive actresses. She accompanied Richard to
Puerto Vallarta, Mexico, where he was shooting Tennessee
Williams's *The Night of the Iguana* with Ava Gardner, a film directed by Monty's nemesis, John Huston. They stayed in houses
across the street from each other, and Richard had a bridge built
to connect the two buildings. Richard bought the two connected
buildings and gave the resulting "house" to Elizabeth as a birthday present, and the two dubbed it Casa Kimberly.[*]

When they were not on movie sets, their life would consist of
yachts and houses and extravagant jewels of various kinds and
throwing the best parties and going to the best parties. They
would own houses all over the world, and when they stayed in hotels, they rented out not only the entire floor but the rooms on
the floors above and below the one on which they'd be staying,
too.

Although it took some time, Eddie Fisher and Sybil Burton agreed to give their spouses a divorce. On March 15, 1964,
nine days following Elizabeth's divorce from Eddie, she and
Richard married in Montreal, where Richard was appearing in a
stage production of *Hamlet.* This was marriage number five for
thirty-two-year-old Elizabeth. Their blended family now included
her two sons from her second marriage, her daughter from her
third, and Richard's two daughters with Sybil. Since Elizabeth

[*]Years later, after it was sold, it was turned into a bed-and-breakfast.

couldn't have any more children, the couple adopted a little girl, a German orphan who had been born with a genetic defect in her hip. She had started the adoption process with Eddie Fisher (his name was on the original adoption papers), but now Richard helped her complete the adoption, and he became her father. With her new parents' support, Maria was able to go through many operations to correct her malformed hip.

In April 1964, Richard Burton would bring his *Hamlet* to Broadway, and it was the hottest ticket of the season. Of course, Monty was invited to the opening; he and Elizabeth hadn't seen each other in a long time, and they were excited at the prospect. On opening night, the entire block had to be blocked off, as thousands of people lined up to get a peek at Elizabeth and Richard, Liz and Dick, their modern-day Cleopatra and Antony. "For some reason, the world has always been amused by us two maniacs," Richard noted wryly.

Elizabeth was dressed regally in dark green attire, with matching emerald earrings and an upswept hairdo. With many hairpieces and flowers interwoven into it, her hair trailed down her back like it belonged to a Grecian goddess. She was sitting regally in her orchestra seat, waiting for the curtain, when Monty arrived in his cups, startling the black-tie audience by wobbling down the theater aisle, chanting, "Bessie Mae! Bessie Mae!" Elizabeth was unfazed by the spectacle and was delighted to hear her best friend's husky voice. But when she turned to greet him and moved in close for a hug, she was shocked by his appearance, by his lined face and emaciated body. That he was broken and fallen was very touching to her.

But she greeted him warmly and embraced him tightly. They weren't really the same two people anymore—the two from *A Place in the Sun*. Their love had gone in a different direction, but it was still there—generating the same warmth, the same comfort, it had always delivered.

As the play unfolded, Monty sat there with a sense of envy and loss—the kind that comes to people over forty when they review their life with regret. Monty had always wanted to play Hamlet, and there had been a time, earlier in his career, when the theater world thought he would be an ideal Hamlet or Romeo. That was past him now, and he squirmed in his seat as a spectator. Richard's performance annoyed him because it seemed fake; he relied too much on his "mellifluous, baritone" voice.

After the play, Monty joined Elizabeth and Richard at the Rainbow Room for the *Hamlet* opening party, but he was still disturbed by the theater experience. He walked around the crowded room, clutching his drink tightly, with a tense look and a fake little smile. The accident showed in his face more than it usually did that night. After a while he quietly left. Elizabeth was busy with the many guests, the focal point of the evening, as usual. But she had felt Monty's unease all evening, and she noticed him slip out early. "If he doesn't work soon, he'll die," she said.

Too antsy to go home, Monty met his brother for a drink; he talked about the play and how much he disliked Richard's Hamlet. He considered it "reciting," not acting, out of step with his introspective approach and sensitive interpretation. After talking for a while, he started reciting lines from the play—he knew big chunks of dialogue by heart. Brooks was extremely moved by his brother's impromptu performance.

Hamlet continued to haunt Monty. He also held a private reading with his doctor, Arthur Ludwig. "It was just him and me," the doctor recalled, "and he was marvelous. There's no question about it. He would have made a great Hamlet if he had the stamina to do the whole play."

During her stay in New York, Elizabeth visited with Truman Capote, and the writer revealed how worried he was about Monty. Often his behavior was out of control, and he acted like an insane person. Capote recounted an incident that had happened that holiday season, when he and Monty had gone Christmas shopping together. At one point they were looking in a boutique that specialized in exquisite handmade Italian sweaters.

Capote recalled: "He pointed at the counter where the sweaters were stacked and counted one, two, three, four, five . . . sixteen. 'How much are all those?' The salesman told him, and Monty picked up all the sweaters in one huge bundle—there was so many, they were falling out of his arms—and somehow got the door open. It had begun to rain by this time—in fact, it was pouring—but he walked out and threw them all in the gutter." While he kicked the sweaters around, Capote asked him for his charge card. "'My face is my charge card,' Monty replied manically. When he came back, the salesman just asked, 'And to what address do I send the bill, Mr. Clift?' I've never seen anyone so cool in my life as that salesman. Monty wouldn't speak to him, but I gave his address and made him sign the bill."

When Capote attempted to drag Monty home, he got into the front seat of a taxicab and tried to take the wheel from the driver. The cabdriver stopped and threatened to call the police. "Please, this man is ill," Capote implored. "Take us to this address and I'll give you a big tip." He had to hold on to Monty, who screamed and shouted the whole way home.

Elizabeth became alarmed. "He can't go on like that," she said. "It will kill him." She persuaded Monty to move into a hotel closer to hers, while she tried to figure out a way to help him. But Monty checked out after a few days. "I can't stand living in a hotel," he declared. "I have to be at home."

The two friends continued to stay in close touch, though, and Elizabeth managed to see Monty almost every day. They fell into their old friendship routine. They'd have dinner together at Monty's apartment or at the Isle of Capri, a small Italian place near his place that had become a favorite. Sometimes the two would dine with Richard at Voisin. "Monty, Elizabeth likes me, but she *loves* you," Richard confided to him, and Monty beamed.

On June 21, 1964, Monty was in the audience as Elizabeth made her own Broadway debut, opposite Richard, in a poetry reading at the Lunt-Fontanne Theatre. The event was a fundraiser for the American Musical and Dramatic Academy. The theater was celebrity packed, at a hundred dollars a seat. It was assumed by the theater people that she would be inaudible, nervous, and shivering with stage fright. Of course, to many of them, that alone would be worth the price of admission.

Richard started the evening, reading in his rich, deep voice. He began with Marvell's "To His Coy Mistress." As he read, anticipation was peaking as the audience waited for Elizabeth. She was wearing a blue, one-shoulder Grecian gown and was dripping with emeralds and diamonds. She appeared at ease, especially after Richard made a few jokes.

Her choices were poems by Elinor Wylie, Elizabeth Barrett Browning, Robert Frost, and Dorothy Parker. The rapt house had no trouble hearing her. Later there was an antiphonal reading of the 23rd Psalm, and a reading of an Act II scene from *The Lady's Not for Burning.* There were some false starts. "So sorry," Elizabeth said. "Let me begin again. I sure screwed that one up."

Later in the evening, Monty joined the couple for drinks. This time he enjoyed Richard's reading of poetry, but he didn't let Elizabeth know how he felt about his performance in *Hamlet*—or his acting in general—and the three of them had a relaxed, easy time together.

The following week, Monty was Elizabeth's escort to the gala world premiere of *The Night of the Iguana,* the film Richard made in Mexico. The premiere was held at Philharmonic Hall, in Lincoln Center for the Performing Arts. They made a grand entrance and were besieged by fans and reporters. At the party afterward, Monty sat at a table with Elizabeth and Richard, and again they had a relaxed, easy time.

When Elizabeth loved, she loved big, and the bond was strong, and her love was lasting. With Monty, where other people saw waste and ruin, Elizabeth still saw beauty.

Through the years, after *Suddenly, Last Summer,* after she won the Oscar for *BUtterfield 8,* after the monumental production of *Cleopatra,* even after her all-consuming passion for Richard Burton, she never forgot Monty. Even though she had become the most powerful player in Hollywood, her loyalty made her want to work with him again. And it was only Elizabeth Taylor who could get anyone to offer him a decent role.

"She was the most loyal friend you could ever have," her assistant Tim Mendelson noted. "I mean, when you were in trouble, you could not have a better friend than Elizabeth. She was also intuitive—sensitive, intuitive, psychic, whatever. And she would know when you needed her help and know exactly what to do. And because she was Elizabeth Taylor, she could move mountains."

Elizabeth knew that Monty needed her. She revealed to him that she would very much like to make another movie with him. Unlike many who rise up to be so powerful, Elizabeth remained kind and loyal to her friends. She knew that the only thing that might bring Monty back to health was for him to get back to work. With the clout to get almost anything she wanted, Elizabeth began talking earnestly with him about teaming up again for a new film. For the first time in a long time, Monty felt enthusiastic about something.

For a while, they considered *The Owl and the Pussycat,* about a romance between a kooky prostitute and a nerdy writer. It was a hit on Broadway, and they had always wanted to do a romantic comedy together, since so much of their earlier relationship had involved black humor and laughter. They both got ahold of the script and would read through it together over the phone. Ultimately, they decided not to do it. (A few years later it would be a hit for Barbra Streisand and George Segal.)

Since Elizabeth and Richard were mainly working together now, sometimes Richard would get on the phone and talk about something the three of them could do. At one point, he suggested *The Macomber Affair.* Monty kept quiet about that, as he had no respect for Richard's acting and would rather he not be in the film, but for the most part, he was full of enthusiasm and ideas, very much like his younger self.

39

REFLECTIONS

I can't get a job. . . . But Elizabeth Taylor is the greatest friend.
She keeps trying to help—everyone else has deserted me.
—Montgomery Clift

Miss Taylor was determined to have [Monty] in Reflections
and to make another picture with an actor she admired greatly
and loved as a friend, and her immense devotion to him was
not only responsible for the acceptance of Clift by John Huston,
[but Taylor] also overcame certain insurance problems.
—Robbie Lantz

*E*LIZABETH HAD ACCOMPLISHED SOMETHING NO ACTOR HAD UP
until that time: she was more powerful than any producer, any
studio executive. Since her name was now synonymous with fame,
wealth, beauty, publicity, and success, she was in demand for almost every project.

Because she had her pick, she was busy lining up an impressive
and diverse array of projects to add to her body of work. In all of
them, she would be acting opposite or alongside Richard. She
signed with Warner Brothers to play the loud, vulgar ball-breaker,
Martha, in the film version of Edward Albee's landmark play
Who's Afraid of Virginia Woolf?, one of the classics of American theater. The character is fiftyish, and in order to age two decades,

Elizabeth gained thirty pounds and wore a frowzy graying wig. Richard would play George, Martha's wimpy history professor husband. For her director, Elizabeth shrewdly chose Mike Nichols, a theater director with no moviemaking experience. The movie was filled with profanity-laced dialogue that violated the production code, but movies were changing, censorship was falling, and producer Ernest Lehman decided that he wouldn't change the script. In that way, the film would be groundbreaking.

Next, she would fulfill one of Richard's dreams by appearing opposite him in *The Taming of the Shrew*, directed by Franco Zeffirelli. All the while, she continued discussing movie ideas with Monty. She assured him she hadn't forgotten—he needed so much reassurance. Elizabeth didn't think of it as being heroic. Sure, she would be helping a friend, but she enjoyed working with Monty, she loved him, and she wanted the project to be right for their particular chemistry.

In April of 1966, when she was in between filming *Who's Afraid of Virginia Woolf?* and *The Taming of the Shrew*, another project was presented to her, *Reflections in a Golden Eye*, based on a novel by Carson McCullers about an army major who is a latent homosexual and his domineering, adulterous wife.

John Huston had talked to her about the book when he was shooting *The Night of the Iguana* with Richard. Elizabeth expressed some enthusiasm for the story as told to her and then put it out of her head. Now Huston approached her again about the possibility of her starring in it. In April, John Huston received a telegram from the producer, Ray Stark: *Elizabeth Taylor's attorney advises she will read book over weekend to give decision about proceeding.*

While Elizabeth read *Reflections in a Golden Eye*, her wheels started turning as her excitement grew. The role of the repressed homosexual husband obsessing over a studly soldier on an army base in the 1940s could be perfect for Monty's comeback. She instinctively knew this was the right project for her and Monty to reunite in.

At first, before she committed to the film or told Monty about it, there were several things that she wanted to be sure of as a star of her stature. First off, aware that there were several really juicy parts in the book, Elizabeth wanted it to be absolutely clear that her role was to be the main role, the best one. The producer, Ray Stark, cabled John Huston: *Miss Taylor concerned about role being starring role and (her lawyer) advises that she wants specific language in contract to the effect that the role must be starring.*

Desperately wanting her to star in the picture, Stark suggested that Huston beef up Elizabeth's part in the script, even if it was just for show. "Please, let's at least write in enough scenes for Elizabeth so there can be no doubt about it being the best of the costarring parts," he urged. "We can always either not shoot them or cut them out later, but until she signs a contract, dear John, let's not rock this shaky canoe!"

After thinking it over, Elizabeth put her reservations aside and decided that her chance to work with Monty again was the most important thing—she didn't care if her part was the best. John Huston received a telegram with the happy news: *Taylor lawyer advises she's planning on going ahead with project and wants us to start as early as possible perhaps end of August He also advices she is worried not having seen script but she feels sure it will be good.*

The producers and director were ecstatic to have Elizabeth as the leading lady, but then she dropped a bombshell: "I will only appear in this film if my costar is Montgomery Clift." They simultaneously balked at the idea. Montgomery Clift was a broken-down has-been. Unusable. Uninsurable. Unacceptable. Elizabeth stood firm: without Monty, there would be no Elizabeth. She was willing to play hardball. Now Huston and Stark were up against a wall. "We'll do our best in getting Monty cast," they assured her.

Elizabeth, giddy with her own power, brushed all their protestations aside. She even called Monty with the news that she had found the project for them. When he heard that she was going to do *Reflections in a Golden Eye,* and that she wanted him to be his costar, he was so overcome with gratitude, he started to cry. He could hardly believe that he'd be going back to work—and with Bessie! He was even willing to work with John Huston again. "If he could stand it, I could stand it," Monty reasoned.

He was aware of the story of *Reflections in a Golden Eye,* but he rushed out to get the book and read it again. He had never done anything homosexual on the screen—it frightened him and excited him. And he had nothing to lose now. He wasn't a romantic figure any longer. He read the book over and over, each time growing more fascinated, excited by the layers he could bring to the role of Major Weldon Penderton, a gay man pretending to be straight in the hypermasculine military and going so far as to marry. Now, in middle age, Penderton finds himself obsessively attracted to a young soldier.

Then Monty would panic. What if the project fell through? Or, worse yet, what if they decided they didn't want him, after all, and chose to cast someone else? Gripped by this anxiety, he would call Elizabeth and reach her at her hotel. Typically, as they chatted, Elizabeth would be crawling under the bed, trying to locate a new puppy or trying to find another dog's squeezy toy, prompting Monty to describe Elizabeth's life away from a movie set as "Where's the dog leash, baby?" During every call he would voice his fears. He wanted it too much! What if it didn't happen? Elizabeth was always patient and would reassure him. "Don't worry, baby," she'd say. "We got them by the balls."

Behind the scenes, preproduction meetings were being held, and heated discussions were taking place. Huston still loathed Monty from their *Freud* feud, but in order to get Elizabeth to sign, he was willing to work with him again. Producer Ray Stark could also live with that casting, but no company was willing to insure Monty. It was the very thing that had kept him from working for nearly four years. There was no way around it. This was to be a substantially budgeted movie, Elizabeth's salary alone saw to that, and no one was willing to take a risk on someone with Monty's reputation.

The dilemma dragged on for several days, until Elizabeth threw up her hands and exclaimed, "Bloody hell! I'll put up the insurance money!" There was a stunned silence. In business terms, this meant that she was willing to put up her million-dollar salary as a guarantee that Monty would complete the movie. Even a loving friend like Elizabeth was aware that this was a risky venture. Knowing that there was a strong possibility that Monty might not make it through the production, Elizabeth was willing to take an expensive chance on him, anyway. After Monty's death producer Ray Stark sent a confidential letter to Elizabeth, in which he revealed, "We finally made a deal, and the problem of a possible replacement for Monty was something we never discussed."

It was astonishing to Monty that Elizabeth would do something so selfless for him. In recent years he had seen many of his friends distance themselves from him or cut him out of their lives completely. He spoke of Elizabeth with wonderment—so many people had let him down, abandoned him, but not her. Not his Bessie Mae. Not only was she putting a movie on the line but a million dollars, too. Elizabeth's gesture on Monty's behalf didn't surprise anyone who knew her. Her fierce loyalty to friends was part of who Elizabeth Taylor was.

Along with Elizabeth, a godsend for Monty during this period was Lorenzo James, who most friends came to call "Larry." People weren't quite sure what his position was. He was spending nearly twenty-four hours a day with Monty, and by now he had moved into a vacant bedroom in the brownstone. He had become an assistant, a nurse, a companion, a lover—a totally devoted friend.

Lorenzo even convinced Monty to rent a house on Fire Island, where he could get some air and sun. (Actress Diahann Carroll, who rented it the following year, affectionately called it the ugliest house on the Island.) And Monty made attempts to be social and mingle with some of the younger gays on the Island. Even at this stage of life—sick, drugged, out of sorts, beauty gone—even then, people still felt the specific magic of what he had inside him. "Being with Monty was like standing in front of a fireplace in the dead of winter and you get all this wonderful kind of sincerity," Lorenzo stated.

No matter where they were, Monty would talk nonstop to Lorenzo about going back to work. "He seemed ecstatic," but he was also "filled with fear." It was apparent that he had significantly changed physically since *Freud*. With help from Lorenzo, he went on an improvement regime in an attempt to look as good as possible. He upped his exercise, and he started eating better. Most importantly, he stopped drinking cold turkey.

He had so much to prove, to Elizabeth for believing in him, to Hollywood for not believing in him, and to himself, but he was full of self-doubt. Would he be able to perform, remember lines, give a performance? He was only forty-four, but his body functioned like that of a man almost double that age.

In an attempt to improve his haggard appearance, Monty decided to have some cosmetic surgery done to remove the bags under his eyes. The doctor, who had done cosmetic surgery on Lorenzo with terrific results, turned out to be another dark figure in Monty's life. Manfred Von Linde, who was gay, was suspected of killing a wealthy socialite fourteen years his senior on their honeymoon in Haiti. To add to Monty's woes, the surgery on his eyes was botched, and he had to have corrective surgery to reverse the plastic surgeon's work.

Still, he worried about the movie deal falling through, and this started him thinking about doing something to prove himself, to others and to himself. He wanted to work on something before he started *Reflections in a Golden Eye*. Something less visible, with less at stake. Monty started looking around for that sort of project, a movie that would work as a kind of test run for *Reflections*.

Through Salka Viertel, Jack Larson heard that director Raoul Lévy was interested in Monty for a role in a low-budget spy movie, *The Defector*, which would be filming in Munich. It was the kind of project Monty was looking for, and he wanted to do it. Setting up the deal, however, involved exhausting phone calls, long distance, to work out the details. The trouble revolved around Monty's insurability. Like *Reflections*, *The Defector* was being produced by Seven Arts, and once again Elizabeth's influence got Monty okayed for the role. Warner producers Ray Stark and Eliot Hyman, on her behalf, intervened, "fighting against great opposition from our banks" to get him cast.

By all accounts, the script for *The Defector* was execrable—it made little sense—but creating a great motion picture wasn't the top priority for Monty. He made it known that he would do the film as a dry run for *Reflections in a Golden Eye*. Still, he wanted to make *The Defector* as good as possible. He immediately began to look around for someone to help him whip the script into shape.

Jack Larson was still seriously involved with the talented writer James Bridges, and at first, Monty thought that Bridges might doctor the script, but he didn't know how to ask. On hearing this, Lorenzo wrote an impassioned letter imploring Bridges to polish the script, stressing how important it was to Monty. "He needs you, Jim," Lorenzo scrawled urgently. "He constantly says, 'If Jim could contribute anything at all to this script, I would walk on that set completely confident.'" He added, "He means it, Jim, and so do I . . . At this moment, Seven Arts could hire a battery of writers—to Monty they would not measure up [to you]. And Monty is right! You could do more with that script in one sitting than all of them have done in two months."

Bridges was unavailable to work on the script. In an attempt to help Monty, he tried to get Christopher Isherwood on board to rewrite it, but that fell through. Monty would have to do any rewriting himself.

Once again, executives insisted that he go through a physical in order to be hired, and on February 2, the president of Seven Arts showed up to personally escort Monty to a 2:00 p.m. doctor's appointment. As the executive waited, he took Lorenzo aside and whispered, "I came because I sincerely have a deep respect and admiration for him. I shall not only accompany him but will stay until the appointment ends and will send him home in my car."

When Leslie Caron came on board as the female lead of *The Defector*, the studio heads became hopeful that between her and Monty, they could make a decent movie, if not a great one. Leslie also had the idea of working on the script, and Monty flew to London so they could work on it together. Apparently, Monty went on to do further rewrites without her, and upon seeing the final script, Leslie backed out.

A lesser-known actress, Macha Méril, was finally brought in as a replacement. For moral support, Monty surrounded himself with people who made him feel safe. He hadn't been close to Mira Rostova for several years, but he asked her if she would accompany him to Germany to coach him on the shoot, as she had on earlier films. She agreed. And Roddy McDowall was cast in a supporting role. Monty also brought Lorenzo James along for moral support.

"He was physically very unwell during the progress of that film," Roddy McDowall recalled. "It was very cold. Munich in March. He didn't have the physical resources left anymore to protect him. But he was totally committed and totally there and fully responsible." Mira kept urging Monty not to give so much. She told him, "[J]ust get through it. It's not worth it." But he wouldn't walk through it.

The biggest hardships of the shoot, Monty inflicted on himself. For a scene where his character falls into a freezing river, a stuntman had been hired to double for him. He wouldn't hear of it. The reason for doing this movie was to prove himself—he had to do everything for himself. "I remember that he fought with director that he wanted to go in the cold water with some kind of rubber suit," Mira recalled. "They wanted to persuade him not to go in, but I don't know why he wanted to make such a big point that he could do it all." Mira didn't understand that his main motivation was to prove that he wasn't past it. He overcompensated by doing all his own stunts.

Monty looks very ill in *The Defector*. His head strangely looks too big for his emaciated body; his face is lined and, even through the makeup, has a grayish pallor. But there are a few flashes where glimpses of the handsome man he once was peek through. Monty got through it and was grateful when he got back home. Shooting would be starting on *Reflections*, and he looked forward to spending some quiet time studying the script.

40

DEFECTOR

It was as though there were two sides of Monty. There was this lovely, incredible human being, and there was another darker side to him, and his whole life was a battle, was a fight—and that side killed him, that side won out. The self-destructive Monty destroyed the other person, and it was a tremendous tragedy. But when I look back, I say that I feel blessed that I knew him. It was a gift.
—**Jean Levy**

WHEN MONTY RETURNED TO HIS TOWNHOUSE IN NEW YORK, HE sank into a deeper depression. He realized that *The Defector* was a personal failure, the first truly terrible movie of his career, and that he looked ravaged in it. (Later the reviews would confirm this.) *The Defector* was supposed to give him confidence for doing *Reflections*; instead, the experience made him more unsure, more frightened. "Nothing went right," he kept saying. "I have never had such a bad time in my life." More than anything, he was very, very tired. He started drinking heavily again, and for a while, he looked as if he was putting on some weight, but it was all bloat. Not a healthy look at all. People that saw him were convinced that he was a dying man.

Reflections in a Golden Eye now had a definite start date, September 15, and with Elizabeth's million-dollar bond hanging over his head, he worried. He had no control over his body, and it consistently betrayed him. "He was in agony," Lorenzo said. The pain in his back never ceased; his legs, covered in varicose veins, would knot and cramp. Lorenzo tried to massage some of the agony away.

The Demerol he injected added another layer of helplessness, because he would hallucinate and grow paranoid. At times he felt that Lorenzo was plotting against him and would even view Elizabeth as an enemy. Then he would do a complete reversal and begin to weep because he was powerless over these unreasonable thoughts. It all seemed so hopeless.

Monty would not live to film *Reflections in a Golden Eye.*

On July 22, 1966, the last full day of Monty's life, he was introspective and quiet. The previous week he had been on a bender, and he was trying to get sober again—he and Lorenzo would be leaving for location in Italy in a few weeks.

That day Monty shut out the world. He kept the door to his bedroom closed for the entire day. In the late evening, Lorenzo peeked into Monty's room to say good night and tell him that *The Misfits* was on the late show. Did he want to watch it with him? "Absolutely not!" Monty shouted. All those memories. The misfits in the desert, the waiting, the heat. Marilyn—gone now. He was in no frame of mind to relive it.

At 6:00 a.m. the following morning, when Lorenzo went in to wake Monty, he noticed he had fallen asleep with his glasses on. He appeared to be out cold, but Lorenzo was used to this. Monty was a lifelong insomniac, and when he finally drifted off, it was usually due to a mixture of drugs and alcohol, and his sleep would be very deep. Lorenzo lifted his naked body and started to carry him to the shower—halfway there, however, he realized Monty was dead.

Shocked, he called Monty's medical doctor, Arthur Ludwig, who was out of town. His associate, Dr. Kline, rushed to the townhouse instead. When the doctor arrived, he saw Monty lying naked on the bed, his fists clenched, his glasses still on. He pronounced Monty dead. At one point, Lorenzo told a medical examiner that Monty "had been hallucinating for a few days and had been trying to stop drinking to get into shape for his new movie."

Monty's body was taken to the city morgue at 520 First Avenue. Dr. Michael Baden performed the autopsy, in which he cited the cause of death as a massive heart attack brought on by "occlusive coronary artery disease." It is generally assumed that Monty's many addictions contributed to his death, in addition to his various illnesses, the lingering effects of chronic colitis and dysentery, the underactive thyroid, which caused calcium deficiencies and lowered his blood pressure. He was forty-five years old.

It was up to Lorenzo to notify Monty's family and friends. Elizabeth was in Italy, shooting *The Taming of the Shrew*. Richard took the call and informed Lorenzo he would give Elizabeth the news himself. Hearing of Monty's death was devastating to her—a piece of herself was gone. Instructing everyone to leave her alone, Elizabeth retreated to her bedroom and locked the door. Moments after, Richard and the staff could hear her wailing in pain.

Later, after she had composed herself, she called Lorenzo and talked to him for a long time—she wanted to know the details of Monty's last days. Afterward, she phoned Dr. Rex Kennamer, Monty's doctor who had become her doctor after they met at Monty's accident. Together they relived that dreadful night—how it had changed Monty in every way. "When you looked at Monty after the accident, you could see the difference—especially in his mouth," she cried. It was something she would never have revealed to Monty. She told the doctor about the shock of seeing him the last time she was in New York, how much he had changed. He had been "the most gorgeous thing I've ever seen" on *A Place in the Sun*. And she spoke of how much they loved each other and how she'd never feel that kind of connection with anyone again.

She regretted that she wouldn't be able to go to his service in New York, because of the tight shooting schedule on *The Taming of the Shrew*. "Elizabeth wanted to go to Monty's funeral," Franco

Zeffirelli said, "but a rupture in the schedule was unthinkable to a professional like Liz. Even that day, after her sobbing had died down, she went on the set." Later she told the press, "I'm in a state of shock. I can barely accept it. I loved him. He was my brother—he was my dearest friend."

As a remembrance, Lorenzo sent Elizabeth some of Monty's exquisite handmade handkerchiefs that he had recently bought in Paris, "delicate white on white." To Richard, he sent some of Monty's favorite soap. "I didn't know him very well, but he seemed a good man," Richard wrote in his diary.

Lorenzo James remembered the suspicion and the racism he experienced because of being in the brownstone alone with Monty when he died. "I've even been stopped in the street, and people said I had something to do with it," he said. Lorenzo was also angry that some didn't acknowledge what his position with Monty had evolved into. "And it all had to do with the racial thing," he said angrily in *Making Montgomery Clift*. "Here's this black man with Montgomery Clift. How dare he!"

"Perhaps his premature death was for the best, because it was very painful to live," Brooks Clift said. If Monty had died ten years earlier, even though he hadn't yet given some of his greatest performances, his death would have been a huge media event. In 1966 news of his death was received relatively sedately. *The Los Angeles Times* said, "This was the enigmatic man who died Saturday in New York City at the age of 45, little understood but always respected for the sensitivity of his approach to any part he played."

None of his famous costars attended the funeral. But there is a reason for some no-shows that has never been disclosed. There was an airport strike at LAX throughout the month of July, and it grounded all outgoing flights. Jack Larson and James Bridges were frantic to get to New York, but with no planes flying, it seemed impossible. Larson was doubly upset because another close friend, the poet Frank O'Hara, had died that week, and he would have to miss both funerals.

Out of the blue, Frank Sinatra called Larson. Sinatra was planning to fly to New York in his private jet to attend Monty's funeral.

Sinatra remained loyal in his friendship. Larson agreed to accompany him, but last-minute problems involving his engagement to Mia Farrow, along with some other pressing issues, made Sinatra call the trip off.

A FUNERAL WITHOUT POMP, a headline read. The people inside the church were very representative of Monty's compartmentalized life. Small clusters and individuals sat in isolated parts of the church. There was a crowd of about two hundred people gathered outside the entrance to St. James Church, there to spot stars coming in and out of Monty's service. They were probably disappointed not to see Elizabeth Taylor, who was filming in Italy. Good friends like Roddy McDowall were also working.

A weeping Lauren Bacall was probably the most recognizable. Libby Holman, haggard and grieving, sat in a back pew. Nancy Walker was also there, along with Monty's family and Lorenzo James. Elizabeth had sent two very large arrangements of chrysanthemums, with a card that read, *Rest, perturbed spirit.* After the service, Monty was buried at Friends Quaker Cemetery in Prospect Park, Brooklyn.

Reflections in a Golden Eye, the movie that Elizabeth planned to make with Monty and that he felt would restore his career, was recast with Marlon Brando, the only actor she would accept. "To me, they tap and come from the same source of energy," Elizabeth explained when discussing their acting styles. "They both have this acute animal sensitivity and the other more animalistic. But it's the same thing. Because, if you think about it, they both have the vulnerability." The movie was not a success, and one could only wonder if Monty's reteaming with Elizabeth would have changed that.

Montgomery Clift is less remembered than Elizabeth Taylor and other movie stars who had his kind of impact in their day. He didn't die young like James Dean or have a body of work like Marlon Brando. He didn't live long enough to reinvent himself over and over, like Elizabeth. But for those who love screen acting, he is revered as a pioneer whose acting style influenced generations of actors to come and continues to do so. "Monty could have been the biggest star in the world if he did more movies," Elizabeth always said.

The impact that Monty's perturbed spirit had on Elizabeth's life would remain with her throughout her life, but she didn't talk publicly about the private man very much. "My feelings are deep and personal," she explained. Yet she never shied away from talking about him as an artist. "You know, we can't speculate what would have happened to Monty's career," Elizabeth mused. "He's safe now. But then he wasn't safe. He was one of the best actors, innovators that the acting world has ever known. His death came at an untimely, unheroic, unpoetic moment in his life. So instead of being revered, he's kind of shuffled aside. But, good God, all you have to do is look at some of his old films. Just look at him. Open a little door of your consciousness and you can be on his wavelength so easily. He just takes you along. That's a great artist."

It wasn't until some years later, after all the chaotic emotions Monty stirred up in her had settled, that Elizabeth was able to sum up her personal feelings in a simple remembrance. "I miss Montgomery Clift," she said, her voice shaking. "I miss talking to him, exchanging thoughts and ideas. I miss laughing together and doing silly things together. He was the best friend I've ever had—and I think he would say the same about me. He was so brilliantly talented and such a tragic figure. Oh, I loved him! And I still do."

41

ELIZABETH IN LATER YEARS

I don't give a shit what people think.
—**Elizabeth Taylor**

AFTER MONTY'S DEATH, ELIZABETH'S LIFE WOULD GO ON FOR FORTY-five more years.

She would win her second Academy Award, for *Who's Afraid of Virginia Woolf?*, this time, undisputedly deserved. As their careers moved forward, their "Liz and Dick" marriage would provide fodder for gossip columns and movie magazines for years: the fantastic jewels Richard presented her with, their international jet-setting, their spats, their drinking.

They continued to make movies together and separately, although by the late 1960s their movie careers began to decline and their marriage faltered, although Elizabeth kept on making films through the 1970s and sporadically in the 1980s and 1990s, mostly for television. They divorced in 1974 and remarried in 1975, "for lovely always." This time *lovely always* came to an end in 1976. They divorced again. But he would remain one of the great loves of her life.

When Richard married model Suzy Miller in August 1976 (one month after his second divorce from Elizabeth), Elizabeth was frantic to marry again. Through it all, she remained a star. Public fascination with Elizabeth Taylor never really subsided, although when she married the Republican politician John Warner (after several prospects) that December, she temporarily gave up show business. She did, however, use her star power in helping Warner's Senate campaign.

After a while, she grew bored with life in Washington DC, and she overate. Also, it was during this time that her alcoholism and drug dependency spiraled out of control. Warner and Elizabeth divorced in 1982. Taking up acting again, she appeared on Broadway in *The Little Foxes* and, to much fanfare, in *Private Lives*, with ex-husband Richard Burton in 1983. By then Richard had remarried again.

Aging is never easy for someone noted for their beauty, but Elizabeth didn't fret over it much. She liked to say, "Before forty you have the face you were born with; after forty you get the face you deserve." For the next several years, the things that became newsworthy about her were her weight gain, another divorce, and her addiction to pills and alcohol. If anyone thought Elizabeth was heading toward being another has-been actor, living on her past glories, they were mistaken. Throughout her life, one of Elizabeth's great talents was to reinvent herself.

In December of 1983, Elizabeth checked into the Betty Ford Center to deal with her addictions. "I used to think that drinking would help my shyness, but all it did was exaggerate all the negative qualities," she concluded. "I was the first celebrity to go to the center," she would say. "Since then, quite a few have gone. Don't get the idea that the center is a spa for stars. All kinds of people go there, including street junkies. It's the great leveler."

At the end of her stay at the Betty Ford Center, Elizabeth emerged healthy, clean, and radiant. Weight loss and some good plastic surgery had restored her lush beauty. When she started a perfume line—joining with Elizabeth Arden—her fragrances Passion, White Diamonds, and Black Pearls would go on to earn her more money than her movie career. She would make hundreds of millions of dollars from her perfumes over the years.

Yet with all her rebirths, her reinventions, her new ventures, her many selves, Elizabeth's greatest accomplishments in her later life were her contributions to AIDS research. By 1985 AIDS was ravaging the gay community. Because it was considered a "gay" disease, it was largely ignored—except in the gay community. People were dying, and no one seemed to be doing anything to help them medically, financially, emotionally. They were invisible, which added to the devastation of an agonizing death. "I first heard about AIDS while reading the newspapers, then, hearing it on television news," Elizabeth recalled. "It was quick, just one sentence. It grabbed me that people were being ignored and dying."

Elizabeth wasn't exactly considered a fag hag, and she actually hated that term. "I think it's a really horrible expression," she stated. "I've had great friendships with men who happen to be homosexual." But it was well known that some of her closest friends, Roddy McDowall, Rock Hudson, and especially Montgomery Clift, were gay. That was one of the reasons seven gay men who were part of the community-based group AIDS Project Los Angeles approached Elizabeth with the request that she sign on as a chairperson for the first major AIDS benefit, the Commitment to Life dinner. "I realized that this town—of all towns—was basically homophobic," Elizabeth told *Vanity Fair*, "even though without homosexuals, there would be no Hollywood, no show business! Yet the industry was turning its back on what it considered a gay disease."

By this point in the epidemic, major celebrities, like Brad Davis, Liberace, and Rock Hudson, had AIDS, but none of them had gone public with it. The shame of getting a gay sexually transmitted disease was overwhelming to many. When Elizabeth first agreed to be a chairperson on the committee, she was unaware that Rock had AIDS. "Oh, God, yes, I knew he was gay," she said, "but I thought he had cancer."

Once Elizabeth signed on to chair the event, it took on a new importance. "So many people were frightened and doing so little about it. The silence was thunderous, and the only way to stop that is to speak out." With Elizabeth on board, people were listening—the guest list began to grow. She got on the phone to rally celebrity friends to get involved. Some did, although not everyone was willing to jump on board and participate. "I knew what I was taking on," she said, "but even after all the people who hung up on me, I did not give up." Then, when Rock Hudson finally released a statement revealing he had AIDS, the response became so great, the dinner, which was originally scheduled to take place at the Century Plaza Hotel, had to be moved to a larger hall, the Westin Bonaventure ballroom.

Eventually, some very big names signed on to lend support: Carol Burnett, Sammy Davis Jr., Diahann Carroll, Cyndi Lauper, Burt Reynolds, and Rod Stewart all participated. Rock Hudson bought ten thousand dollars' worth of tickets but was too ill to attend. He sent a telegram to the guests that said in part: *I am not happy that I am sick. I am not happy that I have AIDS. But if that is helping others, I can, at least, know that my own misfortune has had some positive worth.* The event raised 1.3 million dollars.

Soon after, Rock died. From then on, AIDS would be the main focus of Elizabeth's life. She began a tireless crusade to end the epidemic. Jack Larson stated, "Elizabeth Taylor and Rock Hudson were friends and shared personal memories of making *Giant* and of Michael Wilding, etc. But Elizabeth was closer to Montgomery Clift, and a big reason she became an AIDS activist was her conviction that had Monty lived, he could have easily contracted HIV. Rock Hudson was the catalyst, but Elizabeth did it for Monty and in essence all her gay friends."

In her devotion to her gay friends, she cofounded the Foundation for AIDS Research (amfAR). Later, in 1991, she established the Elizabeth Taylor AIDS Foundation (ETAF) to provide physical care, along with love and moral support, to those suffering the most. Today it is acknowledged that in that era, Elizabeth had a tremendous part in removing the stigma of both homosexuality and AIDS. She brought awareness, and her charities raised millions.

And Elizabeth didn't just use her money and fame to make a difference from a distance; she actually was very hands on, visiting patients at hospices all around the world. "Nobody knows I go," she revealed later. "The press doesn't follow me. When I did my perfume tour, in every city I would find a hospice. We'd have a ball. I'd go to their room, or we'd sit in the kitchen and laugh. I would say, 'No one seems to be listening to you. What can we do for you? What do you need that you don't have?' I'll never forget one answer. 'Somebody to put their arms around me.' So every time that I went to a hospice after that, I hugged and kissed each patient, because they were being treated like lepers."

In 1988 Elizabeth slipped into her bad habits of drinking and pill taking and again checked herself into the Betty Ford Center. "I had the arrogance to think I could be a social drinker," says Taylor, "and I was addicted to painkillers."

It was there Elizabeth met her eighth and last husband, Larry Fortensky. He was controversial for other reasons than her previous husbands. Twenty years her junior, Fortensky was not married, but he was also not in show business, not rich, and he was totally unknown. Elizabeth Taylor's new love interest was a construction worker when she met him in group therapy at her second stint in rehab. In 1991 they married at Michael Jackson's Neverland Ranch and sold the wedding pictures to a magazine for one million dollars (which Elizabeth used toward her AIDS foundation).

Elizabeth had met Michael Jackson when he invited her to a concert in 1984. They formed a bond, partly due to having both been child stars and having their youth sold by their parents to studios, managers, and handlers. "He had one of the worst childhoods ever," she once said about Michael. "I think I had the second."

When Michael was accused of sexually abusing prepubescent children, Elizabeth stood by her friend. She believed in his innocence when many didn't. Even after her death, with the release of the documentary *Leaving Neverland* (which made more people condemn Michael), Elizabeth's assistant, Tim Mendelson, said, "She would have defended him—Elizabeth would defend any friend to the death."

Around this time, she was doing a lot of interviews for the gay press, and Elizabeth told journalist Kevin Sessums that during the making of *A Place in the Sun*, she knew Monty was gay "probably even more than he did." She continued, "And I helped him with it, which is extraordinary, because I was only about sixteen, and I didn't really know anything about it." This is, of course, Elizabeth myth making for her gay audience. Monty had known he was gay for years by 1948, and he had been in relationships with many men. If she did help him in any way, it was by helping him with the realization that he would be unable to have a lasting sexual relationship with any woman.

Elizabeth would always defend Monty against people who claimed that he hated himself because he was gay. "He hated homophobia, not homosexuality," she would say sharply. Once when Elizabeth was watching *A Place in the Sun* with some friends, they came to a court scene with Monty, Raymond Burr, and Keefe Brasselle, and Elizabeth exclaimed, "My God, all three were gay!" Then she shook her head and muttered, "If only the public knew." Monty once said that gay actors, in all their roles—and with the absence of gay characters in films—were always working "in the service of heterosexuality."

The marriage to Fortensky lasted for five years, but they remained on good terms, and they stayed in touch until Elizabeth's death. As she became older, her life slowed down. Her health, always shaky, deteriorated, and she suffered a series of illnesses in the 1990s. Along with treating an irregular heartbeat and respiratory problems, Elizabeth had three hip replacement operations in three years. In 1998 she had a three-hour operation to remove "a golf ball–sized tumor" that was pressing against her brain. The operation was a success, and afterward, she allowed herself to be photographed with a shaved head.

Late in her life, Elizabeth said she loved retiring to her bed, which she outfitted with lush, expensive sheets. She made her bedroom into a sanctuary of comfort and peacefulness, but she didn't shut herself off completely. She attended AIDS events. She was active on Twitter. She saw her children and grandchildren. Ironically, Debbie Reynolds came back into her life in her later years, and she and Elizabeth became good friends, often watching movies together in Elizabeth's bedroom.

Elizabeth gave a last public performance in 2007, when she performed with James Earl Jones in the play *Love Letters* at an

AIDS benefit at Paramount Studios. As she found it increasingly necessary to use a wheelchair, on good days she would venture out to West Hollywood, sometimes going in the late afternoon to the trendy outdoor gay bar the Abbey. But her health continued to fail.

Elizabeth Taylor died on March 23, 2011, at Cedars-Sinai Medical Center in Los Angeles. She was seventy-nine. She had been struggling with congestive heart failure for a number of years, and in early March she had suffered a number of setbacks and had been hospitalized. When she passed away, she was surrounded by her children.

In these last years, Elizabeth often said that the thing she wanted to be remembered for most was her work for AIDS research and charities. She is certainly held in great esteem for that. Still, she is also inevitably remembered for her great beauty and alluring sensuality in photographs and films. And, of course, the scandals.

Yet once when a photographer asked Elizabeth how she felt about being "the most beautiful woman in the world," she replied, "Oh, that's just silly. I see better-looking women every day, just walking down the street."

But perhaps her mirror didn't reflect the qualities that were so clear to others when gazing at her. Yes, when you looked at Elizabeth, you saw the violet eyes with a double set of lashes, the translucent skin, the raven hair cascading. But it isn't just the physical attributes that are the sum of a beautiful woman.

In perfection, there's always something authentic and surprising. When looking at Elizabeth, one can see an exquisite aura—sexual and tempestuous mixed with a loving heart, a gift for friendship, her compelling talent, a compassionate spirit, and a fiery passion for it all. Elizabeth didn't just live life; she explored it, embraced it, tasted it, challenged it, and swallowed it whole. She wrapped her sins and her triumphs around her like an elegant evening shawl as she pranced down a runway. She was a giver, a taker, a passionate lover of life! And when you looked at her, that's what you saw. What you still see. That is her beauty.

EPILOGUE

*L*OVE HAS MANY DEFINITIONS, MANY DIRECTIONS; AND IF LIFE IS A series of entwining roads in which lives cross paths and we have to choose how to proceed with each encounter, Elizabeth and Monty held on to their connection and nurtured it until it turned it into a unique kind of love.

Their relationship was one that neither really could define. It was different than the love felt for a lover and more than the love of a friend. "Monty was my inspiration," Elizabeth once said. "We loved each other with all our hearts. Not sexually, but maybe romantically." Monty would admit that he couldn't explain his love for Elizabeth; it was something that felt as if it had always been there, to simply feel and cherish.

They were called the most beautiful couple in cinema history, and the intense, enthralling chemistry Elizabeth and Monty generated together is immortalized forever in *A Place in the Sun.* Their feelings for each other were so powerful that when they appear in the love scenes, it doesn't matter that we now know they were not of the same sexual persuasion—all the aching hunger and beauty of love, in all its definitions, are there.

They brought out the best in each other; they recognized that early on. It was a friendship that encouraged and supported and moved life forward. They told each other things that they never told anyone else, and they took their secrets with them—as it should be. It was the kind of beautiful, encompassing relationship needed to live a full life, a fulfilling life, a life of accomplishment—in which one grows and improves and becomes more enlightened about life and, yes, love. We all need at least one friend like that. For Elizabeth and Monty, it was each other.

ACKNOWLEDGMENTS

I would like to thank my parents, Gloria and Ralph, not only for their love and support but also for their friendship.

A sincere thank-you goes to my agent, Tom Miller, for his belief in me. Also, I was very lucky to have John Scognamiglio as my editor at Kensington—he was kind and enthusiastic during the writing of this book.

Elizabeth and Monty lived very rich, very hectic lives, and they shared a relationship that was complex and changeable. A myriad of sources and voices have to come together in order to tell their story in full. In that regard, I have been fortunate. Among the many people I interviewed for this project, I am especially grateful to Angela Allen, Diahann Carroll, Ron Chilton, Joan Collins, John Conboy, Robert Forster, Charlotte Henson, Liz Kernen, Sally Kirkland, Robin Leach, Brenda Maddox, Mark Randal, Charles Rappleye, and Susan Rogers.

I would like to express my sincere gratitude to Kimothy Cruse, who knew Elizabeth Taylor starting with *The Little Foxes* period and would often spend time reminiscing with Elizabeth and her personal assistant/press spokesman Chen Sam. Kimothy has wonderful Elizabeth Taylor remembrances and insights, which he tells with humor and passion.

While writing this book, I was also blessed to have the input of Denis Ferrara, who knows almost all there is to know about Elizabeth and often writes about her with wit and candor (and he also happens to be a very dear person and a valued friend).

My heartfelt thanks go to Neal Baer, whose fascinating talks added new information about Montgomery Clift—especially regarding the time he was with Jack Larson. Ken Storer was very generous with his time and with sharing wonderful memories of Larson's relationship with Monty and friendship with Elizabeth—as well as of other people in Monty's life. Ken is a gentleman who went above and beyond in helping me, and I'm very grateful to him.

In 2002, after I completed my biography of the writer John Rechy, I began a book on Montgomery Clift, which I ultimately left unfinished for a number of reasons. But that project led me to the many important interviews that I did at the time, and I am grateful that I was able to put them to good use in this project. Among those I talked to are Ellis Amburn, William Bast, Patricia Bosworth, Michelangelo Capua, Jean Porter, Farley Granger, Don Keefer, Dr. Rex Kennamer, Martin Landau, Jack Larson, Kevin McCarthy, Franklin MacFie, Mira Rostova, Eva Marie Saint, Blaine Waller, and Shelley Winters. Not all of them are mentioned in the text, but all their insights certainly contributed to the atmosphere of the book.

There are also a number of people whom I interviewed for other projects through the years who generously shared their memories and observations about the times of Montgomery Clift and Elizabeth Taylor and contributed to my understanding. They are Don Bachardy, Leslie Caron, C. David Heymann, Gavin Lambert, Skip E. Lowe, Edward Parone, Curtice Taylor, and Mamie Van Doren. In addition, there are several sources who wished to remain anonymous, and I thank them for their input.

Once again, I would like to express my gratitude to the staff at the Margaret Herrick Library, such a pleasant and important place. I would especially like to thank Louise Hilton and Marisa Duron. The main collections I consulted there are the Edward Dmytryk Papers, the Gladys Hall Papers, the Jack Hirshberg Papers, the Hedda Hopper Papers, the John Huston Papers, the Fred Zinnemann Papers, the George Stevens Papers, the Robert LaGuardia Collection, the Joseph L. Mankiewicz Papers, and the Dennis McDougal Research Files. I also utilized the Montgomery Clift Papers in the Billy Rose Theatre Division at the New York Public Library for the Performing Arts, as well as the Patricia Bosworth Papers at that location.

The Facebook group "Montgomery Clift Daily" is a terrific source for all things Monty—for both fans and movie scholars alike. Likewise, "The Great Elizabeth Taylor" page on Facebook is a place where fans come together to share anecdotes and photos.

The relationship between Elizabeth and Monty was a multilayered one that added to both their lives in immeasurable ways. I have some Montgomery Clifts and Elizabeth Taylors in my own life whom I would like to acknowledge. I could never really thank Kelvin Dale enough for all he's done for me. Yet I find myself thanking him every day—even to myself. Thank you, Kelvin. I am grateful to my dear friend Jeff Dymowski simply for being Jeff Dymowski. Indescribable but marvelous. I wish to express my eternal gratitude to Vincent Curcio, a most wonderful, bossy, generous friend, who always advises me, helps me, and pushes me a little further—always in the right direction. I would also like to thank several lovely souls whose friendship during the course of the writing of this book supported and comforted me and whose conversations stimulated me: Rick Brooks, Tricia Civello, and Mary Gaitskill. All always dear to me.

My thanks and affection go out to my glorious red rose, Rossana Scottodivettimo Weitekamp—long of name and big of heart. And also to Cathy Smith, my first friend—and a very dear one.

Mike Prestie is a one-of-a-kind friend, whom I am grateful for, and he assisted me in a variety of ways.

My relationship with journalist J. Randy Taraborrelli is a treasure that was unearthed a long time ago, and I am so thankful for his friendship and the golden times we spend together talking about classic Hollywood and everything else.

A very special thank-you goes to Lisa Santucci and Mike O'Connor for the support and encouragement and good company.

While I'm at it, I would like to thank these other constants in my life: John Rechy, Scott Lesko, Marcella Winn, Debra Tate, David Sloan, Stewart Penn, Frank Fisher, Jacquelyn Michelle, Cindy Negron, Tony Frere, Damian Wild and Marlene, Anthony Jr., Joe, and Adrianna. I'll use the word *love* for all of the above.

There are lovely others who pop in and out of my life, and you know who you are.

Please turn the page for an

exclusive essay from

Charles Casillo!

I HAVE ALWAYS BEEN FRIENDLY WITH THE DEAD. MAYBE IT'S BECAUSE they don't talk as much as the living. Safer and less apt to hurt, they remain frozen and unreachable, knowable only through the things they left behind. In the case of movie stars, it's their films.

When I was a kid I often felt lonely and isolated for a number of reasons. At the time, movies from Hollywood's Golden Age played on television in the afternoons and especially at night on the late, late show. It was there that I found a place where I felt at home. I discovered the classic movie stars. Immediately I felt close to Cary Grant, Ava Gardner, Clark Gable, Rita Hayworth, Humphrey Bogart and many others. The joy they brought in comedies, the danger they projected in film noir, the clever way they expressed themselves in dramas—those were worlds that felt very real to me.

Still today, I sometimes feel like a man out of time. My favorite black-and-white and Technicolor movies almost always present a world I want to visit—if not live in.

I related to those movies in a way that I didn't connect to reality. I loved everything about those distant eras: the clothes, the music, the vernacular and especially the movie personalities. These stars became my first friends, really, and much of the enjoyment I had as a kid came from first watching their movies and later learning about their lives in biographies and documentaries.

Everyone knows that Marilyn Monroe—deceased before I was born—has a place in my heart that's roped off for tragic figures. I saw a photo of her in a magazine and *I had to know more.* I read all the biographies of her, and reading about her led to knowledge of other tragic movie stars. Fallen stars like Jean Harlow and James Dean and Montgomery Clift. It was probably studying Marilyn that led me to Monty. I felt such admiration for him. I recognized that—as beautiful and talented and sought after as he was—he was still lonely. That was something I recognized and responded to immediately. It still touches me to this day.

Elizabeth Taylor was different from the others. She was really special to me because she was still alive and active at the time, a link between the Golden Age and my present day.

And then there was Elizabeth and Monty together! They seduced me in their movies like they did many people before and after. I've loved the three films Elizabeth and Monty co-starred in. *A Place in the Sun* and *Suddenly, Last Summer* are among my all-time favorite movies. I had heard about their friendship but their extraordinary chemistry lead me to believe it was more than just a cookie-cutter relationship. *I had to know more.*

Since they both changed the direction of each other's life, it seemed to me that a book devoted to exploring their friendship was appropriate. They met, they fell into an intense, complex relationship and then it steadied. But they didn't separate and lose touch the way so many other friendships end. Their lives became entangled and through that lasting relationship they brought out the sensitivity and vulnerability in each other.

So I set out to explore them, to know more. It was indeed a fascinating journey; one that compelled me to admire them even more—if that was possible. My hope was to give some readers a more nuanced understanding of these legendary superstars. I'm always gratified and delighted when I hear or read from someone that the book touched them.

* * *

Sometimes people have called the book gossipy, which baffles me. I'm telling the life stories of two extraordinarily colorful and controversial personalities. Elizabeth Taylor was a wonderfully giving person and a talented actress. She also had many affairs and was married eight times. She was at least partially responsible for the breakup of two marriages—after having affairs with the husbands. She checked herself into the Betty Ford Clinic twice for drug and alcohol abuse—and was vocal about it. The lady had a big appetite. She didn't eat life. She devoured it. She loved jewels and men and clothes and she went after what she wanted with gusto. Should a writer not investigate and write about those things in telling her story? I don't think a reader would come away from the book knowing who she really was without seeing that side of her life.

Montgomery Clift was one of the most talented actors the screen has ever known. There were many times he was very kind and witty. Friends and audiences adored him. Monty also had many anonymous sexual encounters and seemed unable to maintain a stable, functioning relationship. He numbed his pain with massive amounts of drugs and alcohol and—when under the influence—could be quite immature and cruel. Does this diminish his accomplishments? Of course not. But, in my opinion, these things should be explored by a biographer in an attempt to piece together a full understanding of the subject.

Many of us are horribly complicated creatures with complex emotions clouding what we really feel at our core, and muddling what we convey to the world. All of that baggage has to be sifted through in order to discover the true person. But I want to let you know again that, through all the complex layers of these personalities, I always think of Elizabeth and Monty with great affection and respect and fondness.

I believe that if you turn away from a person's darkness, then you really can't appreciate their light. All the facets of their personalities combine and make them a genius, particularly a genius like Monty. You have to delve in deep when trying to understand why a man who had so many gifts became so self-destructive.

Yes, part of his pain was because he was a gay man in an era that considered that to be sick and degenerate. How difficult it must have been for him being so loved while knowing that the very people who adored him would despise him if the truth came out. But that was only a fraction of what caused his despair. With someone as sensitive as Monty so many things stung and affected him deeply.

Some have asked me why I mentioned Monty's diminutive endowment. Some have expressed outrage. I did not include that in the text as a bit of gleeful gossip to diminish an icon (one that I admire, no less).

Yes, it's unpleasant. It's unpleasant as hell thinking about something so utterly private, let alone writing about it. But I concluded that if a person becomes a romantic idol and is the subject of countless sexual fantasies, revered for his physicality, how difficult it must have been to realize that he did not always live up to the fantasy. That, at times, the great god was a disappointment. It is known that Monty became aware that people snickered about this behind his back. I feel it played a definite part in his unhappiness and is a piece of the puzzle in understanding his despair. Most of us have self-perceived flaws that have left scars in one way or another.

Monty has been a part of my life for a long time. Years ago, in 2006, when I was in the middle of tentatively researching a book about Montgomery Clift, I had an opportunity to visit the brownstone that he lived and died in. It was a moving experience for me at the time and I wrote a blog entry about it. I thought you might like to see it.

MONTGOMERY CLIFT
SLEPT HERE

*F*OR YEARS, AFTER A LONELY NIGHT ON THE TOWN—HAVING HAD ONE too many—I'd stand in front of Marilyn Monroe's Manhattan apartment on Sutton Place, trying to feel her in some way. Wondering what it would have been like to be waiting there when her limo pulled up in 1962 after she sang Happy Birthday to President Kennedy at Madison Square Garden. Staring up at the thirteenth floor, I'd exclaim to myself, "She was here!" And I stood there on the street waiting for some sign or comfort.

It's because of obsessions like this that I felt a jolt when reading online real estate listings when I noticed a property for sale at 217 East 61st Street. The ad stated: "Lovely four-story, sun-filled, single family townhouse in the Treadwell Historic District has most of its original details intact." Nowhere in the ad did it say that this was the house where actor, tragic figure, and Hollywood legend, Montgomery Clift, had lived from 1960 until his death in 1966. But I immediately knew.

Monty Clift is one of my "dead people" friends. When I was a kid I would watch his movies on *The Late Show* stunned by his awesome talent and intense presence. He was one of the greatest and most influential of our film stars. In the Montgomery Clift fan club world word spread fast that Monty's brownstone was on the market. Soon I began receiving emails from a secretive Monty fan club I had joined while researching a potential biography on the sad, troubled, magnificent actor.

The exceptionally handsome star once rivaled Marlon Brando and James Dean as the most sensitive, interesting, and creative actor in Hollywood. He starred in classic films like *A Place in the Sun* and *From Here to Eternity*. Yet, when he died a broken, tormented man at the age of forty-five, he was considered a forgotten has-been by much of the world. Today Montgomery Clift doesn't have the iconic status of Brando or Dean, but there still is a substantial cult of devotees that recognizes him as the very first of the rebel actors whose broody, naturalistic style set a new standard in screen acting.

Verifying my reputation as a nut—and as a longtime friend of the dead star—no way was I going to miss the opportunity to be inside Monty's house. On an early muggy evening I invited my friend, the writer Michelangelo Capua—who wrote, *Montgomery Clift: A Biography*, (originally published in Italy)—to come to the open house with me. Michelangelo himself has a classic Hollywood appearance, six foot seven and good-looking. Actually, he looks like he could have been a double for Anthony Perkins during the period of the filming of *Psycho*. Wearing our good suits, we headed up the stairs leading to the door of Monty's house.

In previous years, I often walked past Monty's building but I didn't dare ring the doorbell. The previous owners were understandably not welcoming to curiosity seekers who stopped by. For decades Montgomery Clift fanatics rang the bell at all hours, demanding to be let in to explore the house. But now as potential buyers we were welcomed. When we entered the town house we were greeted by a real estate agent, Ms. Lee, of a prestigious real estate brokerage. I told her I was from Los Angeles, "here to look at the house." She seemed impressed. I assumed Michelangelo and I looked like a high-powered show business duo on the market for a Manhattan residence.

"Oh, you live in Los Angeles?" she asked. "You might be interested to know that a one-time famous actor lived here: Montgomery Clift."

My heart started to beat much faster. I was determined not to bring up the subject of Monty and here she was volunteering the information. I acted blasé. "Oh really," I deadpanned. "I think I saw one of his movies once." Through the corner of my eye I saw Michelangelo snicker.

Ms. Lee, whose hair, as well as her sales pitch, had many highlights, could well be the prototype for realtors the world over: attractive, smiling, friendly, perky, eager, knowledgeable. "Shall we go up?" she asked, beginning the tour. "It needs some renovations," she said almost apologetically as she led the way up the rickety stairs. "But you can see that with the original details untouched, wonderful things can be done with the place." I liked it the way it was. A current commercial jokes that when a celebrity dies on a property it's automatically a national landmark. When asked if Clift died in the house Ms. Lee wasn't sure. "Most people die in hospitals," she replied vaguely.

In *A Place in the Sun* Monty urgently whispers to Elizabeth Taylor, "It's wonderful while you're here. While I can hold you, I can see you. And I can hold you next to me. But what's it going to be like next week. . . ?"

In fact, I already knew that Monty died in the house of a heart attack. His live-in nurse/companion, Lorenzo James, found him in bed, naked except for his eyeglasses. By then Monty had become a ravaged, haunted soul. Yet Elizabeth Taylor, who already starred in three pictures with him, had once again come to the aid of her friend and demanded he be cast in a movie with her, *Reflections in a Golden Eye.* She even put up her own salary as insurance.

It was presumed that the near-fatal car accident in 1957 that crushed his face, shattering his looks and confidence, along with the guilt he felt over his homosexuality, caused the emotional pain that made him numb his torment in drugs and alcohol. When he first moved into the house, Monty was still somewhat in demand and many of the huge rooms remained unfurnished for a long time while he was making movies. When decorating, Monty preferred simple classic styles. He painted the walls a light shade of beige. He had a collection of silver objects scattered throughout the living room. He told friends, "I don't like a place cluttered up with stuff. Whatever I have here I bought piece by piece when I saw something I would enjoy living with."

It was here that Monty entertained close friends like Elizabeth Taylor and comedienne Nancy Walker. Monty also had dinners with Marilyn Monroe, who had an apartment four blocks away and it was she who once famously remarked about Monty, "He's the only person I know who's more screwed up than I am."

Monty lived in the townhouse for a number of years with his French lover, Claude Perrin—a handsome young man who said he was a fashion designer but mostly mooched off of Monty. At some point Claude attempted suicide in the house at the end of their relationship before moving back to France. For a while the actor Jack Larson, who had played Jimmy Olsen in the original television series *Superman,* lived with Monty in one of the spare bedrooms.

Further into his disintegration, desperately lonely and some-times stoned out of his mind, Monty would cruise Third Avenue for male prostitutes and bring them home in the middle of the night and, it is said, they would sometimes beat him up. In the morning the house would be overrun with sinister boys slinking through rooms and going through his personal belonging. A bruised Monty would lock himself in his bedroom, not remem-bering the night before, frantically calling friends to come and help him get rid of the strangers.

All of these memories—transfigured into ghosts—could be felt in the house, seeping out of the ancient wood . . . death and love and misery and hope and the laughter of someone now dead . . . all swirling around in the musty air. You could feel it. It is what I wanted to experience and there it was.

In *The Misfits* Monty lays with his injured head in Marilyn Monroe's lap. "Who do we depend on," he asks her. "Who?"

In 1966, after Monty died, a young couple with three children had bought the house from Monty's twin sister, who had inherited it from him. The family has owned the house for over forty years. The matriarch had recently died.

Some of the remnants of Montgomery Clift have not been erased by four decades of family life. Many of the fixtures in the house seemed to be the original ones from the time of Monty's occupancy: wooden floors, pantry, staircase, the banister, windows, doors, and the many floor-to-ceiling bookshelves. He had set up three libraries: one in the main living room and two in the bedrooms. The shelves were once arranged with Monty's books, alphabetically—a task he didn't get to until the year he died.

Ms. Lee pointed out the bar that Monty had built on the second floor. In his final year, Monty had complained to a friend that when he entertained guests he had to mix drinks in the closet. He knocked down a wall so the bar could be built. Monty chose the wood himself. He had been proud of that bar. Earlier biographies made the bar sound quite grand. "Teak and brass and shaped like the prow of a ship," is how one book describes it. The bar—like many things remembered or imagined—is smaller in reality. The bar that Monty built is a tiny, bare, corner affair with a little stainless-steel sink. The counter barely could fit one person standing behind it. Nothing you would expect from a legendary drinker like Monty.

The doors to the rooms and closets are chipped and decaying, the stairs are creaky, the banister old. Continuing up the stairs we came to the master bedroom. Montgomery Clift slept here! Had sex here. Died here. Why is it impossible to describe the feeling I get in these places? Silently the compatible parts of our spirits privately communicated—Monty's and mine. Probably, along with his aura, traces of Monty's DNA could be found in the master bathroom if an FBI unit was called in. The tiles and bathtub seem to be the very same ones Monty stepped on in his bare feet. Michelangelo was looking for the big medicine cabinet that Monty reportedly had custom built to hold his medications, but nothing fitting that description could be found, although the sink is the same one where Monty would discard the syringes he used to pump drugs into his body in a desperate quest for relief from his pain.

For $5.5 million some potential buyers might consider the space neglected. For a Monty fan, it's a bargain. The fact that so little has changed since he lived there is part of its charm. Still, it's the kind of place that—if it wasn't a four-story townhouse with a huge double parlor with terrace, private garden, seven working fireplaces and five and a half bathrooms on the East Side of Manhattan—might be called a dump. I'd buy it in a heartbeat.

Of course, after all these years some vestiges of Monty have disappeared. None of the books I inspected on the shelves could have belonged to the star. Monty mostly bought plays and art books. Many of the books that fill the shelves now are from the '70s, '80s and '90s. Monty's cherished silver objects have been replaced by a curious hippopotamus collection—ceramic renditions—in all shapes and sizes. Some of his tasteful, beige walls have been decorated with amateurish trompe l'oeil murals. Ms. Lee pointed out that the previous owner painted them. "Tacky," whispered Michelangelo, shaking his head as we breezed past the paintings.

"You can explore it yourselves for a while," Ms. Lee told us and Michelangelo and I now exchanged our excitement at being in "the house."

In *From Here to Eternity* Monty says, "Nobody ever lies about being lonely."

In his last years Monty had become unbearably lonely and sad. That car accident on his way home after a dinner party at Elizabeth Taylor's house in the Hollywood Hills had robbed him of his extraordinary beauty. Drugs and alcohol followed—although he still managed to give some shattering performances. By 1963 Monty was virtually unemployable in films—it seemed impossible to get insurance on him. Mercenary young men and male prostitutes continued to straggle in and out of the town house. It wasn't an uncommon sight to see a trembling Monty hobbling down Third Avenue, trancelike, usually leaning on a companion for support. His once flawless face, passersby noted, looked like a death mask.

Because of Monty's lingering aura, the atmosphere in the townhouse—in spite of the dozens of prancing hippopotami—was gloomy and dark, always a vibe that ignites my fantasies. I could imagine myself ringing the doorbell in 1966 and Monty opening the door. I'd be invited in. We'd share a drink. The sound of Ella Fitzgerald singing would be blaring on the hi-fi through the sparsely furnished rooms. We'd hit it off and I'd be the friend to save him, get him in shape, mastermind his come-back. I share this fantasy with Michelangelo but he shakes his head sadly. "When I was working on my book," he replies, "all of Monty's friends kept repeating the same thing to me—they tried very hard to help but it was impossible."

When Michelangelo and I stepped out of the town house in the late afternoon/early evening, a late sun was putting in an appearance. It had stormed earlier. Nowhere in sight in the front of the house was the bronze plaque that Monty's mother requested be attached to the front of the building before selling it. Her stipulation was that the plaque on the house should read, "Montgomery Clift lived here 1960-1966." It had probably been stolen by fans long ago.

Walking down Third Avenue, we passed the Isle of Capri restaurant, which had been Monty's favorite. "It's about the only thing he would still recognize on this street," I said solemnly. It was getting dark. Michelangelo was saying goodbye. Now I was alone, and that's no lie. There are possibilities in this part of Manhattan—things to do—but I wasn't sure where I should go.

My head sometimes gets overloaded with the annoying unan-swerables. It wasn't so long ago, really, that he was here. Things change so fast. We're here for such a short time. And it won't be too long before we will have answers to all the questions. Why are we here? What do we leave? Where do we go?

SOURCE NOTES

PROLOGUE

1. **"like his face had been halved"**: Kelley, *Elizabeth Taylor: The Last Star.*
2. **"I might need it"**: LaGuardia, *Monty: A Biography of Montgomery Clift.*
3. **"the beginning of the end"**: Blaine Waller, interview by Charles Casillo.

1. DEVELOPING MONTY

1. **"because of her lovely lilting laugh"**: Bosworth, *Montgomery Clift: A Biography.*
2. **"They became engaged"**: Krauss, *Male Beauty: Postwar Masculinity in Theater, Film, and Physique Magazines.*
3. **"'I don't want another one.' But a short while later her second son was born"**: *Montgomery Clift: The Hidden Star,* documentary directed by Robert Cassella, Jr., and John Griffin.

4. **"I was always the gentleman. I let my sister see the moon before I did":** "Montgomery Clift," AncientFaces, http://www.ancient faces.com/.

5. **"We were never allowed to trust our own judgment or experience":** Bosworth, *Montgomery Clift*.

6. **"I've been knifed":** *EW* staff, "Remembering Montgomery Clift," *Entertainment Weekly*, updated July 23, 1993, https://ew.com/article/1993/07/23/remembering-montgomery-clift/.

7. **"from our past was released":** Bosworth, *Montgomery Clift*.

8. **"at odds with the American way of life":** *Montgomery Clift: The Hidden Star* documentary.

9. **"he thought, would be his teacher":** Kevin McCarthy, interview by Charles Casillo.

10. **"the theater is my calling":** "Montgomery Clift, 45, Dies of Heart Attack in New York," *Los Angeles Times*, July 24, 1966.

11. **"I should say about forty":** From a taped telephone conversation between Brooks Clift and Sunny Clift in *The Rebels: Montgomery Clift*, documentary directed by Claudio Masenza.

12. **"twelve or thirteen":** Capua, *Montgomery Clift: A Biography*.

13. **"were obvious":** LaGuardia, *Monty*; and Krauss, *Male Beauty*.

14. **"entirely too gentle about the matter":** Bosworth, *Montgomery Clift*.

2. FORMING ELIZABETH

1. **"A jinx . . . seemed to hang over her":** "Who's Who on the Stage," *New York Times*, September 12, 1926.

2. **"he didn't seem to notice":** Taken from a letter written by a childhood friend of Francis Taylor in the Hedda Hopper Collection, Margaret Herrick Library, Fairbanks Center for Motion Picture Study, Beverly Hills.

3. **"liked gay men":** Mann, *How to Be a Movie Star: Elizabeth Taylor in Hollywood*.

4. **"A quality Elizabeth would inherit":** Tavo Amador, "Elizabeth

Taylor Invents Celebrity Culture," *Bay Area Reporter*, November 23, 2009.

5. **"fuzz and inlaid into the sides of her head"**: Sara Taylor "Elizabeth, My Daughter," *Ladies' Home Journal*, March–April 1954.

6. **"a little monkey"**: Heymann, *Liz: An Intimate Biography of Elizabeth Taylor*.

7. **"that doesn't sound so terrible at all"**: Taraborrelli, *Elizabeth*.

8. **"I loved anything that walked or crawled"**: Elizabeth Taylor, documentary, A&E Networks.

9. **"the foreshadowing name Monty"**: Rice, *Cleopatra in Mink*.

10. **"tiny butterflies"**: Walker, *Elizabeth: The Life of Elizabeth Taylor*.

11. **"clapped and cheered, 'Bravo!'"**: Maddox, *Who's Afraid of Elizabeth Taylor?*

12. **"a producer, director, or an actor"**: Taylor, *Elizabeth Taylor: Her Own True Bestselling Story*.

13. **"I gave up my career when I was married"**: Sara Sothern Taylor, "Elizabeth, My Daughter," *Ladies' Home Journal*, February 1954.

14. **"beautiful eight-year-old daughter, Elizabeth"**: Carter, *Elizabeth Taylor*.

3. SURROGATES

1. **"I gave everything I had"**: *Making Montgomery Clift*, documentary directed by Robert Anderson Clift and Hillary Demmon.

2. **"I guess that's the boy"**: Peters, *Design for Living: Alfred Lunt and Lynn Fontanne: A Biography*.

3. **"white marriage, to shield them from gossip"**: Bernstein, ed., *Cast Out: Queer Lives in Theater*.

4. **"we never went to bed together"**: Bosworth, *Montgomery Clift*.

5. **"and didn't ask about"**: Bosworth, *Montgomery Clift*.

6. "'He would double up in pain, in agony,' his friend Jean Green": *The Rebels: Montgomery Clift*, documentary, directed by Claudio Masenza.

7. "All his life, it was misery": "Kevin McCarthy: 'Montgomery Clift Was Brilliant in Every Way,'" *Film Talk*, January 10, 2015.

8. "too gentle about the matter": Bosworth, *Montgomery Clift*.

9. "intolerable strain of living a lie": Bosworth, *Montgomery Clift*.

10. "'We must have assumed that we were more intelligent or something,' McCarthy said": *The Rebels*, documentary.

11. "personification of the young prince": *The Rebels*, documentary; and Kevin McCarthy spoke similarly in the interview by Charles Casillo.

12. "dedicated to the craft of acting": Mira Rostova, interview by Charles Casillo.

13. "dependent on Mira": Lewis, *Slings & Arrows: Theater in My Life*.

14. "would catch an incurable fever": Bradshaw, *Dreams That Money Can Buy*.

15. "friendship and camaraderie": Bradshaw, *Dreams That Money Can Buy: The Tragic Life of Libby Holman*.

16. "affair with a mechanic": Jack Larson told this to Ken Storer.

17. "was repulsive": Parker, *Five for Hollywood*.

4. THE MOST ASTONISHING-LOOKING CHILD

1. "She doesn't look like a kid": Spoto, *A Passion for Life: The Biography of Elizabeth Taylor*.

2. "The mop was supposed to be Lassie": *Elizabeth Taylor*, documentary, A&E Networks.

3. "most astonishing-looking child I had ever seen": *Elizabeth Taylor: An Unauthorized Biography*, documentary.

4. "I stopped being a child the minute I began working in pictures": Amburn, *The Most Beautiful Woman in the World: The Obsessions, Passions, and Courage of Elizabeth Taylor*.

5. "Don't worry. You'll have your breasts": Tom Leonard, "This is Liz Taylor at 16," *Daily Mail*, October 16, 2015.

6. **"But it goes further back than that, since her father was gay"**: Hadleigh, *Elizabeth Taylor: Tribute to a Legend.*
7. **"we bonded for the first time since I was nine"**: Elizabeth Taylor, interview by Barbara Walters, ABC, 1999.
8. **"they were extraordinarily close"**: Elizabeth Taylor, interview by Barbara Walters, ABC, 1999.

5. A TROUBLED, COMPLEX GUY

1. **"along when he was traveling"**: McCarthy talked of his early friendship with Monty in the interview by Casillo. This is also mentioned in the documentary *The Rebels.*
2. **"the true love of Monty's life"**: Tom Vallance, "Kevin McCarthy: Actor Best Known for His Role in the Cold War Science-Fiction Thriller," *Independent*, September 15, 2010. Also, Grobel, *Conversations with Capote.*
3. **"the relationship was protected"**: *The Rebels: Montgomery Clift*, documentary directed by Claudio Masenza.
4. **"We were like children"**: *The Rebels.*
5. **"filling in the decay in my soul, that's all"**: *Making Montgomery Clift*, documentary directed by Robert Anderson Clift and Hillary Demmon.
6. **"none too gorgeous"**: Franklin MacFie, interview by Charles Casillo.
7. **"importance on the size of their cocks"**: Bosworth, *Montgomery Clift.*
8. **"it was all foreskin"**: Amburn, *The Most Beautiful Woman in the World.*
9. **"his friends from that scene were sure he did a lot of cruising"**: MacFie, interview by Casillo.
10. **"dancer-choreographer Jerome Robbins"**: Jowitt, *Jerome Robbins: His Life, His Theater, His Dance.*
11. **"for *West Side Story*"**: Barbara Hoffman, "GANGBUSTERS!" *New York Post*, March 8, 2009.

12. **"very masculine scheme":** Janet Maslin, "Brando, Dean and Clift, the Young Mavericks," *New York Times*, May 26, 1978.

13. **"He seems wholly unaware of the *mores* of the play's period":** Hoskyns, *Montgomery Clift: Beautiful Loser*.

14. **"his choice of parts at any studio":** *Variety*.

15. **"it was very, very appealing":** Jane Fonda quoted in *The Rebels*, documentary.

16. **"sketchy answers to personal questions":** From the William S. Cunningham notes on Montgomery Clift, Margaret Herrick Library, Fairbanks Center for Motion Picture Study, Beverly Hills.

17. **"paint-scarred 1940 convertible":** From the William S. Cunningham notes on Monty at the Margaret Herrick Library, Fairbanks Center for Motion Picture Study, Beverly Hills.

18. **"not a movie star, an actor":** Susan King, "Monty: An Actor of Fragile Brilliance," *Los Angeles Times*, August 29, 2004.

19. **"Who's a Freak":** Leslie Snyder, "Who's a Freak?" *Modern Screen*, March 1951.

20. **"in a profile about Monty":** Leslie Snyder, "Who's a Freak?" *Modern Screen*, March 1951.

21. **"intriguing mysteries of our time":** Bill Tusher, *Variety*.

22. **"caused him great guilt":** LaGuardia, *Monty*.

23. **"raised eyebrows":** McGilligan, *Alfred Hitchcock: A Life in Darkness and Light*.

24. **"scared to death, and they wouldn't do it":** McGilligan, *Alfred Hitchcock*.

25. **"thinly veiled version of their relationship":** Zolotow, *Billy Wilder in Hollywood*.

Note: Additional background information for this chapter also comes from Casillo's interviews with Franklin MacFie, Don Keefer, and Blaine Waller, and also from Malone, *Queer Cinema in America: An Encyclopedia of LGBTQ Films, Characters, and Stories*.

6. CHEMISTRY

1. **"I'm just a Hollywood nothing"**: Elizabeth Taylor, TCM tribute to Montgomery Clift.
2. **"boyish smile"**: Taylor, TCM tribute to Montgomery Clift.
3. **"they reacted to each other"**: *George Stevens: A Filmmaker's Journey*, documentary by George Stevens, Jr.
4. **"regal and sensual"**: Rostova, interview by Casillo.
5. **"her the role of Alice Tripp"**: Winters, *Shelley, Also Known as Shirley*. Also, Shelley Winters, interview by Charles Casillo.
6. **"'I simply go dead,' he explained"**: George Stevens Papers, Margaret Herrick Library, Fairbanks Center for Motion Picture Study, Beverly Hills.
7. **"My goddamn mother is a giant pain in the ass!"**: Winters, interview by Casillo.
8. **"Monty would share his notes with her and then they would go through it again"**: C. David Heymann, interview by Charles Casillo, in *New York Native*.

Note: Some background information that fleshed out this chapter was derived from Casillo's interview with Shelley Winters.

7. WHO IS BESSIE MAE?

1. **"describing his mother"**: Mira Rostova recalled Elizabeth's salty language and disparaging comments about her mother in the interview by Casillo.
2. **"She looked ravishing"**: Bosworth, *Montgomery Clift*.
3. **"that she had fallen in love"**: Heymann, *Liz*.
4. **"She had no one she could be herself with"**: Rostova, interview by Casillo.
5. **"And he crucified himself for it"**: Malone, *Queer Cinema in America*.
6. **"going any further"**: Amburn, *The Most Beautiful Woman in the World*.

7. **"I was supposed to do"**: LaGuardia, *Monty.*
8. **"can shut them off"**: Winters, interview by Casillo.
9. **"not at the moment"**: Langella, *Dropped Names: Famous Men and Women as I Knew Them.*
10. **"woman everyone else sees"**: Winters, interview by Casillo.

8. THE BEAUTIFUL COMMITTED MOMENT

1. **"loved you before I saw you"**: Quoted in director George Stevens's film *A Place in the Sun.*
2. **"not humiliate them in front of anyone"**: Kelley, *Elizabeth Taylor.*
3. **"he was impassioned"**: Bosworth, *Montgomery Clift.*
4. **"what the hell is this"**: Jason Fraley, "A Place in the Sun," *Film Spectrum* (blog), September 24, 2012, https://thefilmspectrum. com/?s=a+place+in+the+sun.
5. **"sophistication beyond her time"**: Moss, *Giant: George Stevens, A Life on Film.*
6. **"one on top of the other"**: Kass, *The Films of Montgomery Clift.*
7. **"It was deeper than that"**: Richard Gere, video interview by Lynn Hirshberg, ed., *W Screen Tests*, released January 2, 2013, https://www.youtube.com/watch?v=m-uE3Y0Navc&lc= UghLSuumc9Sb-HgCoAEC.
8. **"an old gobbler"**: Kelley, *Elizabeth Taylor.*
9. **"What a dish!"**: Mann, *How to Be a Movie Star.*
10. **"'pantywaist' in print"**: Hedda Hopper (column), The *New York Daily News*, November 21, 1949.
11. **"very soon going to be married"**: Bret, *Elizabeth Taylor: The Lady, the Lover, the Legend—1932–2011.*
12. **"I'll take my makeup off at home"**: Waterbury, *Elizabeth Taylor: Her Life, Her Loves, Her Future.*
13. **"You're going to need them for the scene"**: Waterbury, *Elizabeth Taylor.*
14. **"I'm always here for you"**: LaGuardia, *Monty.*

9. MARRIAGE NUMBER ONE

1. **"studio arranged for her to sit in on the graduation cere-mony"**: Amburn, *The Most Beautiful Woman in the World.*
2. **"Nothing comes off until the ring goes on"**: Heymann, *Liz.*
3. **"not only physically but mentally"**: Taylor, *An Informal Memoir.*
4. **"really didn't like women"**: Truman Capote, "Elizabeth Tay-lor," *Ladies' Home Journal,* December 1974.
5. **"With that she slammed down the phone"**: Waterbury and also Ellis Amburn talked of Monty's dislike of Hilton in an in-terview with Charles Casillo.
6. **"Elizabeth walked down the aisle"**: Details of Elizabeth and Hilton's wedding day can be found in many books, including those by Taraborrelli, Heymann, Kelley, Mann, Bret, and Waterbury.
7. **"poodle dyed to match her eyes"**: Maddox, *Who's Afraid of Elizabeth Taylor?*
8. **"I married an institution"**: Ronald Bergan, "Elizabeth Taylor," *The Guardian,* March 23, 2011.
9. **"disillusionment rude and brutal"**: Taylor, *An Informal Memoir.*
10. **"kicked out of my stomach"**: Taraborrelli, *Elizabeth.*
11. **"I fell off my pink cloud with a thud"**: Nick Zegarac, "The Indestructible Elizabeth Taylor," *The Hollywood Reporter,* December 11, 2006.

10. FRIENDS AND LOVERS

1. **"strange yen"**: "Monty Clift's Strange Yen for Older Women," *Inside Story,* December 1956.
2. **"It was a frightening image"**: Bosworth, *Montgomery Clift.*
3. **"She was about sixty years old"**: Winters, *Best of Times, Worst of Times*; and Winters, *Shelley, Also Known as Shirley.*
4. **"kissing her feet"**: Leonard, *Montgomery Clift.*
5. **"he's killing your career"**: LaGuardia, *Monty.*

6. **"sucked my cock"**: Capote, *Answered Prayers: The Unfinished Novel.*
7. **"seemed to sharpen it"**: LaGuardia, *Monty.*
8. **"They both sounded childlike and innocent"**: Bosworth, *Montgomery Clift.*
9. **"newly planted herb garden"**: Gelderman, *Mary McCarthy: A Life.*
10. **"You're right. It's real good pie"**: Griffin, *Merv: An Autobiography.*
11. **"He was trying not to see too much of me, because he felt uncomfortable"**: "McCarthy: 'Montgomery Clift Was Brilliant in Every Way.'"
12. **"might so easily end his career"**: Rod McKuen is quoted as saying this in Hadleigh's *Elizabeth Taylor.*
13. **"the agent assured him that he had not"**: Bosworth, *Montgomery Clift.*

Note: This chapter was also informed by the author's interviews with Franklin MacFie, Farley Granger, and Blaine Waller.

11. MARRIAGE NUMBER TWO

1. **"Dakota apartment building"**: Fisher, *Been There, Done That: An Autobiography.*
2. **"very much in love with Monty"**: Bosworth, *Montgomery Clift.*
3. **"they were very private"**: Bosworth, *Montgomery Clift.* Also, Blaine Waller talked of Elizabeth and Monty's closeness in an interview with the author.
4. **"Mother, you're such a cunt"**: Parker, *Five for Hollywood.*
5. **"trophy that he had overcome her influence"**: Larson, interview by Casillo.
6. **"rumored to be a longtime lover of Stewart Granger"**: Higham, *Howard Hughes: The Secret Life*; and Harrison, *Rex: An Autobiography.*
7. **"dreaded hurting Marlene"**: Wilding, *The Wilding Way: The Story of My Life.*

8. **"Let's pretend we never met, shall we?"**: Walker, *Elizabeth.*

9. **"bought the engagement ring for herself"**: Amburn, *The Most Beautiful Woman in the World.*

10. **"Baby, oh, baby"**: Amburn, *The Most Beautiful Woman in the World.*

11. **"charged the full day rate"**: Rice, *Cleopatra.*

12. **"How could you think of marrying a homosexual?"**: *People,* May 13, 1985.

13. **"Do you know what kind of life you'll have?"**: Mann, *How to Be a Movie Star,* and Higham, *Howard Hughes.*

14. **"in front of fourteen people"**: Rice, *Cleopatra.*

15. **"she knew her gay friends treated her well"**: Richard Knight, Jr., "William J. Mann's Look at Elizabeth Taylor," *Windy City Times,* March 3, 2010.

12. CAREER AND LIFE ADVANCEMENTS

1. **"Actors should be treated like cattle"**: Truffaut, *Hitchcock: A Definitive Study of Alfred Hitchcock.*

2. **"Larson wasn't even sure that Monty was gay"**: Larson, interview by Casillo. Also, *Making Montgomery Clift,* documentary.

3. **"I can't stand him"**: Neal Baer, interview by Charles Casillo.

4. **"first time I ever had a martini"**: Ken Storer, interview by Charles Casillo.

5. **"enormously lively and fun to be around"**: Larson, interview by Casillo.

6. **"I enjoy jokes too much"**: *Making Montgomery Clift,* documentary directed by Robert Anderson Clift and Hillary Demmon.

7. **"in his town house"**: Carlson, "I Am Montgomery Clift," *UnFictional* (podcast).

8. **"but it really hurt Farley's career"**: Baer, interview by Casillo.

9. **"that was important"**: Larson, interview by Casillo.

10. **"He's just so mine!"**: Rex Kennamer, interview by Charles Casillo.

11. **"two young men were completely smitten"**: Storer, interview by Casillo.

12. **"she turned down *Roman Holiday*"**: Parker, *Five for Hollywood*.
13. **"'probably a homosexual,' Cohn ranted"**: Leonard, *Montgomery Clift*.
14. **"foolish pathology"**: Bruce Atkinson, "Theatre: 'Sea Gull' at the Phoenix; Off-Broadway Group Stages Chekhov Play," *New York Times*, May 12, 1954.

Note: For additional background information in this chapter, I used The Fred Zinnemann Papers at the Margaret Herrick Library.

13. JAMES DEAN

1. **"Your mouth looks like a bloody cunt"**: Amburn, *The Most Beautiful Woman in the World*.
2. **"It's not possible to be with him"**: *The Rebels: Montgomery Clift*, documentary directed by Claudio Masenza.
3. **"simpatico with gays"**: Amburn, *The Most Beautiful Woman in the World*.
4. **"wanted to be like him"**: William Bast, interview by Charles Casillo
5. **"gathered to watch the filming"**: Some background information for the making of *Giant* was derived from Don Graham's book *Giant: Elizabeth Taylor, Rock Hudson, James Dean, Edna Ferber, and the Making of a Legendary American Film*.
6. **"I could work with her"**: Winkler, *Dennis Hopper: The Wild Ride of a Hollywood Rebel*.
7. **"Dean called him 'a fairy'"**: Caroline Howe, "How James Dean and Rock Hudson Competed for Elizabeth Taylor's Affection but Had a Secret Gay Flirtation during Filming of *Giant*," *Daily Mail*, updated April 25, 2018, https://www.dailymail.co.uk/news/article-5622973/How-James-Dean-French-kissed-Rock-Hudson-filming-Giant.html.
8. **"things in the middle of the night"**: Dann Dulin, "Elizabeth Taylor," *A&U*, February 2003.
9. **"were friends again"**: Elizabeth Taylor, interview by Larry

King, *Larry King Live*. Also, Elizabeth Taylor, interview on YouTube, in which she talks about the death of James Dean. The interview is uncredited, but it appears to have taken place in the early eighties.

10. **"chocolate martini"**: Taylor, *Elizabeth Takes Off: On Weight Gain, Weight Loss, Self-Image, and Self-Esteem*.

11. **"we could make Bloody Marys"**: Dann Dulin, "Elizabeth Taylor," *A&U: America's AIDS Magazine*.

12. **"'we never needed sleep,' Rock said"**: Excerpt from Hudson and Davidson, *Rock Hudson: His Story*.

13. **"to find out if it was true"**: Allan, *Elizabeth Taylor*.

14. **"I vomited. I don't know why"**: Bosworth, *Montgomery Clift*.

14. RAINTREE COUNTY

1. **"We didn't do much"**: Bob Thomas, "Elizabeth Taylor Was a Prolific Bride," *New York Daily News*, March 23, 2011.

2. **"She was a woman who loved men as much as they loved her"**: Fisher, *Been There, Done That*.

3. **"where she had an abortion"**: Fisher, *Been There, Done That*.

4. **"totally pornographic"**: Heymann, *Liz*.

5. **"A soap opera with *elephantiasis*"**: Girelli, *Montgomery Clift, Queer Star*.

6. **"an interpreter for two people who no longer spoke the same language"**: Wilding, *The Wilding Way*. Also, Wilding, *Apple Sauce*.

7. **"Lately, I'm simply told to shut up"**: Parker, *Five for Hollywood*.

8. **"It's going to be epic"**: Bosworth, *Montgomery Clift*. Also, Jean Porter, interview by Charles Casillo.

9. **"Was this one of his best performances?"**: Edward Dmytryk, "The Making of *Raintree County*" (unpublished manuscript), the Margaret Herrick Library, Fairbanks Center for Motion Picture Study, Beverly Hills.

10. **"funny premonition"**: Bosworth, *Montgomery Clift*.

11. **"impossible to penetrate"**: Eva Marie Saint, interview by Charles Casillo.

15. WRECKED

1. **"the phone rang, and once again it was Elizabeth"**: Larson, interview by Casillo.
2. **"He promised he'd be right over"**: Dmytryk, "The Making of *Raintree County*" (unpublished manuscript).
3. **"white satin cocktail dress and sparkling gems"**: Gates, *My Husband, Rock Hudson*. She also spoke about the night of the accident in a *Larry King* interview conducted on March 21, 2004.
4. **"Monty under the table"**: Fisher, *Been There, Done That.*
5. **"didn't consume too many drinks"**: Gates, *My Husband, Rock Hudson.*
6. **" 'All they'll see is your tits, darling' "**: Kelley, *Elizabeth Taylor.*
7. **"more somber tone"**: Porter, interview by Casillo.
8. **"conversed almost in whispers"**: Gates, *My Husband, Rock Hudson.*
9. **"I'll follow you in my car"**: Amburn, *The Most Beautiful Woman in the World.*
10. **"driving itself"**: McCarthy, interview by Casillo.
11. **"accordion-pleated mess"**: Mann, *How to Be a Movie Star.*
12. **"was like Mother Courage"**: Bosworth, *Montgomery Clift.*
13. **"Monty's broken, battered head"**: *The Rebels*, documentary directed by Claudio Masenza.
14. **"his eyes looked the color of a bright red rose"**: Elizabeth Taylor, interview by Rosie O'Donnell, *The Rosie O'Donnell Show.*
15. **"I didn't cry until later on that night"**: Taylor, interview by Rosie O'Donnell.
16. **"He was bleeding so much, he was in danger of dying from blood loss alone"**: Kennamer, interview by Casillo, 2003.
17. **"most of all Monty's"**: McCarthy, interview by Casillo.
18. **"Get out of here, you fucking bastards!"**: Kelley, *Elizabeth Taylor.*
19. **"it was almost as wide as his shoulders"**: Taylor, *An Informal Memoir.*
20. **"The sick, sweet smell of it made me want to vomit"**: Taylor, *An Informal Memoir.*

21. **"I don't think anybody knows how brutal the accident was"**: *Montgomery Clift: His Place in the Sun*, documentary directed by Robert Guenette.

22. **"cracks rippled through his facial skeleton"**: LaGuardia, *Monty*.

23. **"For nourishment"**: McCarthy, interview by Casillo.

24. **"finally got out of the hospital"**: *Montgomery Clift: Postmortem: Beautiful Loser*, documentary directed by Nicola Jane Black.

25. **"he'd fall asleep talking to you"**: Jack Larson's interview on *Mysteries & Scandals: Montgomery Clift*, documentary directed by Joel K. Rodgers and Liz Flynn. He also commented on this in an interview with Casillo.

26. **"They need me more than Monty does"**: Bradshaw, *Dreams That Money Can Buy*.

16. MIKE TODD

1. **"already very troubled marriage"**: Parker, *Five for Hollywood*.

2. **"before he'll be completely well"**: Kelley, *Elizabeth Taylor*.

3. **"Being broke is only a temporary situation"**: Kennedy, *Joan Blondell: A Life between Takes*.

4. **"a latent intellectual"**: Taraborrelli, *Elizabeth*.

5. **"their shoulders or backs touched"**: Heymann, *Liz*.

6. **"my spine was tingling"**: Amburn, *The Most Beautiful Woman in the World*.

7. **"I would pop right into your face"**: Letter from Montgomery Clift to William LaMassena, July 22, 1956, from the Farley Granger Collection auction.

8. **"But he didn't say 'know'"**: Hopper, *The Whole Truth and Nothing But*.

Note: Additional background information for this chapter was derived from Michael Callahan, "The Legend of Oscar-Winning Producer-Showman Mike Todd," *Hollywood Reporter*, January 23,

2016; Taylor, *Elizabeth Takes Off*; and Todd and Todd, *A Valuable Property: The Life Story of Michael Todd.*

17. NATCHEZ

1. **"across newspapers the next day"**: Leonard, *Montgomery Clift.*
2. **"like a 'lunatic'"**: LaGuardia, *Monty.*
3. **"There was an enormous difference in his behavior after the accident"**: Guenette's documentary *Montgomery Clift: His Place in the Sun.*
4. **"two eyes at the same time"**: LaGuardia, *Monty.*
5. **"he was in constant pain"**: Dmytryk, "The Making of Raintree County" (unpublished manuscript).
6. **"She was the center of attention and dramatic movement"**: Dmytryk, "The Making of Raintree County" (unpublished manuscript).
7. **"doesn't do much of anything"**: Lockridge, *Shade of the Raintree: The Life and Death of Ross Lockridge, Jr.*
8. **"overtly sipped a drink or took a shot"**: Dmytryk, "The Making of Raintree County" (unpublished manuscript).
9. **"Elizabeth seems to have caught some of Clift's aloofness"**: John Maynard, "The Disappearance of Montgomery Clift," *Motion Picture,* June 1958.

18. DANVILLE

1. **"a rack built in his rented house specifically to hold his liquor bottles"**: Liz Kernen, interview by Charles Casillo.
2. **"documenting every move"**: Kernen, interview by Casillo.
3. **"all at the same time"**: Charlotte Henson, interview by Charles Casillo.
4. **"made him an honorary colonel"**: Maynard, "The Disappearance of Montgomery Clift."

5. **"me or with any other crew member"**: Ron Chilton, email messages to Charles Casillo, April 26, 2019.

6. **"He had a lot of things working against him"**: Kernen, interview by Casillo.

7. **"Zanzibar"**: Capua, *Montgomery Clift.*

8. **"were many calls from Todd to Elizabeth"**: Henson, interview by Casillo.

9. **"Elizabeth sighed, admiring the splendor of the jewel"**: Waterbury, *Elizabeth Taylor.*

10. **"Dmytryk instructed the chef not to make them for her"**: Henson, interview by Casillo.

11. **"than anyone I ever met"**: Maddox, *Who's Afraid of Elizabeth Taylor?*

12. **"But a strong sedative put him to sleep for the rest of the day and night"**: Dmytryk Papers at Margaret Herrick Library.

13. **"of physical or mental discomfort"**: Dmytryk Papers at the Margaret Herrick Library.

14. **"the lonely depth of his own feelings"**: Maynard, "The Disappearance of Monty Clift."

15. **"and gives you not-so-playful punches"**: Maynard, "The Disappearance of Montgomery Clift."

16. **"oh dear, how sorry he is for himself"**: Isherwood, *Diaries: Volume One, 1939–1960.*

19. MARRIAGE NUMBER THREE

1. **"Renoir, Pissarro, and Monet"**: The Elizabeth Taylor Archives at www.dameelizabethtaylor.com.

2. **"didn't seem to mind"**: Fisher, *Been There, Done That.*

3. **"That's not bad for luck"**: *Around the World with Mike Todd,* documentary directed by Saul Swimmer, 1967.

4. **"they could cut your throat"**: Callahan, "The Legend of Oscar-Winning Producer-Showman Mike Todd."

5. **"makes her mother look like Frankenstein":** Kelley, *Elizabeth Taylor.*
6. **"We also happen to love each other very much":** Parker, *Five for Hollywood.*
7. **"I mean, that [whack] hurt *me!*":** Debbie Reynolds, interview by Joy Behar, *Joy Behar Show*, aired December 21, 2011.

20. A NEW FACE

1. **"totally relaxed":** Bosworth, *Montgomery Clift.*
2. **"Monty turned around and quickly walked away":** Griffin, *Merv.*
3. **"and he and Thom finally left":** Robert Thom, "Montgomery Clift: A Small Place in the Sun" *Esquire*, March 1, 1967.
4. **"He's not so pretty anymore":** McCarthy, interview by Casillo.
5. **"He told me he was losing weight for a picture":** Winters, interview by Casillo.

21. RUNNING FROM A NIGHTMARE

1. **"Anne had a funny feeling about Kirk flying in that small plane":** Douglas and Douglas, *Kirk and Anne: Letters of Love, Laughter, and a Lifetime in Hollywood.*
2. **"killing everyone on board instantly":** Toby Smith, "50 Years Ago in N.M., a Plane Carrying Elizabeth Taylor's Movie-Producer Husband Crashed; Some Recollect That Fateful Day," *Albuquerque Journal*, Sunday, March 16, 2008.
3. **"Dear God, please, not Mike":** Taraborrelli, *Elizabeth.*
4. **"in the bronze casket":** Geoffrey Johnson, "How a Chicago Detective Found the Stolen Body of Elizabeth Taylor's Third Husband, Mike Todd," *Chicago*, March 24, 2011.
5. **"the time to assume the responsibility":** LaGuardia, *Monty.*
6. **"It was bizarre, unbelievable":** Fisher, *Been There, Done That.*
7. **"Elizabeth remembered that detail, too":** Bosworth, *Montgomery Clift.*

22. THE YOUNG LIONS

1. **"Noah ten years ago"**: "Talk with a Star," *Newsweek*, April 7, 1957.
2. **"He acts throughout the picture as if he were in a glassy-eyed daze"**: Bosley Crowther, "Irwin Shaw's 'Young Lions'; War Story Is Offered at the Paramount, Brando, Martin and Clift Are Starred," *New York Times*, April 3, 1958.
3. **"That was a true nightmare for Monty"**: Thom, "Montgomery Clift."
4. **"virtually flawless"**: "Talk with a Star," *Newsweek*.
5. **"wonderfully funny and touching"**: *Time*.
6. **"but nonetheless genuine"**: Thom, "Montgomery Clift."
7. **"his own private abyss"**: Bosworth, *Montgomery Clift*.
8. **"fact that he was using them"**: LaGuardia, *Monty*.
9. **"important to him that I take it"**: Skip E. Lowe, interview by Charles Casillo.
10. **"looked like a sexagenarian"**: Bradshaw, *Dreams That Money Can Buy*.

23. ELIZABETH THE CAT

1. **"until things got straightened out"**: Todd and Todd, *A Valuable Property*.
2. **"available to take her calls"**: Kennamer, interview by Casillo.
3. **"I began to take sleeping pills"**: Taylor, *Elizabeth Takes Off*.
4. **"on the first take perfectly"**: Walker, *Elizabeth*.
5. **"The rest of the time I was a robot"**: Walker, *Elizabeth*.
6. **"like a brother or a father"**: Fisher, *Been There, Done That*.
7. **"she joined Debbie for Eddie's opening night in Las Vegas"**: Kelley, *The Last Star*.
8. **"Romanoff's with Hedda Hopper"**: Heymann, *Liz*.

24. GOOD MONTY/BAD MONTY

1. **"the night before was funny"**: I based Monty and Nancy Walker's friendship on Bosworth's *Montgomery Clift*, LaGuardia's *Monty*, Guenette's documentary *Montgomery Clift: His Place in the Sun*, and my interview with Jack Larson.
2. **"he needed to be needed"**: Bosworth, *Montgomery Clift*.
3. **"that your talents were limitless"**: Thom, "Montgomery Clift."
4. **"delivered with saintliness, compassion"**: Thom, *Montgomery Clift*.
5. **"aggressive attempts at humor"**: Isherwood, *Diaries*.
6. **"once again seeing Monty"**: LaGuardia, *Monty*.
7. **"a rich fur manufacturer"**: Capua, *Montgomery Clift*.

Note: An interview with Don Bachardy was also a source of background information for this chapter.

25. A VERY UN-PRIVATE AFFAIR

1. **"She had the face of an angel and the morals of a truck driver"**: Bret, *Elizabeth Taylor*.
2. **"he needed me and I needed him"**: Taylor, *Elizabeth Takes Off*.
3. **"she asked breathlessly"**: Amburn, *The Most Beautiful Woman in the World*.
4. **"As soon as possible"**: Fisher, *Been There, Done That*.
5. **"'growing and growing and growing,' Eddie remembered"**: Fisher, *Been There, Did That*.
6. **"We'd make love three, four, five times a day"**: Amburn, *The Most Beautiful Woman in the World*.
7. **"soon after orgasm, he was ready again"**: Spoto, *A Passion for Life*.
8. **"My, how Mike Todd would laugh over all of this"**: Waterbury, *Elizabeth Taylor*.
9. **"forget all Mike meant to me"**: Walker, *Elizabeth*.

10. **"EDDIE FISHER ROMANCE WITH LIZ TAYLOR DENIED":** Bret, *Elizabeth Taylor.*
11. **"Then the car pulled away":** Mann, *How to Be a Movie Star.*

26. A LONELY HEART

1. **"Monty Clift vomited over it":** Isherwood, *Diaries.*
2. **"Not worth the risk":** Thom, "Montgomery Clift."
3. **"the radar but very boldly":** Baer, interview by Casillo.
4. **"been able to remain young":** Thom, "Montgomery Clift."
5. **"because he liked, loved enormously":** Thom, "Montgomery Clift."
6. **"under his social veneer":** Leider, *Myrna Loy: The Only Good Girl in Hollywood.*
7. **"get him into some terrible sweats":** Bosley Crowther, *New York Times* review of *Lonelyhearts,* March 5, 1959.

27. DEBBIE, EDDIE, AND THE WIDOW TODD

1. **"Bitchery, dear, sheer bitchery":** Brian Viner, "Gossip Queen Who Struck Terror in Hollywood," *Daily Mail,* February 17, 2016.
2. **"There is so much feeling about this wherever we go":** Letters to Hedda Hopper, Hedda Hopper Collection, Margaret Herrick Library.
3. **"the luxury of being depressed":** Debbie Reynolds, interview by Craig Ferguson on his late show, 2007.
4. **"like every other dame in this goddamn business":** Taraborrelli, *Elizabeth*; and Wright, *It Ended Badly: Thirteen of the Worst Breakups in History.*

28. SUDDENLY, LAST SUMMER

1. **"no good at all":** Kristin Hunt, "Hollywood Codebreakers: 'Suddenly, Last Summer' Dabbles in Cannibalism," *Medium*, September 23, 2018, https://medium.com/@kristinhunt/hollywood-codebreakers-suddenly-last-summer-dabbles-in-cannibalism-c89c2b1c8dc6.
2. **"thrown in for drama":** Fisher, *Been There, Done That.*
3. **"really had filled out":** Walker, *Elizabeth.*

29. WHAT'S WRONG WITH HIM?

1. **"sober, punctual, and functioning":** Bosworth, *Montgomery Clift.*
2. **"He had this extraordinary presence":** Leonard, *Montgomery Clift.*
3. **"had it absolutely":** Matthew Sweet, "Gary Raymond Interview: The Matinee Idol on Burton, Taylor, and Why Montgomery Clift Was Like a 'Battered Baby,' " *Telegraph*, February 21, 2019.
4. **"That dinner finished it all":** LaGuardia, *Monty.*
5. **"wonder what it might be spiked with":** Geist, *Pictures Will Talk: The Life & Films of Joseph L. Mankiewicz.*
6. **"the rest ended up on the cutting-room floor":** LaGuardia, *Monty.*
7. **"an inferno":** LaGuardia, *Monty.*
8. **"a series of repeated takes":** Geist, *Pictures Will Talk.*
9. **" 'If he goes, I go,' she warned":** Heymann, *Liz.*

30. STRANGE ARRANGEMENTS

1. **"a well-paid hobby":** Fisher, *Been There, Done That.*
2. **"tangled hair, and drab hospital clothes":** Maddox, *Who's Afraid of Elizabeth Taylor?*

3. **"admission to an affair"**: Porter and Prince, *Elizabeth Taylor: There Is Nothing Like a Dame.*

4. **"a little repertory company"**: Leonard, *Montgomery Clift.*

5. **"weaker beings than himself"**: LaGuardia, *Monty.*

6. **"a hulk of gray stone hell"**: McCambridge, *The Quality of Mercy: An Autobiography.*

7. **"heavy drugged sleep"**: McCambridge.

8. **" 'My heart ached for him,' she said"**: LaGuardia, *Monty.*

9. **"I'm fine. Fantastic"**: Bosworth, *Montgomery Clift.*

31. THE FLASHBACK SCENE

1. **"Her body belongs to someone else"**: Maddox, *Who's Afraid of Elizabeth Taylor?*

2. **"opera of madness and death"**: Porter and Prince, *Elizabeth Taylor.*

3. **"Fresh start, my ass"**: Walker, *Elizabeth.*

4. **"She should win the Oscar"**: Porter and Prince, *Elizabeth Taylor.*

5. **"her illusion of youth"**: Geist, *Pictures Will Talk.*

6. **"she spat in his face"**: Kanin, *Tracy and Hepburn: An Intimate Memoir.*

7. **"I can't face waking up in the morning"**: Maddox, *Who's Afraid of Elizabeth Taylor?*

8. **"Sometimes I can't even stand him"**: Porter and Prince, *Elizabeth Taylor.*

9. **"because he needed me"**: Spoto, *A Passion for Life.* Also, Constance Arthur, "Is Liz Taylor Legally Wed?" *Movie Mirror,* July 1965.

10. **"the true love of her life"**: Walker, *Elizabeth.*

11. **"the paper went to print"**: Hunt, "Hollywood Codebreakers."

12. **"climax is sheer histrionic showing off"**: Bosley Crowther, review of *Suddenly Last Summer, New York Times,* December 23, 1959.

13. **"in her dramatic career"**: Dwight Macdonald, "Films: Amateurs and Pros," *Esquire,* April 1960.

14. **"and inexpressive as usual"**: Macdonald, "Films: Amateurs and Pros."

32. TWO DIFFERENT PATHS

1. **"be nice to him"**: Yohana Desta, "A Studio Exec Sexually Propositioned Joan Collins for the Lead in *Cleopatra,* She Says," *Vanity Fair,* April 29, 2019. Also, Collins to Casillo.
2. **"a million dollars"**: Cashmore, *Elizabeth Taylor: A Private Life for Public Consumption.*
3. **"flammable material that caused the fire"**: Various newspaper clippings from the era.
4. **"some hustlers when the fire broke out"**: Capua, *Montgomery Clift.*
5. **"fraternize with her gay circle"**: Bradshaw, *Dreams That Money Can Buy.*
6. **"He lived there until he died"**: Casillo visited the house in 2006, when it went up for sale, and reported on it for *New York* magazine: "His Place in the Sun," *New York,* June 1, 2006.

Note: Also utilized for this chapter was a Charles Casillo interview with Kimothy Cruse.

33. MARILYN

1. **"originally wanted Marlon Brando"**: "*Wild River* (1960)," IMDb, https://www.imdb.com/title/tt0054476/. Also, Kazan, *A Life.*
2. **"Up to now you've done fine. Now lie down"**: The Retro Set, "The Tormented Brilliance of Montgomery Clift," *Retro Set* (blog), http://theretroset.com/?p=7471.
3. **"gods and goddesses of the performing arts"**: "Behind the Camera on The Misfits," TCM, http://www.tcm.com/this-month/article/191117%7C0/Behind-the-Camera-The-Misfits.html.

4. **"They recognized disaster in each other's faces and giggled about it"**: Bosworth, *Montgomery Clift*.

5. **"a gorgeous way to go"**: Edward Parone, interview by Charles Casillo.

6. **"with Marilyn at the Beachcomber"**: Larson, interview by Casillo.

7. **"She even ate it"**: Larson, interview by Casillo. Also, Larson tells this story in the documentary *The Rebels* and in several other interviews regarding Monty.

8. **"in worse shape than I am"**: Anne Helen Petersen, "Scandals of Classic Hollywood: The Long Suicide of Montgomery Clift," *Vanity Fair*, September 23, 2014.

9. **"I would rather work with her than any other actress. I adore her"**: Montgomery Clift quoted in "Five Men, Close to the World's Most famous Blonde, Present a Mosaic of Marilyn," *Coronet*, February1961.

10. **"play an ingenue'"**: Jeanne Martin, interview by Charles Casillo.

11. **"you will have it within twenty-four hours"**: Cruse, interview by Casillo.

12. **"perfect for the part"**: Stanley Kramer interview in Guenette's documentary *Montgomery Clift: His Place in the Sun*.

13. **"I start crying thinking about it"**: *Making Montgomery Clift*, documentary directed by Claudio Masenza.

14. **"as good a performance as I had hoped"**: Kramer, *A Mad, Mad, Mad, Mad World: A Life in Hollywood*.

Note: Details about the making of *The Misfits* were also taken from Charles Casillo's interviews with Angela Allen and Edward Parone, and from Goode, *The Making of the Misfits* and Weatherby, *Conversations with Marilyn*.

34. CLEOPATRA IN LONDON

1. **"only to have her symptoms worsen":** The story of the start of filming *Cleopatra* was informed by the documentary *Cleopatra: The Film That Changed Hollywood*, directed by Kevin Burns and Brent Zacky, aired April 3, 2001; Richard Brody, "The Case for 'Cleopatra,'" *New Yorker*, June 11, 2013; and Spoto, *A Passion for Life*.
2. **"shut down until January 3, 1961":** Parker, *Five for Hollywood*.
3. **"I was pronounced dead four times":** Elizabeth Taylor, interview by Oprah Winfrey, *The Oprah Winfrey Show*, March 4, 1992.
4. **"which must be a record":** David Kamp, "The Death, and Many Near-Deaths, of the Hollywood Cleopatra," *Vanity Fair*, March 23, 2011.
5. **"You cannot give up now":** Dulin, "Elizabeth Taylor."
6. **"I lost to a tracheotomy":** Bernard Weinraub, "And the So-So Winner Is . . . ; Hey, What's Talent Got to Do With It?" *New York Times*, March 24, 1996.
7. **"Marilyn Monroe to be cast as *Cleopatra*":** Kelley, *Elizabeth Taylor*.

35. THE FREUD FEUD

1. **"his gayness particularly offended him":** Allen, interview by Casillo.
2. **"Why didn't you tell me":** Jeffrey Meyers, "The Making of *Freud*: The Secret Passion," *The Kenyon Review New Series* 33, no. 1 (Winter 2011).
3. **"had been polluted":** Meyers, "The Making of *Freud*."
4. **"which is why I offered him *Freud*":** Tuska, ed., *Close-Up: The Hollywood Director*.
5. **"dependent friendships with older woman":** LaGuardia, *Monty*.
6. **"were forced to hold him down the entire trip":** Capua, *Montgomery Clift*.
7. **"I thought he could do *Freud*":** Huston, *An Open Book*.

8. **"they made no sense":** Lyn Tornabene, "Montgomery Clift: Films' Tall Guy," *Cosmopolitan*, May 1963.

9. **"a sadist who takes delight in needling":** *Making Montgomery Clift*, documentary directed by Robert Anderson Clift and Hillary Demmon.

10. **"a very difficult neurotic man to deal with":** *The Rebels*, documentary.

11. **"Unthinkable nonsense":** Huston, *An Open Book*.

12. **"morning and has to get up at 5:30":** Montgomery Clift, interview by Hy Gardner, taped in January of 1963.

13. **"to but it's not going to be me":** Clift, interview by Gardner.

36. THE CLEOPATRA AFFAIR

1. **"cold fish eye":** Kashner and Schoenberger, *Furious Love: Elizabeth Taylor, Richard Burton, and the Marriage of the Century*.

2. **"you're a very pretty girl?":** Kashner and Schoenberger.

3. **"we just kept looking at each other":** *Mirror* staff, "Elizabeth Taylor Dies: Cleopatra Romance Was One of Hollywood's Greatest Love Stories," *Daily Mirror*, updated January 26, 2012, https://www.mirror.co.uk/tv/tv-news/elizabeth-taylor-dies-cleopatra-romance-177134.

4. **"beautiful beyond the dreams of pornography":** Williams, ed. *The Richard Burton Diaries*.

5. **"a needy child":** *Cleopatra: The Film That Changed Hollywood* documentary directed by Kevin Burns and Brent Zacky.

6. **"electricity between Liz and Burton":** David Kamp, "When Liz Met Dick," *Vanity Fair*, March 22, 2011.

7. **"back of my Cadillac!":** Kamp, "When Liz Met Dick."

8. **"and neither do you":** Fisher, *Been There, Done That*.

9. **"always comes home to me":** Fisher, *Been There, Done That*.

10. **"erotic vagrancy":** Chris Nashawaty, "Elizabeth Taylor and Richard Burton's Scandalous Love Story," *Entertainment Weekly*, updated March 23, 2011, https://ew.com/article/2011/03/23/elizabeth-taylor-richard-burton-scandal/.

11. **"the game would never be finished"**: Papa, *Elizabeth Taylor: A Passion for Life: The Wit and Wisdom of a Legend.*

12. **"vomited"**: Tom Dewe Mathews, "She wasn't much of an actress, but . . . ," *Guardian*, May 2, 2000.

37. IT'S VERY HARD

1. **"'Monty, I need some help'"**: Dmytryk quoted in Guenette's documentary *Montgomery Clift: His Place in the Sun.*

2. **"the secrets we shared were sacred"**: Elizabeth Taylor, "Elizabeth Taylor on Montgomery Clift," TCM Tribute to Montgomery Clift.

3. **"I think you're lucky that you can still feel that way"**: Larson, interview by Casillo.

4. **"more than friendship"**: Burton's bisexuality is drawn from a 1974 Richard Burton interview by Michael Parkinson.

5. **"all in the past"**: Jack Larson is quoted as saying this in Hadleigh's *Elizabeth Taylor.*

6. **"'less ashamed' of his homosexual experiences"**: Director Ronald Neame is quoted as saying this in Hadleigh's *Elizabeth Taylor.*

7. **"Richard wants to be famous at any cost"**: Bosworth, *Montgomery Clift.*

8. **"how terribly depressing this is?"**: This October 27, 1962, conversation is from the *Montgomery Clift: The Hidden Star,* documentary.

9. **"shot right in front of them"**: Hoskyns, *Montgomery Clift.*

10. **"a number of young men were seen for the last time"**: Carter, *Stonewall: The Riots that Sparked the Gay Revolution.* Also, "Perry Brass: Lost Gay New York: Truckin' at the Trucks," *Queer New York* (blog), August 3, 2010, http://queernewyorkblog. blogspot.com/2010/08/perry-brass-lost-gay-new-york-truckin.html.

11. **"You can't take him away"**: Bosworth, *Montgomery Clift.*

12. **"I realized he was crying"**: Bogdanovich, *Who the Hell's in It: Conversations with Hollywood's Legendary Actors.*

13. **"and I ain't gonna give it up"**: *Making Montgomery Clift*, documentary.

14. **"that potential was significant, vast"**: Thom, "Montgomery Clift."

15. **"isolation was irredeemable"**: Ralph Zucker, *Backstage*, July 1966.

16. **"My name is Monty Clift"**: Capua, *Montgomery Clift*.

38. HAMLETS IN NEW YORK

1. **"had been intended for Sophia Loren"**: TCM introduction to *The V.I.P.s*, http://www.tcm.com/tcmdb/title/94609/The-V-I-P-s/.

2. **"and the two dubbed it Casa Kimberly"**: "About Casa Kimberly," casakimberly.com.

3. **"us two maniacs"**: Cashmore, *Elizabeth Taylor*.

4. **"Bessie Mae! Bessie Mae!"**: Bosworth, *Montgomery Clift*.

5. **"If he doesn't work soon, he'll die"**: Kelley, *Elizabeth Taylor*.

6. **"my face is my charge card"**: Capote, *Portraits and Observations: The Essays of Truman Capote*.

7. **"screamed and shouted the whole way home"**: Clarke, *Capote: A Biography*.

8. **"It will kill him"**: Truman Capote, "Elizabeth Taylor: Eyes so Liquid with Life," *Ladies' Home Journal*, December 1974.

9. **"Let me begin again. I sure screwed that one up"**: Richard L. Coe, "Elizabeth Taylor's Real Broadway Debut—In 1964," *The Washington Post*, January 25, 1981.

10. **"she could move mountains"**: Hadley Meares, "Elizabeth Taylor's Longtime Assistant Takes a Stroll Through 700 Nimes Road," *Los Angeles Magazine*, April 30, 2019.

11. **"*The Owl and the Pussycat*"**: An annotated copy of the script is among the Montgomery Clift papers (1933–1966) at the New York Public Library.

12. **"*The Macomber Affair*"**: Kashner and Schoenberger, *Furious Love*.

39. REFLECTIONS

1. **"a telegram from the producer, Ray Stark"**: John Huston Collection, the Margaret Herrick Library, Fairbanks Center for Motion Picture Study, Beverly Hills.

2. **"Ray Stark, cabled John Huston"**: John Huston Collection, the Margaret Herrick Library.

3. **"best of the costarring parts"**: John Huston Collection, the Margaret Herrick Library.

4. **"I will only appear in this film if my costar is Montgomery Clift"**: Elizabeth's insistence on Monty as her costar can be found in correspondences regarding *Reflections in a Golden Eye* in the John Huston Collection at the Margaret Herrick Library.

5. **"If he could stand it, I could stand it"**: Bosworth, *Montgomery Clift*.

6. **"Where's the dog leash, baby?"**: Bosworth, *Montgomery Clift*.

7. **"We got them by the balls"**: Kennamer, interview by Casillo.

8. **"I'll put up the insurance money!"**: Kennamer, interview by Casillo.

9. **"Monty made attempts to be social and mingle with some of the younger gays on the Island"**: Verne Gay, "Diahann Carroll spent the summer of '67 on Fire Island," *Newsday* October 4, 2019, https://www.newsday.com/entertainment/celebrities/diahann-carroll-fire-island-1967-1.37154582. Also, LaGuardia, *Monty*; Bosworth, *Montgomery Clift*; and Capua, *Montgomery Clift*.

10. **"you get all this wonderful kind of sincerity"**: *Making Montgomery Clift*, documentary directed by Robert Anderson Clift and Hillary Demmon.

11. **"'fighting against great opposition from our banks' to get him cast"**: John Huston Collection at the Margaret Herrick Library.

12. **"all of them have done in two months"**: Letter from Lorenzo James to James Bridges, February 2, 1966, auctioned off at The Saleroom on September 23 2013.

13. **"Christopher Isherwood on board to rewrite it"**: Isherwood, *Diaries*.

14. **"him home in my car"**: Letter from Lorenzo James to James Bridges, February 2, 1966.
15. **"totally there and fully responsible"**: Roddy McDowall quoted in Guenette's documentary *Montgomery Clift: His Place in the Sun.*

Note: This chapter was also informed by a Casillo interview with Angela Allen.

40. DEFECTOR

1. **"approach to any part he played"**: "Montgomery Clift, 45, Dies of Heart Attack in New York," *Los Angeles Times,* July 24, 1966.
2. **"Sinatra remained loyal in his friendship"**: Storer, interview by Casillo.
3. **"they both have the vulnerability"**: Jonathan Cott, "Elizabeth Taylor: The Lost Interview, A Never-Before-Seen '*Rolling Stone*' Chat with the Hollywood Icon," *Rolling Stone,* March 29, 2011.
4. **"My feelings are deep and personal"**: Taylor, "Elizabeth Taylor on Montgomery Clift," TCM.
5. **"That's a great artist"**: Cott, "Elizabeth Taylor: The Lost Interview."
6. **"And I still do"**: Taylor, "Elizabeth Taylor on Montgomery Clift," TCM.

41. ELIZABETH IN LATER YEARS

1. **"for lovely always"**: Kelley, *Elizabeth Taylor.*
2. **"the face you deserve"**: Celia Walden, "Her Beauty Became a Burden: Behind the Scenes at the First Major Elizabeth Taylor Auction," *The Telegraph,* December 6, 2019.
3. **"It's the great leveler"**: John Duka, "Elizabeth Taylor: Journal of Recovery," *New York Times,* February 4, 1985.
4. **"people were being ignored and dying"**: Dulin, "Elizabeth Taylor."

5. **"men who happen to be homosexual":** Kevin Sessums, "Elizabeth Taylor Tells the Truth," *POZ*, November 1 1997.

6. **"what it considered a gay disease":** Nancy Collins, "Liz's AIDS Odyssey," *Vanity Fair*, November 1992.

7. **"I did not give up":** Dulin, "Elizabeth Taylor."

8. **"had some positive worth":** Aljean Harmetz, "Hollywood Turns Out for AIDS Benefit," *New York Times*, September 20, 1985.

9. **"in essence all her gay friends":** Hadleigh, *Elizabeth Taylor.*

10. **"because they were being treated like lepers":** Dulin, "Elizabeth Taylor."

11. **"I was addicted to painkillers":** Collins, "Liz's AIDS Crusade."

12. **"I think I had the second":** Cashmore, *Elizabeth Taylor.*

13. **"Elizabeth would defend any friend to the death":** Celia Walden, "Her Beauty Became a Burden: Behind the Scenes at the First Major Elizabeth Taylor Auction."

14. **"really know anything about it":** Kevin Sessums, "Elizabeth Taylor Tells the Truth."

15. **"He hated homophobia, not homosexuality":** She told this to Rod McKuen, and he is quoted as saying this in Hadleigh's *Elizabeth Taylor.*

16. **"My God! All three were gay!":** Hadleigh, *Elizabeth Taylor.*

17. **"... in the service of heterosexuality":** Ron Vawter is quoted as saying this in Hadleigh's *Elizabeth Taylor.*

18. **"just walking down the street":** Quote by photographer Tom Gates.

EPILOGUE

1. **"Not sexually, but maybe romantically":** Dulin, "Elizabeth Taylor."

BIBLIOGRAPHY

BOOKS

Allan, John B. *Elizabeth Taylor*. Derby, CT: Monarch Books, 1961.

Amburn, Ellis. *The Most Beautiful Woman in the World: The Obsessions, Passions, and Courage of Elizabeth Taylor*. New York: Harper-Entertainment, 2000.

Beaton, Cecil. *The Unexpurgated Beaton: The Cecil Beaton Diaries as He Wrote Them, 1970–1980*. New York: Alfred A. Knopf, 2003.

Bernstein, Robin, ed. *Cast Out: Queer Lives in Theater*. Ann Arbor, MI: University of Michigan Press, 2006.

Bogdanovich, Peter. *Who the Hell's in It: Conversations with Hollywood's Legendary Actors*. New York: Ballantine Books, 2005.

Borgnine, Ernest. *Ernie: The Autobiography*. New York: Citadel Press, 2009.

Bosworth, Patricia. *Montgomery Clift: A Biography*. New York: Harcourt Brace Jovanovich, 1978.

Bozzacchi, Gianni. *Elizabeth Taylor: The Queen and I*. Madison: University of Wisconsin Press, 2002.

Bradshaw, Jon. *Dreams That Money Can Buy: The Tragic Life of Libby Holman*. New York: William Morrow, 1985.

Bragg, Melvyn. *Richard Burton: A Life*. New York: Little, Brown, 1989.

Bret, David. *Elizabeth Taylor: The Lady, the Lover, the Legend—1932–2011*. Edinburgh, Scotland: Mainstream Publishing, 2011.

Capote, Truman. *Answered Prayers: The Unfinished Novel*. Reissue ed. New York: Vintage Books, 1994.

———. *Portraits and Observations: The Essays of Truman Capote*. Reprint. New York: Modern Library, 2008.

Capua, Michelangelo. *Montgomery Clift: A Biography*. Jefferson, NC: McFarland, 2002.

Carter, David. *Stonewall: The Riots that Sparked the Gay Revolution.* New York: St Martin's Griffin, 2010.

Carter, Grace May. *Elizabeth Taylor.* Boston: New Word City, 2018.

Cashmore, Ellis. *Elizabeth Taylor: A Private Life for Public Consumption.* London: Bloomsbury Academic, 2016.

Clarke, Gerald. *Capote: A Biography.* New York: RosettaBooks, 2013.

Dalton, David. *James Dean: The Mutant King.* Chicago: Chicago Review Press, 2001.

De La Hoz, Cindy. *Elizabeth Taylor: A Shining Legacy on Film.* Philadelphia: Running Press, 2012.

D'Arcy, Susan. *The Films of Elizabeth Taylor.* New York: Beaufort Books, 1982.

Douglas, Kirk, and Anne Douglas. *Kirk and Anne: Letters of Love, Laughter, and a Lifetime in Hollywood.* Philadelphia: Running Press, 2017.

Dunne, Dominick, George Hamilton, Sam Kashner, Nancy Collins, Gwen Davis, David Kamp, Nancy Schoenberger, and William Stadiem. *The Best of Vanity Fair. Elizabeth Taylor: Eight Remarkable Stories About Hollywood's Most Beautiful, Most Controversial Star.* With an introduction by Graydon Carter. New York: Vanity Fair, 2011.

Ehrenstein, David. *Open Secret: Gay Hollywood, 1928–1998.* New York: William Morrow, 1998.

Fisher, Eddie. *Been There, Done That: An Autobiography.* New York: St. Martin's, 1999.

Gates, Phyllis. *My Husband, Rock Hudson.* New York: Doubleday, 1987.

Geist, Kenneth L. *Pictures Will Talk: The Life & Films of Joseph L. Mankiewicz.* Boston: Da Capo Press, 1983.

Gelderman, Carol. *Mary McCarthy: A Life.* New York: St. Martin's, 1988.

Girelli, Elisabetta. *Montgomery Clift, Queer Star.* Detroit, MI: Wayne State University Press, 2013.

Goode, James. *The Making of the Misfits.* New York: Limelight Editions, 1986.

Graham, Don. *Giant: Elizabeth Taylor, Rock Hudson, James Dean,*

Edna Ferber, and the Making of a Legendary American Film. New York: St. Martin's, 2018.

Griffin, Merv. *Merv: An Autobiography.* With Peter Barsocchini. New York: Simon & Schuster, 1980.

Grobel, Lawrence. *Conversations with Capote.* New York: New American Library, 1985.

Hadleigh, Boze. *Elizabeth Taylor: Tribute to a Legend.* Guilford, CT: Lyons Press, 2017.

Harris, Warren G. *Clark Gable: A Biography.* New York: Three Rivers Press, 2005.

Harrison, Rex. *Rex: An Autobiography.* New York: William Morrow, 1975.

Heymann, C. David. *Liz: An Intimate Biography of Elizabeth Taylor.* New York: Citadel Press, 1995.

Higham, Charles. *Howard Hughes: The Secret Life.* Reprinted with a new prologue. New York: St. Martin's Griffin, 2004.

Hirsch, Foster. *A Method to Their Madness: The History of the Actors Studio.* Boston: Da Capo Press, 2001.

———. *Elizabeth Taylor.* New York: Pyramid Publications, 1973.

Hopper, Hedda. *The Whole Truth and Nothing But.* New York: Doubleday, 1963.

Hoskyns, Barney. *Montgomery Clift: Beautiful Loser.* New York: Grove Press, 1992.

Hudson, Rock, and Sara Davidson. *Rock Hudson: His Story.* New York: William Morrow, 1986.

Huston, John. *An Open Book.* Boston: Da Capo Press, 1994.

Inge, M. Thomas, ed. *Truman Capote: Conversations.* Jackson: University Press of Mississippi, 1987.

Isherwood, Christopher. *Diaries: Volume One, 1939–1960.* New York: HarperCollins, 1997.

Jowitt, Deborah. *Jerome Robbins: His Life, His Theater, His Dance.* New York: Simon & Schuster, 2004.

Kaiser, Charles. *The Gay Metropolis: The Landmark History of Gay Life in America.* New York: Grove Press, 2007.

Kanfer, Stefan. *Somebody: The Reckless Life and Remarkable Career of Marlon Brando.* New York: Vintage Books, 2009.

Kanin, Garson. *Tracy and Hepburn: An Intimate Memoir.* New York: Viking, 1971.

Kashner, Sam, and Nancy Schoenberger. *Furious Love: Elizabeth Taylor, Richard Burton, and the Marriage of the Century.* New York: HarperCollins, 2010.

Kass, Judith M. *The Films of Montgomery Clift.* New York: Lyle Stuart, 1984.

Kazan, Elia. *A Life.* New York: Alfred A. Knopf, 1988.

Kelley, Kitty. *Elizabeth Taylor: The Last Star.* New York: Simon & Schuster, 2011.

Kelly, Susan. *Elizabeth Taylor: Her Life in Style.* London: A&C Black, 2011.

Kennedy, Matthew. *Joan Blondell: A Life between Takes.* Reprint. Jackson: University Press of Mississippi, 2014.

Kramer, Stanley. *A Mad, Mad, Mad, Mad World: A Life in Hollywood.* New York: Harcourt, Brace, 1997.

Krauss, Kenneth. *Male Beauty: Postwar Masculinity in Theater, Film, and Physique Magazines.* Albany: State University of New York Press, 2014.

LaGuardia, Robert. *Monty: A Biography of Montgomery Clift.* New York: Arbor House, 1977.

Langella, Frank. *Dropped Names: Famous Men and Women as I Knew Them.* Reprint. New York: Harper Perennial, 2013.

Lawrence, Amy. *The Passion of Montgomery Clift.* Berkeley: University of California Press, 2010.

Leider, Emily W. *Myrna Loy: The Only Good Girl in Hollywood.* Berkeley: University of California Press, 2011.

Leonard, Maurice. *Montgomery Clift.* London: Hodder & Stoughton, 1997.

Lewis, Robert. *Slings & Arrows: Theater in My Life.* New York: Applause Books, 2000.

Lockridge, Larry. *Shade of the Raintree: The Life and Death of Ross Lockridge, Jr.* New York: Penguin, 1995.

Maddox, Brenda. *Who's Afraid of Elizabeth Taylor?* New York: M. Evans, 1977.

Malone, Aubrey. *Queer Cinema in America: An Encyclopedia of*

LGBTQ Films, Characters, and Stories. Santa Barbara, CA: Greenwood, 2019.

Mann, William J. *How to Be a Movie Star: Elizabeth Taylor in Hollywood.* New York: Houghton Mifflin Harcourt, 2009.

McCambridge, Mercedes. *The Quality of Mercy: An Autobiography.* New York: Times Books, 1981.

McGilligan. Patrick. *Alfred Hitchcock: A Life in Darkness and Light.* Reprint. New York: It Books, 2004.

Morley, Sheridan. *Elizabeth Taylor.* New York: Viking, 1989.

Moss, Marilyn Ann. *Giant: George Stevens, A Life on Film.* Madison: University of Wisconsin Press, 2015.

Papa, Joseph. *Elizabeth Taylor: A Passion for Life: The Wit and Wisdom of a Legend.* New York: HarperCollins, 2011.

Parker, John. *Five for Hollywood.* New York: Carol, 1991.

People Magazine, eds. *People Tribute: Elizabeth Taylor, 1932–2011.* New York: Time Inc. Books, 2011.

Peters, Margot. *Design for Living: Alfred Lunt and Lynn Fontanne: A Biography.* New York: Alfred A. Knopf, 2007.

Petersen, Anne Helen. *Scandals of Classic Hollywood: Sex, Deviance, and Drama from the Golden Age of American Cinema.* New York: Plume, 2014.

Porter, Darwin, and Danforth Prince. *Elizabeth Taylor: There Is Nothing Like a Dame.* New York: Blood Moon Productions, 2012.

Rice, Cy. *Cleopatra in Mink.* New York: Paperback Library, 1962.

Spoto, Donald. *A Passion for Life: The Biography of Elizabeth Taylor.* New York: HarperCollins, 1995.

Taraborrelli, J. Randy. *Elizabeth.* New York: Grand Central, 2006.

Taylor, Elizabeth. *An Informal Memoir.* New York: Harper & Row, 1965.

———. *Elizabeth Takes Off: On Weight Gain, Weight Loss, Self-Image, and Self-Esteem.* New York: G. P. Putnam's Sons, 1988.

———. *Elizabeth Taylor: Her Own True Bestselling Story.* New York: Avon, 1967.

———. *My Love Affair with Jewelry.* New York: Simon & Schuster, 2002.

———. *Nibbles and Me.* New York: Simon & Schuster, 2002.

Todd, Mike Jr., and Susan McCarthy Todd. *A Valuable Property: The Life Story of Michael Todd.* With a foreword by Elizabeth Taylor. New York: Arbor House, 1983.

Truffaut, Francois. *Hitchcock: A Definitive Study of Alfred Hitchcock.* Revised ed. New York: Simon & Schuster, 1985.

Tuska, Jon, ed. *Close-Up: The Hollywood Director.* Metuchen, NJ: Scarecrow Press, 1978.

Verlhac, Pierre-Henri, and Yann-Brice Dherbier, eds. *Elizabeth Taylor: A Life in Pictures.* London: Pavilion, 2008.

Vermilye, Jerry, and Mark Ricci. *The Films of Elizabeth Taylor.* Secaucus, NJ: Citadel Press, 1976.

Walker, Alexander. *Elizabeth: The Life of Elizabeth Taylor.* New York: Grove Weidenfeld, 1991.

Waterbury, Ruth. *Elizabeth Taylor: Her Life, Her Loves, Her Future.* With Gene Arceri. New York: Bantam, 1964.

Weatherby, William J. *Conversations with Marilyn.* New York: Mason/Charter, 1976.

Wilding, Michael. *Apple Sauce.* London: Allen & Unwin, 1982.

———. *The Wilding Way: The Story of My Life.* New York: St. Martin's, 1982.

Williams, Chris, ed. *The Richard Burton Diaries.* New Haven, CT: Yale University Press, 2012.

Windham, Donald. *Lost Friendships: A Memoir of Truman Capote, Tennessee Williams, and Others.* New York: William Morrow, 1987.

Winkler. Peter L. *Dennis Hopper: The Wild Ride of a Hollywood Rebel.* London: Robson Books, 2011.

Winters, Shelley. *Best of Times, Worst of Times.* London: Century Hutchinson, 1990.

———. *Shelley, Also Known as Shirley.* New York: William Morrow, 1980.

Wright, Jennifer. *It Ended Badly: Thirteen of the Worst Breakups in History.* New York: Henry Holt, 2015.

Zolotow, Maurice. *Billy Wilder in Hollywood.* New York: Limelight Editions, 2004.

DOCUMENTARY FILMS, PODCASTS, AND TELEVISION INTERVIEWS

Behind the Camera on The Misfits. TCM.com.

BBC. *Elizabeth Taylor: A Tribute.* Documentary. London: British Broadcasting Corporation, 2011.

Black, Nicola Jane, dir. *Montgomery Clift: Postmortem: Beautiful Loser.* Documentary. Glasgow, Scotland: Blackwatch Media, 1997.

Burns, Kevin, and Brent Zacky, dirs. *Cleopatra: The Film that Changed Hollywood,* 2001.

Carlson, Bob, host. "I Am Montgomery Clift." *UnFictional* (podcast). February 19, 2016. Produced by Nick White and Darby Maloney. https://www.kcrw.com/culture/shows/unfictional/i-am-montgomery-clift.

Cassella, Robert Jr., and John Griffin, dirs. *Montgomery Clift: The Hidden Star.* Documentary. Los Angeles: Peter Jones Productions, 1998.

Clift, Robert Anderson, and Hillary Demmon, dirs. *Making Montgomery Clift.* Documentary. Los Angeles: Limbic Productions, 2018.

Elizabeth Taylor. Documentary. New York: A&E Networks, 2003.

Elizabeth Taylor: An Unauthorized Biography. Documentary. San Diego: Legend Films & Jersey Productions, 2013.

Gates, Phyllis. Interview by Larry King. *Larry King Live,* March 21, 2004.

Grant, Lee, dir. *Intimate Portrait: Elizabeth Taylor.* Lifetime Television Documentary. New York: Feury/Grant Entertainment, 2002.

Guenette, Robert, dir. *Montgomery Clift: His Place in the Sun.* Los Angeles: Robert Guenette Productions, 1989.

Masenza, Claudio, dir. *The Rebels: Montgomery Clift.* Documentary. Italy: Ciak Studio 88, 1983.

Rodgers, Joel K., and Liz Flynn, dirs. *Mysteries & Scandals: Montgomery Clift.* Documentary. Los Angeles: E! Entertainment Television, 1998.

Saville, Lyndy, Dir. *Discovering Elizabeth Taylor*. Documentary. London: 3DD Productions, 2015.

Stevens, George Jr. *George Stevens: A Filmmaker's Journey*. Documentary. The Creative Film Center, 1984. (Also in the George Stevens papers at the Academy's Margaret Herrick Library.)

Swimmer, Saul, dir. *Around the World with Mike Todd*, 1967.

Taylor, Elizabeth. Interview by Larry King. *Larry King Live*, 1985.

———. Interview by Larry King. *Larry King Live*, January 15, 2001.

———. Interview by Larry King. *Larry King Live*. May 30, 2006.

———. Interview by Oprah Winfrey. *The Oprah Winfrey Show*, March 4, 1992.

INDEX

Visit us online at
KensingtonBooks.com
to read more from your favorite authors,
see books by series, view reading
group guides, and more!

BOOK CLUB

BETWEEN THE CHAPTERS

Visit us online for sneak peeks, exclusive
giveaways, special discounts, author content,
and engaging discussions with your fellow readers.

Betweenthechapters.net

Sign up for our newsletters and be the first
to get exciting news and announcements about
your favorite authors!
Kensingtonbooks.com/newsletter